CARCIOFI ALLA GIUDIA (ROMAN JEWISH FRIED ARTICHOKES)

THE BEST OF

AMERICA'S TEST KITCHEN

BEST RECIPES, EQUIPMENT REVIEWS, AND TASTINGS

2023

AMERICA'S TEST KITCHEN

AMERICA'S TEST KITCHEN
21 Drydock Avenue, Boston, MA 02210

THE BEST OF AMERICA'S TEST KITCHEN 2023
Best Recipes, Equipment Reviews, and Tastings

ISBN: 978-1-954210-08-0
ISSN: 1940-3925

Printed in Canada
10 9 8 7 6 5 4 3 2 1

Distributed by Penguin Random House Publisher Services
Tel: 800-733-3000

EDITORIAL DIRECTOR, BOOKS: Adam Kowit
EXECUTIVE MANAGING EDITORS: Debra Hudak and Todd Meier
DESIGN DIRECTOR: Lindsey Timko Chandler
GRAPHIC DESIGNER: Sarah Dailey
PHOTOGRAPHY DIRECTOR: Julie Bozzo Cote
PHOTOGRAPHY PRODUCER: Meredith Mulcahy
SENIOR STAFF PHOTOGRAPHERS: Steve Klise and Daniel J. van Ackere
PHOTOGRAPHER: Kevin White
ADDITIONAL PHOTOGRAPHY: Carl Tremblay and Joseph Keller
FOOD STYLING: Catrine Kelty, Chantal Lambeth, Kendra McKnight, Ashley Moore, Christie Morrison, Marie Piraino, Elle Simone Scott, Kendra Smith, and Sally Staub
ILLUSTRATION: John Burgoyne, Sophie Greenspan, and Jay Layman
PROJECT MANAGER, CREATIVE OPERATIONS: Katie Kimmerer
SENIOR PRINT PRODUCTION SPECIALIST: Lauren Robbins
PRODUCTION AND IMAGING COORDINATOR: Amanda Yong
PRODUCTION AND IMAGING SPECIALISTS: Tricia Neumyer and Dennis Noble
LEAD COPY EDITOR: Rachel Schowalter
COPY EDITORS: Katrina Munichiello and April Poole
PROOFREADER: Vicki Rowland
INDEXER: Elizabeth Parson

CHIEF CREATIVE OFFICER: Jack Bishop
EXECUTIVE EDITORIAL DIRECTORS: Julia Collin Davison and Bridget Lancaster

PICTURED ON FRONT COVER: Alfajores de Maicena (Dulce de Leche Sandwich Cookies) (page 259)

CONTENTS

WELCOME TO AMERICA'S TEST KITCHEN

The recipes in this book have been tested, written, and edited by the folks at America's Test Kitchen, where curious cooks become confident cooks. Located in Boston's Seaport District in the historic Innovation and Design Building, America's Test Kitchen features 15,000 square feet of kitchen space, including multiple photography and video studios. It is the home of *Cook's Illustrated* magazine and *Cook's Country* magazine and is the workday destination for more than 60 test cooks, editors, and cookware specialists. Our mission is to empower and inspire confidence, community, and creativity in the kitchen.

We start the process of testing a recipe with a complete lack of preconceptions, which means that we accept no claim, no technique, and no recipe at face value. Instead, we seek out as many versions of a dish as possible, prepare a half dozen of the most promising recipes, and taste the results. We then construct our own recipe and continue to test it, varying ingredients, techniques, and cooking times until we reach a consensus. As we like to say in the test kitchen, "We make the mistakes so that you don't have to." The result, we hope, is the best version of a particular recipe, but we realize that only you can be the final judge of our success (or failure). We use the same rigorous approach when we test equipment and taste ingredients.

All of this would not be possible without a belief that good cooking, much like good music, is based on a foundation of objective technique. Some people like spicy foods and others don't, but we believe that there is a right way to sauté, there is a best way to cook a pot roast, and there are measurable scientific principles involved in producing perfectly beaten, stable egg whites. Our ultimate goal is to investigate the fundamental principles of cooking to give you the techniques, tools, and ingredients you need to become a better cook. It is as simple as that.

To see what goes on behind the scenes at America's Test Kitchen, check out our social media channels for kitchen snapshots, exclusive content, video tips, and much more. You can watch us work (in our actual test kitchen) by tuning in to *America's Test Kitchen* or *Cook's Country* on public television or on our websites. Want to hone your cooking skills or finally learn how to bake—with an America's Test Kitchen test cook? Enroll in one of our online cooking classes. And you can engage the next generation of home cooks with kid-tested, kid-approved recipes from America's Test Kitchen Kids.

Our community of home recipe testers provides valuable feedback on recipes under development by ensuring that they are foolproof. You can help us investigate the how and why behind successful recipes from your home kitchen. (Sign up at AmericasTestKitchen.com/recipe_testing.)

However you choose to visit us, we welcome you into our kitchen, where you can stand by our side as we test our way to the best recipes in America.

facebook.com/AmericasTestKitchen
twitter.com/TestKitchen
youtube.com/AmericasTestKitchen
instagram.com/TestKitchen
pinterest.com/TestKitchen

AmericasTestKitchen.com
CooksIllustrated.com
CooksCountry.com
OnlineCookingSchool.com
AmericasTestKitchen.com/kids

TOMATO AND CHICKPEA SALAD

SOUPS AND SALADS

TANABOUR

WHY THIS RECIPE WORKS Tanabour, or spas, is a nourishing and filling Armenian grain-and-yogurt soup. Though it can be made using a variety of grains, we used pearl barley, since—lacking hulls—it cooks to a tender, plump consistency without breaking down entirely. We used Greek yogurt to give the soup its requisite thickness and dairy richness without leaving it overly tart. We added an egg yolk to provide further richness and a silky consistency. Finally, we garnished the soup with cilantro and Aleppo pepper–infused melted butter. For our madzoon ov kofte variation, we opted for easy-to-make meatballs from ground beef and bulgur instead of the more traditional yet time-consuming stuffed, spiced meatballs.

In his classic 1944 cookbook, *Dinner at Omar Khayyam's*, Armenian American chef and restaurateur George Mardikian explains step one for making yogurt at home in the United States: "Just open any telephone book and find a name ending with 'ian.' Go to that person's address, knock on the door, and ask the Armenian who opens it for a cup of madzoon [yogurt]."

The fact that you could count on just about any "-ian" to have a batch of yogurt in the fridge—in the 1940s, no less, when many Americans were unfamiliar with the ingredient—explains just how important a food it is in my culture.

One of our most beloved uses for yogurt is in the grain-enriched soup known as tanabour, or spas. ("Tan" is a yogurt drink, and "abour" means "soup"; "spas" comes from the verb "spasarkel," which means "to serve," referring to the fact that the dish requires a spoon.) Everyone I serve this soup to is wowed by its silky consistency and savory-tart flavor, even those unfamiliar with eating yogurt in a hot preparation.

They like it even more once they learn how easily it comes together. First, soften chopped onion in butter along with pinches of dried mint, salt, and pepper. Add korkot (dried or roasted cracked wheat—the traditional choice—though other grains can be used), pour in water or broth (I like the savoriness of chicken broth), and simmer until the korkot is tender and the liquid is velvety with its starch.

Next, whisk in lots of whole-milk yogurt (store-bought is fine), taking care to prevent the acidic dairy from curdling. Bolster it with a little flour and/or an egg or yolk and gently warm it through. Ladle out steaming portions, and then perk up the neutral tones with green (fresh herbs) and amber (spiced melted butter).

Since korkot can be hard to source outside of Armenian markets, my first move was to explore the other grains that are used. Wheat berries retained a crunchy edge despite a long simmer, whereas rice, rolled oats, and bulgur threatened to dissolve completely, giving the soup a monotonous consistency. Pearl barley, however, was a standout. The nutty grains plumped into tender nubs as they simmered, releasing a slew of starch that imparted deep silkiness even before the yogurt was incorporated.

Speaking of yogurt, some recipes call for a ratio of 1 or 2 cups of the cultured dairy to 6 cups of broth, while others pack the soup with twice as much. It was hard to decide what to do: A generous hand with yogurt produced a soup that was lush but also strikingly tart. And yet, backing off yielded a thin broth.

As I scanned the dairy section of my supermarket one afternoon, I spied a possible fix: Greek yogurt. Sure enough, with its higher concentration of milk solids, a ratio of 1½ cups of Greek yogurt to 6 cups of broth and water struck the right balance of satiny richness and milky tang.

With my tanabour nearly complete, I circled back to the stabilization measures. Flour turned out to be unnecessary given the ample starch donated by the barley, but I loved the extra body that a single egg yolk mixed into the yogurt provided. It was also crucial to temper the yogurt-yolk mixture before adding it to the broth. Finally, I kept the soup well below the curdling threshold of about 205 degrees by warming it to between 180 and 185 degrees—still plenty hot for serving—before adding a final drizzle of Aleppo pepper–stained melted butter and a shower of chopped fresh cilantro.

Tanabour is not the only Armenian yogurt soup. Some are made even more substantial with add-ins such as lentils or chickpeas, fresh pasta or torn lavash, and stuffed meatballs or braised meat. One—bulked up with lots of lentils and lavash—is called kyalagyosh, which loosely translates as "a meal for a wolf," a poetic way of explaining just how filling it is.

Inspired by the heartiness of kyalagyosh, I took another classic yogurt soup, madzoon ov kofte—made with meatballs augmented with bulgur, earthy Aleppo pepper, citrusy coriander, and grassy cilantro—and fortified it with chickpeas and small dried pasta shells. It's a meal fit for wolves and humans alike.

—ANDREW JANJIGIAN, *Cook's Illustrated*

TANABOUR (ARMENIAN YOGURT AND BARLEY SOUP)

Tanabour (Armenian Yogurt and Barley Soup)

SERVES 6   TOTAL TIME: 1½ HOURS

Dried mint is widely used in Middle Eastern cooking; its flavor is quite different from that of fresh mint, so if you can't find it, it's better to omit it than to substitute fresh. Chicken broth gives the soup added depth, but it can be replaced with water or vegetable broth. We prefer the richness of whole-milk Greek yogurt here, but low-fat can be used; avoid nonfat. Fresh parsley or mint, or a combination of the two, can be substituted for the cilantro. If Aleppo pepper is unavailable, substitute 1 teaspoon of paprika and a pinch of cayenne pepper.

4	tablespoons unsalted butter, divided
1	onion, chopped fine
1	teaspoon dried mint
1	teaspoon table salt
½	teaspoon pepper
	Pinch baking soda
¾	cup pearl barley
4	cups chicken broth
2	cups water
1½	cups plain Greek yogurt
1	large egg yolk
¼	cup chopped fresh cilantro, divided
1	teaspoon ground dried Aleppo pepper

1. Melt 2 tablespoons butter in large saucepan over medium heat. Add onion, mint, salt, pepper, and baking soda. Cook, stirring occasionally, until onion has broken down into soft paste and is just starting to stick to saucepan, 6 to 8 minutes.

2. Stir in barley. Cook, stirring frequently, until grains are translucent around edges, about 3 minutes. Add broth and water. Increase heat to high and bring to boil. Adjust heat to maintain gentle simmer; cook, partially covered, until barley is very tender, 50 minutes to 1 hour, stirring occasionally. Meanwhile, whisk yogurt and egg yolk together in large bowl.

NOTES FROM THE TEST KITCHEN

YOGURT IN THE ARMENIAN KITCHEN

On the Armenian table, yogurt is often enjoyed in its pure, unadulterated form. It's also stirred into a host of dishes, most of which are savory. The thick dairy contributes rich milk fat, gentle acidity, and creaminess—along with plenty of protein—to baked goods, drinks, salads, sauces, and chilled and hot soups.

3. Remove saucepan from heat. Whisking vigorously, gradually add 2 cups barley mixture to yogurt mixture. Stirring constantly, add yogurt-barley mixture back to saucepan. Cover and let sit for 10 minutes to thicken.

4. Heat soup over medium heat, stirring occasionally, until temperature registers between 180 and 185 degrees (do not allow soup to boil or yogurt will curdle). Remove from heat. Soup should have consistency of buttermilk; if thicker, adjust by adding hot water, 2 tablespoons at a time. Stir in 2 tablespoons cilantro and season with salt to taste.

5. Melt remaining 2 tablespoons butter in small skillet over medium-high heat. Off heat, stir in Aleppo pepper. Ladle soup into bowls, drizzle each portion with 1 teaspoon spiced butter, sprinkle with remaining 2 tablespoons cilantro, and serve. (Leftovers can be refrigerated for up to 3 days; reheat gently, being careful not to allow temperature to exceed 180 degrees. If necessary, thin by adding water, 2 tablespoons at a time.)

VARIATION

Madzoon ov Kofte (Armenian Yogurt and Meatball Soup)

SERVES 6   TOTAL TIME: 1¼ HOURS

Fresh parsley or mint, or a combination of the two, can be substituted for the cilantro. If Aleppo pepper is unavailable, substitute 2 teaspoons of paprika and a pinch of cayenne pepper. Dried mint is widely used in Middle Eastern cooking; its flavor is quite different from that of fresh mint, so if you can't find it, it's better to omit it than to substitute fresh. You can substitute small elbow macaroni for the pasta shells. We prefer the richness of whole-milk Greek yogurt here, but low-fat can be used; avoid nonfat.

8	ounces 85 percent lean ground beef
3	tablespoons water
1¾	teaspoons table salt, divided
¼	teaspoon baking soda, divided
½	cup medium-grind bulgur, rinsed
¼	cup chopped fresh cilantro, divided
2	teaspoons ground dried Aleppo pepper, divided
1	teaspoon ground coriander
½	teaspoon pepper, divided
4	tablespoons unsalted butter, divided
1	onion, chopped fine
1	teaspoon dried mint
4	cups chicken broth

1 (15-ounce) can chickpeas, undrained

4 ounces (1 cup) small pasta shells

1½ cups plain Greek yogurt

1 large egg yolk

1. Toss beef with water, 1 teaspoon salt, and ⅛ teaspoon baking soda in bowl until thoroughly combined. Add bulgur, 1 tablespoon cilantro, 1 teaspoon Aleppo pepper, coriander, and ¼ teaspoon pepper and mix by hand until uniform. Transfer meat mixture to cutting board and press into 6-inch square. Using bench scraper or sharp knife, divide mixture into 36 squares (6 rows by 6 rows). Using your lightly moistened hands, roll each square into smooth ball and leave on cutting board.

2. Melt 2 tablespoons butter in large saucepan over medium heat. Add onion, mint, remaining ¾ teaspoon salt, remaining ⅛ teaspoon baking soda, and remaining ¼ teaspoon pepper. Cook, stirring occasionally, until onion has broken down into soft paste and is just starting to stick to saucepan, 6 to 8 minutes.

3. Add broth, chickpeas and their liquid, and meatballs to saucepan. Increase heat to high and bring to boil. Adjust heat to maintain simmer and cook for 5 minutes, stirring occasionally. Add pasta and continue to cook until pasta is tender. While pasta cooks, whisk yogurt and egg yolk together in large bowl.

4. Remove saucepan from heat. Using ladle, transfer 1½ cups broth to liquid measuring cup (try to avoid meatballs, pasta, and chickpeas). Whisking vigorously, gradually add broth to yogurt mixture. Add half of yogurt-broth mixture back to saucepan and stir to combine. Stir in remaining yogurt-broth mixture. Cover and let sit for 10 minutes to thicken.

5. Heat soup over medium heat, stirring occasionally, until temperature registers between 180 and 185 degrees (do not allow soup to boil or yogurt will curdle). Remove from heat. Broth should have consistency of buttermilk; if thicker, adjust by adding hot water, 2 tablespoons at a time. Stir in 1 tablespoon cilantro and season with salt to taste.

6. Melt remaining 2 tablespoons butter in small skillet over medium-high heat. Off heat, stir in remaining 1 teaspoon Aleppo pepper. Ladle soup into bowls, drizzle each portion with 1 teaspoon spiced butter, sprinkle with remaining 2 tablespoons cilantro, and serve. (Leftovers can be refrigerated for up to 3 days; reheat gently, being careful not to allow temperature to exceed 180 degrees. If necessary, thin by adding water, 2 tablespoons at a time.)

CHORBA FRIK

✔ WHY THIS RECIPE WORKS The focal ingredient in this recipe is flavorful freekeh, which is made from roasted durum wheat that has been harvested while the grains are still young and green. The grains are polished, and in Algeria, used cracked. Through simmering, it retains its pleasantly chewy texture and imparts a beautiful, subtly smoky, nutty flavor to the soup. We added two bone-in chicken thighs, which we shredded into bite-size pieces, to the soup, making it even more filling without detracting from the freekeh. A combination of canned tomatoes, pulsed to a puree, and tomato paste imparted acidity, vibrant color, and satisfying body.

Soup is a universal starter on Ramadan iftar dinner tables worldwide, as the warm dish hydrates and prepares digestion after a day of fasting. Chorba, meaning "soup" in Arabic, is widely consumed in Algeria, Tunisia, Morocco, and Libya. Carbohydrate-rich foods are common in Algeria and, especially in the Western part, chorba frik, a freekeh-filled soup, is a favorite and a culinary tradition.

"Chorba frik is a wonderful bowl of nourishing comfort," points out Algerian culinary expert and food blogger Radia SiYoucef, who prepares a superlative version of this savory soup for her family every Ramadan. Versions may vary from household to household, and even from night to night during Ramadan, but its foundation is consistent: an aromatic, well-spiced tomato-based broth simmered with lots of fresh cilantro; plentiful freekeh; morsels of meat (sheep and lamb are most common, but poultry is also used); and sometimes chickpeas, too.

Consumed throughout the Mediterranean for thousands of years, freekeh is made from roasted durum wheat that has been harvested while the grains are still young and green. Algerians use polished, cracked grains that, through simmering, retain their pleasantly chewy texture and give the soup a subtle smoky, nutty signature flavor. Rinsing the freekeh was important to help balance its naturally earthy flavor. While it can be simmered pasta-style in a large amount of water and then drained, for chorba frik, freekeh is traditionally simmered in the soup to ease preparation and to give the soup rich body and savory flavor.

My recipe calls for two bone-in chicken thighs, which make it filling without detracting attention from the

CHORBA FRIK

freekeh. Searing the chicken thighs rendered their fat and created a rich fond, which I used as the base for the soup. I continued to build the flavor base with aromatic celery and onions, sautéed until just softened. I then added a hearty amount of cilantro, a hint of garlic, and a variety of warm spices that I first bloomed in the rendered chicken fat in order to enhance the spices' depth of flavor. Fresh cilantro simmered with the soup for the length of cooking is frequently seen in chorba frik.

A combination of canned tomatoes pulsed to puree and a small amount of tomato paste imparted acidity, vibrant color, and satisfying body, a trademark of this soup. To balance the flavors of the spices, chicken, and freekeh, I used water as the soup base to simmer and blend the flavors together, letting the freekeh's flavor shine. The chicken and the freekeh cook at the same rate, making this soup a one-pot meal that is also simple in preparation. The rich simmered meat is succulent and shredded into bite-size, spoon-friendly pieces. A final pop of acidity from a squeeze of fresh lemon along with dried mint are common serving suggestions with chorba frik that I loved. A sprinkle of fresh cilantro was a vibrant finish that highlighted the cooked cilantro flavor running throughout the soup.

—CARMEN DONGO, *America's Test Kitchen Books*

Chorba Frik

SERVES 4 TO 6   TOTAL TIME: 1½ HOURS

Be sure to use cracked freekeh here. Whole freekeh requires a different cooking method.

- 1 (14.5-ounce) can whole peeled tomatoes, drained with juice reserved
- 2 (5- to 7-ounce) bone-in chicken thighs
- 1¼ teaspoons table salt, divided
- 2 tablespoons extra-virgin olive oil
- 1 onion, chopped fine
- 1 celery rib, minced
- 1 cup minced fresh cilantro, plus ¼ cup leaves for serving
- 2 tablespoons tomato paste
- 3 garlic cloves, minced
- 1 tablespoon ground coriander
- 1 tablespoon paprika
- 2 teaspoons ground cumin
- ½ teaspoon pepper
- ¼ teaspoon ground cinnamon
- ¼ teaspoon cayenne pepper
- 6 cups water
- 1 (15-ounce) can chickpeas, undrained
- ½ cup cracked freekeh, rinsed
- 1 teaspoon dried mint
  Lemon wedges

1. Process tomatoes and their juice in food processor until pureed, about 30 seconds. Pat chicken dry with paper towels and sprinkle with ¼ teaspoon salt. Heat oil in Dutch oven over medium-high heat until just smoking. Cook chicken skin side down until well browned, about 5 minutes; transfer chicken to plate. Pour off all but 2 tablespoons fat from pot.

2. Add onion, celery, and remaining 1 teaspoon salt to fat in pot and cook over medium heat until softened, about 5 minutes. Stir in minced cilantro, tomato paste, garlic, coriander, paprika, cumin, pepper, cinnamon, and cayenne and cook until fragrant, about 1 minute. Stir in pureed tomatoes, water, chickpeas and their liquid, and freekeh, scraping up any browned bits. Nestle chicken and any accumulated juices into pot and bring to simmer. Adjust heat as needed to maintain simmer and cook until freekeh is tender and chicken registers 195 degrees and easily shreds with fork, 35 to 45 minutes.

3. Transfer chicken to clean plate and let cool slightly. Once chicken is cool enough to handle, using two forks, shred chicken into bite-size pieces and discard skin and bones. Stir shredded chicken and any accumulated juices back into pot and season with salt and pepper to taste. Serve with cilantro leaves, dried mint, and lemon wedges.

HAWAIIAN OXTAIL SOUP

✓ **WHY THIS RECIPE WORKS** Oxtail is a collagen-rich cut that typically takes 3 to 4 hours of simmering to turn tender. We dramatically cut down on the cooking time by turning to our multicooker. An hour under high pressure, followed by 30 minutes for the pressure to release naturally, was all it took, giving the oxtails' collagen time to convert to silky gelatin while allowing the meat to still cling gently to the bones. We added the aromatics and other classic ingredients—peanuts, dried jujubes, and dried shiitakes—at the same time as the oxtails. We strained the broth, reheated it on the high sauté function, and then wilted the greens in the stock off the heat. We portioned the oxtails, peanuts, and mushrooms into individual bowls and then ladled the steaming broth and greens over top.

In Hawaii, oxtail soup is steeped in history—and the ghost of homesickness. Early versions date to the mid- to late 19th century, when scores of Chinese people from Guangdong Province arrived on Hawaii's shores as laborers for its sugar and pineapple plantations. With thousands of miles of ocean separating them from their families, the newcomers found consolation in preparing familiar foods. And oxtails, readily available thanks to Hawaii's burgeoning cattle industry, allowed them to recreate some of the nourishing, long-cooked soups from Guangdong that more commonly featured pork or chicken. They loaded up the pot with this cut, along with traditional Cantonese flavorings and vegetables, and an iconic Hawaiian classic was born.

The succulent meat and bits of mineral-sweet marrow clinging to the oxtails' bony hollows are star attractions in the soup. But the whole ensemble is a stunner. The broth is beefy-rich, silky with gelatin, spicy with ginger, and fragrant with star anise and the aged dried orange peel known as chen pi. There's a hint of sweetness from jujubes (Chinese dates) and earthy notes from dried black mushrooms (and in banquet-worthy versions, maybe a whisper of alcohol). Creamy peanuts add texture, and depending on the cook and the occasion, so might other items such as lotus root and winter melon. Mustardy gai choy goes in at the end, and then cilantro and scallions are heaped on before serving. Everyone gets soy sauce and grated ginger at the table for additional seasoning.

The appeal of this dish among locals is so universal that it's as likely to be served in a diner as it is to company for dinner. Lynette Lo Tom, a fifth-generation Hawaiian of Chinese descent and author of *A Chinese Kitchen: Traditional Recipes with an Island Twist* (2015), attributes Hawaiians' special love for the Chinese version (it can also tilt Okinawan, Japanese, or Korean) to its heady aroma. "It's the smell, you know, you just get that feeling," she told me.

For a soup as rich and nuanced as this one, I quickly discovered that pulling it together was straightforward. The trimmed oxtails go into the pot with water and everything save the greens (and other vegetables that can't withstand the long simmer), and then they're cooked until they're tender. The aromatics are then discarded, the broth strained of fat, and the gai choy briefly wilted. My main challenge: getting a rich, gelatinous, clear broth without hours of cooking; laborious skimming; or having to blanch the oxtails first, as many Hawaiian cooks do to remove impurities. I also wanted to figure out the best way to ensure that the gai choy didn't lose its tender chew and that any other vegetables I might include were perfectly cooked, too.

Using a multicooker solved the first issue. It dramatically shortened the usual 3 to 4 hours necessary to cook the oxtails, and because liquid in a pressure cooker doesn't bubble violently except when it's venting, the foam remained intact and was easily strained. One hour under pressure, plus 30 minutes for the pressure to release naturally, gave the oxtails' collagen enough time to convert to silky gelatin while still allowing the meat to cling gently to the bones—a must in the soup, according to Lo Tom. "For us," she noted, "the joy is the meat being the perfect texture, where it's soft but not dissolved off the bone."

For the aromatics, Lo Tom stressed using plenty of ginger for spicy kick. I landed on 8 ounces, bundling it into cheesecloth for easy removal, along with lots of star anise and slivers of the musky, floral chen pi I'd sourced from an Asian market. For the remaining ingredients, after testing recipes from other Hawaiian Chinese cookbooks, I opted to stick with the essentials: peanuts, dried jujubes, and dried shiitakes, all of which could be slipped in with the aromatics at the start of cooking. Gai choy would then be easy to add at the end. For seasoning, soy sauce and salt did the trick.

Once the oxtails were done and the broth enriched by all the other ingredients, I transferred the meat, the shiitakes, and peanuts to a large bowl. I strained the stock, including the jujubes (some cooks chop the dates and add them back, but I found the soup plenty complex without them), to yield a clean, full-bodied broth. Cooking the gai choy was a simple matter of reheating the strained broth on the highest sauté function until it was piping hot and then wilting the greens in the broth with the heat turned off.

I divided the oxtails, shiitakes, and peanuts among bowls; ladled the broth and greens over the top; and capped each with cilantro and scallions, all while luxuriating in the soup's beefy, vibrant aroma.

—NICOLE KONSTANTINAKOS,
America's Test Kitchen Books

SERVES 4 TO 6   TOTAL TIME: 2¼ HOURS

Look for oxtails that are approximately 2 inches thick; thaw them if they're frozen. For the most nuanced flavor, we highly recommend that you avoid substitutions, but if necessary, you can substitute dry-roasted peanuts for the raw peanuts, four Medjool dates for the jujubes, 1½ tablespoons of dried orange peel or 3 strips of fresh orange zest for the chen pi, and 1 pound of stemmed American mustard greens for the gai choy. This dish can also be cooked in a pressure cooker. Place the cooker on medium heat when instructed to use the "highest sauté function." Serve this soup in large, deep soup bowls. For a complete Hawaiian-style meal, serve each diner 2 scoops of white rice.

8   ounces fresh ginger, sliced thin, plus
     4 tablespoons peeled and grated for serving

5   star anise pods

¼   ounce chen pi

3   pounds oxtails, fat trimmed to ¼ inch or less

8   cups water

½   cup raw peanuts

8   dried jujubes

1   ounce dried whole shiitake mushrooms,
     stemmed and rinsed

¼   cup soy sauce, plus extra for serving

½   teaspoon table salt

1   pound gai choy, trimmed and cut into 2-inch pieces

1   cup fresh cilantro leaves

4   scallions, sliced thin on bias

1. Bundle sliced ginger, star anise, and chen pi in single layer of cheesecloth and secure with kitchen twine. Add cheesecloth bundle, oxtails, water, peanuts, jujubes, mushrooms, soy sauce, and salt to multicooker.

2. Lock lid into place and close pressure-release valve. Select high pressure-cook function and cook for 1 hour. Turn off multicooker and let pressure release naturally for 30 minutes. Quick-release any remaining pressure, then carefully remove lid, allowing steam to escape away from you.

3. Discard cheesecloth bundle. Using slotted spoon, transfer oxtails, peanuts, and mushrooms to large bowl; tent with aluminum foil; and let rest while finishing soup. Strain broth through fine-mesh strainer into large bowl or container, pressing on solids to extract as much liquid as possible; discard solids. Let broth settle

for 5 minutes. Using wide, shallow spoon or ladle, skim excess fat from surface. (Broth can be refrigerated overnight before defatting to allow for easier skimming. Reheat oxtails, peanuts, and mushrooms in simmering broth before adding gai choi in step 4.)

4. Return defatted broth to now-empty pot. Using highest sauté function, bring broth to simmer, then turn off multicooker. Stir in gai choy and cook, using residual heat, until wilted, about 3 minutes. Season with extra soy sauce to taste.

5. Slice mushrooms thin, if desired. Divide oxtails, peanuts, and mushrooms among bowls, then ladle hot broth and gai choy over oxtails. Sprinkle each bowl with cilantro and scallions. Serve, passing grated ginger and extra soy sauce separately.

FOUR-CHILE CHILI

✔ **WHY THIS RECIPE WORKS**   To make a rich and flavorful vegetarian chili, we sautéed onion and fresh poblano chile in plenty of olive oil until lightly browned—the oil's fat unlocked the fat-soluble flavor compounds of the chiles and seasonings. Many recipes call for store-bought chili powder, but we toasted torn dried ancho and guajillo chiles, reconstituted them in water, and then blitzed them in a blender with tomatoes and canned chipotle chile to create a significantly more complex chili. To account for the lack of meat, we incorporated soy sauce and dried porcini mushrooms in addition to the tomato paste to contribute umami, or savory flavor. Plus, the soy sauce and tomato paste combined to provide a concentrated salty-sweet tang while the reconstituted mushrooms added depth and a slightly smoky element, too. In lieu of meat, we used a medley of canned beans along with barley, which has a mild taste and adds a pleasant, chewy bite.

On a hot August day in 2015, Mama T (real name: Trisha Gonsalves), a vegan chef, activist, educator, and reggae singer of Kumeyaay Indian heritage, entered her chili into the Chile Pepper Festival chili cook-off in Honolulu. Unbeknownst to the 600 attendees, the chili was vegan. As the votes were being tallied, she revealed her secret to the astonished crowd, who burst into laughter when it was announced that she won first place.

Imagine entering a bowl of plant-based chili that checks all the boxes that the cook-off judges are trained to look for in a traditional chili. An award-winning chili

VEGETARIAN CHILI

must have an appealing color and look, along with a captivating aroma—and that's all before the judges take a bite. Then, the chili itself must be the perfect consistency (not too thick, nor too thin), the meat (or is it . . . ?) must be perfectly cooked and present in the right proportions, and the chile flavor should be distinct and complex without short-circuiting anyone's mouth from the heat.

Inspired by Mama T, I created what I consider to be a competition-worthy vegetarian chili. To make it, start with the flavorful base: Sauté an onion and a fresh poblano pepper in plenty of olive oil until they're lightly browned. (The oil's fat is important to unlocking the flavors of the chiles and seasonings, whose flavor compounds are fat-soluble.) Then add tomato paste and plenty of minced garlic, along with dried oregano and a heap of warm, earthy ground cumin. Let it all sizzle until the tomato paste begins to darken and the sugars caramelize, deepening the flavor. Many recipes call for store-bought chili powder, but using whole dried ancho and guajillo chiles—which you toast and reconstitute in water to soften and then blitz in a blender with tomatoes and canned chipotle chile— creates a significantly more complex chili.

A key to flavorful vegetarian chili is to use ingredients that contribute umami, or savory flavor, to account for the lack of meat. Soy sauce, dried porcini mushrooms, and tomato paste all work to that end here. And on top of the umami, the soy sauce and tomato paste combine to provide a concentrated salty-sweet tang while the reconstituted mushrooms add depth and a slightly smoky element, too.

Since this dish contains no meat, the heft and protein comes from the combination of beans and barley (Mama T's version used eggplant puree and meat alternatives). While I understand that chili purists (looking at you, Texas) may be furrowing their brows, the medley of canned beans—I use black, pinto, and kidney—creates an appealing mosaic of colors, flavors, and textures. All it requires is a few twists of the wrist to open the cans (and for the record, beans are a common ingredient in certain categories of competition chilis). Barley has a mild taste and contributes a pleasant chewy bite.

Like many chilis, this one is delicious (perhaps even more so) the next day. It makes a tasty topper to a hot dog or a Frito pie and is also great stirred into queso. The familiar flavors in this recipe—layers of smokiness, deep savoriness, chiles, tomatoes—make it an easy transition to a delicious, filling, plant-based main course.

—AMANDA LUCHTEL, *Cook's Country*

Vegetarian Chili

SERVES 6   TOTAL TIME: 1¾ HOURS

One ounce of ancho chiles is approximately two or three chiles; ½ ounce of guajillo chiles is about three or four chiles. Use more or fewer chipotle chiles depending on your desired level of spiciness. We like using a mix

---

NOTES FROM THE TEST KITCHEN

CHILES 101

POBLANO	ANCHO	GUAJILLO	CANNED CHIPOTLE IN ADOBO
Poblano chiles vary in color from very dark green (most common in American markets) to dark red or brown when ripe. Spicier than bell peppers but not as spicy as jalapeño or serrano chiles, they add subtle heat and grassy pepper notes to recipes.	Ancho chiles are almost-ripe poblanos that are dried. These chiles are dark, mahogany red and wrinkly skinned, and they have a deep, sweet, raisiny flavor with elements of coffee and chocolate.	Guajillos are dried mirasol chiles. They are a little sweet, with a mild to medium heat. These chiles have a fruity, tangy, smoky flavor profile with notes of berries and green tea.	Chipotles are ripe jalapeño peppers that are smoke-dried. While chipotles are available dried, they are also sold rehydrated and packed in cans with thick, tangy adobo sauce. Both the chiles and the liquid are loaded with spicy, smoky, complex flavors.

of pinto, black, and red kidney beans here, but you can use all of one type or any combination of the three. Do not substitute hulled, hull-less, quick-cooking, or presteamed barley in this recipe (read the ingredient list on the package to determine this). Serve the chili with any of the traditional garnishes: lime wedges, sour cream, diced avocado, chopped red onion, fresh cilantro leaves, and shredded Monterey Jack or cheddar cheese.

1 ounce dried ancho chiles, stemmed, seeded, and torn into 1-inch pieces

½ ounce dried guajillo chiles, stemmed, seeded, and torn into 1-inch pieces

1 (28-ounce) can whole peeled tomatoes

1–3 canned chipotle chiles in adobo sauce

3 tablespoons soy sauce

2¼ teaspoons table salt, divided

¼ cup extra-virgin olive oil

1 onion, chopped

1 poblano chile, stemmed, seeded, and chopped

3 tablespoons tomato paste

6 garlic cloves, minced

2 tablespoons ground cumin

1 tablespoon dried oregano

1 (15-ounce) can pinto beans, rinsed

1 (15-ounce) can black beans, rinsed

1 (15-ounce) can red kidney beans, rinsed

¾ cup pearl barley

½ ounce dried porcini mushrooms, rinsed and chopped fine

½ cup chopped fresh cilantro

1. Place anchos and guajillos in Dutch oven and cook over medium heat, stirring often, until fragrant and darkened slightly but not smoking, 3 to 5 minutes. Immediately transfer anchos and guajillos to bowl and cover with hot water. Let sit until chiles are soft and pliable, about 5 minutes.

2. Drain anchos and guajillos and combine with tomatoes and their juice, 1 cup water, chipotle(s), soy sauce, and 1½ teaspoons salt in blender. Process until smooth, 1 to 2 minutes; set aside.

3. Heat oil in now-empty Dutch oven over medium-high heat until shimmering. Add onion, poblano, and remaining ¾ teaspoon salt. Cook, stirring occasionally, until onion begins to brown, 3 to 5 minutes. Stir in tomato paste, garlic, cumin, and oregano and cook until tomato paste darkens, 1 to 2 minutes.

4. Stir in pinto, black, and kidney beans; barley; mushrooms; chile puree; and 2½ cups water. Bring to boil. Reduce heat to medium-low and simmer, stirring occasionally, until barley is tender, 35 to 45 minutes. Let sit off heat for 10 minutes (chili will continue to thicken as it sits). Season with salt to taste. Stir in cilantro and serve.

CREOLE YAKAMEIN

✓ WHY THIS RECIPE WORKS Browning the beef chuck-eye roast before adding and sautéing our aromatics (the "holy trinity" of onion, bell pepper, and celery) created a deeply flavorful fond. Slowly simmering the roast in beef broth until it was meltingly tender created a concentrated soup stock, and seasoning the broth with Creole spices, savory soy sauce, garlic, and a touch of monosodium glutamate made it as irresistible as those we tasted in New Orleans. To complete the dish, we ladled the delicious soup over bowls of cooked spaghetti, the chopped beef, halved hard-cooked eggs, and sliced scallions, finishing them with dashes of more soy sauce and hot sauce.

I'm sitting in my car, tearing open packets of soy sauce and hot sauce with my teeth. I splash both sauces across my bowl of dark broth, noodles, chopped beef, boiled egg, and scallions. One bite and I get it. This is New Orleans, and this is yakamein (also known as "old sober"), a powerfully seasoned, spicy noodle soup that's purported to cure even the nastiest of hangovers.

Thanks mostly to the tireless efforts of chef Linda Green, known around the city as the "Yakamein Lady," this irresistible Creole amalgamation is becoming increasingly easy to find. In the years since Hurricane Katrina hit in 2005, she's cooked yakamein into a popular resurgence, ladling out her soup to the likes of the late Anthony Bourdain; winning an episode of Food Network's *Chopped*; and garnering profiles in publications such as the *New York Times* and *Rolling Stone*.

Since that first day in my car, I've had the pleasure of slurping down several cups of Green's noodles, along with some other excellent versions from places around the city. As I began work on my own recipe for the dish, I couldn't help but ask myself where this fusion of Creole, Asian, and soul food cuisines came from.

After calling around and doing some initial research, I contacted Winston Ho, a University of New Orleans graduate student researching Chinese American history in New Orleans and an expert on the history of this dish.

Ho has documented what he describes as the "Chinese-American origin theory" of yakamein, explaining to me that he has "menus and photographs from almost fifty restaurants that served yakamein around the country over the past 120 years." His earliest example is a New York City Chinese restaurant menu from 1904 that offers "yet quo mein (noodle soup with pork)." Ho theorizes that yakamein "is an improvised noodle soup, which the Cantonese created in the late 1800s from whatever ingredients they could find in North America—spaghetti noodles instead of Chinese noodles for example." So Cantonese restaurants in cities across America (including San Francisco, New Orleans, New York, and Baltimore) were the first to serve yakamein. And some of these places still have Americanized noodle dishes descended from the original Cantonese noodles—such as "yock" or "yock in a box" in southeastern Virginia, among others. The name, spelled many different ways, loosely translates as "an order of noodles."

Ho is quick to point out that the original Cantonese soup would've been very different from what you can find now in soul food places across New Orleans (yakamein made with Creole spices and a soy sauce–heavy broth and finished with hot sauce). "Creole yakamein and Chinese yakamein are completely different from each other and don't taste or look anything alike. Most Chinese now and in the past would consider Creole yakamein too salty."

When asked about the Chinese influence in New Orleans food in a 2009 interview by chef and food writer Gisele Perez, the famed chef of Dooky Chase's Restaurant and "Queen of Creole Cuisine" Leah Chase echoed Ho's theory, explaining that Chinese and African Americans commingled their food traditions while living side by side. Yakamein became a dish influenced by the many cultures of the great city of New Orleans.

And so yakamein spread and evolved, from Chinese restaurants in the once-bustling New Orleans Chinatown to their Black patrons and then to Black-owned Creole and soul food bars and restaurants. One such establishment, Bean Brothers Bar, is where Shirley Green, Linda Green's mother and culinary inspiration, sold her yakamein. Shirley passed her closely guarded, wildly popular recipe to Linda. And

Linda in turn has served it up for countless others at the jazz festival, in local museums, and at surprise events outside her home. Her efforts have immensely widened yakamein's mysterious appeal.

Linda—who has shared her recipe with only her daughter—continues to guard the family secret. Since not everyone can just walk down the street and order a bowl of yakamein, I quilted together this recipe from my many samples of her version and the variations I tasted in restaurants all over New Orleans, so you can try your hand at making your own.

—MATTHEW FAIRMAN, *Cook's Country*

Beef Yakamein (New Orleans Spicy Beef Noodle Soup)

SERVES 6   TOTAL TIME: 3¼ HOURS

Smaller chuck-eye roasts (such as the one called for in this recipe) are sometimes sold prepackaged and labeled as chuck steak. If you can find only chuck roasts larger than 2 pounds, ask the butcher to cut a smaller roast for you or cut your own 2-pound roast and freeze the remaining meat for another use. Sriracha or Tabasco can be substituted for the Crystal Hot Sauce. We developed this recipe with Kikkoman Soy Sauce and Better Than Bouillon Roasted Beef Base. Monosodium glutamate, an umami-enhancing seasoning that gives the broth a savory boost, is sold under the brand name Ac'cent. Look for it in the spice aisle.

1   (2-pound) boneless beef chuck-eye roast, trimmed
2   teaspoons kosher salt
2   teaspoons pepper
2   tablespoons vegetable oil
1   onion, chopped
1   green bell pepper, stemmed, seeded, and chopped
1   celery rib, chopped
4   garlic cloves, minced
1   tablespoon Tony Chachere's Original Creole Seasoning
1   tablespoon sugar
1   teaspoon onion powder
½   teaspoon Ac'cent (optional)
8   cups beef broth
¼   cup soy sauce, plus extra for serving
12   ounces spaghetti
3   hard-cooked large eggs, halved
6   scallions, sliced ¼ inch thick
    Crystal Hot Sauce

BEEF YAKAMEIN (NEW ORLEANS SPICY BEEF NOODLE SOUP)

BUILDING THE BOWL

The components of yakamein are layered in sequentially, starting with the pasta and ending with the broth.

5. BROTH

4. SCALLIONS

3. EGG

2. BEEF

1. PASTA

1. Pat beef dry with paper towels and sprinkle with salt and pepper. Heat oil in large Dutch oven over medium-high heat until shimmering. Add beef and cook until well browned on all sides, 8 to 12 minutes. Transfer beef to plate.

2. Add onion, bell pepper, and celery to fat left in pot and cook until softened, 5 to 7 minutes. Add garlic; Creole seasoning; sugar; onion powder; and Ac'cent, if using, and cook until fragrant, about 1 minute. Stir in broth and soy sauce, scraping up any browned bits. Return beef to pot and bring to boil over high heat. Cover; reduce heat to low; and simmer until beef is tender, 1½ to 2 hours.

3. Transfer beef to cutting board and let cool until easy to handle, at least 20 minutes. Use wide spoon to skim excess fat from broth. Set colander over large bowl. Strain broth through colander, pressing on solids to extract all liquid. Discard solids in colander. Return broth to pot; cover and keep warm over low heat.

4. Meanwhile, bring 3 quarts water to boil in large saucepan. Add pasta and cook until fully tender. Drain pasta and return it to saucepan. Cover and set aside.

5. Using chef's knife, chop beef into approximate ¾-inch pieces. Divide pasta evenly among 6 serving bowls. Divide beef, eggs, and scallions evenly among serving bowls on top of pasta. Ladle hot broth into serving bowls to cover pasta (about 1½ cups each). Serve, passing hot sauce and extra soy sauce separately.

JAMAICAN STEW PEAS WITH SPINNERS

✓ **WHY THIS RECIPE WORKS** To replicate this homey Jamaican stew using ingredients easily found in American supermarkets, we made some simple substitutions. First, we swapped in dried small red beans for the Jamaican dried red peas. Second, instead of salted pig tails or salted beef, we used smoked ham hocks, which, though not traditional, was not a huge leap since some cooks make stew peas using the leftover ham bone. Fine-tuning the spices and aromatics—allspice berries, garlic, garlic powder, celery, thyme, and a Scotch bonnet chile—gave the stew rich, nuanced flavor, and a combination of chicken broth and coconut milk added savoriness and sweet creaminess. To make the dish even more satisfying, we finished by adding the rustic flour-and-water dumplings known as spinners.

When I left oceanside Montego Bay, Jamaica, to attend cooking school in the hills of New York's Hudson Valley, making a warming batch of my grandmother's stew peas always soothed my homesick heart. And whenever I returned to visit, Grandma invariably welcomed me with a pot bubbling with rich coconut milk; perfumed with fresh thyme, scallions, a fiery Scotch bonnet chile, and allspice berries (known as pimento in the Caribbean); and brimming with red peas, salted pig tails, and the simple dumplings known as spinners.

These days, I am again living on the island, and the homey dish is still woven into our routine: After making a batch, Grandma always packs extra in a food storage container for my lunch—a sweet, silent signal that I was on her mind as she cooked.

To many Jamaicans, stew peas is a poem written just for them, a story that speaks of childhoods spent cooking at their grandma's side, and a lesson that teaches proper seasoning of food and the soul. So as I took on the challenge of developing my own version, I felt a deep sense of responsibility. I wanted to create a recipe that would be accessible to cooks in the United States—particularly the Jamaican diaspora—and rise to the level of my grandmother's. In addition to being an avid cook, she was a home economics teacher for 25 years, so the bar was high.

I considered the beans first. Many Jamaicans, including Grandma, use local dried red peas, a petite variety that cooks up creamy, with a distinctive earthiness. Cooks living in more rural areas of the country tend to use garden-fresh red peas, and still others opt for dried red kidney beans, citing a preference for their mild taste.

Since dried red peas aren't easy to source in the United States, I experimented with dried kidney beans as well as beans labeled "small red beans" that have a similar color and size to dried red peas. The small red beans cooked up velvety soft, whereas the kidneys were slightly grainy, so I chose the former.

After soaking the beans overnight, I sautéed some aromatics. Grandma sizzles a straightforward trio of chopped green bell pepper, onion, and loads of fresh garlic in unrefined coconut oil for a potent hit of coconut. In addition to her mix, I included celery for its subtle bitter qualities, along with garlic powder for its roasty tones.

When the onion was translucent, in went the beans and their ruddy soaking liquid, along with some chicken broth. (Grandma keeps it simple with water only, but I liked the subtlety provided by a couple cups of the savory liquid.) Next, I piled a combination of herbs and spices onto a swath of cheesecloth that I secured with kitchen twine, creating a tidy bundle that would be easy to retrieve at the end of simmering. A bay leaf offered a faint medicinal quality that would offset the sweet-nutty coconut milk that I planned on adding later. Allspice berries hinted of clove, cinnamon, and nutmeg; sprigs of fresh thyme provided an herbal

backdrop; and the requisite neon Scotch bonnet flaunted bright, sweet heat.

For the meat, I deviated from the customary salted pig tails or salted beef, both of which must be desalinated prior to cooking and can be hard to find in the States. Instead, I opted for a pair of smoked ham hocks, which, though not traditional, was not a huge leap since some cooks make stew peas using the leftover bone from a Christmas ham.

Pressure cooking has become a common method for making stew peas, welcomed by many households because of the time and fuel savings. However, I went with an unhurried stovetop approach because I found that the flavors melded together a bit more elegantly during a leisurely simmer.

After 1½ hours, the beans had begun to soften and release their plush starch into the broth, which was slightly reduced. I stirred in some coconut milk and continued to simmer for 30 minutes longer until the beans were tender. Jamaicans are partial toward coconut milk powder reconstituted with water, but the canned type is amply satiny and coconutty.

While the beans finished, I mixed up the dough for the spinners. Children are often encouraged to help prepare these rustic delights, kneading flour, water, and a touch of salt together before "spinning" bits of dough between their small palms and gently dropping the tapered oblong shapes into the stew.

By the time I had produced a plateful of spinners, the ham hocks were tender and the beans soft and creamy. I pulled the hocks out of the pot and dropped in the spinners. While the dumplings poached, I picked off the succulent ham, discarded the bones along with any skin and excess fat, and chopped the meat into small pieces before returning it to the stew.

To finish, I stirred in more fresh thyme—chopped this time—along with a generous handful of chopped scallions, before letting the stew simmer for 10 to 15 minutes longer until the allium just wilted, providing a grassy freshness that most versions lack.

With creamy red beans, smoky ham, and hearty dumplings floating in a silky broth redolent with coconut and bold herbs, spices, and aromatics, my stew peas recipe was complete. To celebrate, my family held a good-natured cook-off: my stew peas versus Grandma's. It was a close battle, but after careful deliberation, my entry was crowned the winner for being slightly more refined and balanced. And yet, I couldn't

FIERY OR MILD? IT'S UP TO YOU

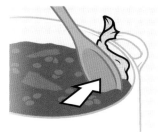

Scotch bonnets are typically dropped whole into a pot of stew peas, where, during simmering, the chile eventually bursts, or "buss," as Jamaicans say, releasing its potent juice into the broth. But wrapping the chile (first pierced with the tip of a paring knife) in a cheesecloth bundle prevents it from breaking apart, thus offering the cook some control over the spiciness level of the stew. Before removing the bundle, taste the broth. If it needs more zing, use the back of a spoon to press the bundle against the side of the pot, squeezing out the pungent liquid that resides in the chile.

claim victory. Nothing could beat the patience, love, and care embodied in Grandma's stew peas. In my eyes, she remains undefeated.

—DIONNE REID, *Cook's Illustrated*

Jamaican Stew Peas with Spinners

SERVES 6 TO 8   TOTAL TIME: 3 HOURS, PLUS 8 HOURS SOAKING

You can substitute dried red kidney beans for the small, dark-red dried beans (usually labeled "small red beans") and vegetable oil for the coconut oil, if desired. If you can't find a Scotch bonnet chile, use a habanero. For the best results, use full-fat coconut milk. Serve with steamed long-grain white rice.

- 1 pound (about 2 cups) dried small red beans, picked over and rinsed
- 6 cups plus 3 tablespoons water, divided
- 4 sprigs fresh thyme, plus 1 tablespoon chopped
- 1 Scotch bonnet chile, pierced once with tip of paring knife
- 1 bay leaf
- 1 teaspoon whole allspice berries
- 1 tablespoon unrefined coconut oil
- 1 onion, chopped
- 1 green bell pepper, stemmed, seeded, and chopped
- 1 large celery rib, chopped (¾ cup)
- 3 tablespoons minced garlic
- 2 teaspoons garlic powder
- 1¼ teaspoons table salt, divided

- ½ teaspoon pepper
- 2 (12-ounce) smoked ham hocks
- 2 cups chicken broth
- 1 (14-ounce) can coconut milk
- ½ cup all-purpose flour
- 6 scallions, chopped

1. Combine beans and 6 cups water in large container and soak at room temperature for at least 8 hours or up to 24 hours.

2. Bundle thyme sprigs, Scotch bonnet, bay leaf, and allspice in cheesecloth; secure with kitchen twine; and set aside. Heat oil in large Dutch oven over medium heat until shimmering. Add onion, bell pepper, celery, garlic, garlic powder, ½ teaspoon salt, and pepper and cook, stirring occasionally, until onion is translucent, 6 to 8 minutes.

3. Add beans and their soaking liquid, ham hocks, chicken broth, cheesecloth bundle, and ½ teaspoon salt. Increase heat to high and bring to boil. Lower heat to maintain a vigorous simmer. Cook uncovered, stirring occasionally, until beans start to soften and liquid is slightly reduced, about 1½ hours. Stir in coconut milk and continue to cook until beans are completely soft (it's OK if some skins crack) and sauce thickens, about 30 minutes longer.

4. While stew simmers, combine flour and remaining ¼ teaspoon salt in bowl. Make well in mixture. Gradually add remaining 3 tablespoons water, stirring until shaggy mass forms. Knead in bowl until dough clears sides of bowl and forms tight ball (if dough seems too dry to shape, add up to 2 teaspoons water, ½ teaspoon at a time). Pinch off about 1 teaspoon dough and roll between your palms to form 3-inch-long dumpling with tapered ends. Transfer to plate and repeat with remaining dough (you should have 14 to 16 dumplings).

5. Taste stew; adjust spiciness, if desired, by pressing cheesecloth bundle against side of pot with back of spoon to release juice of Scotch bonnet. Discard bundle and transfer ham hocks to plate to cool slightly. Gently drop dumplings into stew. Simmer, without stirring, until dumplings are set, about 5 minutes. While dumplings cook, debone ham hocks and cut meat into ½-inch pieces (you'll have ½ to ⅔ cup meat); discard bones, skin, and fat. Stir meat, scallions, and chopped thyme into stew. Season with salt and pepper to taste. Simmer until flavors have melded and scallions have softened slightly, 10 to 15 minutes. Serve.

OKRA AND SHRIMP STEW

✓ **WHY THIS RECIPE WORKS** This long-simmered, complexly flavored mix of vegetables and seafood takes a bit of time, but the investment is worth it. This stew is a gumbo-style dish, but unlike the more familiar Louisiana-style gumbos, it does not rely upon a deep-brown roux or filé powder for flavor and texture. The dish is known by different names, including okra stew and okra gumbo, which can be confusing: The word "gumbo" is derived from the West African word "gombo," which literally means "okra." What is important to know is that all these stews are closely related and the names are used interchangeably; bright-green okra, with its sticky, slimy character, serves as a natural thickener; and the stews often start with a flavorful, slow-simmered broth or stock made from a large smoked ham bone. A ham stock is a common element in African American cookery.

For me, okra and shrimp stew represents home. Its ingredients reflect a wise use of the land and sea, and its cooking methods and simple techniques reveal a cultural wisdom that simmers up both deep flavors and emotions. When I make the thick stew, which is well-known in the Carolina Lowcountry, I'm instantly reminded of my childhood home and memories of happily slurping up second helpings. I am also surprised that so few people outside the region know about the long-simmered, complexly flavored mix of vegetables and seafood. Making okra and shrimp stew takes a bit of time, but the investment is worth it. This is a dish that is meant to be shared among family, friends, and community.

Okra and shrimp stew is a gumbo-style dish, but unlike the more familiar Louisiana-style gumbos, our gumbos in the Lowcountry do not rely upon a deep-brown roux or filé powder for flavor and texture. The dish is known by different names, including okra stew and okra gumbo, which can be confusing: The word "gumbo" is derived from the West African word "gombo," which literally means "okra."

What is important to know is that all these stews are closely related and the names are used interchangeably; bright-green okra, with its sticky, slimy character, serves as a natural thickener; and the stews often start with a flavorful, slow-simmered broth or stock made from a large smoked ham bone. Ham stock is a familiar element in African American cookery. In some Lowcountry kitchens, it is common to see a pot of stock simmering all day on the back burner of the stove, ready for use as a flavorful base for hoppin' John, slow-cooked lima beans, or collard greens as well as in soups, stews, and gumbos.

And while some cooks reserve their soups, stews, and gumbos for when the weather is cooler, I grew up eating this meal all year round, served with simple white rice.

—AMETHYST GANAWAY, *Cook's Country*

Okra and Shrimp Stew

SERVES 8 TO 10 TOTAL TIME: 5 HOURS

If you can find medium shrimp (41 to 50 per pound), use those and leave them whole. Look for meaty ham hocks. If you buy the test kitchen's preferred brand of andouille sausage, Jacob's World Famous Andouille, which tends to be thicker than other products, halve it lengthwise before slicing it crosswise.

4	quarts water
1–1¼	pounds smoked ham hocks
1	onion, quartered
1	bay leaf
1	tablespoon vegetable oil
12	ounces andouille sausage, sliced ¼ inch thick
1	pound frozen or fresh okra (stemmed and cut crosswise ½ inch thick for fresh)
1	(14.5-ounce) can diced tomatoes
1½	cups frozen baby lima (aka butter) beans
4	garlic cloves, minced
2	teaspoons table salt
1	teaspoon pepper
1	teaspoon granulated garlic
1	teaspoon onion powder
½	teaspoon paprika
1	pound large shrimp (26 to 30 per pound), peeled, deveined, and tails removed, cut into thirds
	Cooked white rice

1. Combine water, ham hocks, onion, and bay leaf in large Dutch oven and bring to boil over high heat. Reduce heat to medium-low; cover, with lid slightly ajar; and simmer until ham hocks are fork-tender, 2½ to 3 hours.

2. Remove pot from heat and transfer ham hocks to cutting board. Let ham hocks rest until cool enough to handle; discard onion and bay leaf from broth. Transfer broth to large bowl; measure out 8 cups broth (add enough water to equal 8 cups if necessary; reserve any

OKRA AND SHRIMP STEW

SPOTLIGHT ON OKRA
Finger-shaped okra is the edible seedpod of a plant in the mallow family. At the market, look for relatively small pods, no longer than 3 inches, since bigger pods can be tough. And use them (or freeze them) soon—okra is very perishable. Frozen okra works just as well as fresh in this recipe.

excess for another use). Remove ham from bones, discard bones, and cut ham into bite-size pieces. (Broth and chopped ham can be refrigerated separately for up to 2 days. If fat solidifies on top of broth after chilling, you can discard fat before proceeding, if preferred.)

3. Heat oil in now-empty pot over medium-high heat until shimmering. Add sausage and cook until lightly browned on both sides, about 5 minutes. Add okra, tomatoes and their juice, beans, minced garlic, salt, pepper, granulated garlic, onion powder, paprika, 8 cups broth, and ham to pot. Bring to boil over high heat.

4. Reduce heat to medium and cook at strong simmer, uncovered, until reduced by about half and thickened to stew-like consistency, 55 minutes to 1 hour 5 minutes, stirring occasionally. Reduce heat to low; stir in shrimp; and cook until shrimp are just cooked through, about 3 minutes. Remove from heat and season with salt and pepper to taste. Serve over rice.

CRISPY LENTIL AND HERB SALAD

✓ **WHY THIS RECIPE WORKS** Inspired by lentil preparations in countries such as India, Lebanon, Syria, and Turkey, we decided to fry the lentils for this salad rather than use boiled lentils. Salt-soaking the lentils before frying was crucial to ensure that they turned tender and lightly crispy and didn't burn. We tested various lentils and found that the firm texture of lentilles du Puy held up well when quickly fried in a saucepan. Instead of tossing the components together with a dressing, we used yogurt as an anchor for the other ingredients, spreading it on a platter and topping it with a lightly dressed blend of fresh herbs tossed with the crunchy lentils and sweet bits of dried cherries. Pita was a must for scooping everything up in one perfect bite.

Nutritious, hearty, and filling, lentils work well in salads. But while there are many versions of lentil salads made with simple boiled lentils, not many make crispy lentils the star. For this recipe, we were inspired by crispy lentil preparations where lentils are fried for snacking.

To start, we focused on the preparation of the lentils. We know that soaking beans in a saltwater solution softens their skin. As the beans soak, the sodium ions replace some of the calcium and magnesium ions in the bean skins. Because sodium ions are more weakly charged than calcium and magnesium ions, they allow more water to penetrate the skins, leading to a softer texture. During soaking, the sodium ions travel only partway into the beans, so their greatest effect is on the cells in the outermost part of the beans. And because lentils are smaller and have a thinner coating, they don't need to be brined for as long as beans do. We tested varying soaking times and found that they needed a minimum of 1 hour before frying to produce lentils that were tender on the inside and lightly crispy on the outside.

A shallow fry in a saucepan limited the amount of oil we needed and minimized the mess. As the lentils crisped, the oil mixture bubbled and steamed—a natural part of the dehydration process that occurs when deep-frying food. Stirring the lentils constantly during their short cooking time was crucial to ensuring evenly cooked lentils. If we didn't, some were soggy, while others burned. To boost the flavor, we sprinkled salt and cumin over them when they were still warm.

While these perfectly crisped and seasoned lentils can be stored in an airtight container and enjoyed as a snack, we wanted to showcase them in a salad that was fit for company. We needed to choose other salad components that paired well with the lentils' texture and flavor. To start, we needed an anchor. Thick and creamy Greek yogurt proved a perfect base, as its smooth texture and tart flavor complemented the crunchy texture and savory flavor of the lentils. Seasoning the yogurt with extra-virgin olive oil, lemon, and garlic turned it into a flavorful dressing. For serving, we "schmeared" the yogurt on the platter and arranged the lentils on top.

CRISPY LENTIL AND HERB SALAD

To bulk up the salad, we opted for a medley of fresh herbs. Dressing an ample amount of fresh parsley, dill, and cilantro with a little oil and salt transformed the herbs into the leafy green component. We first tried layering the dressed herbs on top of the yogurt and the lentils on top of the herbs, but we found that the lentils weighed down the herbs and detracted from the final presentation. Gently tossing the crisped lentils with the herbs created vibrancy and balance.

Our salad had a combination of textures and bright, fresh, and savory flavors, but it still needed another flavor component. Sweet and tart dried cherries proved to be a simple addition that worked well stirred in with the crisped lentils and herbs. A final drizzle of pomegranate molasses right before serving completed the meal, but the salad also works great without the pomegranate molasses finish.

This salad is great for sharing at a small dinner party as a starter but is also hearty enough (thanks to the protein boost from the lentils and yogurt) to enjoy as a light meal. We prefer scooping the salad up with pita wedges to get the perfect combination of the rich yogurt base with the fresh herbs, seasoned crispy lentils, and sweet cherries in every bite.

—LEAH COLINS, *America's Test Kitchen Books*

Crispy Lentil and Herb Salad

SERVES 4   TOTAL TIME: 40 MINUTES, PLUS 1 HOUR BRINING

Brown lentils can be substituted for the lentilles du Puy, if desired. Be sure to use a large saucepan to fry the lentils, as the oil mixture will bubble and steam.

    1   teaspoon table salt for brining
    ½   cup dried lentilles du Puy, picked over and rinsed
    ⅓   cup vegetable oil for frying
    ½   teaspoon ground cumin
    ¼   teaspoon plus pinch table salt, divided
    1   cup plain Greek yogurt
    3   tablespoons extra-virgin olive oil, divided
    1   teaspoon grated lemon zest plus 1 teaspoon juice
    1   garlic clove, minced
    ½   cup fresh parsley leaves
    ½   cup torn fresh dill
    ½   cup fresh cilantro leaves
    ¼   cup dried cherries, chopped
        Pomegranate molasses
        Pita, warmed

1. Dissolve 1 teaspoon salt in 1 quart water in bowl. Add lentils and let sit at room temperature for at least 1 hour or up to 24 hours. Drain well and pat dry with paper towels.

2. Heat vegetable oil in large saucepan over medium heat until shimmering. Add lentils and cook, stirring constantly, until crispy and golden in spots, 8 to 12 minutes (oil should bubble vigorously throughout; adjust heat as needed). Carefully drain lentils in fine-mesh strainer set over bowl, then transfer lentils to paper towel–lined plate. Discard oil. Sprinkle lentils with cumin and ¼ teaspoon salt and toss to combine; set aside. (Cooled lentils can be stored in airtight container at room temperature for up to 24 hours.)

3. Whisk yogurt, 2 tablespoons olive oil, lemon zest and juice, and garlic together in bowl and season with salt and pepper to taste. Spread yogurt mixture over serving platter. Toss parsley, dill, cilantro, remaining pinch salt, and remaining 1 tablespoon olive oil together in bowl, then gently stir in lentils and cherries and arrange on top of yogurt mixture, leaving 1-inch border. Drizzle with pomegranate molasses. Serve with pita.

BUTTERNUT SQUASH SALAD

WHY THIS RECIPE WORKS Whisking mayonnaise into a combination of tahini, lemon juice, and water created a flavorful dressing with over-the-top creaminess. We topped the vegetables with rich, crunchy toasted pecans, which added heft and textural intrigue. Briny kalamata olives brought in welcome pops of saltiness, further balancing the sweetness of the squash and onion. Finally, we layered on a fistful of vibrant fresh mint (parsley, dill, and cilantro also work great).

Yotam Ottolenghi, an Israeli-born, London-based chef and cookbook author of well-deserved fame, has been one of the great culinary influences over the past decade. It was in his book *Jerusalem* (2012) (coauthored with Sami Tamimi) that I first encountered the delightful combination of roasted butternut squash and red onion with lemon-tahini sauce, and that recipe is the inspiration and jumping-off point for this salad.

To make this dish my own, I adapted Ottolenghi's side dish into a substantial meal; I serve the roasted butternut squash and onion (seasoned simply with olive oil, cumin, salt, and pepper) on a bed of baby arugula, which adds color contrast, freshness, and a peppery foil to the sweet roasted vegetables. Whisking mayonnaise into a mix of tahini, lemon juice, and water creates a flavorful dressing with over-the-top creaminess. Instead of the pine nuts in the original recipe, I top the vegetables with rich, crunchy toasted pecans, which add heft and textural intrigue. Briny kalamata olives bring in welcome pops of saltiness, further balancing the sweetness of the squash and onion.

Finally, Ottolenghi sprinkles his version with za'atar (a concentrated mix of dried herbs, sumac, and sesame seeds). For something a little fresher and brighter, I layer on a fistful of vibrant fresh mint (parsley, dill, and cilantro also work great). The result is a unique, gorgeous salad that makes a satisfying vegetarian dinner or a beautiful addition to a grand holiday spread.

—MATTHEW FAIRMAN, *Cook's Country*

Roasted Butternut Squash Salad with Creamy Tahini Dressing

SERVES 6   TOTAL TIME: 2 HOURS

We developed this recipe using Ziyad Tahini Sesame Paste. Using other tahini products may result in a thicker or thinner salad dressing. The dressing should be the consistency of buttermilk (or slightly thicker than heavy cream). If the dressing seems thick, thin it out with water, 1 teaspoon at a time, until it's smooth and pourable. If the dressing seems thin, add extra tahini, 1 teaspoon at a time, to thicken it. You can substitute parsley, dill, or cilantro for the mint, if desired.

ROASTED SQUASH

- 1 (2- to 2¼-pound) butternut squash, peeled, seeded, and cut into 1-inch pieces (7 cups)
- 1 red onion, halved and sliced through root end ½ inch thick
- 2 tablespoons extra-virgin olive oil
- 2 teaspoons ground cumin
- 1¼ teaspoons table salt
- ½ teaspoon pepper

DRESSING AND SALAD

- ¼ cup tahini
- ¼ cup water
- 2 tablespoons mayonnaise
- 2 tablespoons lemon juice
- 1 garlic clove, minced

- ½ teaspoon table salt
- ¼ teaspoon pepper
- 5 ounces (5 cups) baby arugula
- ¾ cup pecans, toasted and chopped
- ⅓ cup pitted kalamata olives, chopped
- ¼ cup chopped fresh mint

1. FOR THE ROASTED SQUASH: Adjust oven rack to middle position and heat oven to 425 degrees. Toss all ingredients together in bowl. Spread vegetables in single layer on rimmed baking sheet. Roast until squash and onion are browned and tender, 35 to 45 minutes, stirring halfway through roasting. Remove sheet from oven and let cool for 15 minutes.

2. FOR THE DRESSING AND SALAD: Meanwhile, whisk tahini, water, mayonnaise, lemon juice, garlic, salt, and pepper in now-empty bowl until creamy and thoroughly combined, about 30 seconds.

3. Reserve ¼ cup dressing. Add arugula to remaining dressing in bowl and toss to combine. Season with salt and pepper to taste. Spread arugula

NOTES FROM THE TEST KITCHEN

SQUASH PREP

1. Peel thoroughly, then cut between neck and bulb.

2. Halve each piece (neck and bulb) lengthwise.

3. Remove seeds and pulp from both halves of bulb before cutting neck and bulb into 1-inch pieces.

on large serving platter. Top with squash and onion, pecans, olives, and mint. Drizzle salad with reserved dressing. Serve.

TO MAKE AHEAD: Cooled cooked vegetables can be refrigerated for up to 24 hours. Let sit at room temperature for 1 hour before assembling salad and serving. Dressing can be refrigerated for up to 3 days but may thicken over time. If dressing becomes too thick, adjust consistency with water as needed.

SWISS CHARD SALAD

✓ **WHY THIS RECIPE WORKS** Unlike heartier kale, chard is tender enough to be eaten raw without any pretreatment. It's also lighter, fresher, and slightly less earthy-tasting than cooked chard. The other ingredients create a well-balanced blend of flavors. A bright, sweet vinaigrette of fig preserves, whole-grain mustard, red wine vinegar, and minced shallot complemented not only the chard but also some peppery, pungent blue cheese and salty, rich prosciutto. A handful of shredded fresh basil layered in complexity with its herbal notes of licorice, while toasted walnuts added luxurious nuttiness and crunch.

Looking almost like a tangle of emerald-green fettuccine when plated, this shredded Swiss chard salad is one of the most beautiful recipes you can make with a fresh, vibrantly colored bunch of leafy greens. Happily, chard (which is also commonly known as silver beet and perpetual spinach) is not just exceptionally nutritious, being rich in vitamins, minerals, and fiber—it also makes a delicious salad green when simply stemmed, sliced, and tossed in dressing. Unlike heartier kale, which needs some massaging or light cooking to

NOTES FROM THE TEST KITCHEN

STEMMING SWISS CHARD

Lay leaves flat on cutting board and cut along sides of stems to remove any stems thicker than ¼ inch.

tenderize, chard is tender enough to be eaten raw without any pretreatment. It's also lighter, fresher, and slightly less earthy-tasting than cooked chard.

The other ingredients in this salad make for perfect foils to the mild and pleasantly bitter leafy green, creating a harmonious, balanced blend of flavors. A bright, sweet vinaigrette of fig preserves, whole-grain mustard, red wine vinegar, and minced shallot complements not only the chard but also some peppery, pungent blue cheese and salty, rich prosciutto. A handful of shredded fresh basil layers in complexity with its herbal notes of licorice, while toasted walnuts add luxurious nuttiness and crunch. If it isn't already, with this recipe in your hands, chard could become your new favorite salad green.

—MATTHEW FAIRMAN, *Cook's Country*

Shredded Swiss Chard Salad with Prosciutto, Basil, and Blue Cheese

SERVES 4 TO 6 TOTAL TIME: 20 MINUTES

You can use any color Swiss chard in this recipe.

12 ounces Swiss chard
3 tablespoons extra-virgin olive oil
3 tablespoons red wine vinegar
2 tablespoons fig preserves
1 small shallot, minced
2 teaspoons whole-grain mustard
½ teaspoon table salt
½ teaspoon pepper
½ cup shredded fresh basil
3 ounces thinly sliced prosciutto, torn into bite-size pieces, divided
½ cup walnuts, toasted and chopped coarse, divided
2 ounces blue cheese, crumbled (½ cup), divided

1. Stem Swiss chard, cutting out any stems thicker than ¼ inch from middle of chard leaves. Halve leaves lengthwise, then stack them on cutting board and slice crosswise ¼ inch thick.

2. Whisk oil, vinegar, fig preserves, shallot, mustard, salt, and pepper together in large bowl. Add chard, basil, half of prosciutto, half of walnuts, and half of blue cheese and toss to combine. Transfer salad to platter or individual serving plates and top with remaining prosciutto, walnuts, and blue cheese. Serve.

TOMATO AND CHICKPEA SALAD

✔ WHY THIS RECIPE WORKS To create a fresh, hearty salad based on the flavors of romesco, the classic Spanish sauce, we started by using chopped fresh tomatoes and green bell pepper—instead of the traditional red—for its vegetal flavor and emerald-green color. Two minced garlic cloves, some sliced shallot, plenty of extra-virgin olive oil, and sherry vinegar brought depth and interest. A little smoked paprika gave the salad complex smoky undertones, and some fresh mint balanced out the intensity of the other players with its fresh and cool flavor. To get the most crunch and flavor out of the almonds, it was important to toast them well before adding them to the mix. And for heft, we stirred in a can of chickpeas. Before serving, we allowed the salad to sit for 20 minutes so that the flavors could meld and the chickpeas could soak up their share of the flavorful dressing.

Romesco, a classic sauce that originated in Catalonia, Spain, is a mix of tomatoes, peppers, garlic, onions, almonds, and olive oil all blended (or pounded) together. It makes a great accompaniment to grilled or roasted meats. Since it's prime tomato season, I decided to create a fresh, hearty salad based on the same flavors. Here's how to make it.

Core and chop a pound of ripe tomatoes and transfer them to a bowl. Then chop a green bell pepper and add it to the tomatoes. (Most romescos use red bell peppers, in part because pulverized green peppers turn the sauce a muddy color, but we preferred the vegetal flavor and emerald color of green here.) Follow the peppers with two minced garlic cloves; some sliced shallot; plenty of extra-virgin olive oil; and nutty, sharp sherry vinegar for depth and interest. A little smoked paprika gives the salad complex smoky undertones, and some coarsely chopped mint balances out the intensity of the other players with its fresh and cool flavor.

To get the most crunch and flavor out of the almonds, it's important to toast them well before adding them to the mix. And for heft, stir in a can of drained and rinsed chickpeas. Then let the salad sit for 20 minutes before serving to allow the flavors to meld and to let the chickpeas soak up their share of the flavorful dressing.

—MARK HUXSOLL, *Cook's Country*

NOTES FROM THE TEST KITCHEN

A SPANISH FLAIR
Smoked paprika is a powerhouse ingredient, providing smoky complexity wherever you add it (use it judiciously). Our favorite product is Simply Organic Smoked Paprika. Sherry vinegar has more of a savory punch than most other vinegars: It's nutty, oaky, and rich. Our taste test winner is Napa Valley Naturals Reserve Sherry Vinegar.

Tomato and Chickpea Salad

SERVES 4 TOTAL TIME: 35 MINUTES

This salad is best made with ripe, in-season heirloom tomatoes. If those are not available, opt for ripe tomatoes on the vine that are tender to the touch. Two large shallots, or three medium, should be enough to yield the ½ cup of sliced shallots called for here.

- 1 **pound tomatoes, cored and cut into ½-inch pieces**
- 1 **(15-ounce) can chickpeas, rinsed**
- 1 **green bell pepper, stemmed, seeded, and cut into ½-inch pieces**
- ¾ **cup whole almonds, toasted and chopped**
- ½ **cup thinly sliced shallots**
- ⅓ **cup coarsely chopped fresh mint**
- 3 **tablespoons extra-virgin olive oil**
- 1½ **tablespoons sherry vinegar**
- 2 **garlic cloves, minced**
- 1½ **teaspoons table salt**
- ¾ **teaspoon smoked paprika**
- ½ **teaspoon pepper**

Combine all ingredients in bowl. Let sit for 20 minutes to allow flavors to blend. Serve using slotted spoon.

LAO HU CAI (TIGER SALAD)

✔ WHY THIS RECIPE WORKS This vibrant Chinese salad, named for its bold flavors and textures, is served to stimulate the appetite at the beginning of a meal or to reset the palate between courses. We balanced the bracing vinaigrette, piquant scallions, and hot chiles with the herbal freshness of cilantro and the juicy crunch of celery. The earthy sweetness of the nuts and seeds and the rich sesame oil further tempered the dish.

The essay "A Word for Autumn" by A. A. Milne is, in part, a tribute to the end of summer and a meditation on the changing seasons—but it's mostly about Milne's unfettered passion for celery.

"It is as fresh and clean as a rainy day after a spell of heat," he rhapsodizes about the vegetable, which he feels best captures the "crispness" of the cold months. "How delicate are the tender shoots unfolded layer by layer. Of what a whiteness is the last baby one of all, of what a sweetness his flavour."

The *Winnie the Pooh* author is hardly the lone member of celery's fan club. For centuries, enthusiasts around the world have flocked to the plant: from Egypt and China, where wild varieties were used medicinally as a hangover cure or aphrodisiac, to Greece and Rome, where victorious athletes were crowned with celery leaves. And after cultivation of wide, crisp stalks began in the 1800s, the vegetable became downright trendy in the United States—Americans in the late part of that century ordered celery prepared myriad ways in restaurants (mashed, fried, as tea, as jelly) and also used it to adorn their dining tables at home, presenting stalks in elaborate crystal "celery vases" for their dinner guests to munch on.

If you ask me, the vegetable is well worth the attention. The three commercially grown varieties of celery—each cultivated for a unique purpose—produce parts with complex flavors, textures, and hues, offering cooks a wealth of possibilities in the kitchen. The *dulce* variety most popular in the West produces tall, grassy, herbaceous stalks. The *rapaceum* variety produces a bulbous underground stem known as celery root or celeriac that boasts an earthy-sweet flavor and takes well to braising, roasting, and pureeing. Finally, leaf celery, or the *secalinum* variety, grows more delicate-looking but more intensely flavored leaves and stems, often used in stir-fries and soups.

My version of lao hu cai, or Northern Chinese tiger salad, enlivens juicy, crunchy celery ribs with a bracing vinaigrette, piquant scallions, and plenty of hot chiles and cilantro.

—STEVE DUNN, *Cook's Illustrated*

NOTES FROM THE TEST KITCHEN

ONE SPECIES, THREE VARIETIES

While all celery belongs to the same species, *Apium graveolens*, there are three unique varieties of the celery plant that are cultivated commercially, each bred for different purposes.

STALK CELERY	CELERY ROOT	LEAF CELERY
var. dulce	*var. rapaceum*	*var. secalinum*
Commonly known in the West as just "celery," this plant is cultivated to grow tall, crisp stalks. It's grassy, with hints of sweetness and bitterness.	This plant produces celery root (celeriac). It has been bred to produce an underground base much more substantial and bulbous than that of the *dulce* variety, and its stalks are small and thin.	Known variously as leaf celery, Chinese celery, and smallage, this plant is more diminutive, aromatic, and leafy than the *dulce* variety. Its strongly flavored stems, stalks, and leaves are often used in soups and stir-fries.

Lao Hu Cai (Tiger Salad)

SERVES 4 AS AN APPETIZER OR A SIDE DISH

TOTAL TIME: 25 MINUTES

For a spicier salad, include the chile seeds. For less spice, substitute half of a small green bell pepper (cut into 2-inch-long matchsticks) for the serrano. Serve as a light appetizer or as a palate cleanser between courses.

- 1 tablespoon unseasoned rice vinegar
- 1 teaspoon sugar
- ½ teaspoon table salt
- ½ teaspoon soy sauce
- ¾ teaspoon toasted sesame oil
- 1 Thai chile, stemmed, halved, seeded, and sliced thin
- 3½ cups fresh cilantro leaves and tender stems, chopped into 2-inch lengths
- 4 celery ribs, sliced on bias ¼ inch thick

3 scallions, white and green parts sliced thin on bias

1 serrano chile, stemmed, quartered, seeded, and sliced thin

2 teaspoons sesame seeds, toasted

2 tablespoons chopped salted dry-roasted peanuts

1. In small bowl, stir vinegar, sugar, salt, and soy sauce until sugar and salt are completely dissolved. Add oil and Thai chile and stir to combine.

2. In large bowl, combine cilantro, celery, scallions, and serrano. Sprinkle with sesame seeds and dressing and toss to combine.

3. Transfer salad to platter, sprinkle with peanuts, and serve immediately.

CHOPPED VEGETABLE AND STONE FRUIT SALAD

✓ **WHY THIS RECIPE WORKS** Chopped vegetable salads—frequently composed of finely diced tomatoes, cucumbers, and parsley tossed in olive oil and lemon juice—can be found across the eastern Mediterranean. They are known by a variety of names and typically served with most meals. We took inspiration for our interpretation from both traditional versions and from modern takes, opting to swap out tomatoes for stone fruit and add radishes, bell pepper, and lemony sumac, along with generous amounts of fresh mint and parsley. Salting and lightly sugaring the fruit first helped intensify its flavor and extracted some of the juice that would have resulted in a watery salad.

Nearly every cuisine of the eastern Mediterranean serves a refreshing, crunchy, raw chopped vegetable salad with most meals. There are as many names as there are versions: çoban salatası (shepherd's salad) in Turkey, salata baladi (country salad) in Egypt, and salat aravi (Arab salad) in Israel are just a few. My first encounter with a version of this salad was while on my honeymoon in Istanbul, where ordering a shepherd's salad produced a small plate of sweet juicy tomato wedges, crisp chunks of Persian cucumbers, thinly sliced red onion, and a sprinkle of minced parsley, all tossed together with lemon juice and olive oil. It was simple but perfect in its composition of flavors and textures, and I subsequently ordered it at every meal. Sometimes it

arrived at the table sprinkled with crumbled feta cheese or accompanied by a few olives. No matter the accompaniments, I enjoyed its bright, crunchy, juicy, fresh, and palate-cleansing effect alongside the more richly seasoned dishes in our meze spread.

Regardless of its name or provenance, this simple side salad's one requirement—and where it derives its depth of flavor despite relatively simple ingredients—is fresh, ripe, in-season vegetables. While cucumbers, tomatoes, parsley, lemon juice, and olive oil are standard, the ingredient list doesn't have to stop there: Some renditions include peppers, radishes, red onions, or scallions along with mint, sumac (a lemony, puckery spice made from the ground berries of a plant indigenous to the Mediterranean), Aleppo pepper, or za'atar. Adding a fried or grilled leftover pita that has been torn into pieces creates fattoush, another branch of this ubiquitous salad's family tree. As Sami Tamimi and Yotam Ottolenghi relate in their cookbook *Jerusalem* (2012), "Each cook, each family, each community has their own variation."

Years later, while working at the eastern Mediterranean–inspired restaurant Sarma in Somerville, Massachusetts, I encountered additional variations of this classic salad. There, Chef Cassie Piuma creates modern interpretations of classic eastern Mediterranean meze with punchy, bold flavors. Her lamb kofte sliders, harissa barbecue duck, and sesame-and-nigella fried chicken with tahini rémoulade are beloved menu mainstays, but her interpretations of vegetable dishes, redolent of fresh herbs and filled with imaginative combinations that frequently incorporate non-Mediterranean ingredients, including sweet potatoes and smoked maple syrup or shishito peppers with halloumi and honey, were most inspirational to me. A chopped vegetable salad was common on her seasonally rotating menu, and while the bones of the traditional salad were there, there was always a twist, sometimes the addition of fruit—nectarines or persimmons depending on the season—combined with an unexpected dressing such as tamarind and lime. I would make, and eat, that salad night after night and never tire of it.

So when tasked with developing a chopped vegetable salad for our *More Mediterranean* cookbook, I knew that my version would draw on both experiences and possess the classic simplicity of a traditional salad, but with a twist. However, the biggest challenge I would

CHOPPED VEGETABLE AND STONE FRUIT SALAD

face was how to account for the lack of in-season fruit and vegetables in the dead of winter in Boston, when I happened to be developing this recipe.

I started with the basics: Persian cucumbers, shallots, lemon juice, olive oil, puckery sumac, and lots of fresh parsley and mint. I added chopped radishes for peppery crunch and bell peppers for sweet juiciness. Instead of the traditional tomatoes, I swapped in stone fruit—plums, peaches, nectarines, or apricots would all work—knowing from my time at Sarma that the fruit's juicy yet firm texture would match well with the chunky ingredients and provide a pop of intense sweetness that would contrast with the tarter ingredients. I tossed it all in olive oil and lemon juice and dug in.

While this fruit and vegetable hybrid was gorgeous to look at—the fuchsia chunks of plums speckled with dark-red sumac glistened in their light coating of lemon juice and olive oil—as I feared, the fruit's flavor was wan, lacking sufficient sweetness to contrast with the acidic elements. Having broken the cardinal rule of this salad—using only fresh in-season ingredients—I wondered how we could make off-season fruit taste closer to their in-season selves.

Then I remembered two techniques that might come in handy here: salting and sugaring. Tossing a vegetable with salt and draining it before adding it to a salad is a common technique to pull out moisture that would otherwise leach into the salad and create a watery mess. In fact, in several versions of chopped vegetable salad recipes I looked at, salting the ingredients and then placing them in a colander was a first step in waterlog prevention. Tossing fruit as well as vegetables in sugar can do the same thing: I recalled the technique we used in a shredded carrot salad, where a toss with salt and sugar not only drew out moisture that would leave the carrot shreds limp and soggy but also made the carrots taste more "carrot-y" by adding a touch of sweetness. Perhaps I could use the same technique to do double duty here: adding sugar to intensify the flavors of out-of-season fruit, and adding salt to draw out extra moisture (particularly when I was fortunate enough to have juicier in-season fruit).

I gave it a shot, tossing the plums in a small amount of salt and sugar and letting them drain in a colander while I prepped the remaining ingredients. Sure enough, the extra touch of sweetness made the plums taste more "plummy," and to my delight, the salting/sugaring step had also improved their texture, making them a bit more juicy and tender instead of dry and mealy. The contrast between the salad's sweeter and tarter elements was now where I wanted it, rounded out by the cooling parsley and mint and full of juicy, crunchy texture. This version was not only beautiful but also worthy of a place on my table at any meal, and at any time of year.

—CAMILA CHAPARRO, *America's Test Kitchen Books*

Chopped Vegetable and Stone Fruit Salad

SERVES 4 TO 6   TOTAL TIME: 30 MINUTES

We call for plums here, but, depending on the season, you can substitute peaches, nectarines, or apricots for the plums, if desired. Ground sumac is made from dried berries that are harvested from a shrub grown in southern Europe and in the Middle East. It is an essential component of za'atar, another spice blend common in the Middle East, but it's also used as an ingredient in spice rubs or sprinkled over foods as a finishing touch. It's bright, with a clean, citrusy flavor and a slight raisiny sweetness—both more balanced and more complex-tasting than lemon juice. You can buy both ground sumac and sumac berries, which you can grind yourself.

- 1 pound ripe but firm plums, halved, pitted, and chopped
- ½ teaspoon plus ⅛ teaspoon table salt, divided
- ½ teaspoon sugar
- 2 tablespoons extra-virgin olive oil
- 2 tablespoons lemon juice
- ¼ teaspoon pepper
- 4 Persian cucumbers, quartered lengthwise and chopped
- 1 red bell pepper, stemmed, seeded, and chopped
- 4 radishes, trimmed and chopped
- ¼ cup minced fresh mint
- ¼ cup minced fresh parsley
- 1 shallot, minced
- 2 teaspoons ground sumac

1. Toss plums with ½ teaspoon salt and sugar in bowl. Transfer to fine-mesh strainer and let drain for 15 minutes, tossing occasionally.

2. Whisk oil, lemon juice, pepper, and remaining ⅛ teaspoon salt together in large bowl. Add drained plums, cucumbers, bell pepper, radishes, mint, parsley, shallot, and sumac and toss gently to combine. Season with salt and pepper to taste, and serve immediately.

LEMON PEPPER WINGS

STARTERS

LEMON PEPPER
CHICKEN WINGS

✓ **WHY THIS RECIPE WORKS** From the mayor on down to the common folks, lemon pepper wings are the undisputed favorite food of the people of Atlanta. An increasingly popular style is called "lemon pepper wet," where crispy fried wings get tossed with a bright, tart, peppery dry seasoning blend and draped with either clarified butter or buffalo sauce. For our version, we created a homemade lemon pepper seasoning by quickly dehydrating fresh lemon zest in the microwave before crumbling it into a mix of coarsely ground black pepper, granulated garlic, onion powder, coriander, sugar, cayenne, and turmeric. Adding ½ teaspoon of citric acid to our seasoning blend gave it the signature mouthwatering tartness of classic lemon pepper blends. Tossing our wings in lemon juice and then a mixture of cornstarch, flour, and a bit of baking powder not only gave them a light, crispy coating out of the fryer but also gave the luscious, bright, buttery sauce something to cling to.

If it's pizza in New York City, po' boys in New Orleans, and fried clams in coastal New England, then it's chicken wings in Atlanta. And not just any wings. With outspoken advocates such as rappers Waka Flocka Flame and Rick Ross, writer Rembert Browne, and even Mayor Keisha Lance Bottoms, it's more or less official: People in this city love lemon pepper wings.

Increasingly it's a version called "lemon pepper wet," a riff on the classic dry-rubbed lemon pepper wing that's doused in a glistening splash of either clarified butter or buffalo sauce (depending on which wing joint you hit up in the city). Though Atlanta natives in the know have likely been customizing their own versions of lemon pepper wet at neighborhood wing joints for years beforehand, the phrase gained widespread attention in 2016 after appearing in Donald Glover's FX television series *Atlanta*. In one scene, up-and-coming rapper Paper Boi is treated by the cook at J.R. Crickets, a beloved chicken spot, to a secret, off-menu special described as "the lemon pepper joints, but [with] the sauce on 'em." Paper Boi and his friend Darius unbox the wings with awe and joy bordering on tears. The scene crystallizes how Atlanta natives feel about their lemon pepper wings.

So if a wing recipe can so captivate one of America's sprawling metropolises, it's worth trying at home. This one is unapologetically wet, taking cues from both the buffalo-based wet sauce and the butter-based style, with every decision made to hype the star of the show: that bright, zesty lemon pepper.

The bedrock of the recipe is a freshly crafted, homemade lemon pepper seasoning blend that's pantry-friendly and comes together quickly and easily. Microwaving grated lemon zest dehydrates it in record time (while retaining its vibrancy), making it shelf-stable and easy to crumble into a complex rub whose other primary ingredient is freshly cracked black pepper. Granulated garlic, onion powder, coriander, cayenne, and sugar (to balance the pepper) round out the flavor profile while a bit of turmeric adds depth and shades

NOTES FROM THE TEST KITCHEN

PREP, COAT, FRY, AND SAUCE!

1. Using kitchen shears or sharp chef's knife, cut through joint between drumette and flat. Cut off and discard wingtip.

2. Toss wings in lemon juice mixture and then in cornstarch mixture, pressing so cornstarch mixture adheres to wings.

3. Fry wings in 375-degree oil in 2 batches until crispy.

4. Add fried wings and lemon pepper seasoning to sauce and toss to coat evenly.

the whole thing bright yellow, reinforcing the visual appeal of the lemony wings.

Most wings in Atlanta aren't dredged in flour before frying, but the addition of a light, crisp coating in this version gives the copious sauce something to cling to. Tossing the uncooked wings in a mix of lemon juice, salt, and pepper not only seasons them but also hydrates the coating of cornstarch, flour, and baking powder, ensuring that the wings fry up crispy and crunchy. After 10 minutes bubbling away in 375-degree oil, the wings emerge golden and ready for a toss in lemon pepper seasoning and that special sauce: rich melted butter, a hit of fresh lemon juice, and Frank's RedHot sauce for kick. Touches of mayo and honey bring not only tang and sweetness but also gloss and body to the sauce, helping it cling to the crispy wings and providing the glorious glow they need to be worthy of the name "lemon pepper wet."

So the next time you gather with friends and loved ones (or simply can't go on without a batch of quality, freshly made wings), serve these up crispy and hot. (True confession: They're also really good cold.) You'll understand what wing aficionados in Atlanta already know and what the rest of us are finally figuring out.

—MATTHEW FAIRMAN, *Cook's Country*

Lemon Pepper Wings

SERVES 4 TO 6   TOTAL TIME: 1¼ HOURS

Citric acid gives our homemade lemon pepper seasoning the signature punchy tartness present in most commercial lemon pepper blends. We developed this recipe using Ball brand citric acid. Look for it in the canning and jarring section of your supermarket or online. When possible, buy whole wings and butcher them yourself because they tend to be larger than wings that come split. If you can find only split wings, look for larger ones. Twelve whole wings should ideally equal 3 pounds and will yield 24 pieces (12 drumettes and 12 flats, with the tips discarded). Serve with blue cheese dressing.

LEMON PEPPER SEASONING

- 3   tablespoons grated lemon zest (3 lemons)
- 1   tablespoon coarsely ground pepper
- 1   teaspoon kosher salt
- 1   teaspoon granulated garlic
- 1   teaspoon onion powder
- 1   teaspoon ground coriander
- ½   teaspoon sugar
- ½   teaspoon citric acid (optional)
- ½   teaspoon ground turmeric
- ¼   teaspoon cayenne pepper

WINGS

- ¾   cup cornstarch
- ¼   cup all-purpose flour
- 2   teaspoons baking powder
- 3   pounds chicken wings, cut at joints, wingtips discarded
- 3   tablespoons lemon juice
- 1   tablespoon kosher salt
- 1   teaspoon pepper
- 2   quarts peanut or vegetable oil for frying

SAUCE

- 8   tablespoons unsalted butter, melted
- 1½   tablespoons Frank's RedHot Original Cayenne Pepper Sauce
- 1½   tablespoons lemon juice
- 1   tablespoon mayonnaise
- 1   tablespoon honey

1. FOR THE LEMON PEPPER SEASONING: Spread lemon zest evenly on plate and microwave until dry and lemon zest separates easily when crumbled between your fingers, about 2 minutes, stirring halfway through microwaving.

2. Combine pepper; salt; granulated garlic; onion powder; coriander; sugar; citric acid, if using; turmeric; cayenne; and lemon zest in bowl. Set aside. (Seasoning can be stored in airtight container at room temperature for up to 1 month.)

3. FOR THE WINGS: Adjust oven rack to middle position and heat oven to 200 degrees. Line rimmed baking sheet with triple layer of paper towels. Whisk cornstarch, flour, and baking powder together in bowl. Toss wings with lemon juice, salt, and pepper in large bowl until wings are evenly coated. Add cornstarch mixture and use your hands to toss and thoroughly coat wings in cornstarch mixture, pressing and rubbing cornstarch mixture into wings to adhere; set aside while heating oil.

4. Heat oil in large Dutch oven over medium-high heat to 375 degrees. Using tongs, add half of wings to oil and fry until golden and crispy, about 10 minutes. Using slotted spoon or spider skimmer, transfer fried wings to prepared sheet. Transfer sheet to oven to keep warm. Return oil to 375 degrees and repeat with remaining wings.

5. FOR THE SAUCE: Meanwhile, whisk all ingredients in second large bowl until uniform.

6. Add wings and 2 tablespoons lemon pepper seasoning to bowl with sauce and toss until wings are uniformly coated. Serve, sprinkled with extra lemon pepper seasoning as desired.

LUMPIANG SHANGHAI

✔ **WHY THIS RECIPE WORKS** Our lumpiang Shanghai feature a savory pork and vegetable filling flavored with soy sauce, pepper, garlic, and ginger. We pulsed the vegetables and aromatics in a food processor until they were finely chopped before pulsing in the pork along with 2 tablespoons of beaten egg. The vegetable juices freed by the whirring blades of the processor, along with the egg, moistened and softened the filling, making it easy to pipe into neat strips on the wrappers. We rolled up the filling carefully, making sure to work out any air pockets. This prevented the lumpia from floating as they cooked, which can cause them to cook and crisp unevenly. We sealed the lumpia with beaten egg and then fried them in 350-degree oil until their exteriors were golden brown and crisp. We paired the rolls with white cane vinegar seasoned with garlic, pepper, and soy sauce.

Read a recipe for lumpiang Shanghai, and you'll notice the brevity of the ingredient list: vegetables, ground meat or seafood, a few seasonings and aromatics, and wrappers for rolling. Ask Chicago chef Tim Flores, the co-owner of the Filipino restaurant and bakery Kasama, about the dish, and his description is even pithier: "They're a no-BS egg roll," he told me. "Just crispy pork goodness."

Lumpiang Shanghai (often referred to as "lumpia," though that term can technically be used to refer to a wide variety of Filipino spring rolls) are relatives of Chinese egg rolls, which were introduced to the Philippines by traders sometime between the ninth and 11th centuries. Today, lumpia are a staple at Filipino holidays and celebrations, where they're piled onto platters with various dipping sauces. Their straightforward flavor profile makes them a popular and crowd-pleasing snack.

But don't be fooled by their simplicity. Lumpia are more than a party food; they symbolize a fundamental Filipino value: hospitality. According to Ellie Tiglao,

chef and worker-owner of the Boston-area Filipinx restaurant Tanám, setting out a tray of lumpia at a gathering sends a wordless message of gratitude or welcoming. "We want to show you that we appreciate you being here," she told me. Making lumpia is an investment, Tiglao explained, both of ingredients (meat is a rarity in some regions of the Philippines) and of time and labor. Often, the process of forming and frying the rolls is a family affair, with multiple generations gathering around bowls of filling and piles of wrappers to speed the process along, assembly-line-style. Lumpia, therefore, are "something to be treasured," Tiglao said.

Over time, cooks across the 7,000-plus islands of the Filipino archipelago have tweaked the filling, cooking, assembly, and frying processes, adapting these rolls to suit their tastes. Yet there are a few traits that most lumpiang Shanghai share. The filling is savory, punctuated by soy sauce, garlic, and black pepper. They're rolled into slender, easy-to-eat cylinders. And they're fried until they're golden brown and shatteringly crisp.

Broadly speaking, there are two styles of filling for lumpia: raw and cooked. Some cooks sauté the vegetables and meat before rolling them into the wrappers, while others merely mix the components together before filling the lumpia, allowing the meat mixture to cook during the frying process. I prefer the latter method since it's quicker; plus, the raw meat's sticky proteins bind the filling together, making it easier to shape tidy rolls. Precooked fillings also sometimes dry out during the frying process, resulting in crumblier, less cohesive lumpia.

LUMPIANG SHANGHAI WITH SEASONED VINEGAR

Fillings are often pork-based, but it's not unusual to see recipes with beef, poultry, shrimp, and any number of vegetables. For simplicity, I settled on ground pork, along with onion, carrot, and celery. I also added four garlic cloves, soy sauce, and salt to punch up the savoriness. Some ginger and pepper contributed a subtly sweet zing.

Both Tiglao and Flores save prep time by buzzing the vegetables in a food processor, and I followed their lead, appreciating how the blades caused the vegetables to release their juices and render a more malleable filling. The finely minced food processor filling also cooked up more tender than versions using hand-cut vegetables, which can't cook through in lumpia's brief 5-to-7-minute deep-frying time.

Traditionally, lumpia wrappers are made with a sticky wheat dough that's swiped onto a hot pan, forming a paper-thin layer on the surface that cooks in seconds. But prepackaged wrappers are affordable and easy to use; the only work required is separating the thin sheets from one another.

Rolling lumpia is a simple if repetitive task: Apply a strip of filling to the wrapper, fold over the corners, roll, and seal with a swipe of lightly beaten egg. While many cooks dollop the filling with a spoon, Flores uses a pastry bag for cleaner, faster, and more uniform assembly. I borrowed this trick but used a zipper-lock bag instead. This way, a whole assembly line of lumpia makers could wield bags of filling.

I did need to thin out the filling some so that it would pipe smoothly, but fortunately the perfect fix was right in front of me: excess egg wash. I added 2 tablespoons to the filling and still had plenty left over to seal the wrappers. Another trick? Take time to work out air pockets between the wrapper and the filling to keep your lumpia from floating in the hot oil. They must be fully submerged for most of the frying time (they'll eventually float to the surface) to cook and crisp evenly.

For me, one of the most appealing aspects of Filipino cuisine is its encouragement of customization through sawsawan, the dipping sauces and condiments that diners use to tweak a dish's flavor, aroma, and texture to their tastes. Sweet chili sauce, banana ketchup, and seasoned vinegar are common accompaniments for lumpia. The first two are thick, sweet-and-sour condiments, but I love the vinegar because it's easy to make and surprisingly complex. I use sukang maasim (Filipino white cane vinegar) because its sourness is

NOTES FROM THE TEST KITCHEN

THIS IS HOW WE ROLL

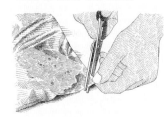

1. Load filling into large heavy-duty zipper-lock bag. Snip 1 corner to create 1-inch opening.

2. Pipe even 5 by ¾-inch strip of filling just below center of wrapper.

3. Apply light layer of egg wash onto top corner of wrapper with pastry brush, making sure to brush all the way to edges.

4. Fold bottom corner of wrapper over filling and gently press along length of filling to remove air pockets.

5. Fold side corners over to enclose filling and gently roll to form tight cylinder.

approachable and devoid of the funky notes of cider or wine vinegars. Lightly tempered by soy sauce, garlic, pepper, and sugar, it's the perfect finishing touch for lumpia: Now all that's missing is a flock of hungry family and friends to share them with.

—LAN LAM, *Cook's Illustrated*

Lumpiang Shanghai with Seasoned Vinegar

SERVES 6 TO 8 AS AN APPETIZER (MAKES 18 TO 20 LUMPIA)

TOTAL TIME: 1½ HOURS

Use a Dutch oven that holds 6 quarts or more. You can substitute distilled white vinegar for the sukang maasim. Look for spring roll wrappers or lumpia wrappers in the frozen foods section of an Asian market. Crisp leftover lumpia by baking them in a 425-degree oven for 8 to 10 minutes. When removed from the oven, the rolls will be soft; they will crisp as they cool. Serve warm or at room temperature. Instead of the dipping sauce, you can serve the lumpia with a store-bought sweet chili sauce or banana ketchup.

DIPPING SAUCE

- ⅔ **cup sukang maasim**
- 1 **tablespoon soy sauce**
- 1½ **teaspoons pepper**
- 1 **teaspoon sugar**
- 1 **garlic clove, minced**
- **Pinch table salt**

LUMPIA

- ½ **cup chopped onion**
- ⅓ **cup chopped carrot**
- ⅓ **cup chopped celery**
- 4 **garlic cloves, peeled**
- 1 **(½-inch) piece ginger, peeled**
- 1 **large egg**
- 1 **pound ground pork**
- 1 **tablespoon soy sauce**
- 1 **teaspoon pepper**
- ¼ **teaspoon table salt**
- 18–20 **(8-inch) square lumpia wrappers or spring roll wrappers**
- 1½ **quarts vegetable oil for frying**

1. FOR THE DIPPING SAUCE: Stir all ingredients together in bowl. Let stand at room temperature for at least 30 minutes to let flavors meld or refrigerate for up to 4 days.

2. FOR THE LUMPIA: Process onion, carrot, celery, garlic, and ginger in food processor until finely chopped, scraping down sides of bowl as needed, about 20 seconds. Beat egg in small bowl until homogeneous. Add 2 tablespoons beaten egg to food processor, reserving remainder. Add pork, soy sauce, pepper, and salt and process until combined, scraping down sides of bowl as

needed, 10 to 15 seconds. Transfer mixture to large heavy-duty zipper-lock bag and snip 1 corner to create 1-inch opening. Peel wrappers apart to separate; stack neatly and cover with very lightly dampened dish towel.

3. Place 1 wrapper on counter so 1 corner points to edge of counter. Pipe 5 by ¾-inch strip of filling parallel to counter, just below center of wrapper. Using pastry brush, apply light layer of egg wash onto upper 1½ inches of top corner of wrapper, making sure to brush all the way to edges. Fold bottom corner of wrapper over filling and press gently along length of filling to remove air pockets. Fold side corners over to enclose filling snugly and gently roll to form tight cylinder. Transfer, egg-washed corner down, to rimmed baking sheet or large platter. (Do not stack.) Wipe any excess egg from counter and repeat with remaining wrappers and filling, filling two at a time if you feel comfortable with it. (Lumpia can be refrigerated in single layer in airtight container for up to 24 hours. Alternatively, freeze in single layer and then stack in airtight container and freeze for up to 1 month. Do not thaw before frying.)

4. Heat oil in Dutch oven over medium heat to 350 degrees. Set wire rack in rimmed baking sheet. Line rack with paper towels. Using tongs, transfer 6 lumpia to oil and fry, adjusting burner, if necessary, to maintain oil temperature of 340 to 360 degrees, until lumpia are golden brown, 5 to 7 minutes (frozen lumpia will take 1 to 2 minutes longer). Transfer to prepared rack. Repeat with remaining lumpia in 2 batches. Let cool for at least 5 minutes before serving with dipping sauce.

HOT CHEDDAR CRAB DIP

✓ **WHY THIS RECIPE WORKS** This dip was inspired by one from French-influenced Cajun Louisiana, where it's called crab au gratin. For our perfectly creamy, irresistibly dippable version, we began by making a base that was essentially a traditional French Mornay sauce (a cheese-laden cream sauce) that was boldly seasoned with distinctly Cajun ingredients. We built the sauce by sautéing onion, bell pepper, and celery in a generous amount of butter before flavoring the mix with fresh garlic, thyme, cayenne, and black pepper; adding ultrasavory Worcestershire sauce layered in spice and umami. We took care when sourcing the two starring ingredients, seeking out a good-quality aged cheddar and the best crabmeat available. Aged cheddars are not only salty and sharp but also pleasantly sour and buttery. When melted into the already flavorful base of this crab dip, they added incomparable depth. We found that we preferred freshly cooked and picked unpasteurized crab here, but we also loved the test kitchen's winning refrigerated pasteurized crabmeat, Phillips Premium Crab Jumbo. It's fresh-tasting and sweet, with a pleasant mild brininess. When carefully stirred into the delightful Mornay sauce, topped with more good-quality cheddar, and broiled briefly until beautifully browned and bubbling, it lightened and invigorated the dip.

When I cook at home, I usually just want to get dinner on the table as efficiently and affordably as possible, but when I'm cooking for holiday gatherings, I pull out all the stops. That's the spirit of this crab dip: everything from scratch, no shortcuts, and the best ingredients available.

Crab-loving coastal regions in the United States have myriad traditions for creamy, gooey crab dishes, including deviled crab and baked crab, but this dip was inspired by one from French-influenced Cajun Louisiana, where it's called crab au gratin. The base is essentially a traditional French Mornay sauce (a cheese-laden cream sauce) that's boldly seasoned with distinctly Cajun ingredients.

You build the sauce by sautéing onion, bell pepper, and celery (the foundation of Cajun and Creole cooking that's known as the holy trinity) in a generous amount of butter before flavoring the mix with fresh garlic, thyme, cayenne, and black pepper. After sprinkling flour on the vegetables and briefly toasting it all together, you whisk in whole milk and a spoonful of ultrasavory Worcestershire sauce.

Now you're ready for the two crucial ingredients: the cheese and the crab. Seek out the best of these, and you'll be rewarded with a dish that's truly worthy of a celebration. I look for aged cheddar, the kind I'd be excited to get on a cheese plate. The best aged cheddars are a bit firmer and crumblier than younger cheeses and are not only salty and sharp but also pleasantly sour and buttery. When melted into the already flavorful base of this crab dip, they add incomparable depth.

Finally, it's worth your time and money to do your research when sourcing the crab. If you're able to find it, freshly cooked and picked unpasteurized crab is usually best, but keep in mind that it has a short shelf life. On the other hand, the refrigerated pasteurized crabmeat sold in containers at the seafood counter in your supermarket can be really great, but not all products are created equal. Phillips Premium Crab Jumbo, our taste test winner, makes an excellent choice if you can find it. It's fresh-tasting and sweet, with a pleasant mild brininess. When carefully stirred into this delightful Mornay sauce, topped with more good-quality cheddar, and broiled briefly until beautifully browned and bubbling, it lightens and invigorates the dip. With a final topping of fresh thyme leaves and some toasted baguette slices on the side, this dip will fly from the dish.

—MATTHEW FAIRMAN, *Cook's Country*

Hot Cheddar Crab Dip

SERVES 6 TOTAL TIME: 45 MINUTES

If you can't find fresh crab, refrigerated pasteurized crab is the next-best option. Lump, backfin (special), and claw meat all work well here. This recipe can be easily doubled to serve a crowd. For the best results, we recommend using good-quality aged cheddar cheese and shredding it on a box grater. The finished dip goes great with a little extra Worcestershire and some Tabasco sauce on top. Serve with toasted baguette slices or crackers.

- 2 tablespoons unsalted butter
- ½ cup finely chopped onion
- ¼ cup finely chopped celery
- ¼ cup finely chopped red bell pepper
- 2 garlic cloves, minced
- 2 teaspoons fresh thyme leaves, divided
- 1 teaspoon table salt
- ½ teaspoon cayenne pepper
- ¼ teaspoon pepper
- 1½ tablespoons all-purpose flour
- ⅔ cup whole milk
- 2 teaspoons Worcestershire sauce
- 6 ounces sharp or extra-sharp cheddar cheese, shredded (1½ cups), divided
- 8 ounces crabmeat, picked over for shells
- 1 teaspoon paprika

1. Adjust oven rack 8 inches from broiler element and heat broiler. Melt butter in medium saucepan over medium heat. Add onion, celery, and bell pepper and

HOT CHEDDAR CRAB DIP

cook until softened, 5 to 7 minutes. Stir in garlic, 1 teaspoon thyme, salt, cayenne, and pepper and cook until fragrant, about 30 seconds. Sprinkle flour over vegetables and cook, stirring constantly, for 1 minute.

2. Slowly whisk in milk and Worcestershire and bring to simmer. Cook until sauce thickens, about 2 minutes. Whisk in ¾ cup cheddar until melted. Off heat, gently stir in crabmeat. Transfer crab dip to shallow broiler-safe 1-quart baking dish.

3. Sprinkle remaining ¾ cup cheddar over crab dip, followed by paprika. Broil until cheese is well browned, 3 to 5 minutes. Remove dish from oven and sprinkle dip with remaining 1 teaspoon thyme. Let dip cool for 5 minutes. Serve.

TO MAKE AHEAD: At end of step 2, let dip cool completely, cover with plastic wrap, and refrigerate for up to 24 hours. When ready to serve, unwrap and bake at 400 degrees until hot throughout, 20 to 25 minutes. Stir dip and continue with step 3.

AIR-FRYER ROMESCO

✔ **WHY THIS RECIPE WORKS** Wanting to see how far we could go with using the air fryer to cook different ingredients, we made romesco, a classic Catalan sauce from the Spanish province of Tarragona. Traditionally used as a spread; an accompaniment to meats, fish, or vegetables; or the base of a stew, we put romesco, a sweet, tangy combination of dried ñora chiles, roasted tomatoes, garlic, toasted nuts, bread, olive oil, and vinegar, to use as a dip. We rehydrated dried ñora chiles in hot water. Meanwhile, we used the air fryer to roast tomatoes until lightly browned, toast bread and nuts, and roast garlic cloves, too. Then we processed the cooked ingredients with the rehydrated chiles, water, olive oil, and vinegar to create an earthy, creamy sauce.

Romesco is a classic Catalan sauce that has its roots in the province of Tarragona (about 100 kilometers down the Mediterranean coast from Barcelona). It is an earthy, sweet, tangy, coarse combination of roasted tomatoes and garlic, dried chiles (known as ñoras, a species of *capsicum*), toasted nuts (usually hazelnuts or almonds), bread, olive oil, and sherry vinegar. The exact proportions of ingredients can vary depending on whether the sauce is intended as a dip or spread; an

accompaniment to meat, fish, or vegetables; or the base of a fish stew. A romesco-style sauce known as salvitxada is eaten with calçots, a seasonal delicacy in Catalonia. In the early part of the year, calçots, or large green onions, are grilled at an outside gathering known as a calçotada and served with a kind of romesco called salsa calçots.

I came to love romesco, along with other classic Catalan sauces such as allioli, samfaina, and picada, thanks to my Catalan husband and his family. So when we decided to include romesco in our *Healthy Air Fryer* cookbook, it naturally fell to me to develop a recipe. I knew the tangy, nutty flavors I wanted to re-create, but could this be done in an air fryer? I already knew from previous testing that the air fryer was a great way to cook vegetables. But what I learned while developing this recipe was that the air fryer's even heat actually made cooking ingredients for romesco a speedy, one-vessel job. The conventional method requires time to cook the tomatoes, bread, garlic, and nuts individually in a skillet (it takes even longer if you use the oven).

For my romesco, I first sourced ñoras online. They are easily available in the United States, but I made sure to test other chiles, too, so that we could offer options. Ancho chiles had a similar fruitiness, color, and flavor to ñoras, and I found that they gave the romesco a similar rich hue and texture. Now I was ready to cook. My first step was to rehydrate the stemmed and seeded dried chiles in hot water. While they were softening, I prepped my other ingredients, tossing sliced baguette, cloves of garlic, and hazelnuts in a tablespoon of olive oil. After 20 minutes, I drained the softened chiles.

As for using the air fryer, I gave the halved tomatoes a head start until their skins became spotty brown and blistered and their flesh softened. Then I simply arranged the bread, garlic, and hazelnuts around the tomatoes and air-fried everything a bit longer until they were all a deep golden brown.

Instead of using a mortar and pestle to pound the cooked ingredients together, I transferred them to a food processor and added the softened chiles and salt. A few pulses and I was ready to pour in some water (romesco is not a smooth sauce, so you don't need to add too much liquid while processing it), a tablespoon of olive oil, and aromatic sherry vinegar (red wine vinegar works great, too). I processed the mixture for

AIR-FRYER ROMESCO

2 minutes until it was the consistency of thick mayonnaise. Then I tasted the aromatic sauce, adjusting salt, pepper, and vinegar for a salty, sweet, fragrant romesco that I wanted to eat with everything. Since I'd made romesco in different ways, the benefits of using an air fryer were clear to me: You save time, use less oil, and get even browning on ingredients. It definitely is a great way to make romesco.

I was also the cook charged with making pita chips in the air fryer. The air fryer cooks the chips so quickly and evenly that it's easy to make them fresh at home. Since our cookbook was focused on healthier foods, I used whole-wheat pita bread. Separating one pita into its two layers with scissors and then cutting each into eight wedges yielded 16 chips. I flavored them simply with olive oil spray, salt, and pepper. These chips make a delicious snack on their own, but they are even better dipped into the romesco.

—NICOLE KONSTANTINAKOS,
America's Test Kitchen Books

Air-Fryer Romesco

SERVES 6 (MAKES ABOUT 1½ CUPS) TOTAL TIME: 40 MINUTES

You can substitute ancho chiles for the ñora chiles, if desired. This recipe can be easily doubled. Serve with toasted baguette slices, pita chips (recipe follows), crackers, and/or crudités.

- 1 ounce dried ñora or ancho chiles, stemmed and seeded
- 1 (3-inch) piece baguette (1½ ounces), cut into 4 slices
- ¼ cup whole blanched hazelnuts and/or almonds
- 6 garlic cloves, lightly crushed and peeled
- 2 tablespoons extra-virgin olive oil, divided, plus extra for serving
- 6 plum tomatoes, cored and halved lengthwise
- 1 tablespoon sherry or red wine vinegar, plus extra for seasoning
- ½ teaspoon table salt

1. Place ñoras in bowl; cover with hot water; and let sit until softened, 20 to 30 minutes. Drain chiles and discard soaking liquid. Meanwhile, toss baguette slices, hazelnuts, and garlic with 1 tablespoon oil.

2. Arrange tomatoes cut side up in air-fryer basket. Place basket into air fryer; set temperature to 400 degrees; and cook until tomatoes are spotty brown,

skins are blistered, and tomatoes have begun to collapse, 12 to 18 minutes. Arrange bread, hazelnuts, and garlic around tomatoes in air-fryer basket and cook until bread, hazelnuts, and garlic are deep golden brown and tomatoes are well browned, 5 to 7 minutes.

3. Transfer tomato-bread mixture to food-processor bowl and add ñoras and salt. Pulse until mixture is coarsely ground, 6 to 8 pulses, scraping down sides of bowl as needed. Add 3 tablespoons water, vinegar, and remaining 1 tablespoon oil and process until mixture is mostly smooth, about 2 minutes. (Add up to ¼ cup extra water, 1 tablespoon at a time, as needed to achieve consistency of thick mayonnaise.) Season romesco with salt, pepper, and extra vinegar to taste. Transfer to serving bowl and drizzle with extra oil. Serve. (Romesco can be refrigerated for up to 2 days; bring to room temperature and whisk to recombine before serving.)

Air-Fried Whole-Wheat Pita Chips with Salt and Pepper

SERVES 2 (MAKES 16 CHIPS)

TOTAL TIME: 20 MINUTES, PLUS 30 MINUTES COOLING

To use a traditional oven, arrange the pita wedges in a single layer on a baking sheet to facilitate even cooking and skip the redistribution step. This recipe can be easily doubled.

- 1 (8-inch) 100 percent whole-wheat pita
  Olive oil spray
- ⅛ teaspoon table salt
- ⅛ teaspoon pepper

1. Using kitchen shears, cut around perimeter of pita and separate into 2 thin rounds. Lightly spray both sides of each cut round with oil spray and sprinkle with salt and pepper. Cut each round into 8 wedges.

2. Arrange wedges into two even layers in air-fryer basket. Place basket into air fryer and set temperature to 300 degrees. Cook until wedges are light golden brown on edges, 3 to 5 minutes. Using tongs, toss wedges gently to redistribute and continue to cook until golden brown and crisp, 3 to 5 minutes. Let cool completely, about 30 minutes, before serving. (Chips can be stored in airtight container for up to 3 days.)

OYSTERS ON THE HALF SHELL

✔ **WHY THIS RECIPE WORKS**   To serve oysters on the half shell the way they'd be served in a restaurant or raw bar, the first step was to crush ice by hand. Filling a heavy-duty zipper-lock bag about three-quarters full with ice; wrapping the bag in a dish towel; and using a mallet, skillet, or rolling pin to break up the ice yielded pieces that were small enough to pack tightly but not so fine that they melted quickly. The ice chilled the oysters and bowls of condiments and also kept them securely nestled on the platter so that they didn't tip. Wrapping a dish towel over our thumb and tucking the end between our thumb and forefinger was the easiest, most effective way to protect our hand during shucking.

Everyone remembers their first oyster. I had mine back in 2004, when I was working as a garde-manger at UpStairs on the Square, the iconic azalea-pink dining room that for decades graced the top three floors of a Harvard Square brownstone. When I admitted to my sous chef that I'd never tried a raw oyster, he plucked one from my station, shucked it, and offered it to me. I was unprepared to be transported to the cold, blue waters of Wellfleet, Massachusetts, as the liquor that I tipped from that gently gnarled gray-and-green shell flooded my palate with salt. But as I chewed, that brininess was tempered by the umami-rich, creamy flavors packed in the oyster's plump body. It was, as author and oyster expert Rowan Jacobsen recently described to me, "a little bit of the sea come to life."

I was immediately won over, and I have downed at least 1,000 oysters since then—not only in bars and restaurants but also at home with friends, which has become one of my favorite ways to entertain. Plattering up a dozen or two on the half shell is simple and makes an impressive starting point for any gathering.

If you're nervous about shucking or eating raw oysters or simply want a new way to serve them on the half shell, roasting is a great option (see page 46). Warming them makes them much easier to shuck, and the mustard butter melds with the liquor to form a punchy sauce.

—LAN LAM, *Cook's Illustrated*

OYSTERS ON THE HALF SHELL

Oysters on the Half Shell

SERVES 2 OR 3   TOTAL TIME: 15 MINUTES

Serve the oysters with lemon wedges and/or an accompaniment (recipes follow); embed the serving bowl in the ice and then fill it. You'll need an oyster knife and a large, deep, chilled serving platter.

3   pounds crushed ice
12   oysters, well scrubbed

Arrange ice in even layer on chilled serving platter. Shuck 1 oyster and discard top shell; place oyster on ice, being careful not to spill much liquid. Repeat with remaining oysters.

Red Wine Vinegar Mignonette Granité

SERVES 8 (MAKES ABOUT ⅔ CUP)

TOTAL TIME: 10 MINUTES, PLUS 1 HOUR FREEZING

For a traditional mignonette, skip the freezing and scraping steps, cover the bowl, refrigerate the sauce for at least 30 minutes or up to two days, and serve it chilled.

½   cup red wine vinegar
3   tablespoons water
2   teaspoons finely grated shallot
¾   teaspoon sugar
1   teaspoon coarsely ground pepper

In shallow bowl, stir together vinegar, water, shallot, and sugar. Freeze until fully frozen, at least 1 hour or up to 2 days. One hour before serving, place small serving bowl in freezer. To serve, scrape frozen mixture with fork to create ice crystals. Stir in pepper. Transfer to chilled serving bowl; serve or cover and freeze until ready to use.

Lime-and-Soy-Marinated Scallions

SERVES 8 (MAKES ABOUT ½ CUP)   TOTAL TIME: 20 MINUTES

Marinating scallions in a mixture of soy sauce, lime juice, and sugar makes for a savory, concentrated alternative to the sauces typically served with oysters.

3   tablespoons lime juice (2 limes)
2   scallions, sliced thin
1   tablespoon water
1   tablespoon soy sauce
½   teaspoon sugar

Stir all ingredients together and refrigerate for at least 15 minutes or up to 24 hours before serving.

NOTES FROM THE TEST KITCHEN

HOW TO SHUCK

With an oyster knife, a dish towel, and some practice, you'll be able to shuck safely and confidently.

1. Fold dish towel several times into thin, tight roll. Grip towel in fist of hand that will be holding oyster, wrapping 1 end over your thumb and tucking it between your thumb and forefinger.

2. Using your towel-protected thumb, hold oyster in place with hinge facing away fro ... of oyste ... oyster.

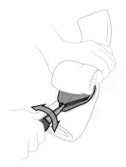

3. Work tip of knife into hinge using twisting motion. When shells begin to separate, twist knife to pop hinge.

4. Run knife along top shell, scraping abductor muscle from shell to release oyster. Slide knife under oyster to scrape abductor muscle from bottom shell.

Roasted Oysters on the Half Shell with Mustard Butter

SERVES 4 TO 6   TOTAL TIME: 55 MINUTES

You'll need an oyster knife and a large serving platter for this recipe. Using oysters that are 2½ to 3 inches long ensures that they will cook evenly. Placing the oysters on crumpled foil prevents them from tipping.

    5   tablespoons unsalted butter, softened
    3   tablespoons minced fresh parsley, divided
    1   tablespoon whole-grain mustard
    24 oysters, 2½ to 3 inches long, well scrubbed
        Lemon wedges

1. Adjust oven rack to middle position and heat oven to 450 degrees. Stir butter, 2 tablespoons parsley, and mustard in bowl until well combined. Gently crumple and uncrumple two 24-inch lengths of aluminum foil. Place 1 piece in 18 by 13-inch rimmed baking sheet and second piece on large serving platter; cover foil on platter with dish towel for presentation, if desired. Nestle oysters, cupped side down, into foil on prepared sheet and bake until oysters open slightly, about 5 minutes. (It's OK to eat oysters that don't open.) Let oysters rest until cool enough to handle, about 5 minutes.

2. Shuck 1 oyster and discard top shell. Return oyster to foil, being careful not to spill much liquid. Repeat with remaining oysters.

3. Distribute mustard butter evenly among oysters, about ¾ teaspoon per oyster. Bake until thickest part of largest oyster registers 160 to 165 degrees, 5 to 8 minutes. Let rest for 5 minutes. Using tongs, carefully transfer oysters to prepared platter, nestling them into foil or towel to hold them level. Sprinkle remaining 1 tablespoon parsley over oysters. Serve, passing lemon wedges separately.

CARCIOFI ALLA GIUDIA (ROMAN JEWISH FRIED ARTICHOKES)

✓ **WHY THIS RECIPE WORKS** To make carciofi alla giudia, the fried artichokes that Roman Jews have prepared for centuries during the thistle's spring harvest, cooks trim the thistles to expose their tender inner leaves, and then they deep-fry the artichokes a few at a time—twice. The first round softens up the vegetable's dense heart, and the second makes the petals unfurl and crisp. After plucking off the tough outer bracts, we made four angled cuts with a sharp knife to remove the top half of the remaining leaves. Halving the artichoke exposed its hairy choke, which we scooped out with a spoon after the first fry, when it had softened considerably. Using very fresh, tightly closed blossoms minimized the amount of leaves lost during prep. Double frying delivered a stunning range of textures: The first fry, done low and slow, rendered the dense heart soft and creamy. The second, a 1-minute flash in hot oil, browned and crisped up the leaves so that they offered a range of potato chip–like crunch and crispness. The leaves also unfurled so that the finished product resembled a copper-dipped chrysanthemum. Frying in a combination of neutral canola oil and a small amount of olive oil minimized cost and also allowed the delicate artichoke flavor to stand out. Straining the used oil meant that it could be reused more than half a dozen times.

To make carciofi alla giudia, the fried artichokes that Roman Jews have prepared for centuries during the thistle's spring harvest, cooks start by plucking the tough bracts off a bunch of very fresh blooms. Next, they trim and strip the stalks of their fibrous skin and carve the blossoms to expose their inner cone of tender, chartreuse leaves. Then they deep-fry the artichokes a few at a time—twice. Once to soften up the vegetable's dense heart, and again to make the petals unfurl and crisp.

It's a lot of ceremony for a simple primo, but according to Joyce Goldstein, chef and author of several books, including *Cucina Ebraica: Flavors of the Italian Jewish Kitchen* (1998), the fuss was intentional for Renaissance-era Jews. When they were banished to the ghetto along the Tiber River and stripped of their livelihoods, they made the very best of what they could get—which, food-wise, was mostly produce.

"The vegetables were like a festival of food," Goldstein said, "and you wanted to make each one sort of special so that you didn't feel you were being neglected, you know? You had the good stuff."

The payoff really was spectacular. For cooks, carciofi alla giudia became an architectural showpiece: a bouquet of blossoms so dramatically splayed and browned, they looked like copper-dipped chrysanthemums. For eaters, it's always been fried food nirvana: crunchy, crispy, and creamy from petal to heart, with nothing but salt and a spritz of lemon juice amping up the vegetable's sweet, nutty, delicate savoriness.

"The first time you eat one of these artichokes, it is so delicious, you will want to cry," Goldstein raves in her book. It's also one of few preparations that doesn't require dismantling the artichoke leaf by leaf at the table; thanks to all that aforementioned pruning and peeling, everything is edible.

The only real hang-up to replicating the dish in the States is the artichoke itself. Common Italian varieties such as the mammole (sometimes called cimaroli) are thornless and mature before the hairy choke develops, saving cooks and diners the trouble of dodging it. But the globe (sometimes called French) plant grown in the United States is a veritable fortress of a vegetable, with imposing spine-tipped bracts and a choke that develops by the time the vegetable is large enough to harvest. Those botanical hurdles didn't dissuade me from trying, though; the stunning visual and potato-chip crunch of the leaves would be worth it.

Artichoke prep is a bit like wood carving, where the cook whittles away the raw, rougher exterior to make something clean and usable. The spiny bracts go first, the

NOTES FROM THE TEST KITCHEN

FRESH ENOUGH TO FRY?

Very fresh artichokes are a must when frying. They should feel heavy for their size and boast bright-green, tightly closed leaves. Squeeze them gently; they should squeak a little. Avoid drab artichokes with loose or dry leaves, which will fall apart and literally lose their bloom in the hot oil.

GREEN
AND TIGHT

DRAB AND
LOOSE

goal being to remove enough of them that the color at the base of the leaves fades from dark to light green. After trimming and peeling the stem, you carve away the tops of the inner leaves, which many Italian cooks do by "turning" the artichoke with a coltello da carciofi curvo, a paring knife curved like a bird's beak, until the vegetable resembles a tight rosebud. I found turning tricky to do, so instead I switched to a chef's knife and made four angled cuts that exposed the artichoke's tender core.

The choke is burrowed in there and incredibly dense when raw, so my options were to chisel it out—and inevitably lose a lot of precious leaves in the process—or halve the artichoke lengthwise to expose it and then dig out each portion. Severing the blossom wasn't my first choice, but it made the surgery much easier while preserving almost all the leaves—and the dish's striking aesthetics. Then I waited until after the first fry to remove the choke. At that point, it was soft enough to scoop out with a spoon, but the leaves still clung tightly to the core. (Don't use anything less than superfresh artichokes; when I used older ones, the thistle fell apart during frying.)

Fried food has always been popular in Jewish communities and olive oil a default fat since it was a local and kosher alternative to lard and butter. Most contemporary recipes for carciofi alla giudia still call for it exclusively, but after a few fry tests I opted to replace most of the 2 quarts of olive oil I was using with canola oil. The cost savings were huge; good-quality extra-virgin olive oil can cost upwards of eight times more per ounce than canola oil. And I preferred the more neutral flavor of the oil hybrid, which imparted just enough fruitiness to the artichokes without obscuring their delicate flavor. (Another cost-saving benefit: You can strain and reuse the oil multiple times.)

The first fry is really more of a long, lazy oil poach, its goal being to soften the artichokes before the second, hotter fry crisps them. So I poured the oils into a large saucepan and didn't let the temperature tick above 275 degrees. Ten or so minutes later, when the artichoke hearts were tender and the leaves were just starting to brown, I fished them out and carefully scooped out the chokes. Then I upped the heat so that the oil hit 350 degrees and carefully lowered two halves into the pot cut side down, gently pressing with my spider skimmer to spread the leaves and keep them submerged.

HOW TO PREP ARTICHOKES FOR FRYING

1. Snap off outer leaves.

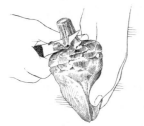

2. Trim and peel stem.

3. Cut top at 45-degree angle.

4. Rotate quarter turn; repeat 3 times.

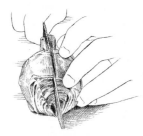

5. Halve lengthwise through stem.

6. After first fry, scoop out choke.

Barely a minute later, I had a pair of bronzed blossoms with the most fantastic textural spectrum: luxuriously creamy hearts surrounded by leaves as lacy and brittle as LAY'S Classic Potato Chips and an outer layer of thicker ones that crunched like kettle chips. I repeated the frying with the other halves, piling them on a platter and sprinkling them with salt and lemon juice. They were gobbled up in minutes, the way all the best fussed-over cooking projects are.

—STEVE DUNN, *Cook's Illustrated*

Carciofi alla Giudia (Roman Jewish Fried Artichokes)

SERVES 4 AS AN APPETIZER   TOTAL TIME: 1¼ HOURS

Look for artichokes that are uniformly green, have tightly closed leaves, feel heavy for their size, and squeak a little when squeezed—all indications of freshness; avoid any that are browning and dried out. Don't worry when the artichokes discolor as you prep them; any oxidation won't be visible after frying. If your large saucepan holds less than 4 quarts, use a large Dutch oven and add 2 cups more canola oil so that the artichokes are completely covered. We like to season these artichokes with flake sea salt. The stem makes a useful handle when prepping and cooking the artichokes but is usually too fibrous to eat.

> 4   artichokes (10 to 12 ounces each)
> 6   cups canola oil for frying
> 2   cups extra-virgin olive oil for frying
>   Lemon wedges

1. Working with 1 artichoke at a time, snap off tough outer leaves until you reach tender inner leaves (they'll be pale yellow at their base). Trim stem to 1½-inch length. Peel stem and base with paring or bird's beak knife to remove dark-green layer. Starting halfway up leaves, use chef's knife to make 45-degree angled cut toward top of artichoke to remove tips of leaves. Repeat same cut 3 more times, rotating artichoke quarter turn before each cut.

2. Set wire rack in rimmed baking sheet and line with double layer of paper towels. Heat canola oil and olive oil in large saucepan over medium-high heat to 275 degrees. Cut each artichoke in half through stem.

3. Using spider skimmer or slotted spoon, carefully add artichokes to oil. Cook until paring knife slipped into thickest part of base meets little resistance and leaves are medium brown, 10 to 12 minutes. Using spider skimmer or slotted spoon, transfer artichokes to prepared rack cut side down to drain. Remove saucepan from heat. Let artichokes cool for 15 minutes. (Artichoke halves can be wrapped well and refrigerated for up to 24 hours.)

4. Using spoon, scoop out choke from center of each artichoke half, being careful not to dislodge leaves attached to base. Replace paper towels with double layer of fresh paper towels. Heat oil over high heat to 350 degrees.

5. Place 2 artichoke halves cut side down in oil and, using spider skimmer or slotted spoon, lightly press on artichokes to submerge. Cook until outer leaves are dark brown, 45 to 60 seconds. Transfer to prepared rack cut side down to drain. Return oil to 350 degrees and repeat with remaining artichoke halves in 3 batches. Sprinkle artichokes on both sides with flake sea salt to taste. Serve, passing lemon wedges separately.

SPICED CAULIFLOWER FRITTERS

✔ **WHY THIS RECIPE WORKS** Cooked cauliflower, bound with flour and eggs and then fried into golden fritters, can be found in various parts of the Mediterranean. This recipe, lightly crisp and delectable, takes inspiration from Middle Eastern spiced versions. We started by steaming the cauliflower rather than boiling it to preserve its sweet, nutty, vegetal flavor. We mashed it, purposefully leaving a few small chunks for contrasting texture. We used the bare minimum amount of flour so that the fritters held together but were still delicate. Shallow frying was easier to manage—and clean up after—than deep frying. Dipping the hot fritters into our fresh, turmeric-dyed, cool and creamy yogurt sauce after cooking was a delight.

Golden, tender, and bursting with sweet-nutty cauliflower flavor, crispy cauliflower fritters are enjoyed throughout the Middle East. Fried food and vegetables are two of my favorite things, so I jumped at the chance to develop my own recipe for these versatile fritters while working on recipes for our *More Mediterranean* cookbook.

Though these fritters come in a wide variety of styles, the basics of making them are the same. You start by

FRESH TURMERIC
Turmeric, the rhizome (underground stem) of a plant in the ginger family, might be more familiar to you as the ground spice with a bright-yellow color; earthy, slightly bitter flavor; and touch of gingery heat. Fresh turmeric has its own beautiful qualities, however, bringing brightness and complexity. It's most perceptible in raw foods; in cooked applications, it can be hard to tell fresh turmeric from dried. You can buy just a small amount of fresh turmeric (which makes it inexpensive) and refrigerate any extra for up to four weeks in an airtight container or zipper-lock bag to keep it fresh. A spoon makes quick work of removing turmeric's thin skin, and a rasp-style grater breaks it down in a flash.

coarsely mashing cooked cauliflower, bind the cauliflower batter with egg and flour, spice it with an array of fragrant seasonings and some kind of allium, and then fry until crispy. Many recipes also call for adding baking powder to the batter, claiming that doing so results in fritters that are lighter and airier than their unleavened counterparts. I was particularly inspired by a Palestinian version spiced with cumin, cinnamon, and turmeric, so I decided to keep this profile in mind as I moved forward with my testing.

But before I could get my fry on, I had to nail down the cauliflower cooking method. I wanted the fritters to have a rustic, slightly chunky texture, so it was crucial that I cooked the cauliflower until it was tender enough to mash, but no further. I also wanted each bite to be loaded with intense cauliflower flavor. Roasting is a terrific method for concentrating vegetable flavor, so I started there.

Roasting the cauliflower until it was tender and spotty brown brought out its natural nuttiness, but there was one big downside: The fritters I made with it turned out dry. I briefly considered adding dairy to the batter to counter the dryness but quickly discarded that idea since dairy is not a traditional component of Middle Eastern fritters. Moving on, I found that boiling the cauliflower worked, but the very best results came when I steamed the cauliflower in just ¼ cup of water, which preserved the cauliflower's flavor and moisture. Fifteen minutes of steaming was all it took to reach the perfect just-tender consistency.

Next, I took a closer look at the batter. Some recipes called for mixing in a full cup of flour or more. This made for fritters that were sturdy and easy to work with but a little light on cauliflower flavor. I gradually whittled away at the flour until I found that a mere ½ cup would suffice to create delicate and light (but not crumbly) fritters where the cauliflower flavor was front and center. I also tested adding the baking powder that many cooks swear by, but with so little flour to weigh down my fritters, I found that it didn't make a noticeable difference and so I left it out.

The catch was that the batter was now much looser and more difficult to work with. Allowing the mashed cauliflower to cool slightly before combining it with the other ingredients (a 10-minute resting period did the trick) helped, allowing the cauliflower mash to firm up slightly and become more workable. Still, it was next to impossible to form the batter into fritters and drop them into the hot oil without causing them to break apart—to say nothing of the messy sticking and splattering. I was loath to go back up on flour and compromise the cauliflower flavor I'd worked so hard for, but forming the patties by hand just wasn't working out. So instead, I simply scooped up a portion of batter using a greased measuring cup, dropped it directly into the hot oil, and then gently flattened and smoothed the fritters into their final shape. This kept my hands clean and resulted in prettier fritters to boot, a win-win.

All that was left was to doll the fritters up a bit. Into the batter I mixed a few thinly sliced scallions plus cumin, allspice, and black pepper for earthy-floral warmth. I also incorporated some grated fresh turmeric (which is brighter and more floral than the ground stuff)—not into the fritters themselves, but instead by whisking it into a creamy yogurt sauce where its color and flavor would really shine. So far, my recipe had cleaved pretty closely to tradition, but now, in the *More Mediterranean* spirit of embracing global flavors, I added my own spin, mixing a tablespoon of minced fresh tarragon into the yogurt sauce where the herb's pungent, licorice-y flavor brought a unique depth and complexity.

Though they look impressive and taste even better, especially when accompanied by the creamy yogurt dipping sauce, these fritters are an example of simple Middle Eastern home cooking at its finest. They're also just as good cold from the fridge the next day as they are straight out of the pan—not that you're likely to have many left over, as they're even quicker to devour than they are to make.

—JOSEPH GITTER, *America's Test Kitchen Books*

Spiced Cauliflower Fritters

SERVES 4   TOTAL TIME: 45 MINUTES

When taking the temperature of the frying oil, tilt the skillet so that the oil pools on one side. Use two spatulas to flip the fritters to prevent splattering. Make them the vegetable side to your dinner or give them star status next to a beautiful vegetable salad. The fritters can also be enjoyed at room temperature, stuffed into sandwiches.

YOGURT SAUCE

- ½ cup whole-milk Greek yogurt
- 1 tablespoon minced fresh tarragon
- 1½ teaspoons grated fresh turmeric
- ½ teaspoon grated lemon or lime zest plus 2 teaspoons juice
- 1 small garlic clove, minced to paste

FRITTERS

- 1 head cauliflower (2 pounds), cored and cut into 1-inch florets
- ¼ cup water
- 1 teaspoon table salt
- ½ cup all-purpose flour
- 2 large eggs
- 4 scallions, sliced thin
- 1½ teaspoons ground cumin
- ½ teaspoon ground allspice
- ½ teaspoon pepper
- ½ cup extra-virgin olive oil for frying

1. FOR THE YOGURT SAUCE: Combine all ingredients in bowl. Let sit for 30 minutes for flavors to meld, then season with salt and pepper to taste. Set aside.

2. FOR THE FRITTERS: Combine cauliflower, water, and salt in large saucepan. Cover and cook over medium-low heat, stirring occasionally, until just tender, 15 to 20 minutes. Remove from heat. Using potato masher, mash cauliflower until mostly smooth with some small chunks remaining. Transfer to large bowl and let cool slightly, about 10 minutes.

3. Set wire rack in rimmed baking sheet and line half of rack with triple layer of paper towels. Stir flour, eggs, scallions, cumin, allspice, and pepper into cooled cauliflower mixture until fully combined.

4. Heat oil in 12-inch nonstick skillet over medium heat to 350 degrees. Using greased ¼-cup dry measuring cup, place 6 portions of cauliflower mixture in skillet, evenly spaced. Gently press and spread

SPICED CAULIFLOWER FRITTERS

portions into approximate 3-inch disks with back of spoon. Cook fritters until well browned, 3 to 5 minutes per side, using 2 spatulas to carefully flip.

5. Transfer fritters to paper towel–lined side of prepared rack to drain for 15 seconds on each side, then move to unlined side of rack. Return oil to 350 degrees and repeat with remaining cauliflower mixture. Serve warm or at room temperature with yogurt sauce.

PAKORAS

✓ **WHY THIS RECIPE WORKS** Pakoras are spiced vegetable fritters from the Indian subcontinent that are made with a thick batter of besan (flour milled from skinned and split brown chickpeas) and water. Traditionally served with hot cups of masala chai, the crispy, craggy fritters make a cozy, satisfying snack. For vegetable-forward pakoras, we used a 4:1 ratio of chopped and shredded vegetables—a colorful trio of spinach, potato, and red onion worked nicely—to batter. Pakoras are often generously spiced, and ours are no exception, with liberal doses of earthy cumin; citrusy coriander; ocher turmeric; mildly spicy Kashmiri chile powder; fruity, maple syrup–esque fenugreek; and ajwain, which is frequently added to fried foods to support digestion. Finally, a minced serrano chile added bright, zingy heat. Baking powder kept the pakoras light and fluffy on the inside, and frying just five at a time in 370- to 380-degree oil created evenly cooked interiors that weren't greasy. We also created two chutneys that came together easily to serve alongside the fritters.

If you have a few vegetables in the fridge, a sack of besan (flour milled from skinned and split brown chickpeas) in the pantry, and a well-stocked spice cabinet, you've got everything you need to fry up a batch of pakoras, the crispy, savory, two-bite fritters that are treasured throughout the Indian subcontinent.

Most vegetables fit neatly into the pakora template, offering loads of use-it-up flexibility: Chop or shred a mix of whatever vegetables you have on hand; season them liberally with fragrant spices and minced fresh chiles; add a little besan; and drizzle in water to create a scoopable batter. Deep-fry spoonfuls until the fritters develop a jumble of brown, spiky tendrils, and then serve them piping hot with assorted chutneys and milky cups of masala chai.

It's a cozy, comforting snack that many, including Indian-born British chef Asma Khan, have a deep fondness for. The cookbook author and owner of London's Darjeeling Express told me that she's been hooked on pakoras since she was a child: "In my haste to ensure that I got my fair share . . . I would make the mistake of eating them while they were still excruciatingly hot," she recalled before admitting that even as an adult, it's still hard to wait: "Somehow the temptation is too much."

I understand. When New Delhi native Gulshan Singh, cooking instructor and author of *Masala Magic: Unlocking the Secret to Indian Home Cooking* (2014), taught me how to make the golden nuggets more than a decade ago, I too found them irresistible.

Eager to assemble my own recipe, I started with a common trio of vegetables that Singh uses: sliced red onion for sweetness; chopped spinach for a pop of color; and a shredded russet potato to bulk up the fritters. But that's just one of many possible combinations—lean into the versatility of pakoras and substitute whatever is in your garden or fridge (see "Vegetable Pakoras, Your Way").

Next, I assembled a selection of whole and ground spices that would enhance a variety of produce: earthy cumin; citrusy coriander; turmeric for an ocher tint; mildly spicy Kashmiri chile powder; fruity, maple syrup–esque fenugreek; and ajwain, which is frequently added to fried foods to support digestion. Finally, a minced serrano chile added bright, zingy heat.

Three-quarters of a cup of besan hydrated with ¼ cup of water produced a batter that was thick enough to suspend 4 cups of vegetables in a loose tangle. Singh taught me that many cooks also add baking powder, and I followed suit, finding that it gave the fritters a lightness that unleavened versions lacked.

As I lowered heaping tablespoonfuls of the vegetable-packed batter into a pot of gently bubbling oil, I reflected on Khan's account of a perfectly fried pakora: "crunchy-textured on the outside and soft and cooked all the way through in the middle." Closely monitoring the oil temperature—370 to 380 degrees—produced deeply browned fritters that weren't greasy, and frying just five at a time ensured that each one cooked thoroughly and evenly with crisp, scraggly threads around the edges.

For the requisite chutney, cilantro-mint is common, as is a syrupy tamarind type. Tomato ketchup works, too: "[It was] my fallback option when I was young and I found chutney too spicy," remembered Khan.

I'm fond of a carrot-tamarind style inspired by a recipe from chef and author Hari Ghotra. To make it, I buzz raw carrot and red onion in a food processor along with sweet-tart tamarind juice concentrate, lemon juice, water, sugar, and salt. Cumin and coriander echo the earthy, citrusy notes of the pakoras.

You'll find that the lively mixture is an ideal complement for the crispy, spiced fritters. And a generous dunk may just prevent you from burning your mouth.

—ERICA TURNER, *Cook's Illustrated*

Pakoras (South Asian Spiced Vegetable Fritters)

SERVES 4 TO 6 (MAKES ABOUT 15 PAKORAS)   TOTAL TIME: 1 HOUR

Use the large holes of a box grater to shred the potato. For the best texture, we recommend measuring the prepped onion and potato by weight. Besan (also known as gram flour) is made by milling skinned and split brown chickpeas. To substitute standard chickpea flour (made from white chickpeas), add an additional 2 tablespoons of water to the batter. Besan, along with ajwain and Kashmiri chile powder, can be found in South Asian markets. If ajwain is unavailable, substitute dried thyme. If fenugreek is unavailable, it can be omitted. Use a Dutch oven that holds 6 quarts or more. Serve with Carrot-Tamarind Chutney and/or Cilantro-Mint Chutney (recipes follow).

- 1 **large red onion, halved and sliced thin (1½ cups/5 ounces)**
- 1 **large russet potato, peeled and shredded (1½ cups/6½ ounces)**
- 1 **cup baby spinach, chopped**
- 1 **serrano chile, stemmed and minced**
- 1 **teaspoon ground cumin**
- 1 **teaspoon ground coriander**
- 1 **teaspoon ajwain**
- ½ **teaspoon table salt**
- ½ **teaspoon Kashmiri chile powder**
- ¼ **teaspoon ground fenugreek**
- ¾ **cup besan**
- 1 **teaspoon baking powder**
- ½ **teaspoon ground turmeric**
- ¼ **cup water**
- 2 **quarts canola oil for frying**

BESAN VERSUS CHICKPEA FLOUR

The golden, powdery staple called besan is made by milling skinned and split brown chickpeas (aka gram chickpeas, desi chickpeas, or chana dal) into a fine flour. In addition to pakoras, the mildly nutty, nutritious ingredient appears in missi roti (savory flatbreads), laddoos (dessert balls made with sugar and ghee), and numerous other sweet and savory dishes. Chickpea flour is not an identical swap for besan; it's milled from white chickpeas into a slightly coarser grind and requires extra water to hydrate.

1. In large bowl, combine onion, potato, spinach, serrano, cumin, coriander, ajwain, salt, chile powder, and fenugreek. Toss vegetables until coated with spices. Using your hands, squeeze mixture until vegetables are softened and release some liquid, about 45 seconds (do not drain).

2. In small bowl, mix together besan, baking powder, and turmeric. Sprinkle over vegetable mixture and stir until besan is no longer visible and mixture forms sticky mass. Add water and stir vigorously until water is well incorporated.

3. Adjust oven rack to middle position and heat oven to 200 degrees. Set wire rack in rimmed baking sheet. Add oil to large Dutch oven until it measures about 1½ inches deep and heat over medium-low heat to 375 degrees.

4. Transfer heaping tablespoonful of batter to oil, using second spoon to ease batter out of spoon. Stir batter briefly and repeat portioning until there are 5 pakoras in oil. Fry, adjusting burner, if necessary, to maintain oil temperature of 370 to 380 degrees, until pakoras are deep golden brown, 1½ to 2 minutes per side. Using spider skimmer or slotted spoon, transfer pakoras to prepared rack and place in oven. Return oil to 375 degrees and repeat with remaining batter in 2 batches. Serve immediately.

PAKORAS (SOUTH ASIAN SPICED VEGETABLE FRITTERS)

Carrot-Tamarind Chutney

SERVES 6 (MAKES ABOUT 1 CUP) TOTAL TIME: 15 MINUTES

Tamarind juice concentrate can be found at South Asian markets.

- ½ **cup chopped peeled carrot**
- ¼ **cup chopped red onion**
- 3 **tablespoons tamarind juice concentrate**
- 2 **tablespoons water**
- 1 **tablespoon lemon juice**
- 2 **teaspoons sugar**
- ½ **teaspoon ground cumin**
- ½ **teaspoon ground coriander**
- ½ **teaspoon table salt**

Process carrot and onion in food processor until finely chopped, about 20 seconds, scraping down sides of bowl halfway through processing. Add tamarind concentrate, water, lemon juice, sugar, cumin, coriander, and salt and process until combined, about 20 seconds, scraping down sides of bowl halfway through processing (mixture will not be completely smooth). Transfer to bowl and serve. (Chutney can be refrigerated for up to 3 days.)

Cilantro-Mint Chutney

SERVES 4 (MAKES ABOUT 1 CUP) TOTAL TIME: 10 MINUTES

You can adjust the salsa's heat level by reserving and adding the jalapeño seeds, if desired.

- 2 **cups fresh cilantro leaves**
- 1 **cup fresh mint leaves**
- ½ **cup water**
- ¼ **cup sesame seeds, lightly toasted**
- 1 **(2-inch) piece ginger, peeled and sliced into ⅛-inch-thick rounds**
- 1 **jalapeño chile, stemmed, seeded, and sliced into 1-inch pieces**
- 2 **tablespoons vegetable oil**
- 2 **tablespoons fresh lime juice**
- 1½ **teaspoons sugar**
- ½ **teaspoon salt**

Process all ingredients in blender until smooth, about 30 seconds, scraping down sides of jar with spatula after 10 seconds. Transfer to bowl and serve.

NOTES FROM THE TEST KITCHEN

VEGETABLE PAKORAS, YOUR WAY

To riff on our recipe using produce that's already in your garden or crisper drawer, swap the spinach for chopped greens or herbs and/or replace the potato with a shredded firm vegetable.

INSTEAD OF SPINACH, TRY

- Kale
- Swiss chard
- Arugula
- Parsley
- Cilantro
- Collard greens
- Cabbage

INSTEAD OF POTATO, TRY

- Carrot
- Cauliflower
- Zucchini
- Summer squash
- Sweet potato
- Butternut squash

LENTILLES DU PUY WITH SPINACH AND CRÈME FRAÎCHE

CHAPTER 3

SIDE DISHES

BRAISED ASPARAGUS WITH LEMON AND CHIVES

BRAISED ASPARAGUS

✓ **WHY THIS RECIPE WORKS** Braising produces asparagus with a tender, silky texture and sweet, nutty flavor. To achieve consistently cooked spears, we eschewed the tradition of slow cooking in a minimal amount of liquid. Instead we vigorously simmered the vegetable in a copious amount of liquid. We also allowed the braising liquid to evaporate, leaving behind a light glaze that coated the asparagus. Finishing the dish with a small amount of acidity and fresh herbs accentuated the vegetable's sweet flavor.

Braising renders asparagus neither crisp-tender nor browned nor vibrant green—yet it's about to become your favorite way to cook the vegetable. Hear me out: While I'm a fan of the grassy, snappy spears that are the goal of grilling, roasting, and sautéing, braising coaxes asparagus's gentler side into the spotlight. The crisp bite gives way to silkiness; the fresh vegetal flavor evolves into more-complex sweet nuttiness; and the braising liquid can travel into the spears, seasoning them inside and out.

Cooking the most tender asparagus starts not on the stovetop but at the supermarket. Asparagus spears range from pencil-thin to thick and hearty, so I bought an assortment to cook (for the moment, just in salted water in a skillet) to determine the optimal size for braising. I hypothesized that thinner spears were too flimsy for this treatment—and sure enough, the spears were limp and sodden after their stint in the liquid—but I was surprised to discover that the thinner specimens were also more fibrous than the thicker ones when cooked whole. Why? Thick and thin spears of asparagus contain similar amounts of stringy fibers, and the fibers are more concentrated in thin spears, creating a chewier texture. For this application, thicker spears were the way to go.

Another benefit of heartier asparagus? I could peel off their firm, waxy skin without whittling them down to toothpicks. I also wondered if removing the skin would help with absorption. To test, I jazzed up my braising liquid, swapping out some water for chicken broth and adding 2 tablespoons of olive oil for richness, and then cooked peeled and unpeeled spears in the delicately flavored bath. A tasting revealed that the liquid flavored the unpeeled spears only superficially, while the peeled were seasoned to their cores.

I liked the taste of my new braising liquid, but the method still needed a tweak to help the spears cook evenly. Cooking over low heat in a small amount of liquid proved inconsistent; some spears overcooked while others remained crisp. Increasing the amount of liquid so that the asparagus was half-covered and turning up the heat to keep the liquid at a vigorous simmer created more steam—and more evenly cooked spears. In 10 minutes, the bases of all the spears were meltingly tender, yet the tips maintained their shape. The higher heat also helped the braising liquid reduce to a thin, glossy sauce that coated the vegetable.

When it came to finishing touches, I took a "less is more" approach, adding just a splash of acidity and a handsome sprinkle of fresh herbs to my platter of sweet, silky spears. Bright-green asparagus, you've finally met your match.

—KEITH DRESSER, *Cook's Illustrated*

Braised Asparagus with Lemon and Chives

SERVES 4   TOTAL TIME: 30 MINUTES

This recipe is best with asparagus spears that are at least ¾ inch thick.

- 1 **pound thick asparagus**
- 1 **cup water**
- ¼ **cup chicken broth**
- 2 **tablespoons extra-virgin olive oil**
- ¼ **teaspoon table salt**
- ¼ **teaspoon grated lemon zest plus 1 teaspoon juice**
- 2 **teaspoons minced fresh chives, divided**

1. Trim bottom inch of asparagus spears; discard trimmings. Peel bottom two-thirds of spears until white flesh is exposed. Bring water, broth, oil, and salt to simmer in 12-inch skillet over high heat. Add asparagus in even layer. Reduce heat to maintain vigorous simmer and cover. Cook, gently shaking skillet occasionally, until asparagus is tender and can be easily pierced with tip of paring knife, 8 to 10 minutes.

2. Remove lid and continue to cook, shaking and swirling skillet, until skillet is almost dry and asparagus is glazed, 1 to 3 minutes longer. Off heat, add lemon zest and juice and half of chives and toss to coat. Transfer asparagus to platter, sprinkle with remaining chives, season with salt to taste, and serve.

Braised Asparagus with Orange and Tarragon

Substitute orange zest and juice for lemon, increasing amount of orange juice to 1 tablespoon. Substitute minced fresh tarragon for chives.

Braised Asparagus with Sherry Vinegar and Marjoram

Substitute 1 teaspoon sherry vinegar for lemon zest and juice and 1 teaspoon minced fresh marjoram for chives.

ROASTED CAULIFLOWER WITH MINT AND OLIVE SAUCE

✔ WHY THIS RECIPE WORKS Inspired by the simple yet bold ingredients of Sicily, we wanted a roasted cauliflower dish with a bright and zesty sauce that bolstered the roasty notes of the cauliflower. To ensure that the cauliflower had plenty of browning on the bottom, we simply tossed the pieces in olive oil, spread them evenly on a baking sheet (with as many pieces cut side down as possible), and roasted them on the lowest rack of a 475-degree oven. When roasted this way, the cauliflower turned dark brown, caramelized, and nutty, with a tender, creamy center. For the sauce, we combined fresh mint and parsley with Castelvetrano olives, garlic, red pepper flakes, and lemon juice in a food processor before tossing in pine nuts for a quick blitz.

In Sicily, cooks pair cauliflower with a number of big-flavored regional ingredients—from tomatoes, capers, and umami-rich anchovies to golden raisins and wine. In the spirit of this concept, here cauliflower is roasted until it's browned and tender and then topped with a bright and zesty sauce that comes together with a few pulses in the food processor.

To make it, simply break down the cauliflower, toss the pieces in olive oil, spread them evenly on a baking sheet (with as many pieces cut side down as possible), and roast them on the lowest rack of a 475-degree oven. These steps ensure that the cauliflower gets plenty of browning on the bottom. When roasted this way, cauliflower turns caramelized and nutty, with a tender, creamy center. Be sure to roast it until the bottom and some small pieces are dark brown.

A fresh mint and parsley sauce with buttery Castelvetrano olives and toasted pine nuts—other Sicilian favorites—bolsters the roasty notes of the cauliflower. In a food processor, roughly chop pitted Castelvetrano olives, fresh mint and parsley, garlic, and red pepper flakes along with lemon juice and olive oil. Then add the toasted pine nuts and briefly pulse to lightly chop them and combine them with the other ingredients.

The vivid green from the herbs and olives against the chocolaty-brown roasted cauliflower will draw you to the table. But the saucy, almost crispy cauliflower edges and the chopped olives and pine nuts that get caught in the nooks and crannies of the florets will keep you coming back.

—AMANDA LUCHTEL, *Cook's Country*

NOTES FROM THE TEST KITCHEN

AN OLIVE THAT APPEALS TO ALL

Grown primarily in a Sicilian town of the same name, Castelvetrano olives are harvested young and cured in lightly salted water. They have a green-apple color and a meaty, firm texture. And their flavor is mild and buttery, not metallic or overly briny, making them a hit even among those who don't think they like olives. They oxidize quickly, so keep them submerged in their brine until you're ready to use them.

Roasted Cauliflower with Mint and Olive Sauce
SERVES 4   TOTAL TIME: 55 MINUTES

Kitchen shears make easy work of cutting the cauliflower florets away from the core, but you can use a paring knife if you prefer. We like Castelvetrano olives here, but if you can't find them, you can substitute pitted green olives without pimentos. For the best results, use a good-quality extra-virgin olive oil here.

- 1 head cauliflower (2 pounds)
- ½ cup extra-virgin olive oil, divided
- 1 teaspoon table salt, divided
- ¾ teaspoon pepper, divided
- ½ cup pitted Castelvetrano olives

½ cup fresh mint leaves

¼ cup fresh parsley leaves

2 tablespoons lemon juice

1 garlic clove, chopped

¼ teaspoon red pepper flakes

¼ cup pine nuts, toasted

1. Adjust oven rack to lowest position and heat oven to 475 degrees. Trim outer leaves of cauliflower and cut stem flush with bottom of head. Place cauliflower stem side up. Using kitchen shears, cut stems vertically around core to remove large florets. Cut florets through stems into 1- to 1½-inch pieces. Cut core into ½-inch pieces. (You should have about 7 cups cauliflower total.)

2. Toss cauliflower, ¼ cup oil, ½ teaspoon salt, and ½ teaspoon pepper together on rimmed baking sheet. Spread cauliflower into even layer, cut side down. Roast until cauliflower is tender and browned on bottom, about 25 minutes.

NOTES FROM THE TEST KITCHEN

CAULIFLOWER PREP

1. Cut stem flush with bottom of head.

2. Using kitchen shears, cut stems vertically around core to remove large florets.

3. Cut florets through stems into 1- to 1½-inch pieces. Cut core into ½-inch pieces.

3. Meanwhile, combine olives, mint, parsley, lemon juice, garlic, pepper flakes, remaining ¼ cup oil, remaining ½ teaspoon salt, and remaining ¼ teaspoon pepper in food processor. Pulse until roughly chopped, about 6 pulses, scraping down sides of bowl as needed. Add pine nuts and pulse until just combined, about 2 pulses.

4. Transfer cauliflower to platter. Spoon half of sauce evenly over cauliflower. Serve, passing remaining sauce separately.

SAUTÉED RADISHES

✓ **WHY THIS RECIPE WORKS** Cooking radishes is an easy way to mute their assertive spicy flavor and bring out their subtle sweet notes. We began by quickly sautéing quartered radishes in butter over medium heat to ensure light browning and a crisp-tender interior texture. Sautéed scallions provided some textural variety and color. To retain a slight crispness that complemented the heartier radish pieces, we added the scallions near the end of cooking, just to soften and wilt. Briny capers, fresh dill, and lemon zest—more spring favorites—tossed in with the sautéed radishes made for a gentle yet vibrant side dish.

Sweet and mildly spicy radishes are a spring staple. But some people find them a bit too assertive when raw. Cooking radishes is an easy way to mute some of their spiciness and bring out their subtle sweet notes. When paired with scallions, dill, and lemon zest and juice—more spring favorites—sautéed radishes make for a gentle yet vibrant side dish. And they're really easy to prepare.

Begin by quickly sautéing quartered radishes in butter over medium heat to ensure light browning and a crisp-tender interior texture. Scallions provide some textural variety and color. To retain a slight crispness that complements the heartier radish pieces, add the scallions near the end of cooking, just to soften and wilt.

Stir in briny capers and minced garlic with the scallions to add some high notes and depth, respectively. Finish the dish with citrusy lemon zest and juice and fresh dill. Transfer it to a serving dish and enjoy this light, spring-y side dish with a simple piece of seared or grilled chicken or fish.

—AMANDA LUCHTEL, *Cook's Country*

SAUTÉED RADISHES AND SCALLIONS WITH GARLIC, DILL, AND CAPERS

Sautéed Radishes and Scallions with Garlic, Dill, and Capers

SERVES 4   TOTAL TIME: 30 MINUTES

If you buy radishes without the greens attached, you'll need only about 1 pound. Radishes with greens will be fresher. If the diameters of your radishes are less than 1 inch, cut them in half. If your scallions are thicker than a pencil, halve them lengthwise. We like to serve this dish as an accompaniment to seared or grilled chicken or fish.

- 3 tablespoons unsalted butter, divided
- 1½ pounds radishes (1¼ to 1½ inches in diameter) with their greens, trimmed and quartered
- ½ teaspoon table salt, divided
- 5 thin scallions, cut into 1-inch lengths
- 1 tablespoon capers, rinsed
- 2 garlic cloves, minced
- ½ teaspoon pepper
- 3 tablespoons chopped fresh dill
- ½ teaspoon grated lemon zest plus 2 teaspoons juice

1. Melt 2 tablespoons butter in 12-inch nonstick skillet over medium heat. Add radishes and ¼ teaspoon salt and cook until radishes are lightly browned and crisp-tender, 7 to 10 minutes, stirring halfway through cooking.

2. Stir in scallions, capers, garlic, pepper, remaining 1 tablespoon butter, and remaining ¼ teaspoon salt and cook until scallions are wilted, about 2 minutes.

3. Stir in dill and lemon zest and juice. Season with salt and pepper to taste. Transfer to serving dish and serve.

NOTES FROM THE TEST KITCHEN

RADISHES: SHOP SMALL
Round red radishes (Cherry Belle or Scarlet Globe are the most common) are harvested in both spring and fall and store well, making them easy to find in markets year-round. These radishes are best when they are smaller, about 1¼ to 1½ inches in diameter; larger ones may be tough, woody, and hollow.

LEEKS VINAIGRETTE

✔ WHY THIS RECIPE WORKS Leeks are part of the onion family, but when they're cooked, their flavor is sweeter and milder than that of their pungent relations, making them a great base for a starter or side dish. We started by trimming away the dark-green tops and then halved each leek lengthwise, leaving the base intact, so we could rinse away any grit concealed between the layers. Though some recipes call for steaming the leeks to prevent their becoming waterlogged, we preferred simmering them in heavily salted water because it enabled us to get seasoning all the way to their bases. Tying up each leek with a piece of kitchen twine prevented the layers from splaying out and becoming detached as they cooked, and a brief squeeze after cooling removed any excess water. A punchy, mustardy vinaigrette, served both under and atop the leeks, balanced their sweet creaminess, and crispy bread crumbs spiked with a little bit of Parmesan for added savor and richness provided a pleasing textural contrast to the tender leeks.

Leeks need a new PR campaign, and I might be just the person for the job. The sweetest, gentlest allium is best known to American audiences as a soup ingredient—but its quiet character also permits it to play a leading role without being overpowering. Case in point: France's leeks vinaigrette, which is simply silky leeks overlaid with a veil of mustardy dressing. Mellow yet piquant, leeks vinaigrette can accompany chicken or fish, but the dish also works well as a main course with some additions, accompanied by a hunk of bread and a glass of wine.

It comes together quickly: Trim and wash the leeks, simmer or steam them until they're softened, and drizzle them with vinaigrette. Eat them warm or let them sit for hours; they'll only get tastier as the vinaigrette permeates their layers. Here are some lessons I learned from developing my own recipe.

Farmers mound soil around growing leeks to encourage them to develop elegant long, pale stalks, but doing so traps dirt between their concentric layers. Brush any exterior dirt from your leeks before trimming their dark-green tops. Then, starting an inch from the base of each leek, halve them lengthwise and gently open the layers to rinse them under running water. Keep the bases tilted up so that the water washes the dirt out instead of deeper into the layers.

Though I initially dismissed the traditional practice of tying the halved leeks back together, I realized its purpose when my untied leeks' layers splayed out haphazardly during cooking. Tidy leeks are more aesthetically pleasing when they're arranged on a platter, so it's well worth taking this extra step.

Though some cooks advocate steaming to prevent the leeks from becoming waterlogged, submersion in heavily salted water seasons them thoroughly, and any excess water can be expelled by gently squeezing the slightly cooled leeks over the sink.

Many recipes I tried called for dousing the leeks with vinaigrette. This seemed like a cruel injustice to inflict upon the handsomest member of the onion clan, so instead I spread half of my punchier-than-usual Dijon vinaigrette on the platter before placing the leeks on top. The leeks peeked through the remaining vinaigrette enticingly. A sprinkle of Parmesan-spiked bread crumbs, prepared while the leeks cooled, added contrast to the plate of soft, creamy leeks and vinaigrette. Elevating the dish to a main course is as simple as swapping out the crumbs for crumbled bacon and chopped hard-cooked eggs.

—ANDREA GEARY, *Cook's Illustrated*

Leeks Vinaigrette

SERVES 4   TOTAL TIME: 1¼ HOURS

You can use almost any unseeded bread for the bread crumbs; if you're using a rustic loaf, remove the crust before grinding in a food processor. This dish is usually served on its own as a starter, but it could also work as an accompaniment to a simple fish or chicken main course. For a bistro-style lunch for two, omit the bread crumbs and top the dressed leeks with two chopped hard-cooked eggs and two slices of crumbled crispy bacon; serve with crusty bread and a glass of wine.

- 3 leeks (1 to 1½ inches in diameter, with 8 to 9 inches of white and light-green parts), white and light-green parts only
   Table salt for simmering leeks
- 2 teaspoons plus 3 tablespoons extra-virgin olive oil, divided
- ¾ cup fresh bread crumbs
- 2 tablespoons finely grated Parmesan cheese
- 2 tablespoons finely chopped fresh parsley, divided

- ¼ teaspoon pepper
- 1½ tablespoons red wine vinegar
- 1 tablespoon Dijon mustard
- 1 garlic clove, minced to paste

1. Trim roots from leeks, leaving base intact so layers stay together. Starting 1 inch above base, halve leeks lengthwise (they'll still be joined at base). Rinse thoroughly between layers to remove any dirt. Tie halves of each leek together with kitchen twine about 2 inches from top.

2. Bring 3 quarts water to boil in Dutch oven. Add leeks and 3 tablespoons salt and return to boil. Adjust heat to maintain simmer. Cover and cook until area just above base can be pierced easily with paring knife, 15 to 20 minutes. Using tongs, grasp 1 leek close to base and hold vertically over pot to drain briefly. Transfer to paper towel–lined plate and repeat with remaining leeks. Let sit until cool enough to handle, about 10 minutes. While leeks cool, make crumbs and vinaigrette.

3. Heat 2 teaspoons oil in 8-inch nonstick skillet over medium heat until shimmering. Add bread crumbs and cook over medium heat, stirring frequently, until deep golden brown, 4 to 5 minutes. Off heat, sprinkle

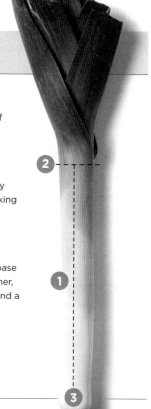

NOTES FROM THE TEST KITCHEN

PREPARING LEEKS

1. Buy leeks with 8 to 9 inches of white and light-green parts to reduce waste.

2. Trim the dark-green tops (they are too tough for this quick-cooking recipe), but save them for use in soups and stocks.

3. Trim the roots, but leave the base intact. It will hold the leek together, and it has a sweet, nutty flavor and a buttery texture when cooked.

with Parmesan and let sit until crumbs are just warm, about 5 minutes. Add 1 tablespoon parsley and pepper and stir, breaking up any clumps.

4. Whisk vinegar, mustard, 1 tablespoon water, and garlic in small bowl until combined. Whisking constantly, drizzle in remaining 3 tablespoons oil. Whisk in remaining 1 tablespoon parsley. Squeeze leeks over sink to remove excess water. Remove twine and finish cutting leeks in half lengthwise. Cut each half crosswise into thirds (do not remove bases of leeks; they're delicious). Spread half of vinaigrette over bottom of serving platter. Arrange leeks on platter, cut side up, opening layers slightly. Drizzle evenly with remaining vinaigrette. (Dressed leeks can be covered loosely and stored at room temperature for up to 3 hours.) Sprinkle with bread crumb mixture and serve.

PA AMB TOMÀQUET (CATALAN TOMATO BREAD)

✓ **WHY THIS RECIPE WORKS** Pa amb tomàquet—Catalan bread with tomato—is simple cooking at its finest. Ciabatta mimicked the airy, open structure of traditional pan de cristal. Halving the loaf laterally, opening it like a book, and cutting the halves into slices maximized its surface area. Toasted dry under the broiler, the bread charred lightly and quickly so that its interior crumb remained tender—a textural contrast that was just right for both supporting and absorbing the tomatoes' liquid. Rubbing a garlic clove over the toasts infused them with subtle savoriness. Halving and grating ripe round tomatoes on a box grater yielded loads of sweet, skin-free pulp that could be uniformly seasoned and spooned onto the toasts. Great olive oil, drizzled over the tomato bread for serving, complemented the bright tomato and lean bread.

Whether you know it as pan con tomate, as many Spaniards do, or by its native Catalan name, pa amb tomàquet ("pam two-MAH-cat"), the dish is bread with tomato, and it's as simple as cooking gets.

"If you have a piece of bread, you have a piece of bread with tomato," said Alex Montiel, a native of Catalonia and chef/owner of La Cuchara de San Telmo in San Sebastián, who grew up eating pa amb tomàquet daily. The crunchy yet tender toasted bread and brilliantly ripe tomato pulp make for an unbeatable combination, he

explained, especially when the tomato-topped toast is seasoned with coarse salt and lavished with great olive oil.

Once you've had it, the appeal is obvious. In addition to the contrasting flavors and textures of the elements, you're charmed by the dish's deceptively complex character. On the one hand, it's routine, humble food—something that "everybody eats in Catalonia," according to Montiel. On the other hand, the purity of the ingredients conveys a certain sense of luxury. Owen Royce-Nagel, chef at Tres Gatos, my go-to tapas bar in the Jamaica Plain corner of Boston, said pa amb tomàquet reminds him of "picking snap peas right out of the garden while they still have the sweetness of coming off the vine."

It may seem like a dish this simple doesn't need a recipe. But given pa amb tomàquet's weight in Catalan cuisine, and that best practices can guarantee truly sublime results when you're using high-quality ingredients such as these, I wanted to work out every detail. After all, said Montiel, "it's one of the most important meals in the world."

Pa amb tomàquet uses only the tomato's vibrant, umami-rich pulp; in fact, tomàquets de ramallet (tomatoes on the vine) and tomàquets de penjar (hanging tomatoes) are thick-skinned, juice-heavy varieties bred in Catalonia specifically for this purpose. But ripe, in-season American varieties—the bigger, the better to maximize the yield—were also terrific.

To harvest the pulp, cooks halve tomatoes through the equator to expose as much of the interior as possible and then either rub the cut side directly onto the toast or grate it on a box grater and spoon it over the top. Montiel said that putting the tomato directly to the bread is an older, more traditional approach, but some cooks prefer grating because the pulp is easy to prepare ahead, uniformly season, and portion on the bread. I chose to grate, running the fruit over the coarse holes until the flesh was reduced to a puree and the skin a mere slip. Two large tomatoes netted about 1½ cups of pulp—enough to coat a loaf's worth of toast.

Pan de cristal ("glass bread"), a rustic loaf with an exceptionally open, airy crumb, is the gold standard for pa amb tomàquet. It's often compared to ciabatta, so that's what I used in its place, halving the oblong loaf horizontally and slicing each half 2 inches thick.

The bread is always toasted dry (olive oil is drizzled on at the table) and quickly so that the exterior browns and crisps while the inside stays tender. Royce-Nagel

PA AMB TOMÀQUET (CATALAN TOMATO BREAD)

said that structural contrast allows the bread to both absorb and withstand the tomato's liquid: "You still get that crunch from the bottom of the bite, and then all of that flavor kind of seeps into the top."

Some cooks grill it, but broiling works, too. I placed the bread slices cut side up on a wire rack set in a baking sheet and toasted them 6 inches below the broiler element until they crisped and browned. Then I rubbed the hot toasts with garlic—an optional step that infuses the crumb with a mellow savoriness. Its flavor complemented the tomatoes so nicely that it felt essential.

—ANNIE PETITO, *Cook's Illustrated*

Pa amb Tomàquet (Catalan Tomato Bread)
SERVES 4 TO 6   TOTAL TIME: 30 MINUTES

If possible, use ripe local tomatoes here. Avoid plum tomatoes; they're not juicy enough. If ciabatta is unavailable, substitute a crusty baguette, cut into 4-inch pieces. Use a fresh, robust, high-quality olive oil here. Serve as an accompaniment to any meal or as an appetizer or a snack.

- 2 large ripe tomatoes, halved through equator
- ½ teaspoon table salt
- 1 loaf ciabatta, halved horizontally and sliced crosswise 2 inches thick
- 1 large garlic clove, peeled and halved crosswise
- 3 tablespoons extra-virgin olive oil, plus extra for serving

1. Place box grater in medium bowl. Rub cut side of tomatoes against large holes of grater until tomato flesh is reduced to pulp (skins should remain intact). Discard skins. (You should have about 1½ cups pulp.) Stir in salt.

2. Adjust oven rack 6 inches from broiler element and heat broiler. Set wire rack in rimmed baking sheet and arrange bread slices cut side up on rack. Broil until browned, crisp, and starting to char at edges, 2 to 4 minutes. Rub toasts with cut side of garlic (apply more pressure for more-potent flavor; rub lightly for delicate flavor).

3. Arrange toasts on serving plate. Distribute tomato pulp evenly among toasts and spread to edges. Drizzle with oil and season lightly with flake sea salt. Serve immediately, passing extra oil and sea salt separately.

OKRA: A VEGETABLE SUPERSTAR

WHY THIS RECIPE WORKS For well-browned and tender okra with lightly crisp edges, we split similar-size pods lengthwise and tossed them with oil and salt. We arranged the pods cut sides down on a rimmed baking sheet and covered them with foil so that the thicker parts could steam and turn tender before the thin tips withered and scorched. Finally, we uncovered the okra to allow their cut sides, which rested flush against the baking sheet, to brown and crisp lightly. For a full-bodied, spiced, and smoky okra stew, we started by rendering bacon fat until a rich fond formed on the bottom of the pot, and then we built on its flavor base by sautéing onion along with onion and garlic powders, smoked paprika, and black and cayenne peppers. Next, we deglazed the fond with juicy chopped fresh tomato and added the okra, along with water and lemon juice. As the okra simmered, its polysaccharides dissolved in and thickened the broth.

There are many ways to reveal okra's charms: The fresh pods can be breaded and deep-fried, pickled in a vinegary brine, charred over fiery coals, gently stewed, or used to thicken soup, to name just a few. The vegetable is even good lightly steamed; in Southern barbecue joints, you'll often find a single downy pod draped atop a dish of black-eyed peas, seductively flaunting tenderness, grassy sweetness, and viscosity. And purists such as Chris Smith, gardener and author of *The Whole Okra* (2019), appreciate the joys of okra without even bringing it into the kitchen: "I like eating it raw in the field," he enthused on a recent call from his home in Asheville, North Carolina.

It's no wonder that okra is used in such a variety of preparations, as its roots run deep and wide. The vegetable's origin is debated by botanists, though many agree that *Abelmoschus esculentus* grew wild in Asia and was later domesticated in East Africa. From there, the velvety pods became popular across large swaths of the globe, where they were given many names—including gombo, bamia, and okro—and incorporated into a variety of recipes and culinary traditions. In India, where the majority of the world's crop is grown and consumed, one of the most beloved dishes is bhindi masala, a deeply fragrant, spice-heavy celebration of the pods.

And anywhere in the Americas where the culinary traditions of enslaved Africans took hold, we see okra and the recipes of Black cooks. Along with gumbo—perhaps the most famous of all American okra dishes—a variety of other okra soups are seen in early U.S. recipe collections, and menus from the late 19th and early 20th centuries feature the likes of "Scalloped Okra," "Strained Okra in a Cup," and "Okra Jelly." Which brings us to the sticking point.

Or is it the slipping point? The most intriguing part of okra might just be its mucilage (the technical term for the slimy substance within the cells of its pod and seeds). As it turns out, this goo is quite easy to manipulate (for details, see "Using Science to Dictate Texture"). Here, I celebrate the wonderful versatility of okra with two distinctly different preparations.

Roasting is a terrific way to cook okra. The high, dry heat of the oven concentrates the pods' nuanced vegetal flavors and encourages browning reactions that create even more complexity. Heat also dehydrates the okra's mucilage, so it becomes nearly undetectable.

Roasting is also simple by nature. My method starts with selecting pods that are similar in diameter (depending on the variety, okra can be elegantly long and thin or barrel-shaped and short, grassy green or burgundy, ridged or smooth, and straight or curved) so that they will cook at the same rate. Just lop off their caps and then split them lengthwise to expose their interiors, which are clustered with small round seeds.

After quickly tossing the okra with vegetable oil and salt, arrange them cut sides down on a baking sheet, and then seal them in with aluminum foil before sliding the assembly into a 425-degree oven. A steaming period prevents the pointed tips from withering and charring before the thicker upper sections turn tender. After 15 minutes, remove the foil and allow the flat surfaces of the okra to brown for about 10 minutes. The results are remarkable: tender, with graceful streaks of brown at the edges—and virtually absent of slipperiness. Serve the pods as a side dish with almost any entrée or offer them as finger food with a dipping sauce. Either way, they'll disappear fast.

In the South, where okra is a pillar of the kitchen, the pods are often chopped and simmered with tomatoes and alliums—and sometimes smoky pork—until they turn supple and their mucilage acts similarly to a roux, thickening the savory broth.

NOTES FROM THE TEST KITCHEN

USING SCIENCE TO DICTATE TEXTURE
Okra can have two distinctly different characters, depending on how it's cooked. Its slick texture is formed by polysaccharides that dissolve in water to make a slippery gel. Thus, slowly stewing the vegetable exploits its gooey properties, eventually releasing most of its polysaccharides to create a thick, silky consistency. Conversely, a dry cooking method such as roasting bypasses slipperiness: In the heat of the oven, okra's mucilage dehydrates and clings to the inside of the pod. When the okra is chewed, this mucilage doesn't have time to dissolve and form a gel.

H_2O IS KEY
Add or limit water, depending on the outcome you desire.

Soul food expert and James Beard Award–winning author Adrian Miller told me he considers the simple stew "a very complete meal" when served atop a heap of white rice, and he grinned broadly at the memory of his last batch, recalling "grubbin' on it for days."

I start my version by frying bacon pieces with onion, cayenne and black peppers, smoked paprika, and onion and garlic powders. Chopped fresh tomato goes in next so that the juice can deglaze the bottom of the saucepan. Finally, I stir in the okra, along with water—key for encouraging the mucilage to bring viscosity to the stew—and fresh lemon juice and let it bubble for about 25 minutes, until the okra becomes soft and tender and cloaked in a rich, velvety broth.

—LAN LAM, *Cook's Illustrated*

Roasted Okra

SERVES 4   TOTAL TIME: 45 MINUTES

Don't use frozen okra in this recipe. For even cooking and browning, select okra pods that have approximately the same diameter. If you use a dark baking sheet, the browning time after removing the foil will be on the shorter end of the range. If desired, serve with Spicy Red Pepper Mayonnaise (recipe follows) by spreading the mixture onto a serving platter and arranging the okra on top. Alternatively, squeeze lemon or lime juice onto the roasted okra and/or sprinkle it with your favorite spice blend.

1 **pound fresh okra, trimmed and halved lengthwise**

2 **teaspoons vegetable oil**

½ **teaspoon table salt**

1. Adjust oven rack to middle position and heat oven to 425 degrees.

2. Toss okra with oil and salt in bowl until well combined. Arrange okra, cut sides down, in single layer on rimmed baking sheet. Cover tightly with aluminum foil and roast until okra is bright green, 12 to 15 minutes (cut sides of a few pieces may be beginning to brown). Remove foil and roast until cut sides are well browned, 7 to 12 minutes.

3. Let okra rest on sheet for 5 minutes. Serve.

Spicy Red Pepper Mayonnaise

SERVES 4   TOTAL TIME: 25 MINUTES

For a less spicy mayonnaise, use just a pinch of cayenne pepper.

- 2 teaspoons vegetable oil
- 5 garlic cloves, minced
- ¾ teaspoon smoked paprika
- ¾ teaspoon ground coriander
- ¾ teaspoon ground cumin
-   Pinch to ⅛ teaspoon cayenne pepper
- ⅓ cup jarred roasted red peppers, patted dry and minced
- ½ teaspoon table salt
- ¼ teaspoon sugar
- 3 tablespoons mayonnaise
- ¼ teaspoon grated lime zest plus ½ teaspoon juice

1. Heat oil in 8-inch skillet over medium heat until shimmering. Add garlic and cook, stirring frequently, until garlic just starts to brown, about 2 minutes. Add paprika, coriander, cumin, and cayenne and cook, stirring constantly, until fragrant, about 30 seconds. Immediately transfer to bowl. Stir in red peppers, salt, and sugar and refrigerate for at least 5 minutes.

2. Stir mayonnaise and lime zest and juice into red pepper mixture and serve.

Stewed Okra

SERVES 4 TO 6   TOTAL TIME: 55 MINUTES

Don't use frozen okra in this recipe. We like the sharp tang that a few drops of a particularly vinegary hot sauce add here. Serve as a side dish or with steamed white rice as an entrée.

- 1½ teaspoons garlic powder
- 1 teaspoon onion powder
- 1 tablespoon plus 1¼ cups water, divided
- 3 slices bacon, cut into ½-inch pieces
- 1 small onion, chopped
- ½ teaspoon table salt
- ¼ teaspoon smoked paprika
- ¼ teaspoon pepper
- ⅛ teaspoon cayenne pepper
- 1 vine-ripened tomato, cored and chopped
- 12 ounces fresh okra, trimmed and cut into ½-inch pieces
- 2 teaspoons lemon juice
-   Hot sauce

1. Stir garlic powder, onion powder, and 1 tablespoon water together in small bowl. Cook bacon in medium saucepan over medium heat, stirring occasionally, until fat is rendered and dark fond forms on bottom of saucepan, 5 to 7 minutes. Add onion and salt and cook, stirring frequently, until onion is translucent, about 5 minutes. Add paprika, pepper, cayenne, and garlic powder mixture and cook, stirring constantly, until fragrant, about 30 seconds.

2. Add tomato and cook, scraping browned bits from bottom of saucepan. Stir in okra, lemon juice, and remaining 1¼ cups water. Increase heat to high and bring to simmer. Adjust heat to maintain gentle simmer. Cover and cook, stirring occasionally, until okra is tender and liquid has consistency of thin gravy, 25 to 30 minutes (gravy will thicken as it cools). Season with salt and pepper to taste. Serve, passing hot sauce separately.

ROASTED KALE

✓ **WHY THIS RECIPE WORKS** We used curly kale for roasting because it retained some volume and featheriness when cooked. After tearing the leaves into large pieces and rinsing them, we spun the pieces in a salad spinner to remove most of the excess moisture that would otherwise need to be cooked off in the oven. Massaging oil and salt into the kale evenly seasoned all the pieces and kick-started the wilting process. Roasting the kale in a hot oven cooked it relatively quickly and encouraged browning. By skipping any stirring while cooking, we ended up with kale that had a delightful mix of textures: tender, crisp, and crunchy. The classic combination of garlic, red pepper flakes, and lemon brightened up the earthy green. In a second version, grated ginger wIth coriander plus unsweetened coconut chips (added after cooking) gave the greens a rich, citrusy sweetness. For a third take, Parmesan, shallot, and nutmeg offered a warm, nutty profile.

Even cynics have to admit: Kale has range. Raw, its leaves are tenacious and hearty, but a brief stint on the stovetop renders the vegetable moist and tender, and a long period in a low oven produces crispy, shattery chips. And as I recently discovered, roasting can capture the many faces of cooked kale on a single baking sheet. In just 10 minutes in a hot oven, the leaves turn a deep emerald color and take on a delightful mélange of textures: crunchy, browned edges; crisped centers; and still-tender wilted spots. It's the most versatile of dishes, equally capable of accompanying a simple entrée and melding seamlessly into pastas, scrambles, or grain bowls.

There are generally two widely available options when it comes to kale—Tuscan (also known as dinosaur or lacinato) and curly. Tuscan kale leaves are more tender, but the frilly, more fibrous curly kale leaves actually work better here: They retain some volume, and the crinkly edges crisp and brown dramatically.

After rinsing and stripping the stems from a pound's worth of kale leaves (enough to serve four but still roast on a single sheet), I tore the leaves into 1½- to 2-inch pieces. To get the kale to brown, I knew it was crucial to rid it of most of its excess moisture, so I spun the leaves in batches in my salad spinner until most of the water was whisked away. (Leaving a few beads of water on the leaves helped them soften during roasting.)

Oil is key to attaining browning during roasting, but a quick toss didn't thoroughly coat the ruffled leaves. Instead, I spread the spun leaves on the sheet where they'd roast; drizzled them with 2 tablespoons of vegetable oil, along with some salt; and massaged the oil and salt into the leaves. In addition to being the most efficient way to coat the kale, kneading and squeezing also broke down the kale's cell walls, darkening and tenderizing the leaves. Sure enough, just a minute later, the leaves began to soften, transforming the mountainous pile into something manageable.

With that, all that was left to do was roast. I slid the sheet into a 400-degree oven for 10 minutes; the relatively high temperature encouraged browning and cooked the greens through quickly without drying them out. It wasn't necessary to toss the leaves; in fact, leaving them be was key to attaining myriad textures: Pieces near the bottom were tender, as if sautéed; those closer to the top were crisp; and others made an audible crunch when eaten because of their deep browning.

Roasted kale can stand on its own, but I found that adding garlic, red pepper flakes, and lemon to the mixture before roasting made the kale downright snackable. What's more, the dish is so versatile that it's easy to swap out the seasonings: Grated fresh ginger with coriander and unsweetened coconut chips (added after cooking) provided a rich, citrusy sweetness, and Parmesan, shallot, and nutmeg turned the kale warm and nutty.

—ANNIE PETITO, *Cook's Illustrated*

Roasted Kale with Garlic, Red Pepper Flakes, and Lemon

SERVES 4   TOTAL TIME: 30 MINUTES

Washing the kale and drying it in the salad spinner leaves it with just the right amount of surface moisture to facilitate cooking; kneading and squeezing the kale helps soften its texture and evenly distributes seasonings—do not skip these steps. Kale bunches can vary in the amount of usable leaves; buy 1 pound to ensure that you end up with 12 cups (10 ounces) of kale pieces. To minimize waste, look for bunches where leaves run the length of the stem. Serve the kale as a side dish or mix it into pastas, scrambles, or grain bowls.

1   pound curly kale, stemmed and torn into 1½- to 2-inch pieces (12 cups)
2   tablespoons vegetable oil
2   garlic cloves, minced
1   teaspoon grated lemon zest
½   teaspoon table salt
¼   teaspoon red pepper flakes

1. Adjust oven rack to upper-middle position and heat oven to 400 degrees. Working in 3 batches, wash kale and spin in salad spinner until leaves are mostly dry. Transfer to rimmed baking sheet.

2. Combine oil, garlic, lemon zest, salt, and pepper flakes in small bowl. Drizzle over kale. Gently knead and squeeze kale until leaves are evenly coated in oil mixture, have started to soften, and are slightly wilted, about 1 minute.

3. Roast kale until leaves are tender and some edges of leaves are crisp and brown, about 10 minutes. Serve immediately (leaves will soften as they stand).

ROASTED KALE WITH PARMESAN, SHALLOT, AND NUTMEG

SHOPPING FOR CURLY KALE

When shopping for curly kale, you're likely to see some leggy bunches with leaves limited to the upper half of the stem alongside fuller bunches with greens running the entire length of the stem. Because the stem is too tough to eat, maximize the usable leafy portion by looking for fuller bunches, which can have as much as 15 percent more.

And what about bagged precut kale? You might be tempted by the opportunity to skip some prep, but you won't actually save much time—or money, for that matter. We found that bagged kale contained irregularly sized pieces, from large, 2-inch pieces to some that measured less than an inch, which wilted to almost nothing when roasted. The bags also contained more than half their weight in inedible stem pieces, which needed to be sorted out and replaced. What's more, some usable leaves had been cut crosswise, which left the stem intact, contributing an unpleasant woodiness to finished dishes. With all that in mind, it's safe to say that prepping your own leafy bunches is your best bet.

AVOID PRECUT KALE

FULLER IS BETTER
Look for leaves that run the entire length of the stem.

VARIATIONS

Roasted Kale with Coriander, Ginger, and Coconut
Omit lemon zest. Substitute 2 teaspoons grated fresh ginger for garlic and ½ teaspoon ground coriander for pepper flakes. Sprinkle ½ cup unsweetened coconut chips over kale after roasting.

Roasted Kale with Parmesan, Shallot, and Nutmeg
Substitute ½ cup grated Parmesan for garlic, 2 tablespoons minced shallot for lemon zest, and ground nutmeg for pepper flakes.

HASSELBACK POTATO CASSEROLE

✔ **WHY THIS RECIPE WORKS** To make this recipe failproof, we chose large russets, which, when sliced, fit neatly in three rows in an 8-inch square metal baking pan. We used a mandoline to ensure that the potato slices would be uniformly thin and result in an unfailingly tender interior and an extra-crispy top. Then we layered in complementary flavors: crispy bacon and caramelized onions for a sweet, savory, smoky flavor base; ample garlic for a pungent bite; and minced fresh rosemary for bright, piney notes. Finally, we incorporated Gruyère and Parmesan to provide nuttiness and sharpness while melding the slices into a cohesive whole as they melted.

Hasselback potatoes, a dish purportedly created by Leif Elisson in 1953 at the Hasselbacken Restaurant Academy in Stockholm, are whole potatoes that are sliced thin almost all the way through to create a fanned effect. They look cool, but they take some care and precision to prepare. This revised, easier version features potato coins arranged on their sides in a baking pan. Standing the potato slices upright exposes more potato flesh to flavorings and creates gorgeous caramelized edges.

Chef and author J. Kenji López-Alt, an ATK alumnus, deserves credit for melding Hasselback potatoes with potato gratin. His recipe inspired this one as well as countless recipes for Hasselback potato casseroles from food bloggers and celebrity chefs alike.

The key to making our utterly delicious and failproof version is layering in our own complementary flavors and testing rigorously to find the best way to stack the potatoes (see "Slice Spuds; Then Stand Them Up"). Crisping bacon before caramelizing onions in the rendered bacon fat builds a sweet, savory, smoky flavor base. Ample garlic adds a pungent bite, and minced fresh rosemary (both baked in and sprinkled on top before serving) brings piney high notes that brighten the dish. Gruyère and Parmesan provide nuttiness and sharpness while melding the slices into a cohesive whole as they melt.

Choosing large russets makes for slices that will fit neatly when arranged in three rows in an 8-inch square metal baking pan, and slicing the potatoes uniformly thin on a mandoline results in an unfailingly tender interior; an extra-crispy top; and a refined, impressive

HASSELBACK POTATO CASSEROLE

presentation. This casserole is stylish enough for a fancy dinner party but so delectable that you might not be able to resist making it every Sunday.

—MATTHEW FAIRMAN, *Cook's Country*

Hasselback Potato Casserole

SERVES 8 TOTAL TIME: 3 HOURS

Look for oblong russets that are 4 to 6 inches long and about 3 inches in diameter at their widest. Large potatoes are easier to peel and to slice on a mandoline and fit well when stacked in an 8-inch square pan. If you can find only small russets, you may need more than 4¼ pounds to yield enough slices to fill the pan. Do not pack the potatoes in too tightly or they may not cook through in the stated time; it's OK to have a few unused slices. Use the mandoline's finger guard and stop slicing when you've got about a 1-inch nub of potato left.

- 6 slices bacon, chopped fine
- 2 cups finely chopped onion
- 1¼ cups chicken broth, divided
- 4 garlic cloves, minced
- 1 tablespoon minced fresh rosemary, divided
- 1 tablespoon unsalted butter
- 4¼ pounds large russet potatoes, unpeeled
- 6 ounces Gruyère cheese, shredded (1½ cups), divided
- 2 ounces Parmesan cheese, grated (1 cup), divided
- 2 teaspoons table salt
- 1 teaspoon pepper

1. Adjust oven rack to middle position and heat oven to 400 degrees. Cook bacon in 12-inch nonstick skillet over medium-high heat until crispy, 5 to 8 minutes, stirring frequently.

2. Stir in onion and ½ cup broth. Cover and cook until most of liquid has evaporated, 5 to 7 minutes, stirring occasionally. Uncover and continue to cook until onion is well browned, about 5 minutes longer. Add garlic and 2½ teaspoons rosemary and cook until fragrant, about 1 minute. Set aside off heat.

3. Grease 8-inch square baking pan with butter. Peel potatoes. Using mandoline, slice potatoes crosswise ⅛ inch thick. Combine potatoes, ¾ cup Gruyère, ½ cup Parmesan, salt, pepper, bacon-onion mixture, and remaining ¾ cup broth in large bowl and toss to thoroughly combine, breaking up any stacked potatoes and making sure potatoes are coated.

SLICE SPUDS; THEN STAND THEM UP

1. Slice potatoes crosswise ⅛ inch thick using mandoline.

2. Working with 2-inch stacks of potatoes, lay stacks on their sides in pan.

4. Stack 2 inches of potatoes, then lay stack on its side in 1 corner of prepared pan. Continue stacking and laying down potatoes until pan is filled with 3 rows of potatoes. (Potato slices should fit snugly without having to be squeezed in. You may not need all of them; save any extra slices for another use.) Pour remaining broth mixture in bowl over potatoes. Brush any pieces of bacon or onion on top of potatoes down into valleys between rows.

5. Cover pan tightly with aluminum foil and place on foil-lined rimmed baking sheet. Bake for 1¼ hours. Uncover pan and continue to bake until tops of potatoes are golden brown and paring knife inserted into potatoes meets very little resistance, about 30 minutes longer.

6. Combine remaining ¾ cup Gruyère and remaining ½ cup Parmesan in bowl. Remove potatoes from oven and sprinkle with cheese mixture. Continue to bake until potatoes are well browned, about 15 minutes longer.

7. Remove potatoes from oven. Sprinkle with remaining ½ teaspoon rosemary. Let cool for 15 minutes and serve.

LENTILLES DU PUY WITH SPINACH

✓ **WHY THIS RECIPE WORKS** This recipe is made with lentilles du Puy, which are grown under strict French and European Union origin laws. We chose a mix of onion, carrot, and celery as the primary aromatics in this dish. We sweated the aromatics in olive oil before cooking the lentils in chicken broth for depth of flavor. When cooked properly and with the right amount of liquid, the lentils held their shape but had a creamy mouthfeel. We folded in spinach for a bit of greenery and Dijon for a mustard kick. A dollop of crème fraîche made for a luxurious finish.

The French Government goes through painstaking measures to protect certain French foods. For instance, their appellation d'origine contrôlée (AOC) seal certifies strict geographical identities to maintain the quality and authenticity of wines; cheeses; and, yes, lentils. It's a way of preserving culinary heritage at the sourcing level. For centuries, the Le Puy community in the Auvergne region of France has been cultivating its namesake lentils with the utmost care to ensure that the legumes are of consistently high quality. Lentilles du Puy enjoy AOC status in France as well as Protected Designation of Origin (PDO) certification from the European Union.

Lentilles du Puy have a deep-green color and are often referred to as the "caviar of lentils." Though their price is lower than that of actual caviar, they are typically more expensive than other lentils. Lentilles du Puy have a rich, earthy flavor, and when cooked properly, they have a silky texture but still hold their shape. Thanks to the internet (and some big-box and department stores as well as large supermarkets), they are widely available.

This recipe is simple enough to allow the lentils to shine. To make it, gently cook mirepoix (a mixture of two parts chopped onion to one part each of chopped carrots and celery) in extra-virgin olive oil with a touch of salt until it's just softened. Add the lentils and some chicken broth (or vegetable broth if you prefer); bring the mixture to a simmer; and gently cook it, covered, for about 30 minutes, until the lentils are soft and creamy inside and still hold their shape and almost all the broth is absorbed or has evaporated. Next, stir in some mineral-y spinach and a few spoonfuls of fiery Dijon mustard. Let the mixture sit for 5 minutes, and then top it with a dollop of rich, tangy, creamy crème fraîche. Dig in!

—MARK HUXSOLL, *Cook's Country*

NOTES FROM THE TEST KITCHEN

KEY INGREDIENTS

Lentilles du Puy are French lentils that have rich, earthy, complex flavor and a firm yet tender texture. Because they hold their shape, they work well in dishes where they are the main ingredient.

Crème fraîche, which is made by adding bacteria (or cultures) to heavy cream, has a lush, fluid consistency; a subtle tang; and a nutty flavor. It can be used to boost creaminess in dishes or add richness as a topping.

Lentilles du Puy with Spinach and Crème Fraîche

SERVES 4 TO 6   TOTAL TIME: 1 HOUR

You can substitute other French green lentils for the lentilles du Puy, but do not substitute other types of green lentils or black, brown, or red lentils—the cooking times of the other lentil varieties can vary greatly. By the end of step 2, the lentils should have absorbed most, but not all, of the chicken broth. If the bottom of the saucepan looks dry and the lentils are still somewhat firm, add hot water, ¼ cup at a time, and continue to cook until the lentils are tender. For a vegetarian version, substitute vegetable broth for the chicken broth. If you can't find crème fraîche, sour cream works well.

- 1 **tablespoon extra-virgin olive oil**
- ½ **cup finely chopped onion**
- ¼ **cup finely chopped carrot**
- ¼ **cup finely chopped celery**
- ½ **teaspoon table salt**
- 2 **cups chicken broth**
- 1 **cup dried lentilles du Puy, picked over and rinsed**
  Hot water
- 2 **ounces (2 cups) baby spinach**
- 2 **tablespoons Dijon mustard**
- ¼ **cup crème fraîche**

1. Heat oil in large saucepan over medium heat until shimmering. Add onion, carrot, celery, and salt; cook until vegetables are tender, about 5 minutes.

2. Add broth and lentils and bring to simmer. Reduce heat to medium-low; cover; and cook, stirring occasionally, until lentils are tender but still hold their shape, about 30 minutes. (Add hot water, ¼ cup at a time, if saucepan becomes dry before lentils are cooked through.)

3. Gently fold in spinach and mustard. Let sit off heat for 5 minutes. Transfer to serving bowl and dollop with crème fraîche. Serve.

INSTANT POT BARBECUE BEANS

✔ **WHY THIS RECIPE WORKS** Using a multicooker to make baked beans can save time without sacrificing flavor; it just requires a little strategy. We employed a three-part method: brining, pressure cooking, and simmering. The brined beans took less time to cook, held their shape better, and were well seasoned due to the added salt. We used the Instant Pot's sauté function to create a tasty base of aromatics and spices before adding the brined beans. After pressure-cooking the beans for only 9 minutes, we stirred in ketchup, brown sugar, Dijon mustard, and molasses and simmered the beans to create that signature flavor.

Tender, lightly sweet, and deeply savory barbecue baked beans, a mainstay at potlucks today, are believed to have originated with Native American tribes whose crops included beans. According to Jasper White in *Jasper White's Cooking from New England* (1989), "The [tribes] of New England slow-cooked beans in underground pits inside deer hides, with maple sugar and bear fat. This dish evolved into cooking beans with salt pork and molasses in a bean pot very slowly, often overnight." Today's baked beans, inspired by these early methods, are typically made with navy beans—though great northern or pinto are also common—plus a pork product for richness and a sweet-tangy sauce to tie it all together.

Baked beans are often cooked low and slow on the stovetop or in the oven for a just-right texture and plenty of flavor development. But does reaching this ideal have to take so long? As it turns out, no. Cooking baked beans in less time just requires a little strategy and a switch to a popular time-saving appliance: the multicooker (see "Key Equipment"). As for strategy, a three-part method—brining, pressure cooking, and

simmering—produces the best results. The brining (soaking in a saltwater solution for at least 8 or up to 24 hours) means preparing dried beans requires some advance planning, but it's well worth it, as brined beans take less time to cook, hold their shape better, and are well seasoned due to the added salt.

The next step is moving the brined beans to the Instant Pot. The steady, even heat and closed environment cook them in minutes rather than hours, all the while coaxing flavor into the beans. To create a tasty base, sauté smoky thick-cut bacon and finely chopped onion in vegetable oil in the Instant Pot until the fat is rendered and the onion is caramelized, and then add a liberal amount of minced garlic, chili powder, salt, and cayenne. For enhanced depth, stir in broth, instead of water, along with the beans. A mere 9 minutes under pressure is all it takes to achieve tenderness, but these beans aren't quite ready yet.

Stir sweet-tart ketchup, brown sugar, punchy Dijon mustard, and complex molasses into the Instant Pot. Then, using the sauté function, cook the combination for about 8 minutes to concentrate the flavors and thicken the sauce. Transfer the beans to a serving bowl, and let them sit for 10 minutes—they are too hot to enjoy straight from the pot. Swirl in a little cider vinegar just before serving to add a pleasant tang and welcome brightness. Then dig in and enjoy these delicious barbecue "baked" beans.

—LAWMAN JOHNSON, *Cook's Country*

Instant Pot Barbecue Beans

SERVES 4 TO 6   TOTAL TIME: 1¼ HOURS, PLUS 8 HOURS BRINING

Regular bacon can be used in place of the thick-cut bacon, if desired. If you are short on time, you can quick-brine your beans: In step 1, bring 1½ tablespoons of salt, 2 quarts of water, and the beans to a boil in the

---

NOTES FROM THE TEST KITCHEN

KEY EQUIPMENT
The Instant Pot Pro 8Qt is our top pick among multicookers. We love its many features, such as its flat bottom for even searing, its stay-cool handles, and its steaming and sautéing functions. We were impressed with the well-cooked food it produced.

INSTANT POT PRO 8QT
Pressure-cooking rock star

INSTANT POT BARBECUE BEANS

Instant Pot using the highest sauté function; turn off the pot; and let the beans sit for 1 hour. Drain and rinse the beans and proceed with step 2.

1½   tablespoons table salt for brining
  1   pound (2½ cups) dried navy beans,
      picked over and rinsed
  1   tablespoon vegetable oil
  1   pound thick-cut bacon, cut crosswise ½ inch thick
  1   onion, chopped fine
  4   garlic cloves, minced
  1   tablespoon chili powder
1½   teaspoons table salt
  ½   teaspoon cayenne pepper
  3   cups chicken broth
  1   cup ketchup
  ⅓   cup packed brown sugar
  ¼   cup molasses
  ¼   cup Dijon mustard
  2   teaspoons cider vinegar

1. Dissolve 1½ tablespoons salt in 2 quarts cold water in large container. Add beans and let soak at room temperature for at least 8 hours or up to 24 hours. Drain and rinse well.

2. Using highest sauté function, heat oil in Instant Pot until shimmering. Add bacon and onion and cook, stirring occasionally, until bacon fat is rendered and onion is softened, 8 to 10 minutes.

3. Add garlic, chili powder, salt, and cayenne and cook, stirring frequently, until fragrant, about 30 seconds. Stir in broth, scraping up any browned bits. Stir in beans.

4. Lock lid into place and close pressure-release valve. Select high pressure-cook function and cook for 9 minutes. Turn off Instant Pot and let pressure release naturally for 15 minutes. Quick-release any remaining pressure. Carefully remove lid, allowing steam to escape away from you.

5. Stir in ketchup, sugar, molasses, and mustard. Using highest sauté function, bring to simmer. Cook, stirring occasionally and scraping bottom of pot, until slightly thickened, 8 to 10 minutes. Transfer to serving bowl and let cool for 10 minutes (beans will continue to thicken as they cool). Stir in vinegar and serve.

GRITS WITH FRESH CORN

✅ **WHY THIS RECIPE WORKS** Corn on corn is a grits recipe for success. Grits are mild on their own since they are made from dried corn. To bump up their flavor and add texture, we used fresh corn kernels. Those cobs came in handy; rather than throwing them away, we easily scraped off the sweet pulp left behind with the back of a butter knife for concentrated corn flavor. We added milk, water, some corn kernels, and the corn pulp to a saucepan and brought the mixture to a boil. Next we stirred in the grits, minced garlic, salt, and pepper; returned the mixture to a boil; lowered the heat; and cooked the grits covered— whisking often to avoid scorching—until they thickened. We added a knob of butter off the heat and seasoned the grits to taste before moving on to the topping. Sautéing some reserved corn kernels in more butter with garlic and scallion whites for just a few minutes allowed them to lose their raw crunch. We stirred scallion greens into the sautéed corn and topped portions of the porridge with this delightfully sweet-savory mixture.

Grits aren't just for breakfast—they can be dressed up for any meal. Grits, of course, are simply a cornmeal mush (the word is also used for the raw meal itself) often enriched with milk, cream, and/or cheese. How do you make them taste their best?

On their own, grits are mild; since they are made from dried corn, it makes sense to bump up the flavor with fresh corn. Begin by husking three ears of the best corn you can find, and then cut the kernels off the cobs. Think you're done with those cobs? Think again—the pulp left behind on the cobs after cutting off the kernels is packed with sweet, concentrated corn flavor. All you

need to do to harvest it is run the bowl of a spoon or the flat side of a butter knife down the cob, scraping as you go to make a pile of rich corn pulp on your board.

Add milk, water, corn kernels, and corn pulp (in our carefully determined ratio) to a saucepan and bring them to a boil. Stir in the grits—along with minced garlic, salt, and pepper—return the mixture to a boil, and then turn down the heat. Cook the grits, covered but whisking often, until they have thickened. Take the saucepan off the heat, plop in a knob of butter (because corn and butter), taste and adjust for seasoning, and then cover the saucepan while you get on with the topping.

Sauté some reserved corn kernels in butter, garlic, and scallion whites for just a few minutes until the corn loses its raw crunch. Stir scallion greens into the sautéed corn, and you're ready to top portions of the porridge with this beautiful, delightfully sweet-savory topping. These grits are special, and I hope that you make and enjoy them as much—and as often—as I do.

—LAWMAN JOHNSON, *Cook's Country*

Grits with Fresh Corn

SERVES 4 TO 6   TOTAL TIME: 1 HOUR

If you use fresh-milled grits such as Anson Mills Colonial Coarse Pencil Cob Grits, you will need to increase the simmering time by 25 minutes and may need to add more water during simmering in step 2.

3	ears corn, husks and silk removed
2¼	cups whole milk
2	cups water
1	cup old-fashioned grits
2	garlic cloves, minced, divided
1¾	teaspoons table salt, divided
¼	teaspoon plus ⅛ teaspoon pepper, divided
4	tablespoons unsalted butter, divided
2	scallions, white parts sliced thin, green parts sliced thin on bias

1. Cut kernels from cobs (you should have about 2¼ cups). Scrape pulp from cobs, keeping separate from kernels.

2. Combine milk, water, two-thirds of kernels (about 1½ cups), and pulp in large saucepan. Bring to boil over medium-high heat. Whisk in grits, half of garlic, 1½ teaspoons salt, and ¼ teaspoon pepper and return

to boil. Reduce heat to low; cover; and simmer, whisking often, until thick and creamy, about 25 minutes. Off heat, stir in 2 tablespoons butter and season with salt and pepper to taste. Cover to keep warm.

3. Meanwhile, melt remaining 2 tablespoons butter in 10-inch nonstick skillet over medium heat. Add scallion whites, remaining garlic, remaining ¼ teaspoon salt, and remaining ⅛ teaspoon pepper and cook until fragrant, about 30 seconds. Add remaining one-third of kernels (about ¾ cup) and cook until tender, 2 to 3 minutes, stirring occasionally.

4. Off heat, stir scallion greens into skillet. If grits are too thick, adjust consistency by gradually whisking in additional hot water as needed until creamy. Serve grits, topping individual portions with corn-scallion mixture.

HOMEMADE JELLIED CRANBERRY SAUCE

✓ **WHY THIS RECIPE WORKS**   We simmered fresh cranberries with cranberry juice, a modest amount of sugar, and salt. A touch of vanilla brought everything to life. Cranberries are both rich in pectin and naturally acidic, which helped them form a gel. Cooking the mixture at a full boil for 25 minutes helped extract more pectin, resulting in a more stable gel and a sliceable consistency.

Jellied cranberry sauce—indented by the ridges of the can from which it slithers—is my secret Thanksgiving love. It's not the flavor that keeps drawing me back, since the overt, one-note sweetness dominates the fruity tang. I'm more captivated by its physical qualities: the alluring smoothness, the playful jiggle, and the way the semitranslucent ruby gel catches the light. This year I set out to create a DIY version with those attributes and more. I'd be in full control of the sugar, and the sky would be the limit in terms of flavoring and molding options.

I started by adding a modest amount of granulated sugar along with a little salt to a saucepan filled with 12 ounces of fresh cranberries. I poured in 3 cups of water, simmered the mixture until the berries popped, and then strained out the skins and seeds. After stirring in a whisper of vanilla to bring everything to life, I poured the garnet liquid into a mold and chilled it for 4 hours.

JELLIED CRANBERRY SAUCE

It gelled beautifully. That's because cranberries are both rich in pectin and naturally acidic. Pectin is a polysaccharide found in the cell walls of fruit; these walls break down when the fruit is heated, releasing the pectin. In a sugary, acidic environment, the long-chain molecules interact and tangle, trapping liquid and dissolved sugar to form a gel as the mixture cools.

And yet, this attempt had neither the coveted smoothness nor the translucence of the canned stuff. Instead, it was somewhat grainy and as stodgy and opaque as tomato paste.

Increasing the ratio of liquid to solids in the final gel would dilute the mixture, resulting in a clearer jelly. But extra water would also dilute the acidity and therefore impede gelling. Cranberry juice was the answer. It not only preserved the acidic pH, allowing me to use more liquid and still achieve the degree of translucency I was after, but also boosted the tart fruitiness of the jelly. Four cups of juice produced a glossy, delicious gel.

Along the way, I also learned that cooking the cranberry mixture at a full boil for 25 minutes helped extract more of the berries' pectin, resulting in a more stable gel and the firm, sliceable consistency that came with it.

As a final test, I tried using an empty can as a mold. To my (perhaps childish) delight, I found that it resulted in a cylinder with perfectly imprinted ridges, hoodwinking my guests into thinking they were getting the canned type—until they tasted it, that is.

—ADAM RIED, *Cook's Illustrated*

Jellied Cranberry Sauce

SERVES 12 (MAKES ABOUT 2¾ CUPS)

TOTAL TIME: 50 MINUTES, PLUS 5 HOURS COOLING AND CHILLING

If you don't wish to unmold the sauce, transfer the mixture to a glass serving bowl in step 3. To control evaporation, use a saucepan with a diameter no greater than 9 inches, and be sure to follow the timings in the recipe. Do not use unsweetened cranberry juice here.

- 4 **cups sweetened cranberry juice**
- 12 **ounces (3 cups) fresh or frozen cranberries**
- 1⅓ **cups (9⅓ ounces) sugar**
- ¼ **teaspoon table salt**
- ¼ **teaspoon vanilla extract**

1. Bring cranberry juice, cranberries, sugar, and salt to boil in large saucepan over medium-high heat, stirring to dissolve sugar. Cook, lowering heat slightly if mixture threatens to boil over, for 10 minutes. Mash cranberries with potato masher. Continue to cook, stirring frequently, until mixture is slightly thickened, 15 minutes longer. (Mixture will be very foamy, but foam will subside as mixture cooks.)

2. Carefully strain mixture through fine-mesh strainer set over 4-cup liquid measuring cup. Stir and press solids with back of small spoon or ladle until about ¼ cup skins, seeds, and pulp remains in strainer. You should have about 2¾ cups strained mixture (it's fine if you have a little less; if you have more than 2¾ cups, return strained mixture to saucepan and cook over medium-high heat until reduced to 2¾ cups). Use clean spoon to scrape mixture from bottom of strainer into liquid measuring cup. Discard solids. Add vanilla and stir until mixture is smooth.

3. Transfer mixture to 3-cup mold or clean 15-ounce can (put leftover mixture in small mold or bowl). Let cool completely, at least 1 hour. Cover tightly and refrigerate until firm, at least 4 hours or up to 4 days. To unmold, use your fingers to gently pull sauce away from all edges of mold to loosen. Holding plate firmly over mold, invert mold and shake sharply until sauce releases. Remove mold and serve.

VARIATIONS

Jellied Cranberry Sauce with Ancho Chile

Add 2½ tablespoons ancho chile powder and pinch cayenne pepper (optional) with cranberries in step 1.

Jellied Cranberry Sauce with Lemon and Rosemary

Before combining ingredients in saucepan, add sugar, 3 tablespoons grated lemon zest (3 lemons), and 3 tablespoons minced fresh rosemary to bowl. Stir and mash with potato masher until sugar is moist and fragrant.

Jellied Cranberry Sauce with Orange and Cardamom

Before combining ingredients in saucepan, add sugar, 3 tablespoons grated orange zest (2 oranges), and ¾ teaspoon ground cardamom to bowl. Stir and mash with potato masher until sugar is moist and fragrant.

TARTIFLETTE (FRENCH POTATO AND CHEESE GRATIN)

CHAPTER 4

PASTA, SANDWICHES, AND MORE

GNOCCHI À LA PARISIENNE WITH ARUGULA, TOMATOES, AND OLIVES

GNOCCHI À LA PARISIENNE WITH ARUGULA, TOMATOES, AND OLIVES

✓ **WHY THIS RECIPE WORKS** For an easier take on tricky-to-make Italian potato gnocchi, we turned to their French cousin, gnocchi à la Parisienne. French gnocchi are made with pate a choux, the eggy French pastry dough also used to make éclairs, profiteroles, and beignets. We made our dough quickly on the stovetop and then transferred it to a food processor to incorporate the eggs. We piped and cut the dough into simmering water to form the gnocchi and then seared them in a hot skillet to lightly brown and puff them to tender, melt-in-your-mouth perfection. We finished our gnocchi by tossing them with sweet tomatoes, briny olives, and peppery arugula dressed with lemon and thyme.

Pate a choux has been a workhorse of the French culinary canon since the 1500s, serving as the foundation for a number of airy pastries, including gougères, profiteroles, éclairs, and beignets. But my favorite use for the eggy dough is as the base of a somewhat lesser-known puffed delicacy: gnocchi à la Parisienne.

It's a real game changer for gnocchi lovers. Mixing a light dough for Italian potato gnocchi and individually shaping each dumpling requires practice—an artist's touch, even—for airy results, but replacing the dough with pate a choux promises tender, ethereal puffs, even if you're a newbie.

That's because instead of crafting each of the gnocchi by hand from potato-rich dough, you just pipe pate a choux—which is naturally light—directly into simmering water, cutting off short lengths with a knife. The gnocchi are guaranteed to inflate as they poach and can then be sautéed to create a crisp crust. Before you know it, you'll be rewarded with piles of soft, airy pillows gently held in golden cases.

Pate a choux dough comes together easily: Bring water and butter to a boil in a saucepan, and then stir in flour and cook the mixture over low heat until it turns into a stiff paste. Off the heat, incorporate whole eggs—by hand, in a stand mixer, or with a food processor (my favorite method)—for structure and flavor; the dough will tell you it's ready by flaunting a glossy sheen. Give the dough a savory edge with shredded cheese, salt, and pepper.

I tweaked the test kitchen's standard pate a choux dough to make it just right for this application, finding that too many eggs caused the dumplings to overinflate when they hit the hot water and too few eggs resulted in insufficient inflation. Also, if the hydration level was too high, the resulting batter-like dough was hard to cut into tidy, uniform gnocchi.

The simple formula that I landed on combines three large eggs with equal amounts (¾ cup each) of water and all-purpose flour. Two ounces of shredded Gruyère (or Emmentaler) imparts cheesy nuttiness while still keeping the dough light enough to puff when sautéed; any more impedes their rise.

With my dough perfected, I loaded it into a pastry bag fitted with a ½-inch round tip and let it cool for 30 minutes to help it firm up while I brought a large pot of water to a boil. I worked in batches of 20 to 30 gnocchi: As the water bubbled, I gripped the pastry bag with one hand, angling it to make it easier to manage, and squeezed lightly to extrude the golden dough. As it emerged from the pastry tip, I used a sharp paring knife to quickly cut off ¾-inch nuggets, which dropped into the water. After 2 minutes, the gnocchi floated, signaling that they were ready to be scooped onto a baking sheet to await the next step.

Recipes take one of two roads at this point. The gnocchi can be bathed in cheese sauce and slipped under a broiler to brown, or they can be crisped in a hot skillet with butter before being finished with a flourish of herbs or a bright sauce. I've always favored the latter, since the thin, crisp crust produced via sautéing makes an irresistible contrast to the gnocchi's airy interior.

For a summery, salad-like feel, I like to toss the sautéed gnocchi with quartered sweet-tart cherry tomatoes and briny kalamata olives, along with peppery arugula, lemon juice, and thyme. Another good option is a pistou—I make mine with loads of fresh basil, lemon, and garlic, plus Parmesan and anchovies. The gleaming emerald sauce is a lovely bed on which to rest the petite, hot-from-the-skillet pillows.

—STEVE DUNN, *Cook's Illustrated*

Gnocchi à la Parisienne with Arugula, Tomatoes, and Olives

SERVES 4   TOTAL TIME: 1¼ HOURS, PLUS 30 MINUTES RESTING

Emmentaler can be used in place of the Gruyère, if desired. You'll need a pastry bag and a ½-inch round tip for this recipe. If these are unavailable, substitute a large zipper-lock bag with one corner snipped off to create a ½-inch opening. For a simpler dish, follow the recipe through step 6 and then toss the sautéed gnocchi with 4 tablespoons of browned butter, 2 teaspoons of minced fresh sage, and a pinch of salt. Or follow the recipe through step 6, plate the sautéed gnocchi on top of a generous layer of pistou, and serve with extra Parmesan cheese. Serve the gnocchi in wide, shallow pasta bowls.

3	large eggs
9	tablespoons unsalted butter, divided
1	teaspoon table salt, divided
¾	cup (3¾ ounces) all-purpose flour
2	ounces Gruyère cheese, shredded (½ cup)
⅛	teaspoon pepper
20	cherry tomatoes, quartered
20	pitted kalamata olives, quartered
2	teaspoons minced fresh thyme
2	teaspoons lemon juice
1½	ounces (1½ cups) baby arugula
1	tablespoon minced fresh chives
	Grated Parmesan cheese

1. Fit pastry bag with ½-inch round tip. Beat eggs in 2-cup liquid measuring cup.

2. Bring ¾ cup water, 4 tablespoons butter, and ¾ teaspoon salt to boil in small saucepan over medium heat, stirring occasionally. As soon as mixture boils, remove saucepan from heat and stir in flour until incorporated. Return saucepan to low heat and cook, stirring constantly, using smearing motion, until mixture looks like shiny, wet sand, about 2 minutes.

3. Immediately transfer mixture to food processor. Add Gruyère and pepper and process, with feed tube open, for 10 seconds. With processor running, gradually add eggs in steady stream. When all eggs have been added, scrape down sides of bowl with rubber spatula. Continue to process until smooth, thick, sticky paste forms, about 30 seconds longer.

4. Fill prepared pastry bag with warm mixture. Twist top of bag to close and let rest at room temperature for at least 30 minutes or up to 1 hour.

PIPING GNOCCHI

Using 1 hand, hold pastry bag at 45-degree angle so tip is about 3 inches away from surface of water, then squeeze bag to force dough out of tip. Using paring knife, cut off ¾-inch lengths of dough and let them fall into water.

5. Lightly grease rimmed baking sheet. Bring 4 quarts water to boil in large Dutch oven. Reduce heat to maintain gentle simmer. Using 1 hand, hold pastry bag at 45-degree angle so tip is about 3 inches away from surface of water and squeeze bag to force dough out of tip. Using paring knife, cut off ¾-inch lengths and let them fall into water. Continue to pipe until 20 to 30 gnocchi are in pot. Simmer until gnocchi float and are slightly firm, about 2 minutes. Using spider skimmer or slotted spoon, transfer gnocchi to prepared sheet. Repeat until all dough is cooked (4 to 6 batches). (If not proceeding immediately, allow gnocchi to cool completely. Transfer to airtight container and refrigerate for up to 3 days. Alternatively, freeze on sheet until solid, then transfer to zipper-lock bag and store in freezer for up to 2 months; sauté from frozen, adding 1 to 2 minutes to sautéing time.)

6. Melt 3 tablespoons butter in 12-inch nonstick skillet over medium heat. Add all gnocchi and shake skillet gently until gnocchi fall into single layer. Cook, tossing every 2 minutes, until gnocchi are golden brown and slightly puffed, about 6 minutes. Return cooked gnocchi to sheet.

7. Melt remaining 2 tablespoons butter in now-empty skillet over medium heat. Add tomatoes, olives, thyme, and remaining ¼ teaspoon salt and cook, tossing occasionally, until tomatoes start to soften, about 2 minutes. Add lemon juice and gnocchi to skillet and gently stir until gnocchi are evenly glazed. Off heat, add arugula and stir until it just starts to wilt, about 15 seconds. Top with chives and serve immediately, passing Parmesan separately.

PESTO DI PREZZEMOLO (PARSLEY PESTO)

✅ **WHY THIS RECIPE WORKS** This recipe features handfuls of fresh Italian parsley paired with subtle and creamy untoasted walnuts (a common substitute for pine nuts in parsley pesto recipes). Since we were already using the food processor to bring the sauce together, we saved ourselves some work and used it to process the cheese. We processed the base of parsley, untoasted walnuts, briny capers, and garlic with plenty of oil and salt until it was smooth, and then we added that to the bowl of cheese and stirred everything together; the processed Parmesan provided concentrated pops of flavor. To balance the pesto, we added a few spoonfuls of lemon juice for brightness along with a dash of red pepper flakes and anchovies for depth of flavor. The resulting vibrant green pesto radiates with parsley's grassy, peppery notes.

The beauty of pesto is that it can be made with just about any combination of herbs and nuts; it is a flexible recipe. In Liguria, where pesto alla genovese (basil pesto) was born, many cooks switch to fresh parsley when the basil growing season is waning.

In basil pesto recipes, buttery pine nuts pair well with the herb's bold licorice aroma, but in parsley pesto, untoasted walnuts are a common substitute, preferred for their subtle nuttiness and creamy texture. While both Parmesan and Pecorino Romano are traditional in pestos, the milder, rounder flavor of Parmesan beautifully complements the parsley here. Grinding the Parmesan right in the food processor makes quick work of breaking it down. In addition to the parsley and walnuts, a full cup of extra-virgin olive oil, a few tablespoons each of capers and lemon juice, garlic cloves, anchovies (these are optional but deepen the savory quality of the pesto), some red pepper flakes, and salt and pepper also go into the processor. The resulting vibrant green pesto radiates with the grassy, peppery notes of parsley.

—AMANDA LUCHTEL, *Cook's Country*

Pesto di Prezzemolo (Parsley Pesto)

SERVES 4 TO 6 (MAKES ABOUT 1¾ CUPS)   TOTAL TIME: 15 MINUTES

Use a good-quality, relatively mild extra-virgin olive oil for the best results. You will need about two bunches of parsley to yield 3 ounces of parsley leaves. It's OK to use the tender, thin stems at the base of the parsley sprigs. This recipe yields enough to sauce 1 pound of pasta (our recipe for Linguine with Pesto di Prezzemolo follows). This pesto is also good on crostini, in sandwiches, on fish, stirred into soup, or as a dip with crudités.

- 2 ounces Parmesan cheese
- 3 ounces fresh parsley leaves (about 5 cups)
- 1 cup extra-virgin olive oil
- 1 cup walnuts
- 2 tablespoons capers, rinsed
- 2 tablespoons lemon juice
- 2 garlic cloves, peeled
- 2 anchovy fillets, rinsed (optional)
- ½ teaspoon red pepper flakes
- ½ teaspoon table salt
- ¼ teaspoon pepper

Process Parmesan in food processor until finely ground, about 30 seconds; transfer to medium bowl. Process parsley; oil; walnuts; capers; lemon juice; garlic; anchovies, if using; pepper flakes; salt; and pepper until smooth, about 1 minute, scraping down sides of bowl as needed. Transfer pesto to bowl with Parmesan and stir to combine. Season with salt and pepper to taste. Serve.

TO MAKE AHEAD: Place pesto in sealable 1-pint container and cover with additional 1 tablespoon extra-virgin olive oil. Cover and refrigerate for up to 2 days or freeze for up to 1 month.

NOTES FROM THE TEST KITCHEN

PESTO WITH EXTRA PIZZAZZ

Herbs, nuts, garlic, and cheese are traditional in pestos. To make this one especially enticing, we pack it with some additional strongly flavored ingredients. Anchovies (optional, but recommended!), capers, lemon juice, and red pepper flakes add brightness, savory notes, and a little heat that complement the fresh, green flavor of the parsley and the richness of the Parmesan, walnuts, and olive oil.

LINGUINE WITH PESTO DI PREZZEMOLO

SERVES 4 TO 6   TOTAL TIME: 40 MINUTES

Use a rasp-style grater to grate the Parmesan.

  1   **pound linguine**
      Table salt for cooking pasta
  1   **recipe Pesto di Prezzemolo (Parsley Pesto) (page 87)**
      Grated Parmesan cheese

Bring 4 quarts water to boil in large pot. Add pasta and 1 tablespoon salt and cook, stirring often, until al dente. Reserve ¾ cup cooking water, then drain pasta and transfer to large bowl. Add pesto and ½ cup reserved cooking water to pasta and toss to combine. Season with salt to taste. Adjust consistency with remaining reserved cooking water as needed. Serve immediately, passing Parmesan separately.

PASTA CACIO E UOVA (PASTA WITH CHEESE AND EGGS)

WHY THIS RECIPE WORKS   Our pasta with cheese and eggs comes together quickly. We gently heated crushed garlic cloves in lard while the water for the pasta came to a boil. And while the fat became infused with the garlic's flavor, we stirred together Pecorino Romano, Parmesan, eggs, salt, pepper, and parsley. We drained the pasta and tossed it with the lard, which provided a subtly sweet, nutty, toasted garlic flavor, in addition to 1 tablespoon of the pasta cooking water and the egg-and-cheese mixture. While the sauce seems straightforward—mix beaten eggs and cheese with lard, hot pasta, and some of its cooking water—the mixture can turn out grainy and curdled if it overheats. To keep our sauce from scrambling, we mixed the sauce and pasta together off the heat, melting the cheese and bringing the eggs up to temperature using only the residual heat in the pasta and the saucepan.

There's lots to love when it comes to pasta cacio e uova ("CAH-chee-oh eh WOE-va"). The cheese and egg pasta, called cas 'e ov in its native Naples, doesn't dirty many dishes, calls for just a handful of ingredients, and makes its way to the table in a flash. The method is simple: Cooked and drained pasta is returned to its cooking pot and tossed with a garlic-infused fat, such as lard, olive oil, or butter. The magic happens when a mixture of

Pecorino Romano, Parmesan, and beaten eggs is poured into the pot—as the egg, cheese, and still-hot pasta are stirred together, the cheese melts, the egg cooks, and a smooth and glossy sauce forms to complete the dish.

With such a straightforward cooking method, the keys to success lay in ingredient selection and proportions. Choosing a pasta was simple—I'd stick with the traditional choice of tubetti, a tubular shape that's about twice as long as ditalini—but I had a few options when it came to choosing a fat. Lard seemed to be the most traditional choice, but in the past I had found that most lards tasted plain, so I ruled it out, doubting it would bring much flavor to the dish. A test using butter demonstrated that it got lost amid the cheese and egg, so I settled on toasting a couple garlic cloves in olive oil, which lent the dish a subtle complexity.

With that, I thought I was ready to move on to the rest of my ingredient selection—but then a chat about the dish with Italian food historian Francine Segan stopped me in my tracks. "Lard!" Segan enthused. "Somehow in English the word just doesn't sound as delicious as it does in Italian. 'Strutto'—so musical, it melts in your mouth." With a description like that, how could I not try swapping in lard at least once? And from the first bite of that batch, my mind was made up. The cacio e uova made with lard not only tasted fuller and richer, with the cheese flavor heightened, but also felt lighter and cleaner on the palate.

Next, it was on to the sauce. I liked the flavor and textural balance offered by using 1 ounce each of tangy Pecorino Romano and nutty Parmesan, but I dithered on the eggs—some recipes call for whole eggs, while others add richness through additional yolks. I saw no need to involve extra yolks, because I liked the consistency that resulted from using whole eggs, but how many to use? A side-by-side test made the answer clear: Made with only one egg, the sauce overheated in the final mixing step and became grainy and curdled. With two eggs, on the other hand, the residual heat contained in the pasta and the saucepan could melt the cheese and cook the eggs without overheating them, leaving the sauce silky-smooth.

With the sauce worked out, there was just one small tweak left to make. I had been cooking the tubetti until it was al dente but found that the finished pasta was a bit too chewy. I realized that this is because most al dente pasta is tossed with very hot sauce and some of the pasta cooking water, which helps the pasta cook

PASTA CACIO E UOVA (PASTA WITH CHEESE AND EGGS)

just a little more so that it's the perfect firmness when it reaches the table. The tubetti in this dish, however, doesn't see much pasta cooking water or heat, so to make sure that it would be tender at the table, I had to cook it just past al dente.

As I tucked into a bowl, I couldn't believe this decadent dish had come together so speedily: That's the power of delicate heat, emulsifying eggs, and a little bit of strutto.

—LAN LAM, *Cook's Illustrated*

Pasta Cacio e Uova (Pasta with Cheese and Eggs)

SERVES 4   TOTAL TIME: 35 MINUTES

Tubetti is traditionally used for this dish, but you can substitute 8 ounces (2 cups) of elbow macaroni. Lard contributes an incomparably rich, savory flavor to the sauce. Look for it in the meat section, in the oil or baking supply aisle near the shortening, or in the refrigerated section near the butter. Our favorites are U.S. Dreams Lard and John Morrell Snow Cap Lard. Because this dish is very rich, we recommend serving it in small portions with a light salad.

- 3 tablespoons lard or extra-virgin olive oil
- 2 garlic cloves, lightly crushed and peeled
- 2 large eggs
- 1 ounce Parmesan cheese, grated (½ cup)
- 1 ounce Pecorino Romano cheese, grated (½ cup)
- 2 tablespoons minced fresh parsley
- ¼ teaspoon table salt, plus salt for cooking pasta
- ¼ teaspoon pepper
- 8 ounces (1½ cups) tubetti

1. Melt lard in 8-inch skillet over medium-low heat. Add garlic and cook, swirling skillet and flipping garlic occasionally, until garlic is pale golden brown, 7 to 10 minutes. (Tiny bubbles will surround garlic, but garlic should not actively fry. Reduce heat if necessary.) Turn off heat, but leave skillet on burner. Discard garlic.

2. While garlic cooks, bring 2 quarts water to boil in large saucepan. Beat eggs in medium bowl until very few streaks of white remain. Stir in Parmesan, Pecorino, parsley, salt, and pepper and set aside.

3. Stir pasta and 1½ teaspoons salt into boiling water and cook, stirring often, until pasta is tender (slightly past al dente). Reserve ¼ cup cooking water, then drain

pasta and return it to saucepan. Immediately add lard, egg mixture, and 1 tablespoon reserved cooking water to pasta and stir until cheese is fully melted. Adjust consistency with remaining reserved cooking water, 1 tablespoon at a time, as needed. Serve immediately.

CAULIFLOWER PASTA WITH BROWNED BUTTER–SAGE SAUCE

WHY THIS RECIPE WORKS Aromatic sage and rich hazelnuts infuse a browned butter sauce that envelops crispy cauliflower and tender pasta. Campanelle, the bell-shaped noodles, are beautiful and do a great job of capturing a special sauce made only with starchy water and butter that emulsifies and clings to every forkful. Lemon zest and juice add brightness and acidity.

These days, it seems like cauliflower is incorporated into everything (pizza crust, rice, "chicken" wings). These recipes can be delicious, but I wanted to let the nutty, slightly sweet flavor of cauliflower shine in this dish, not transform it into something unrecognizable. For our *Five-Ingredient Dinners* book, my editor challenged me to develop recipes that packed a punch with just (you guessed it) five ingredients. The only exceptions (what we call our "staple" ingredients) were salt, pepper, and oil or butter. What better way to showcase cauliflower than to pair it with pasta and a luxurious browned butter–sage sauce? Plus, using butter as the base of the sauce would count as a freebie ingredient.

As decadent as I wanted this pasta to taste, I also wanted to keep the preparation as simple as the ingredient list. I started by forgoing the oven and opting for a strictly stovetop cooking method, choosing to roast the cauliflower in a skillet instead of fussing with an oven and additional equipment. Cooking the florets in the skillet until they were crisp-tender and browned not only kept things simple but also ensured the browned bits in the skillet could be incorporated into the sauce. Once the cauliflower was cooked, I transferred it to a bowl and added a hefty amount of butter to the skillet. (Don't be shy—it's the main component of the sauce here.) A handful of hazelnuts was added to the butter, imparting a nutty flavor to the sauce. Once the butter was browned, I added a combination of

CAULIFLOWER PASTA WITH BROWNED BUTTER–SAGE SAUCE

chopped and whole sage leaves and cooked them until the whole leaves were crispy. The chopped sage flavored the sauce, and the whole leaves were reserved for a final garnish. Garnishing with fried sage leaves adds a wildly aromatic flavor and looks beautiful, too.

Butter was not the only key to a silky sauce in this recipe. When I cooked the pasta, I made sure to use half the amount of water we typically recommend to ensure the starchiest cooking water. That way, I could ladle that liquid gold into the sage-and-hazelnut-infused butter for a silkier, more emulsified sauce that would cling to every forkful. Campanelle "bells" are perfect for scooping up the sauce and cauliflower, jam-packing every bite with maximum flavor. Right at the end, a squeeze of lemon juice and some lemon zest brightened up the sauce (and kept it from feeling too rich). I served it all with lemon wedges and a sprinkle of the fried sage leaves.

One of my favorite things about this pasta is that each ingredient is used in an intentional way and often pulls double duty. That was the creative puzzle of developing recipes for *Five-Ingredient Dinners*: We had to make the most of every ingredient. There's a no-waste angle that I try to employ in my own kitchen. Sometimes that meant reserving shrimp shells and turning them into a stock, or sautéing the white parts of a scallion in place of onion and chopping up the green parts as a fresh garnish. Here, I used both the zest and juice of a lemon to add floral sweetness and a bright, citrusy zip, and I used sage as a part of the sauce as well as a garnish. (Using aromatic sage instead of a milder herb such as parsley also helped kick things up a notch flavor-wise.) Butter (a "staple ingredient") was the base of the sauce, bolstered by usually drained-away pasta water. Waste not, want not, right?

Five ingredients but oh-so-much more, this veggie-packed meal is rich without being overly so, and is easy to pull together on a weeknight when you're looking for something comforting (and fast). Step aside, cauliflower pizza.

—CARMEN DONGO, *America's Test Kitchen Books*

Cauliflower Pasta with Browned Butter–Sage Sauce

SERVES 4 TO 6   TOTAL TIME: 35 MINUTES

This recipe is from our cookbook, *Five-Ingredient Dinners*. Pantry staples such as salt, oil, and butter are not included in the five-ingredient total.

1	pound campanelle or orecchiette
1¼	teaspoons table salt, divided, plus salt for cooking pasta
2	tablespoons olive oil
1	head cauliflower (2 pounds), cored and cut into 1-inch florets
6	tablespoons unsalted butter
½	cup hazelnuts, skinned and chopped coarse
2	tablespoons chopped fresh sage, plus 12 leaves
½	teaspoon grated lemon zest plus 1 tablespoon juice, plus lemon wedges for serving

1. Bring 2 quarts water to boil in large pot. Add pasta and 1½ teaspoons salt and cook, stirring often, until al dente. Reserve 1½ cups cooking water, then drain pasta and return to now-empty pot.

2. Meanwhile, heat oil in 12-inch skillet over medium-high heat until shimmering. Add cauliflower and 1 teaspoon salt and cook, stirring occasionally, until florets are crisp-tender and browned in spots, 10 to 12 minutes. Transfer to bowl and set aside.

3. Melt butter in now-empty skillet over medium heat, then add hazelnuts and remaining ¼ teaspoon salt. Cook, swirling skillet constantly, until butter begins to brown and has nutty aroma, 1 to 2 minutes. Add chopped and whole sage leaves and cook until sage darkens in color and is fragrant, about 1 minute. Remove from heat and transfer whole sage leaves to paper towel–lined plate, leaving remaining sage, hazelnuts, and browned butter in skillet.

4. Add 1 cup reserved cooking water to skillet with browned butter mixture and bring to boil over high heat, scraping up any browned bits. Remove from heat and stir in lemon zest and juice. Add browned butter sauce and cauliflower to pasta in pot and toss to coat. Adjust consistency with remaining reserved cooking water as needed and season with salt and pepper to taste. Serve with lemon wedges and reserved whole sage leaves.

ULTRACREAMY SPAGHETTI WITH ZUCCHINI

✅ **WHY THIS RECIPE WORKS** In our version of the well-known dish called spaghetti alla Nerano, we microwaved the thinly sliced rounds of zucchini with salt and water and then sautéed the drained, softened coins until they were lightly browned. This was easier than frying, and it proved to be almost as effective at moisture removal. Tossing al dente spaghetti with the zucchini, black pepper, basil, starchy pasta water, and butter created an emulsion that served as the base of a sauce, and adding a combination of mild provolone and Parmesan (to replicate the special blend of local cheeses traditionally used) made the sauce luxuriously creamy.

What do you get when you cross a clever cook, some leftover zucchini, and a prince?

Spaghetti alla Nerano—at least, so the story goes. According to legend, the dish was born in 1952 when Francesco "Pupetto" Caravita, the Prince of Sirignano, turned up at Ristorante Maria Grazia, a favorite restaurant of his located in the charming Amalfi Coast fishing village of Nerano. He told the owner, his friend Rosa Mellino, that he had brought a guest whom he wanted to impress, so the pair sized up the ingredients on hand, got cooking, and emerged from the kitchen with a never-before-seen pasta dish—spaghetti tangled with basil, black pepper, and delicate, golden coins of fried zucchini, all napped with a creamy, lightly cheesy sauce.

The dish is enchantingly simple. It's rich but eats light, and the zucchini's sweetness is concentrated and heightened by the frying. Nowadays, versions of the dish abound in restaurants across Nerano, and tourists flock to its shores just to get a taste of the town's eponymous piatto.

"The whole world talks about spaghetti alla Nerano," Rosa Andreone, Mellino's granddaughter, told me through her translator Kylie Caraco.

Andreone, who, along with several other members of her family, is now part owner of Ristorante Maria Grazia, closely guards her grandmother's original recipe (though she says most everything is done "all'occhio," or "by eye," anyway). However, she was happy to give me some advice in creating my own version of the dish.

From its verdant hue to its basil-tinged aroma, spaghetti alla Nerano is a celebration of summertime, a dinner for eating al fresco, if not beachside. But for cooks, its appeal at this time of the year is also practical: When gardens and farmers' markets are teeming with zucchini, Nerano is a way to put pounds of the squash to work. At Maria Grazia, Andreone told me, chefs slice small zucchini (they're denser and contain fewer seeds) into thin rounds and deep-fry them until they're golden brown. The zucchini is cooked and refrigerated for a few hours before it will be mixed with the pasta so that the crisp golden coins will soften and mingle with the spaghetti.

THE EMULSIFYING POWER OF MANTECARE

The final step in spaghetti alla Nerano (and an abundance of risotto and pasta dishes) is mantecare: the tossing together of pasta with fat, often in the form of butter, oil, or cheese, and its starchy cooking water. This process forms a luxurious, creamy sauce by creating an oil-in-water emulsion: water with tiny droplets of fat suspended throughout. Water and fat molecules don't naturally cling to one another, but in this case, the constant stirring of the pasta forcibly combines them, breaking up the oil into droplets that (at least temporarily) can't separate from the water. The butter and cheese help, too, encouraging the sauce to emulsify because they're already made up of emulsified droplets.

I began my testing by following Andreone's lead, and while I loved the complex, nutty sweetness of the fried zucchini, the restaurant method posed a challenge for home cooks. To fry the dainty, delicate coins, I needed to cook them in very small batches—a tedious process when you're working with pounds of squash. I theorized I could get close to the concentrated flavors I enjoyed in the fried zucchini by finding a method that would drive off comparable amounts of the vegetable's water, so I tested out sundry techniques, weighing the zucchini before and after cooking to get a sense of how much water was lost. A hybrid method of microwaving and sautéing did the trick. First, I combined the coins with some salt and ¼ cup of water in a bowl (adding liquid might seem counterintuitive, but the steam actually helps the zucchini cook and lose its moisture faster), and then I covered it and placed it in the microwave. I found that after 10 minutes, the zucchini coins were softened and had already lost about 20 percent of their water weight—plus, they had collapsed so much that I could fit them all into a single 12-inch skillet for browning. I drained the coins in a colander and slid them into a skillet slicked with oil. I stirred once every few minutes until light golden browning developed on about half the slices (since flavor concentration was also coming from moisture loss, it wasn't essential to brown every piece). The shrunken, bronzed zucchini was sweet and tender, and when I weighed the cooked slices, they'd lost just over 50 percent of their original weight, a substantial difference in such a short time.

The zucchini squared away, I turned to the cheeses. Andreone uses three: Parmigiano-Reggiano and two local products, Provolone del Monaco and caciocavallo. All three are aged cheeses made from cow's milk, and mixing them creates a blend of nutty, sweet, and buttery flavors. Provolone del Monaco and caciocavallo are tough to come by in the United States, but I found that a block of mild provolone purchased at my local market (and shredded at home) made an apt substitute. The cheese melted beautifully, and when combined with Parmesan in a 2:1 ratio, it imparted a milky, mellow sweetness that complemented the Parmesan's nutty depth.

I cooked a pot of spaghetti to al dente and drained it, reserving some of the starchy liquid. With that, it was time to bring all the components of the Nerano together and, in the process, create the rich, creamy sauce that binds it all. According to Andreone, the quality of the final dish hinges almost entirely upon this process—so in her restaurant, only she and other members of the family are permitted to perform this final step, tossing the zucchini coins, pasta and its cooking water, and grated cheeses off the heat until the mixture reaches an even, velvety consistency. "That's the secret," she shared with me.

As I tossed the pasta off the heat, I found myself wishing that I could pass the pot over to Andreone. The spaghetti was tasty, but it looked dry. Without Andreone's special touch, I'd need to give my sauce a little help: A knob of butter, though untraditional, finally created the luxe creaminess that is the dish's calling card.

Along with the butter, I added a cup of the starchy pasta water, the cooked zucchini, a couple tablespoons of chopped fresh basil, and a healthy dose of black pepper to the spaghetti. When the butter was melted and the spaghetti strands were slicked with fat, I took the pot off the heat and then added the provolone and Parmesan, stirring and tossing until they were melted and a creamy, lightly thickened sauce coated the pasta.

I twirled the pasta on a fork and spun the nest into a bowl. I marveled at how beautiful it was, and I knew that I'd gotten it right. Deep yellow with just a hint of green, it was, as Andreone had described, "almost the color of a really good extra-virgin olive oil." The sauce was silky and full of sweetness from the tender zucchini, which was tamed by the fresh basil, pepper, and savory undertones from the cheese. As I took my first bite, I swear I heard the waves lapping on the beach in Nerano.

—ANNIE PETITO, *Cook's Illustrated*

Ultracreamy Spaghetti with Zucchini

SERVES 4 TOTAL TIME: 45 MINUTES

Be sure to use zucchini that are smaller than 8 ounces because they contain fewer seeds. Using a mandoline will make quick work of slicing the zucchini. Use a 2½-ounce block of mild provolone from the deli counter rather than presliced cheese.

- 2 pounds small zucchini, sliced ⅛ inch thick
- 1 teaspoon table salt, plus salt for cooking pasta
- 2 tablespoons extra-virgin olive oil
- 12 ounces spaghetti
- 2 tablespoons unsalted butter
- 2 tablespoons chopped fresh basil
- ½ teaspoon pepper
- 2½ ounces mild provolone cheese, shredded (⅔ cup)
- ⅓ cup grated Parmesan cheese

1. In large bowl, stir together zucchini, ¼ cup water, and salt. Cover and microwave until zucchini is softened (some slices will curl at edges) and liquid is released, 10 to 12 minutes, stirring halfway through microwaving. Drain zucchini in colander and let cool slightly, about 5 minutes.

2. Heat oil in 12-inch nonstick skillet over medium-high heat until shimmering. Add zucchini (do not wash colander) and spread into even layer. Cook, stirring every 4 minutes and then reflattening into even layer, until zucchini is very tender and about half of slices have browned, 10 to 12 minutes (it is OK if some pieces fall apart). (Zucchini can be refrigerated for up to 2 days.)

3. Meanwhile, bring 4 quarts water to boil in large pot. Add pasta and 1 tablespoon salt and cook, stirring often, until al dente. Reserve 1½ cups cooking water, then drain pasta and return it to pot.

4. Add 1 cup reserved cooking water, zucchini, butter, basil, and pepper to pasta. Set pot over low heat and cook, stirring and tossing pasta constantly, until ingredients are evenly distributed and butter is melted, about 1 minute. Off heat, add provolone and Parmesan. Stir vigorously until cheeses are melted and pasta is coated in creamy, lightly thickened sauce, about 1 minute, adjusting consistency with remaining reserved cooking water as needed. Transfer pasta to platter and serve immediately.

MAFTOUL WITH CARROTS AND CHICKPEAS

✔ **WHY THIS RECIPE WORKS** Maftoul, also known as Palestinian couscous, is traditionally made by hand-rolling grains of bulgur wheat in moistened wheat flour to create small balls of pasta. While maftoul in Palestine is usually served with a brothy stew of chicken, onions, and chickpeas, we instead created a vegetable-and-legume-forward dish, fragrant with warm spices. Because maftoul can vary in size and cook time, we chose to cook it like pasta rather than simmering in a measured amount of water or steaming (which would require specialized equipment). Simmering sweet carrots and hearty chickpeas in a spice-scented broth infused them with rich flavor, and stirring in the cooked maftoul at the end to absorb the remaining liquid pulled this dish together.

Maftoul's beige color, slightly irregular spherical shape and size, and extra-nutty whole-wheat flavor make it a unique addition to the hand-rolled pastas of the Mediterranean, such as North African couscous (from which maftoul likely derived) and Sardinian fregula, both made from semolina. The first time I tasted maftoul, I was blown away by its depth of flavor and texture—warm and nutty, and tender with a little bit of chew; it was completely unlike other semolina-based pastas I had tried. Sometimes referred to as Palestinian couscous, maftoul should not be confused with extruded Israeli couscous (aka pearl couscous or "ptitim" in Hebrew). Maftoul, derived from an Arabic word meaning "to twist or roll," is bulgur that has been rolled in a mix of moistened whole-wheat and white flours to create small, irregularly shaped balls of pasta; these tiny balls are then sun-dried.

Maftoul is traditionally served with a brothy stew of chicken, onions, and chickpeas and frequently spiced with allspice, cumin, cinnamon, and sometimes caraway; the entire dish is also referred to as maftoul. To familiarize myself with the dish and how it is cooked and served, I prepared three different recipes, all including maftoul, chicken, onions, a vegetable (carrots and butternut squash were common), and in most cases, an array of warm spices. Two of the recipes cooked the chicken similarly: Skin-on chicken parts were simmered in water to create a flavorful broth and then placed in a hot oven so that the skin could crisp. The maftoul and any additional vegetables were simmered or steamed in the cooking broth. The third recipe was a bit more streamlined: Coat the chicken with spices and roast it, simmer the maftoul and vegetables in store-bought chicken stock flavored with garlic and lots of spices, and then combine the two for serving. While all versions were hearty and delicious, I wanted a simple method that didn't rely on too many pots and baking sheets or steaming equipment yet still captured the warming and comforting essence of the dish. The most delicious bites of the versions we tried, other than the maftoul, were the chunks of carrots and butternut squash that were simmered in the spiced broth. With chickpeas for protein, could a chicken-free version stand on its own? I set out to find out.

I focused first on figuring out how to cook the maftoul. An online search and a trip to my local Mediterranean grocery store yielded a few different brands of maftoul, each with varying sizes and regularity. While maftoul is traditionally steamed, I didn't want my recipe to call for steaming equipment. Instead, to make it failproof and to account for the variability in grain size, I relied on the pasta method to cook the maftoul (in lots of salted boiling water).

As for the other components, chickpeas and onions were essential to the dish, and we really liked the addition of carrots or squash in the recipes—they added sweetness and color to an otherwise pale composition. I peeled and chopped some carrots and simmered them in store-bought chicken broth that I'd fortified with onions; garlic; and baharat, a spice mixture common throughout countries of the eastern Mediterranean that relies heavily on cumin, coriander, cinnamon, cardamom, allspice, and pepper. The carrots were tender in just about 10 minutes, when I added the cooked maftoul to absorb the remaining broth. A short rest off heat brought the components together, creating a hearty, flavorful, and warming dish. All that it needed was a splash of lemon juice and a handful of parsley to round out the flavors and colors.

—CAMILA CHAPARRO, *America's Test Kitchen Books*

Maftoul with Carrots and Chickpeas

SERVES 4   TOTAL TIME: 35 MINUTES

Maftoul is available at well-stocked Middle Eastern grocery stores or online. If you are unable to find maftoul, you can substitute an equal amount (by weight) of fregula or moghrabieh. Because the size of maftoul

MAFTOUL WITH CARROTS AND CHICKPEAS

grains can vary considerably, we provide a wide range of cook times; cook until the maftoul is just tender. Be sure to choose carrots that measure between 1 to 1½ inches in diameter.

8 ounces (1⅓ cups) maftoul
½ teaspoon table salt, plus salt for cooking maftoul
2 tablespoons extra-virgin olive oil
1 red onion, sliced ½ inch thick
1 tablespoon Baharat (page 160)
2 garlic cloves, minced
1 pound carrots, peeled, cut crosswise into 1½- to 2-inch lengths, and halved lengthwise or quartered if thick
2 cups chicken broth or vegetable broth
1 (15-ounce) can chickpeas, rinsed
½ cup minced fresh parsley
1 tablespoon lemon juice

1. Bring 2 quarts water to boil in medium saucepan. Add maftoul and 1½ teaspoons salt, and cook, stirring occasionally, until just tender, 10 to 25 minutes. Drain and set aside.

2. While maftoul cooks, heat oil in large saucepan over medium-high heat until shimmering. Add onion and cook until softened and beginning to brown, 5 to 7 minutes. Reduce heat to medium; stir in baharat and garlic; and cook until fragrant, about 30 seconds. Add carrots, broth, chickpeas, and salt and bring to boil. Reduce heat to maintain simmer and cook, stirring occasionally, until carrots are tender, 8 to 10 minutes.

3. Remove saucepan from heat; stir in maftoul; and let sit, covered, until most of broth has been absorbed but dish is still saucy, 3 to 5 minutes. Stir in parsley and lemon juice and season with salt and pepper to taste. Serve.

CHEDDAR-CRUSTED GRILLED CHEESE

✓ **WHY THIS RECIPE WORKS** To give the beloved grilled cheese sandwich an added dimension, we decided to work on a version that featured cheese both inside and out. We focused on the interior first. Covering the skillet trapped the heat and steam, helping the cheese melt as the bread slowly browned. After wiping out the skillet, we sprinkled shredded sharp cheddar cheese directly into the skillet in the shape of the bread; put the sandwiches on top, taking care not to let the cheese mound in the center; and returned the skillet to medium heat. As the cheese in the skillet melted, it fused to the sandwiches and eventually crisped up to develop a cheese crust. Letting the sandwiches cool for 5 minutes before eating allowed the cheesy crust to become even crispier. Switching out cheddar for Gruyère and layering in additional ingredients such as bacon, pepper jelly, tomato, and smoked salmon bring these sandwiches to another level.

One of the defining (and most frequently consumed) foods of my childhood was a grilled cheese sandwich. To this day, I still love to make and eat them for lunch or a quick snack. Obviously I'm not alone: Grilled cheese sandwiches are an institution of American cuisine. Knowing that they are endlessly adaptable, I wanted to perfect a variation that I'd seen online and that I hoped would carry this sandwich to an even higher plane of deliciousness. But first, the basics.

As with any supremely popular food, there is a heated debate about the best way to make a standard grilled cheese sandwich. While I would never try to force my method on anyone—to each their own—I do have a tried-and-true procedure that results in fantastic grilled cheese sandwiches. I start by melting butter over medium heat in a nonstick skillet.

Once the butter is liquefied, into the pan goes the sandwich, which consists of a combination of American cheese (a good melting cheese) and sharp cheddar cheese (for flavor), a little mayo on the inside (for extra richness), and white bread. Covering the skillet traps the heat and helps the cheese melt. Once the bottom is a beautiful, deep golden brown, I flip the sandwich, melt more butter, and brown the second side. Perfection. But why stop there?

Here's where things get fun. Cheese crisps (also known as frico) have become one of America's favorite snacks—they are especially popular among keto dieters. In restaurants, cheese crisps are used to garnish soups and salads. I am not sure who originally thought to combine the crunchy appeal of cheese crisps with grilled cheese sandwiches, but I knew it was an idea worth exploring.

After experimenting with several recipes, I eventually landed on the following process—a rousing success. Make two grilled cheese sandwiches as previously described, remove them from the skillet, and then

CHEDDAR-CRUSTED GRILLED CHEESE

sprinkle more sharp cheddar cheese (which I preferred to Parmesan here for its crunchy-chewy texture when crisped) in two piles in the now-empty skillet. Then lay the sandwiches on top of the cheese in the skillet, taking care not to move them until the cheese has crisped and fused onto the bottoms of the sandwiches. Gently remove the sandwiches from the skillet and let them rest for a few minutes, crisped-cheese side up, on a wire rack to allow the cheesy crusts to crisp even more as they cool (and to let the molten cheese centers cool enough to eat). I did try adding the cheese crust to both sides of the sandwiches but found that it was too much and made the sandwiches hard to eat.

I know it sounds like hyperbole, but this recipe has changed my life . . . or at least the way I'll make grilled cheese sandwiches moving forward. Inspired by this success, I developed three variations that keep the combination of crunchy exterior and melty cheese but bring some other distinct flavors to the party. Enjoy!

—MARK HUXSOLL, *Cook's Country*

Cheddar-Crusted Grilled Cheese

MAKES 2 SANDWICHES   TOTAL TIME: 35 MINUTES

It's important to use a good nonstick skillet here to avoid sticking. While crisping the cheese crust in step 5, avoid flipping the sandwiches too early. At first the cheese will be soft and melty, but it will crisp as it continues to cook. When sprinkling the cheese in the skillet for the crust, be sure to leave enough room between the portions so that the cheese doesn't run together. For the best flavor, buy the American cheese at the deli counter, not the presliced cheese that comes wrapped in cellophane.

NOTES FROM THE TEST KITCHEN

PATIENCE REQUIRED

Making the crispy cheese crust is easy: You simply have to wait. OK, so maybe waiting isn't easy, but it's important to make sure that the shredded cheese is well browned and crisp before sliding a spatula under the sandwiches and transferring them to a wire rack to rest.

2 teaspoons mayonnaise

4 slices hearty white sandwich bread

2 slices deli American cheese (1½ ounces)

4 ounces white sharp cheddar cheese, shredded (1 cup), divided

2 tablespoons unsalted butter, divided

1. Spread mayonnaise evenly on 1 side of each slice of bread. Layer 1 slice of American cheese and ¼ cup cheddar on mayonnaise side of each of 2 slices of bread. Top with remaining 2 slices of bread, mayonnaise side down.

2. Melt 1 tablespoon butter in 12-inch nonstick skillet over medium heat. Place sandwiches in skillet. Cover and cook until deep golden brown on bottom, 4 to 7 minutes.

3. Using spatula, carefully flip sandwiches. Add remaining 1 tablespoon butter to center of skillet between sandwiches and tilt to distribute butter as it melts. Cover and continue to cook until second side is deep golden brown and cheese is visibly melted around edges of sandwiches, 2 to 5 minutes longer. Transfer sandwiches to wire rack.

4. Remove skillet from heat and wipe clean with paper towels. Sprinkle two ¼-cup portions of remaining cheddar into rectangles just larger than slices of bread, about 6 by 4 inches, on opposite sides of now-empty skillet. Place sandwiches directly on top of cheddar.

5. Return skillet to medium heat and cook until edges of cheddar beneath sandwiches are well browned and crisp, 2 to 4 minutes. (Do not slide spatula under sandwiches before cheddar is crisp; it will pull cheddar and ruin crust.) When cheddar is browned along edges, slide spatula underneath sandwiches and transfer, cheddar crust side up, to rack. (For decorative purposes, you can upturn edges of cheddar crust, if desired.)

6. Let sandwiches sit for 5 minutes to allow cheese to set. Transfer sandwiches to cutting board and cut diagonally. Serve.

VARIATIONS

Cheddar-Crusted Grilled Cheese with Bacon and Pepper Jelly

Substitute ¼ cup pepper jelly for mayonnaise and yellow sharp cheddar for white sharp cheddar. Place 4 half slices of cooked bacon between cheese layers in each sandwich.

Shingle 2 thin tomato slices on top of American cheese in each sandwich. Sprinkle tomato slices with 1 tablespoon grated Parmesan and pinch each of table salt, pepper, red pepper flakes, dried oregano, and granulated garlic. Sprinkle cheddar over tomato layer.

Gruyère-Crusted Grilled Cheese with Smoked Salmon

Substitute Gruyère for cheddar. Layer 3 slices smoked salmon on top of American cheese in each sandwich. Sprinkle salmon with 1 tablespoon fresh dill leaves, 2 teaspoons minced shallot, ½ teaspoon grated lemon zest, and pinch pepper. Sprinkle Gruyère over salmon layer.

AIR-FRYER LENTIL AND MUSHROOM BURGERS

✓ **WHY THIS RECIPE WORKS** The complex flavor and satisfying texture of this vegetarian burger is well worth the prep. Using the air fryer to cook the patties meant that they were ready from fresh or frozen in just 10 minutes. An earthy mix of canned lentils, bulgur, and panko paired with shallot and celery gave our burgers a flavorful, hearty meatless base. Cremini mushrooms and a surprising addition—chopped cashews—created rich meatiness. Chopping everything in the food processor made for a cohesive and even-textured mix, and olive oil provided fat to bind the patties. Microwaving the mixture helped to soften the bulgur and allowed the flavors to meld.

Every so often, we enjoy eating a burger made with a good vegan or vegetarian patty. What we don't like is the long list of ingredients that a store-bought patty contains. So, we decided to develop a tasty, healthy vegetarian patty with a few simple ingredients and cook it in an air fryer. We turned to a recipe from our archives, the Ultimate Veggie Burger, for inspiration. We liked all the ingredients in that patty: brown lentils and bulgur for bulk; celery, onions, leeks, and garlic for flavor; and cremini mushrooms and cashews for rich, meaty umami. Our challenge was to make cooking that recipe in the air fryer possible, which meant heavily simplifying it. As we tested the original recipe, we reduced the number of ingredients and the number of steps and time needed to make it.

First we pared down the number of ingredients in the patty. We could build flavor without the use of aromatics such as onion, garlic, and leek and found that we didn't need to sauté the mushrooms and aromatics that we did use (shallot and celery), so we could cut out the step that required the stovetop. Next, instead of soaking and cooking dried brown lentils, we used canned brown lentils, making prep much quicker.

Our next challenge was soaking the bulgur until it was soft enough to shape into a patty. We started by first soaking it for 15 minutes, as called for in the original recipe, but since the lentils didn't need to cook and the vegetables didn't need to be sautéed, we had some time on our hands. We tried soaking the bulgur in hot water for less time, but that didn't give us the result we wanted. Then we discovered that if we used the food processor to chop the mushrooms, celery, shallot, and cashews, we could omit chopping from our prep altogether. We could soak the bulgur with the chopped ingredients and some oil, and briefly microwave them. This way the bulgur was soft and ready to shape in just 6 minutes. The other advantage to this method was that we reduced the amount of water needed to soak the bulgur, using a mere ¼ cup instead of 2 cups, because of the moisture released by the mushrooms and celery. An added benefit was that we did not have to boil water to pour over the bulgur since the microwave brought it to temp for us and cooked the wheat quickly.

Next, it was a matter of vigorously stirring the ingredients together with panko and the lentils to create cohesion. Nevertheless, the patties were delicate and required gentle handling, but here, too, we found an advantage to using the air fryer. Patties cooked traditionally in a skillet need to be turned over, which increases the chance of their breaking. The even heat of the air fryer circulates all around the patty, which means it does not have to be turned during cooking and results in a patty that is nicely browned on both sides. We just had to handle the patties gently and be sure to oil the air-fryer basket well before adding the patties in to cook.

This recipe is a total win. You can cook the burgers right away or freeze them for up to a month; they cook from frozen in just 10 minutes in the air fryer. Once the patties are ready, all that remains is to heat the buns, which can also be done in the air fryer. That means a healthy burger is available whenever anyone wants one.

—DAN ZUCCARELLO AND SAMANTHA BLOCK,
America's Test Kitchen Books

AIR-FRYER MAKE-AHEAD LENTIL AND MUSHROOM BURGERS

MAKES 6 PATTIES   TOTAL TIME: 45 MINUTES

Look for medium-grind bulgur (labeled "#2"), which is roughly the size of mustard seeds. Avoid coarsely ground bulgur; it will not cook through in time. The number of patties you can cook at one time will depend on the size of your air fryer. Serve with your favorite burger toppings and sides.

8   ounces cremini or white mushrooms,
     trimmed and quartered
½   cup raw cashews
1   celery rib, cut into 1-inch pieces
1   shallot, quartered
½   cup medium-grind bulgur
¼   cup water
3   tablespoons extra-virgin olive oil
½   teaspoon table salt
1   (15-ounce) can brown lentils, rinsed
½   cup panko bread crumbs
1-6 slices deli cheese (optional)
1-6 hamburger buns, toasted if desired

1. Pulse mushrooms, cashews, celery, and shallot in food processor until finely chopped, about 10 pulses, scraping down sides of bowl as needed. Transfer vegetables to large bowl and stir in bulgur, water, oil, and salt. Microwave, stirring occasionally, until bulgur is softened and most of liquid has been absorbed, about 6 minutes. Let cool slightly.

2. Lightly spray base of air-fryer basket with canola oil spray. Vigorously stir lentils and panko into vegetable-bulgur mixture until well combined and mixture forms cohesive mass. Using your lightly moistened hands, divide mixture into 6 equal portions (about ½ cup each), then tightly pack each portion into ½-inch-thick patty.

3. Space up to 4 patties at least ½ inch apart in prepared basket. Place basket into air fryer and set temperature to 400 degrees. Cook until patties are golden brown and crisp, 10 to 15 minutes. Turn off air fryer. Top each burger with 1 slice cheese, if using; let sit in warm air fryer until melted, about 1 minute. If desired, arrange bun tops and bottoms cut side up in now-empty basket. Return basket to air fryer, set temperature to 400 degrees, and cook until buns are lightly toasted, 4 to 6 minutes. Serve burgers on buns.

TO MAKE AHEAD: At end of step 2, evenly space patties on parchment paper–lined rimmed baking sheet and freeze until firm, about 1 hour. Stack patties between pieces of parchment, wrap in plastic wrap, and place in zipper-lock freezer bag. Patties can be frozen for up to 1 month. Cook frozen patties as directed in step 3; do not thaw.

TARTIFLETTE (FRENCH POTATO AND CHEESE GRATIN)

✔ WHY THIS RECIPE WORKS   For this luscious potato gratin, we used half-moon slices of Yukon Gold potatoes since they maintained their shape well and cooked evenly. To maximize their earthy taste, we left their skins on and steamed them. Six slices of thick-cut bacon, cut into pieces and cooked until they turned chewy-crisp, delivered meaty smokiness, and cooking a chopped onion in the bacon fat ensured that the smoky essence permeated the whole dish. Cream contributed silkiness while a splash of white wine brought welcome acidity to temper the gratin's richness. Finally, topping the potatoes with cubes of a ripe, semisoft cow's-milk cheese such as Camembert evoked the flavor of Reblochon, the French cheese traditionally used in tartiflette. A quick stint in a hot oven melted the cheese, enveloping the dish in a melty, creamy blanket.

Years ago, when my family and I were living in Paris, we would spend our spring vacations in the French Alps. The skiing was magnificent, and so was the food. In fact, I'm still haunted (in the best way possible) by memories of tartiflette, the luscious gratin of tender potatoes, crisp-chewy poitrine fumée (smoked bacon), white wine, and cream, generously topped with nutty, milky Reblochon cheese. My sons and I would tuck into individual crocks, still bubbling from the heat of the oven and dolloped with tangy crème fraîche, for lunch most days at a slopeside restaurant in Courchevel. I would sip a cold, crisp Chablis, and the boys, chocolat chaud, as we took in the glittering Mont Blanc.

I always figured that this dish dated back generations, but tartiflette actually came into being in the 1980s. It was the brainchild of the Syndicat Interprofessionnel du Reblochon, a cheese consortium that hoped the dish would encourage sales of their eponymous washed-rind, cow's-milk specialty. The group came up with the idea of melting Reblochon on top of Péla, a rustic preparation of fried potatoes, onions, and bacon, and renaming it tartiflette. The concept was brilliant: The dish went on to dominate ski resort menus throughout France and became a Haute-Savoie specialty.

Before I got to work on my own tartiflette—one I hoped would capture the magic of the dish I fell so hard for in France—I wanted to prepare a few existing recipes. Alas, I ran into an obstacle before I even got into the kitchen. It turns out that Reblochon is not available in the United States because in 2004 the U.S. Food and Drug Administration banned the import of raw-milk cheeses that haven't been aged long enough to satisfy the administration's food safety regulations.

I nervously wondered how this would impact my dream of crafting a realistic tartiflette, but a quick call to a local cheesemonger alleviated my concern. He suggested that a high-quality, ripe Camembert (a bloomy-rind cheese) would be a suitable replacement for the creamy, slightly funky, hazelnut-scented Reblochon, so I bought several wheels and got started.

The recipes I tried all shared a similar method: Precooked potatoes, onion, aromatics, and bacon were layered in a baking dish with wine and sometimes a glug of cream; topped with a whole round of cheese; and baked until the cheese melted. The Camembert was indeed a good swap for the Reblochon, but differences in ingredient proportions across the recipes made for starkly contrasting gratins. One was so laden with cream and cheese that eating more than a few bites was impossible. Another eschewed the cream; was skimpy with the cheese; and was blasted in such a hot oven that the potatoes crisped and the cheese seemingly evaporated, leaving behind only the skeletal remains of its white rind. I could do better.

Moderately waxy potatoes are typically used in tartiflette since they hold their shape well in the creamy gratin. I selected buttery Yukon Golds and experimented with prepping and parcooking options: peeled and unpeeled; boiled and steamed; and whole, halved, cubed, and sliced. Leaving the thin skins on accentuated the potatoes' earthiness, and steaming rather than boiling prevented them from tasting waterlogged. I found that 1¾ pounds of half-moon slices fit snugly into an 8-inch baking dish, and cutting the spuds prior to steaming helped them cook quickly and evenly (and

eliminated the need to slice hot potatoes). Once the slices were just tender, I set them aside to cool while I prepped the other ingredients.

In France, tartiflette is made with lardons of smoked bacon in a nod to the smoky essence of its ancestral Péla, which cooks over a wood fire. Thick-cut American bacon was a great replacement; I cut six slices of bacon into ½-inch pieces and fried them until they were chewy-crisp. To prevent a greasy gratin, I then removed the pieces from the skillet and poured off all but 2 tablespoons of the rendered fat.

This modest amount of fat was enough to sauté a chopped onion, a bit of garlic, and some minced fresh thyme. Once the onion had softened and just started to color, I hit it with a liberal splash of dry white wine and let it reduce by half; the liquid that remained would infuse the rich gratin with gentle acidity.

Finally, I needed to decide whether or not to add cream. Passions are split: Some feel that cream takes away from the prominence of the cheese, and others say that without it, the meal hews too closely to the simpler Péla. In a two-way test, I compared gratins made with and without a modest amount of heavy cream and found that the silky, lush feel of the former most reminded me of the tartiflette that I so fondly remember. I tossed the potatoes together with ½ cup of cream and the onion before layering the glorious mix with the bacon in a greased baking dish.

To finish my tartiflette journey, I was curious to try other cheeses, specifically some washed-rind types that promised to be close style matches for Reblochon. After a highly enjoyable streak of cheese-filled days, I identified several that delivered a richly flavored, decadent tartiflette (see the recipe headnote for my recommendations).

I cut an 8-ounce portion of cheese into cubes so that I could distribute it evenly over the top, rind side up, before sliding the casserole into a 400-degree oven for about 20 minutes, until it attained creamy, molten perfection. After giving the piping-hot tartiflette 10 minutes to cool to serving temperature, I dolloped a spoonful of crème fraîche onto a portion and dug in. My ski vacation memories came once again into sharp focus, and I was transported to the cozy lunches I enjoyed with my boys, soaking up the sun in the crisp mountain air while we ravenously enjoyed the best potato gratin on the planet.

—STEVE DUNN, *Cook's Illustrated*

Tartiflette (French Potato and Cheese Gratin)

SERVES 4   TOTAL TIME: 1¾ HOURS

Reblochon, the French cow's-milk cheese traditionally used in tartiflette, is unavailable in the United States, but Camembert or Taleggio make good substitutes. Other alternatives include Pont l'Évêque, Delice du Jura, and Vacherin Mont d'Or or domestic cheeses such as Jasper Hill's Harbison and Winnimere. If your cheese is very runny, chill it before cutting it and hold the pieces in the freezer until you're ready to use them. A 2-quart baking dish of any dimensions can be used in place of the 8-inch square baking dish. Serve the tartiflette with bread and a crisp green salad.

8   ounces ripe Camembert or Taleggio cheese, rind left on

1¾   pounds Yukon Gold potatoes, unpeeled, halved lengthwise and sliced into ¼-inch half-moons

6   slices thick-cut bacon, cut into ½-inch pieces

1   large onion, chopped fine

1¼   teaspoons table salt, divided

2½   teaspoons minced fresh thyme

2   garlic cloves, minced

½   cup dry white wine

½   cup heavy cream

¼   teaspoon pepper

Crème fraîche (optional)

1. Adjust oven rack to middle position and heat oven to 400 degrees. Line large plate with paper towels. Grease 8-inch square baking dish. Cut Camembert in half horizontally to create 2 pieces of equal thickness. Cut each half into ¾-inch pieces.

2. Place steamer basket in large saucepan. Add water to barely reach bottom of steamer and bring to boil over high heat. Add potatoes, cover, and reduce heat to medium (small wisps of steam should escape from beneath lid). Cook until potatoes are just cooked through and tip of paring knife inserted into potatoes meets little resistance, 15 to 17 minutes. Leaving potatoes in steamer, remove steamer from saucepan; set aside and let cool slightly, at least 10 minutes.

3. While potatoes cool, cook bacon in 12-inch skillet over medium heat, stirring occasionally, until browned and chewy-crisp, 4 to 6 minutes. Using slotted spoon, transfer bacon to prepared plate; pour off all but 2 tablespoons bacon fat. Add onion and ½ teaspoon salt to fat left in skillet and cook over medium heat, stirring occasionally, until onion is softened and beginning to brown, about 7 minutes. Add thyme and garlic and continue to cook, stirring occasionally, until fragrant, about 2 minutes longer. Add wine and cook until reduced by half, about 2 minutes. Off heat, stir in cream, pepper, and remaining ¾ teaspoon salt.

4. Add potatoes to skillet and stir gently to coat with onion mixture. Transfer half of potato mixture to prepared dish and spread into even layer. Top evenly with half of bacon. Add remaining potatoes and top evenly with remaining bacon. Arrange Camembert, rind side up, in even layer on top. Bake until bubbling and lightly browned, about 20 minutes. Let cool for 10 minutes before serving. Top each serving with spoonful of crème fraîche, if using.

BRIAM

✓ **WHY THIS RECIPE WORKS** Briam is a simple but dynamic dish of potatoes, onions, bell peppers, tomatoes, and zucchini bathed in olive oil. We sliced our vegetables ¼ inch thick and strategically layered them in the dish, with potatoes serving as a sturdy base and tomatoes an attractive, browned top. Loosely covering the dish with a foil lid for the first 30 minutes of cooking allowed moisture to evaporate, hyperconcentrating the vegetables' flavor; we then removed the foil, which encouraged browning, rendering the tomatoes on top slightly collapsed and caramelized but still moist and tender. Warm, room temperature, or chilled, our briam made for a satisfying vegetarian main course, especially when accompanied by crusty bread and a slice of feta cheese.

Making the Greek dish briam feels like a magic trick. A rainbow of summer produce—tomatoes, zucchini, bell peppers, onions, potatoes—enters the oven simply sliced, seasoned, and bathed in olive oil and emerges a meltingly soft and velvety melange, each vegetable an amplified version of itself. Heaped onto a plate alongside a hunk of crusty bread and a crumbly slice of feta, it's a dish that makes an inarguable case for vegetables as a main course.

"Natural sweetness and good fat—there's something very craveable about that," Greek chef and cookbook author Diane Kochilas told me on a call from her home in Athens. In speaking with Kochilas and other Greek chefs about briam, I quickly learned that, while there are few hard-and-fast rules when it comes to the dish (some recipes call for the vegetables to be thinly sliced and meticulously shingled; others, breezily chunked and mixed together before going in the oven), the desired result is universal: vegetables that are meltingly soft but not soggy, with hyperconcentrated flavor. In a successful briam, Kochilas said, the only liquid left at the end of cooking should be olive oil, perfect for sopping up with bread.

In my take on the dish, I sliced about 4 pounds of vegetables ¼ inch thick, large enough to keep them from turning to mush but thin enough that they'd cook up tender. When it came time to arrange the slices in my baking dish, I opted for a simple but strategic approach. I placed the potatoes in first, to serve as a sturdy base, tossing them with minced garlic, some

NOTES FROM THE TEST KITCHEN

STEAMED SPUDS

For earthy-tasting potatoes, we keep the skins on sliced Yukon Golds and steam them rather than boil them to preserve their flavor.

salt, and ⅓ cup of olive oil. Next came the other, more delicate vegetables: half the onion (cut through the root end so that it would maintain its shape), 2-inch lengths of green bell pepper, the rest of the onion, sliced garlic, and a layer of zucchini coins. I topped the briam with tomato rounds, overlapping them to cover the entire surface like a quilt. This way, the tomatoes could develop some flavorful browning; plus, their juice would trickle down through the layers of the dish during cooking, infusing all the vegetables with their brightness. I topped off the (very full) dish with another ⅓ cup of olive oil and sprinkles of salt and pepper.

With the layering settled, it was time for me to finesse the cooking method. Simply sliding the baking dish into a 400-degree oven dried out the tomatoes on top before the rest of the vegetables could cook through, leaving them shriveled and leathery at the edges. So, in my next batch, I loosely covered the dish with foil for the first 30 minutes, leaving the sides open to allow some moisture to evaporate. After that, I uncovered the dish for the rest of the cooking time to encourage browning. This time, the tomatoes were perfect: slightly collapsed, concentrated, and caramelized but still bright, moist, and tender.

I scattered some chopped fresh parsley over the top and scooped a portion onto my plate. Peering at the shallow, gleaming olive oil left behind in the baking dish, I knew even before I dug in that it was right. The vegetables were tender, luxurious but not greasy, and substantial. As I swiped up the warm, garlic-infused olive oil with a hunk of bread, I could barely contain my excitement at the prospect of eating my briam again the next day, when, I was told, it would be even better.

—ANNIE PETITO, *Cook's Illustrated*

BRIAM

SERVES 6 AS A MAIN COURSE OR 8 AS A SIDE DISH

TOTAL TIME: 1½ HOURS, PLUS 20 MINUTES COOLING

Use small or medium zucchini, which contain more flesh and fewer seeds, for this recipe. We prefer local seasonal tomatoes here, but supermarket tomatoes will work; plum tomatoes are too dry for this dish. High-quality olive oil is vital. Some oil will pool in the bottom of the baking dish; spoon it over the portioned briam or sop it up with bread. Briam is usually served with crusty bread and feta cheese, but it also can be served over pasta or rice or alongside meat or fish. Serve this dish warm, at room temperature, or chilled.

1 **pound Yukon Gold potatoes, peeled and sliced crosswise ¼ inch thick**

⅔ **cup extra-virgin olive oil, divided**

6 **garlic cloves (3 minced, 3 sliced thin)**

1¼ **teaspoons table salt, divided**

1 **onion, halved and sliced through root end into ¼-inch-thick pieces, divided**

1 **teaspoon pepper, divided**

1 **teaspoon dried oregano, divided**

1 **green bell pepper, stemmed, seeded, and cut into 2-inch-long matchsticks**

12 **ounces zucchini (2 small), sliced crosswise ¼ inch thick**

1½ **pounds tomatoes (3 large), cored and sliced ¼ inch thick**

¼ **cup chopped fresh parsley**

1. Adjust oven rack to middle position and heat oven to 400 degrees. Place potatoes, ⅓ cup oil, minced garlic, and ½ teaspoon salt in 13 by 9-inch baking dish and toss to combine thoroughly. Spread into even layer. Scatter half of onion slices over potatoes. Sprinkle with ½ teaspoon pepper and ½ teaspoon oregano.

2. Scatter bell pepper over surface, followed by remaining onion, sliced garlic, ¼ teaspoon salt, ¼ teaspoon pepper, and remaining ½ teaspoon oregano. Arrange zucchini in single layer. Top with tomato slices, overlapping pieces slightly so they cover entire surface (it should be snug). Pour remaining ⅓ cup oil evenly over tomatoes and sprinkle with remaining ½ teaspoon salt and remaining ¼ teaspoon pepper.

3. Cover dish loosely with aluminum foil, leaving sides open so moisture can escape. Bake for 30 minutes. Remove foil and bake until potatoes can be easily pierced with tip of paring knife and tomatoes have collapsed slightly and started to brown at edges, 40 to 50 minutes. Let cool for at least 20 minutes. Sprinkle parsley over top and serve.

TOMATO COBBLER

✓ WHY THIS RECIPE WORKS Our skillet tomato cobbler is packed full of chunky fresh tomatoes that are seasoned with garlic and thyme and topped with a pastry crust. Cooking the tomatoes on the stovetop for just a minute before transferring the cobbler to the oven ensured that they maintained their natural sweetness and vibrant acidity. Tomato paste brought rich depth to the filling, and a touch of cornstarch gave it body. Our all-butter pie crust balanced the brightness of the tomatoes. To account for their abundant juice, we cut the round of dough into six wedges and arranged them on the filling with gaps between each wedge. As the cobbler baked, the spaces promoted evaporation and concentration of the liquid, giving the filling a scoopable texture.

Growing up in the suburbs of Atlanta as the youngest of five kids, I was immersed in my family's ancestral food traditions, rich with recipes passed down orally through six generations. One of the most treasured is our peach cobbler, a treat that my mom prepared on summer weekends with me nearby helping mix the dough and gobbling up the velvety fruit skins as she peeled them away.

My family's method calls for precooking chunks of fruit with sugar and spices until they just soften, thickening the filling with cornstarch, transferring it to a baking dish, and laying pie pastry on top before sliding the assembly into the oven. I adore the way the flaky pie crust complements the soft, plump fruit, its buttery crumb mellowing out the sweetness and tang. The recipe is as steeped in history as it gets, and I wanted to

NOTES FROM THE TEST KITCHEN

PRECUT CRUST

Spacing six wedges of pie dough on top of the filling allows the abundant tomato juices to evaporate and concentrate during baking. It also creates neat, individual portions.

apply our knowledge to a much more recent invention: savory tomato cobbler, a luscious main- or side-dish twist on the sweet dessert.

I started with the seasonings: Minced garlic and a spoonful of tomato paste sizzled in olive oil provided depth; fresh thyme added an herbal touch that steered clear of marinara territory; and salt, pepper, and sugar focused the flavors. After coating 2 pounds of chopped tomatoes in this garlicky-tomatoey base, I stirred in a slurry of 1 tablespoon of water and 2½ teaspoons of cornstarch, enough to give the filling body without making it jam-like.

For convenience (and a homey look), I left the filling in the skillet instead of moving it to a baking dish to receive the pie dough topping. After some tinkering, I landed on an unusual treatment for the dough to account for the fact that tomatoes tend to bake up more liquid-y than peaches: I rolled a small batch of our all-butter pie dough into a round and cut it into six tidy wedges that I brushed with an egg wash and arranged on the filling with gaps between each wedge and around the edge of the skillet. As the cobbler bubbled in the oven, the crust turned golden and delicately crisp. The spaces around the wedges promoted evaporation and concentration of the abundant juice, which gave the filling a scoopable texture.

I tucked into a warm, inviting portion graced with a dollop of tangy sour cream. The seventh generation of the Turner family is in for a treat.

—ERICA TURNER, *Cook's Illustrated*

Skillet Tomato Cobbler

SERVES 6

TOTAL TIME: 1½ HOURS, PLUS 2 HOURS 20 MINUTES CHILLING AND COOLING

We strongly recommend weighing the flour. Use in-season tomatoes that are ripe but firm; do not use plum tomatoes. Serve the cobbler as a side dish or as a light meal with a green salad. We like to dollop servings with sour cream, ricotta, or mascarpone.

CRUST

- 5 tablespoons unsalted butter, chilled, divided
- ⅔ cup (3⅓ ounces) all-purpose flour, divided
- 1½ teaspoons sugar
- ¼ teaspoon table salt
- 2 tablespoons ice water, divided

FILLING

- 1 tablespoon water
- 2½ teaspoons cornstarch
- 2 tablespoons extra-virgin olive oil
- 3 garlic cloves, minced
- 1 tablespoon tomato paste
- 1½ teaspoons minced fresh thyme
- 1½ teaspoons sugar
- ¾ teaspoon table salt
- ½ teaspoon pepper
- 2 pounds tomatoes, cored and cut into ¾-inch pieces

- 1 large egg beaten with 1 tablespoon water and pinch table salt

1. FOR THE CRUST: Grate 1 tablespoon butter on large holes of box grater and place in freezer. Cut remaining 4 tablespoons butter into ½-inch cubes. Pulse ⅓ cup flour, sugar, and salt in food processor until combined, 2 pulses. Add cubed butter and process until homogeneous paste forms, 20 to 30 seconds. Using your hands, carefully break paste into 1-inch chunks and redistribute around processor blade. Add remaining ⅓ cup flour and pulse until mixture is broken into pieces no larger than ½ inch (most pieces will be much smaller), about 3 pulses. Transfer mixture to bowl. Add grated butter and toss until butter pieces are separated and coated with flour.

2. Sprinkle 1 tablespoon ice water over mixture. Toss with rubber spatula until evenly moistened. Sprinkle remaining 1 tablespoon ice water over mixture and toss to combine. Press with spatula until dough sticks together. Wrap dough in plastic wrap and press to form compact, fissure-free 4-inch disk. Refrigerate for at least 2 hours or up to 2 days. Let dough soften on counter for 10 minutes before rolling.

3. FOR THE FILLING: Adjust oven rack to middle position and heat oven to 400 degrees. Whisk water and cornstarch together in small bowl. Heat oil in 10-inch ovensafe skillet over medium heat until shimmering. Add garlic and cook until fragrant, about 30 seconds. Add tomato paste and cook, stirring constantly, until oil is tinted red, about 30 seconds. Add thyme, sugar, salt, and pepper and stir to combine. Add tomatoes and stir until coated. Whisk cornstarch mixture to recombine. Stir into tomato mixture and cook, stirring occasionally, until juice is slightly thickened, 1 to 2 minutes. Remove from heat.

4. Roll dough into 8-inch round on lightly floured counter. Cut into 6 equal wedges. Brush wedges with egg wash. Using bench scraper or spatula, place wedges on filling, spacing rounded edges ½ inch from edge of skillet and leaving gaps between wedges. Bake until crust is deep golden brown, 40 to 45 minutes. Let cool for 20 minutes and serve.

INSTANT POT SAVORY OATMEAL WITH SAUTÉED WILD MUSHROOMS

✔ **WHY THIS RECIPE WORKS** We've had great success cooking risottos, farrottos, pilafs, and polentas in the Instant Pot, so why not savory oatmeal? For a rounded meal, we sautéed almost a pound of leeks. After sautéing the steel-cut oats to give them toasty flavor, we deglazed the pot with wine and cooked the mixture under pressure. This yielded a supercreamy porridge, as the oat starch gelled without the need for butter or cream. For serving, we sautéed a portion of the sliced leeks until they were golden brown; we loved how these sweet, crispy strands melded with the savory mushrooms.

Years ago, my wife and I shared an unforgettably garlicky and savory bright-green oatmeal at Harvest restaurant in Cambridge, Massachusetts. It was my first encounter with a savory oatmeal, and its comforting nature left me wanting to create my own version. When it came time to develop recipes for our *Healthy and Delicious Instant Pot* cookbook, I knew a savory oatmeal would be perfect because the test kitchen has successfully cooked risottos, pilafs, and polentas in a multicooker, where the pressure function does a great job of efficiently hydrating starches. As the oatmeal cooks, it releases starch that forms a creamy emulsion and binds the cooked grains. As I thought through the rest of my ingredients, I looked to New Nordic cuisine and my own love of foraging for inspiration; both approaches promote the idea of using local, natural, and seasonal produce. Herbs, mushrooms, and alliums were at the forefront of my list.

You know when you walk into someone's house and think, "What are they cooking? That smells so amazing!" and you find out that it's just sautéed onions? I wanted that intoxicating smell for my oatmeal, so

I chose what I consider to be onion's fancier cousin: the leek. I wanted to turn a portion into a crisp topping to contrast against the creamy, but unitextured, porridge base. However, I needed to be cautious because leeks can overcook quickly and turn bitter. Instant Pots, especially new and powerful ones, really hold on to their heat, so there was a real risk of this happening. To guard against this, I cooked the leeks for a few minutes using the pot's fierce sauté function and then let them finish with the power off, using the residual heat to turn them golden brown.

I removed the leeks with a slotted spoon in order to save the leek-infused oil for cooking the mushrooms. You can use a single type of mushroom or a combination for variety. I love mushrooms and really wanted them to shine. I knew putting them directly into the oatmeal would be a mistake; all their intensity would leach out during cooking and they'd end up pallid and lacking flavor. Instead, I cooked the mushrooms over direct heat, using the sauté function so that they would release their moisture and brown nicely, become firm, and maintain their distinctly earthy flavor. I added fresh thyme to the pot (its woodsy flavor is a classic with mushrooms) for the last 30 seconds, just long enough for everything to become fragrant. Then I removed them, reserving them to be stirred in at the end so that their specific and distinct flavor would be preserved.

To make this a hearty meal, I bulked up the base of the dish by adding more leeks, almost a whole pound, into the pot to soften. Before adding liquid, I stirred in my oats to brown them for a few minutes to eke out some extra-toasty flavor. As a nod to risotto, I deglazed the pot with white wine before mixing in water and closing the lid to cook everything under pressure. The starches in the oats needed only 10 minutes to gel into a thick, comforting consistency and create a supercreamy porridge. When the time was up, I quick-released the pressure so that the oatmeal wouldn't overcook and then let the mixture settle, partially covered, for 5 minutes to achieve the right thickness.

The finishing accompaniments really brought the dish together and elevated it in the way I had envisioned. Whisking in a few tablespoons of olive oil helped enrich the emulsion with an appetizing, yet still healthful, amount of fat. Ricotta salata cheese, which is made from sheep's milk, added creaminess with a bit of tang. Stirring in fresh parsley (I wanted some green to recall my original inspiration) and

INSTANT POT SAVORY OATMEAL WITH SAUTÉED WILD MUSHROOMS

WASHING LEEKS

Leeks grow in layers of concentric circles, which means that they can trap a lot of dirt. After halving the leeks lengthwise and slicing them thin, wash the pieces well (a salad spinner works great).

lemon juice brought freshness and brightness. Topping it all with the remaining mushrooms, extra cheese, added parsley, and frizzled leeks before drizzling with oil made the final oatmeal so appealing and abundant that you'd never guess it came from an Instant Pot. For many years I'd wanted to re-create this dish, but I never thought I'd be able to do it so effectively in an Instant Pot. This was definitely an experience that deepened my affection for that wonderfully efficient, time-saving multitasker.

—JOSEPH GITTER, *America's Test Kitchen Books*

Instant Pot Savory Oatmeal with Sautéed Wild Mushrooms

SERVES 4 TOTAL TIME: 1¼ HOURS

You can use a single type of mushroom here or a combination for variety.

    5 tablespoons extra-virgin olive oil, divided,
       plus extra for drizzling
    1 pound leeks, halved lengthwise, sliced thin, and
       washed thoroughly, divided
    1 pound cremini, chanterelle, shiitake, and/or oyster
       mushrooms, stemmed and cut or torn into
       1½-inch pieces
   ½ teaspoon table salt, divided
    1 teaspoon minced fresh thyme
 1½ cups steel-cut oats
   ½ cup dry white wine
 4½ cups water, plus extra as needed
    3 ounces ricotta salata cheese, shredded (¾ cup),
       plus extra for serving
   ½ cup chopped fresh parsley,
       plus whole leaves for garnish
    1 tablespoon lemon juice

1. Using highest sauté function, heat 2 tablespoons oil in Instant Pot until shimmering. Add ¼ cup leeks and cook, stirring often, until beginning to brown, 2 to 3 minutes. Turn off Instant Pot and continue to cook, using residual heat, until leeks are evenly golden brown and crisp, 2 to 3 minutes. Using slotted spoon, transfer leeks to paper towel–lined bowl; set aside.

2. Add mushrooms and ¼ teaspoon salt to fat left in pot. Partially cover and cook, using highest sauté function, stirring occasionally, until mushrooms release their liquid, about 5 minutes. Uncover and continue to cook until liquid has evaporated and mushrooms begin to brown, 8 to 10 minutes. Add thyme and cook, stirring frequently, until fragrant, about 30 seconds; transfer to separate bowl.

3. Add remaining leeks and 1 tablespoon oil to now-empty pot and cook, using highest sauté function, until leeks are softened, 3 to 5 minutes. Stir in oats and cook until fragrant, about 2 minutes. Stir in wine and cook until nearly evaporated, about 30 seconds. Stir in water and remaining ¼ teaspoon salt, scraping up any browned bits. Lock lid into place and close pressure-release valve. Select high pressure-cook function and cook for 10 minutes.

4. Turn off Instant Pot and quick-release pressure. Partially uncover with care, allowing steam to escape away from you, and let sit for 5 minutes. Add ricotta salata and remaining 2 tablespoons oil and stir vigorously until oatmeal becomes creamy. Adjust consistency with extra hot water as needed. Stir in parsley, lemon juice, and half of mushrooms. Season with salt and pepper to taste.

5. Divide oatmeal among individual serving bowls. Top with remaining mushrooms, reserved leeks, extra ricotta salata, and whole parsley leaves. Drizzle with extra oil before serving.

AIR-FRYER HEARTY VEGETABLE HASH WITH GOLDEN YOGURT

✓ WHY THIS RECIPE WORKS Magic happens when you air-fry vegetables. In minutes, you get the crisped, caramelized exteriors and tender interiors usually associated with oven roasting. We transformed that roasted veggie concept into a quick, flavorful hash. We used nutrient-dense sweet potatoes and meaty mushrooms along with shallots, which crisped up nicely in the air fryer. To start our day with some fresh greens, we also incorporated raw baby kale that we tossed with the warm vegetables to wilt it. A silky-smooth yogurt sauce, flavored with cumin, turmeric, and cilantro, and a sprinkling of pistachios finished the dish.

When it comes to breakfast hash, there's a lot to love. It's hearty and savory; plus, it can be quick and easy, especially when made in an air fryer. But a typical hash can also be heavy and greasy. My goal here was to develop a healthier air-fryer hash recipe that was superhearty and packed with vegetables.

First up, the vegetables. I settled on kale, mushrooms, and potatoes for the base of my hash, as their flavors meshed well together. Since this air-fryer recipe would serve two, using part of an onion was annoyingly wasteful. Two shallots worked perfectly.

My original idea was to toss the vegetables with a little oil and air-fry them together. The sweet potatoes, mushrooms, and shallot cooked together beautifully, but the kale was too bulky to fit in the basket. To simplify the recipe, I decided to opt for baby kale and not cook it. Tossing it with the cooked vegetables helped wilt it.

Many hash recipes call for fried eggs, as their runny yolks provide a saucy coating. But cooking eggs in an air fryer can be tricky. Instead, I created a zippy yogurt sauce that incorporated the warm flavors of turmeric and cumin. I microwaved the spices with a little oil to draw out their flavors. A tablespoon of minced fresh cilantro stirred into the sauce added a pop of freshness.

As a finishing touch, I added a sprinkling of toasted pistachios on top. The textures of the caramelized vegetables were very tender, so the crunch the pistachios added was welcome. They also contributed a protein boost to make this a hearty vegetarian breakfast meal.

—SAMANTHA BLOCK, *America's Test Kitchen Books*

NOTES FROM THE TEST KITCHEN

TOASTING NUTS AND SEEDS IN AN AIR FRYER
Arrange nuts or seeds in 6-inch round nonstick or silicone cake pan. Place pan in air-fryer basket and place basket into air fryer. Set temperature to 350 degrees. Cook, shaking basket occasionally, until nuts or seeds are fragrant, 1 to 3 minutes. Immediately remove from pan.

Golden Yogurt
SERVES 2   TOTAL TIME: 35 MINUTES

This recipe can be easily doubled. If your air fryer has a capacity of 6 quarts or more, you can double the recipe and still cook it in a single batch, increasing the cooking time to about 45 minutes and stirring twice during cooking. However, it is critical to leave enough room for air circulation around the ingredients to ensure even cooking. If you have a smaller air fryer (less than 6 quarts), you will need to cook in batches.

4   teaspoons extra-virgin olive oil, divided
¼   teaspoon ground cumin
¼   teaspoon ground turmeric
¼   cup plain yogurt
1   tablespoon minced fresh cilantro
½   teaspoon table salt, divided
1   pound sweet potatoes, peeled and cut into ½-inch pieces
12   ounces cremini mushrooms, trimmed and quartered
2   shallots, sliced thin
¼   teaspoon pepper
2   ounces (2 cups) baby kale
¼   cup shelled pistachios, toasted and chopped

1. Combine 1 teaspoon oil, cumin, and turmeric in small bowl and microwave until fragrant, about 1 minute. Stir in yogurt, cilantro, and ¼ teaspoon salt; set aside for serving.

2. Toss potatoes, mushrooms, and shallots with pepper, remaining 1 tablespoon oil, and remaining ¼ teaspoon salt in large bowl; transfer to air-fryer basket. Place basket into air fryer and set temperature to 400 degrees. Cook until vegetables are tender and golden brown, 18 to 20 minutes, stirring halfway through cooking.

3. Return vegetables to now-empty bowl. Add kale and toss gently to combine. Drizzle individual portions with yogurt sauce and sprinkle with pistachios before serving.

PASTELÓN (PUERTO RICAN SWEET PLANTAIN AND PICADILLO CASSEROLE)

CHAPTER 5

MEAT

PASTELÓN (PUERTO RICAN SWEET PLANTAIN AND PICADILLO CASSEROLE)

✓ **WHY THIS RECIPE WORKS** This plush, meaty Puerto Rican casserole is a savory-sweet mash-up of two island staples—plátanos maduros fritos (fried ripe plantains) and the briny, sofrito-laced filling called picadillo. For appropriately sweet, velvety-soft plantains, it was critical to start with fruit that had ripened sufficiently (see "Buying Plantains"). To ensure evenly thick planks for frying, we cut the peeled fruit in half before slicing it into slabs; these stubbier pieces were also easier to manipulate in the hot oil. We used just ¾ cup of oil—enough that the plantains could move freely without sticking. For a dish that was filling but not overly rich, we chose 90 percent lean ground beef for the picadillo. For the meatiest taste, we browned the beef first with a healthy dose of sazón, the Puerto Rican seasoning blend, before combining it with the sofrito; tomato sauce; and alcaparrado, a briny blend of olives, capers, and pimentos. A pour of distilled white vinegar brought all the flavors into focus. After fanning half the plantains across the bottom of a baking dish, we drizzled beaten egg on top to give the casserole a sturdier structure. We topped the pastelón with a light sprinkling of Monterey Jack, which made the dish all the more appealing and comforting.

My Puerto Rican grandmother stockpiled plantains in the pantry of our New York City apartment like preserves in a root cellar. While they were green and as starchy as potatoes, she'd double-fry them for tostones or pound them into a mash with flavorful fats. As they transitioned to yellow, softening slightly and taking on a touch of sweetness, she'd grate them into soups or turn them into dumplings. But for me, the real prize came days or even weeks later, when their skins were mostly black and their flesh creamy and sweet: She'd fry up a batch of plátanos maduros fritos (fried ripe plantains) to make the meaty casserole called pastelón. Then she'd layer the caramelized slices with a swath of picadillo—ground beef simmered in sofrito and tomato sauce and studded with olives, capers, and pimentos—drizzle beaten egg over the top, and bake the casserole in the oven, where its flavors would meld.

More elaborate preparations featuring plantains layered with meat and other fillings exist across Latin America, but I can't imagine any that would make me feel happier or more replete than pastelón. Every Puerto Rican family has their own version of the dish, whose name translates as "big pie." Here is mine, based largely on my grandmother's, but with tweaks to ensure that its savory-sweet flavors pop.

There is only one thing essential to pastelón: The fruit must be very ripe so that it has the requisite softness and sweetness to provide a counterpoint to the picadillo. Typically, the peeled plantains are each sliced along their length into planks, but I found it challenging to make even slices with such long cuts. Instead, I first halved the plantains crosswise and then sliced each half lengthwise into three thin slabs. When I slipped these stubbier pieces into a skillet with hot oil (¾ cup did the trick—just enough to allow them to move freely), they were also easier to flip during cooking. Once the plantains darkened to a deep golden brown and crisped at the edges, I drained them on paper towels. A little salt and they were good to go.

On to the picadillo: I wanted a casserole that didn't taste overly rich, so I opted for 90 percent lean ground beef. For the sofrito, I pulsed onion and garlic in a food processor with plenty of cilantro, its grassy-citrusy cousin culantro, and a musky Cubanelle pepper. But instead of sautéing this flavor base and then cooking the raw meat in it with tomato sauce, I browned the beef in the skillet first to amplify its meatiness and then further boosted its savory flavor by sprinkling it with a healthy dose of sazón, a heady Puerto Rican mix of salt, dried garlic, onion, black pepper, oregano, cumin, and achiote. I removed the browned beef from the pan, added my sofrito, and sautéed it for several minutes before stirring in tomato sauce (the canned kind is perfect) and simmering the mixture long enough for a flavorful fond to begin forming on the bottom and edges of the pan. I added the beef back to the skillet with a couple tablespoons of alcaparrado, a jarred combination of green olives, capers, and pimentos that gives the island's version of picadillo its characteristic punch. Some cooks chop the mixture, but I love the tangy burst of biting into a meaty olive, so I left it whole. I cooked the picadillo until the sauce tightened and clung to the meat. A pour of white vinegar brought all the sweet, savory, and vibrant flavors into focus.

I fanned half the fried plantains across a baking dish and, after some experimentation, poured beaten eggs over just this bottom layer instead of the whole assembly, which gave the casserole a sturdier structure

BUYING PLANTAINS

Color is one way to determine ripeness, but assessing texture is also important, because overly cool temperatures can cause darkening but slow ripening.

GREEN
Intensely green. Mildly nutty with no hint of sweetness. Should feel firm and full in their skins.

HALF-RIPE
Yellowy green, with a few dark spots. Faintly sweet. Should yield slightly to the touch.

VERY RIPE
Heavily to entirely blackened. Fruity and sweet. Should be soft like a fully ripe avocado.

for lifting slices out of the pan. I smoothed on the picadillo, shingled the remaining plantains over the top, and debated the final question: cheese or no cheese? The most traditional versions, including my grandmother's, eschew it, but I decided on a smattering of shredded Monterey Jack. After 20 minutes in the oven, it melted oozily over the velvety-soft plantains and tender bits of beef, making this already ridiculously good dish even more comforting and appealing.

—DAVID PAZMIÑO, *Cook's Illustrated*

Pastelón (Puerto Rican Sweet Plantain and Picadillo Casserole)

SERVES 6 TO 8   TOTAL TIME: 1½ HOURS

If culantro is unavailable, increase the cilantro to 1 cup. You can substitute one small green bell pepper for the Cubanelle, if desired. Buy the largest plantains you can find; they should be almost completely black and yield to firm pressure, like a ripe avocado. The seasoning mix sazón can be found in the international section of your supermarket; we like versions that include cilantro and achiote for this dish, but any will work. Alcaparrado, a mixture of pitted Manzanilla olives, capers, and pimento strips, can be found there, too. If you can't find it, substitute pimento-stuffed Manzanilla olives. Serve the pastelón with rice and beans.

¾   **cup fresh cilantro leaves and stems**

1   **small Cubanelle pepper, stemmed, seeded, and chopped coarse**

½   **onion, quartered**

¼   **cup fresh culantro, chopped coarse**

2   **tablespoons vegetable oil**

3   **garlic cloves, peeled**

3–3½   **pounds very ripe plantains, peeled**

¾   **cup vegetable oil for frying**

½   **teaspoon plus pinch table salt, divided**

1   **pound 90 percent lean ground beef**

2½   **teaspoons sazón**

2   **teaspoons distilled white vinegar**

1   **(8-ounce) can tomato sauce**

2   **tablespoons pitted alcaparrado**

2   **large eggs**

4   **ounces Monterey Jack cheese, shredded (1 cup)**

1. Adjust oven rack to middle position and heat oven to 400 degrees. Pulse cilantro, Cubanelle, onion, culantro, 2 tablespoons oil, and garlic in food processor until coarsely chopped, 12 to 14 pulses.

2. Line rimmed baking sheet with double layer of paper towels. Halve 1 plantain crosswise; cut each half lengthwise into thirds. Repeat with remaining plantains.

3. Heat ¾ cup oil in 12-inch nonstick skillet over medium-high heat until shimmering. Carefully lay one-third of plantain pieces in skillet and fry until deep golden brown on 1 side, 3 to 4 minutes. Using 2 spatulas, flip and fry on second side until deep golden brown, 2 to 3 minutes. Transfer plantains to prepared sheet. Repeat with remaining plantains in 2 batches. Discard excess oil, leaving any browned bits in skillet. Sprinkle ½ teaspoon salt over plantains.

COOKING WITH CULANTRO

Culantro, also known as recao or ngò gai, is an essential ingredient in the sofritos that form the base for many Puerto Rican dishes (including pastelón). Culantro is native to Mexico, Central and South America, and the Caribbean, but it also grows in tropical areas around the globe and is popular in Vietnamese and other Southeast Asian cuisines.

The herb is often likened to its close relative cilantro, though its appearance is quite different—culantro has long, flat, sturdy leaves instead of cilantro's petite frilly ones, with no separation between leaf and stem (making it easier to prep than cilantro, since its ribs are also tender). And while culantro shares a similar aroma and flavor, its earthy, herby, citrusy taste is much more potent than cilantro's. If you are trying culantro in place of cilantro in a raw application, start with about half the amount called for and adjust to your taste. Since their differences are more muted in cooked applications, a one-to-one swap in such instances is fine. –Annie Petito

4. Add beef to now-empty skillet and cook over medium-high heat, breaking up meat with wooden spoon, until beef is no longer pink and begins to brown. Sprinkle sazón over meat and cook until aromatic, about 1 minute. Drizzle vinegar over meat and stir to combine. Transfer meat to bowl.

5. Transfer cilantro mixture to now-empty skillet. Cook over medium-high heat, stirring frequently, until onion softens, 3 to 4 minutes. Add tomato sauce and continue to cook until mixture thickens and fond begins to form on edges and bottom of skillet, 2 to 4 minutes longer. Stir in beef and alcaparrado and continue to cook until sauce is thickened and coats meat, 2 to 3 minutes longer. Off heat, season with salt and pepper to taste.

6. Arrange half of plantain pieces in lightly greased 13 by 9-inch baking dish (plantains will not cover bottom of dish completely). Whisk eggs with remaining pinch salt and pour evenly over plantains. Spread beef over plantains. Arrange remaining plantains in single layer over beef. Sprinkle evenly with Monterey Jack. Bake until cheese is melted and beginning to brown, 20 to 25 minutes. Transfer to wire rack; let cool for 5 minutes before serving.

SMOKED PRIME RIB

✓ **WHY THIS RECIPE WORKS** Smoking a prime rib can elevate this already grand cut of meat to a whole new level. We seasoned it simply with salt and pepper and let the grill smoke add the rest of the flavor. We used a grill setup called a charcoal snake; this C-shaped array of smoldering briquettes provided low, slow, indirect heat to the center of the grill for the entire time it took to cook the roast without needing to reload the grill with more coals. Cooking the meat to 115 degrees in the center allowed it to carry over to a rosy medium-rare. A temperature probe was the most fail-safe way to know that the beef was cooked properly. After letting the roast rest (for the juiciest results), we carved the meat and served it with a spicy horseradish sauce.

Texas brisket is arguably the holy grail of barbecue in the United States. But some Lone Star State pit masters, such as Roy Perez of Kreuz Market and Tim McLaughlin of Lockhart Smokehouse, occasionally add prime ribs to their smokers. And when they do, they elevate this already grand cut of meat to a whole new level.

Start at the butcher counter; we recommend calling in advance, as many grocery stores carry rib roasts only around the holidays. Order a 6- to 7-pound bone-in prime rib, specifically a first-cut (the section closer to the loin that's more uniform and tender) standing rib roast. If you're willing to spend extra, go for the prime grade (choice also works well). The roast should have an even fat cap on top and three big bones. It's a special-occasion cut that usually costs more than $100.

Since this prime rib is done in the Texas style (which is meant to highlight the beef flavor), the only seasonings are kosher salt and black pepper. But you need to apply this simple rub at least 24 hours (or up to four days) in advance of cooking so that the salt can penetrate and fully season the meat; the salting process helps keep the meat juicy, too.

We are not afraid of snakes at *Cook's Country*—charcoal snakes, that is. In Texas, pit masters smoke prime rib in commercial smokers where the low heat gradually brings the meat up to temperature. A charcoal snake is a grill setup that allows a kettle grill to mimic this without the need to refuel. To make it, you arrange coals in a two-layered C shape around half of the bottom grill grate. Then you place wood chunks over the charcoal and a water pan in the center (to help keep the grill temperature stable) and light just one end of the charcoal so that the briquettes slowly ignite each other as the fire works its way across the entire arrangement, creating a low and slow burn. Just three wood chunks give the prime rib a gentle dose of smoke without overwhelming the rich, beefy flavor.

A temperature probe is the most fail-safe way to know that your beef is cooked properly; you can monitor the exact temperature without having to open the grill lid and lose heat (and thus delay the cooking). It's an investment, sure, but one that protects your investment in the meat.

Some barbecue spots choose to smoke their prime rib until it's well-done, but we call for smoking it to medium-rare for a delightful mix of textures. Although we remove the prime rib from the grill when the center registers 115 degrees, the temperature will continue to rise to 125 degrees—a phenomenon known as "carry-over cooking."

After letting the roast rest (for the juiciest results), carve the meat off the bones. (And trust us, you are going to want to gnaw on those bones.) Then slice the meat into thick slabs. The outside of the roast gets a deep, dark crust, and the meat just below it is very tender, just a little shy of shreddable; it's similar to nicely cooked barbecue brisket. At the center of the roast is the juicy, rosy, medium-rare eye. The beauty of this recipe is that you get to experience all these textures in one piece of meat. Our spicy horseradish sauce is the perfect complement to the rich, tender slices. And if you have the willpower to save some meat, you will thank yourself the next day when you make our Smoked Prime Rib Sandwiches with Green Chile Queso (page 121).

—MORGAN BOLLING, *Cook's Country*

Smoked Prime Rib

SERVES 8 TO 10

TOTAL TIME: 3¼ HOURS, PLUS 24¾ HOURS SALTING AND RESTING

We developed this recipe using a 22-inch Weber kettle charcoal grill. If you intend to make the Smoked Prime Rib Sandwiches with Green Chile Queso on page 121, reserve a 12-ounce chunk of meat after carving the roast in step 7. Be sure to also reserve 3 tablespoons of the horseradish sauce.

PRIME RIB

- 1 (6- to 7-pound) first-cut beef standing rib roast (3 bones), fat cap trimmed to ¼ inch
- 2 tablespoons kosher salt
- 1 tablespoon pepper
- 3 (3-inch) wood chunks
- 1 (13 by 9-inch) disposable aluminum pan

HORSERADISH SAUCE

- ½ cup mayonnaise
- ⅓ cup prepared horseradish
- 2 tablespoons lemon juice
- 1 garlic clove, minced
- 1 teaspoon Worcestershire sauce
- 1 teaspoon pepper
- ¾ teaspoon kosher salt
- Pinch cayenne pepper

1. FOR THE PRIME RIB: Using sharp knife, cut 1-inch crosshatch pattern in fat cap of roast, being careful not to cut into meat. Rub salt and pepper over entire roast and into crosshatch. Transfer to large plate and refrigerate, uncovered, for at least 24 hours or up to 4 days.

2. Open bottom vent of charcoal grill completely. Arrange 40 charcoal briquettes, 2 briquettes wide, around half of perimeter of grill, overlapping slightly so briquettes are touching, to form C shape. Place second layer of 40 briquettes, also 2 briquettes wide, on top of first. (Completed arrangement should be 2 briquettes wide by 2 briquettes high.)

3. Place 2 wood chunks on top of charcoal 2 inches from each end of C. Place remaining chunk in center of C. Place disposable pan in center of grill, running lengthwise into arc of C. Pour 6 cups water into disposable pan.

4. Light chimney starter filled with 10 briquettes (pile briquettes on 1 side of chimney so they catch). When coals are partially covered with ash, use tongs to place them at 1 end of C.

5. Set cooking grate in place, then clean and oil grate. Place roast over water pan, fat side up, with bones facing arc in C. Insert temperature probe into center of roast. Cover grill, open lid vent completely, and position lid vent over roast. Cook until meat registers 115 degrees (for medium-rare), 2½ to 3¼ hours.

SMOKED PRIME RIB

6. FOR THE HORSERADISH SAUCE: Meanwhile, combine all ingredients in bowl. Cover and refrigerate for at least 30 minutes to allow flavors to meld. (Sauce can be refrigerated for up to 2 days.)

7. Transfer roast to carving board, tent with aluminum foil, and let rest for 45 minutes. Carve meat from bones and slice ¾ inch thick. Serve with sauce. (Leftover meat can be refrigerated for up to 2 days.)

SMOKED PRIME RIB SANDWICHES WITH GREEN CHILE QUESO

✓ **WHY THIS RECIPE WORKS** For this sandwich, we saved a chunk of our Smoked Prime Rib. We chilled the leftover meat to make sure that we could slice it thin across the grain. We then sautéed the slices to warm them and crisp the fat. For a topping, we made a quick green chile queso in the microwave using spicy pepper Jack, creamy American cheese, jarred green salsa, and a little milk. All that was left to do was assemble the hot, cheesy sandwiches and dig in (with plenty of napkins on hand).

Lewis Barbecue in Charleston, South Carolina, sells a Beef N' Cheddar special on Fridays that nods to Arby's signature sandwich. The Lewis version features delightfully rich smoked prime rib; shaved onion; horseradish sauce; Hatch green chile queso; and a buttered, toasted bun. The sandwich is well worth waiting in the hour-plus-long line that forms to get it.

So from Arby's to Lewis Barbecue to *Cook's Country*, here's our version. To make the sandwich, start by thinly slicing leftover Smoked Prime Rib (page 119); this is much easier to do when the meat is cold and firm. Then sauté the slices in a skillet until they're warmed through and the fat just begins to crisp up.

The queso comes together quickly in the microwave following a tried-and-true test kitchen method for queso fundido: Simply microwave a combination of creamy American cheese, spicy pepper Jack cheese, jarred salsa verde, and milk. To build the sandwich, layer a hefty amount of the beef on a bun with sliced onion, "horsey sauce" (as the Lewis menu calls it), and plenty of that bubbling-hot queso. Wow.

—MORGAN BOLLING, *Cook's Country*

Smoked Prime Rib Sandwiches with Green Chile Queso

SERVES 2 TOTAL TIME: 20 MINUTES

We recommend chilling the leftover meat overnight to make it easier to slice thin.

- 3 tablespoons horseradish sauce from Smoked Prime Rib (page 119)
- 2 kaiser rolls, split and toasted
- ½ small white onion, sliced into thin rounds
- 1 tablespoon vegetable oil
- 12 ounces Smoked Prime Rib (page 119), sliced thin on bias
- 1 ounce American cheese, shredded (¼ cup)
- 1 ounce pepper Jack cheese, shredded (¼ cup)
- 2 tablespoons jarred salsa verde
- 2 tablespoons whole milk

1. Spread horseradish sauce on cut sides of bun tops (1½ tablespoons per bun top). Divide onion between bun bottoms.

2. Heat vegetable oil in 12-inch nonstick skillet over medium-high heat until just smoking. Add prime rib and cook until warmed through and fat is lightly crisped, about 3 minutes. Cover to keep warm.

3. Combine American cheese, pepper Jack, salsa verde, and milk in medium bowl. Microwave until cheeses begin to melt around edges of bowl, 30 to 60 seconds. Stir and continue to microwave until cheeses are completely melted and just beginning to bubble around edges of bowl, 1 to 2 minutes longer, whisking halfway through microwaving.

4. Divide prime rib between bun bottoms. Pour half of queso (or more if desired) over prime rib. Cap with bun tops. Serve, passing any extra queso separately.

NOTES FROM THE TEST KITCHEN

THE RIGHT SLICE

Holding knife at angle, slice leftover prime rib thin on bias. (Note that meat is easier to slice when cold.)

KOUSA MIHSHI (LEBANESE STUFFED SQUASH)

✓ **WHY THIS RECIPE WORKS** Kousa mihshi, which translates as "stuffed squash" in Arabic, is a satisfying yet light preparation that's popular across the Levant. The dish consists of hollowed-out zucchini filled with a mixture of spiced ground lamb and rice and slowly braised in cinnamon-accented tomato sauce until the meat is succulent and the rice tender. Soaking the rice for 10 minutes before combining it with the lamb ensured that the grains cooked evenly and thoroughly. Browning the stuffing and breaking it up with the back of a spatula created small, distinct pieces that packed lightly into the squash cavities. To give the sauce a meaty underpinning, we sautéed the aromatics in the fatty juices we drained from the lamb. After 40 minutes of braising in the velvety sauce, the zucchini was tender but not mushy and the filling was cooked through.

In late summer, when zucchini and tomatoes are bursting from their vines, I crave kousa mihshi, one of the great Middle Eastern stuffed vegetable traditions that's long been treasured across the Levant, and one that I grew up preparing with my mother in our Lebanese American home. We'd hollow out the mildly bitter zucchini ("kousa mihshi" means "stuffed squash" in Arabic), fill it with a mixture of spiced rice and lamb, and slowly braise it in tomato sauce until the meat was succulent and the rice tender. A drizzle of olive oil and a spoonful of cooling yogurt completed the ensemble: a vibrant mix of flavors, textures, and temperatures that to me epitomizes all that is special about Lebanese cooking.

In many households, these "delectable pockets of nourishment and care," as my Aunty Karen calls them, are reserved for special occasions. My mother also made kousa mihshi for Sunday brunch, presenting it to family at our backyard picnic table in a gleaming copper pot.

All the women on my mother's side prepare the squash using a recipe that dates to my Lebanese-born great-great-grandmother. I've tweaked that basic approach, incorporating tips from my family as well as innovations of my own, careful to keep it tasting as it has for generations. The sauce must be layered with the flavors of fruity fresh tomatoes, warm cinnamon, and peppery olive oil. The squash should be tender and intact and the filling rich but light in texture and flecked with fluffy grains of rice. Not least of all, every bite must taste balanced and cohesive.

To make the stuffing, called "hashweh" in Arabic, most recipes start by rinsing the rice. I prefer to rinse it and then soak it in water for 10 minutes before combining it with the lamb, which helps the grains plump evenly and shaves minutes off the cooking time—all the better for ensuring that the zucchini doesn't overcook. The hashweh is usually left raw, but I brown mine, breaking it up as it cooks to create small, distinct pieces that pack more lightly into the squash.

Lebanese cooks often lay the stuffed squash atop lamb bones and simmer it in tomato broth. My family makes a thicker, brighter-tasting sauce, but to get that same meaty underpinning that's critical for uniting all the flavors, I sauté onion and garlic (seasoned with more spices) in the fatty juices drained from cooking

NOTES FROM THE TEST KITCHEN

THREE SIMPLE STEPS TO CORING THE ZUCCHINI
With the right tools, hollowing out the zucchini is a quick and easy task.

1. CORE the zucchini with an apple corer, pressing it into the squash as far down as it will go.

2. SCOOP out more pieces of core with a melon baller until the hollow is ½ inch from the bottom.

3. RINSE the cavity to remove seeds and debris clinging to the walls, and drain on a dish towel.

KOUSA MIHSHI (LEBANESE STUFFED SQUASH)

the lamb. Then I puree those lamby-tasting alliums in a blender with a couple pounds of farmers' market tomatoes, tomato paste to bolster their fresh flavor, and cider vinegar for extra brightness.

As the sauce bubbles in the skillet, I core the squashes, replacing the squatter Lebanese variety that's sometimes called grey zucchini with the conventional kind sold in the United States. Coring is easily done with an apple corer and a melon baller (though my grandfather once resorted to using his drill to core dozens of zucchini for a big family gathering—a story I love, as it demonstrates the lengths Lebanese cooks will go to feed the people they love). Filling them is a simple matter of dropping spoonfuls of stuffing into their cavities and periodically tapping each zucchini gently on the counter to encourage the hashweh to settle lightly on the bottom.

To cook the kousa mihshi, I arrange them on their sides in the skillet, which allows some of the filling's meaty juices to trickle into the ruddy sauce, further enriching and unifying its flavors. After 40 minutes of braising, this beautiful symbol of Lebanese hospitality is ready to serve.

—DOMINIQUE KHOURY, *Cook's Illustrated*

Kousa Mihshi (Lebanese Stuffed Squash)

SERVES 4   TOTAL TIME: 2¼ HOURS

For this recipe, you'll need an apple corer, the type that removes the core only but does not slice the apple; the small end of a melon baller or a long-handled bar spoon is also helpful. We like ground lamb here, but you can substitute 90 percent lean ground beef, if preferred. Select zucchini that are similarly sized to ensure even cooking, and to make them easier to core, choose the straightest ones you can find. Use fresh, in-season tomatoes for the best flavor. For a refreshing accompaniment, reserve the zucchini cores and trimmings (but not the stems) to make Zucchini-Cucumber Salad with Pine Nuts and Mint (recipe follows).

HASHWEH

- ½ cup long-grain white rice
- 8 ounces ground lamb
- 2 tablespoons extra-virgin olive oil, divided
- 1 teaspoon table salt
- ½ teaspoon pepper
- ¼ teaspoon ground cinnamon

SAUCE

- 2 tablespoons extra-virgin olive oil
- ½ teaspoon pepper
- ¼ teaspoon ground cinnamon
- 1 small onion, chopped coarse
- 2 garlic cloves, minced
- 2 pounds tomatoes, cored and chopped coarse
- 2 tablespoons tomato paste
- 2 teaspoons cider vinegar
- 1 teaspoon table salt

ZUCCHINI

- 6 zucchini (6 to 7 inches long and at least 1½ inches wide)
- 2 tablespoons extra-virgin olive oil
- ¼ cup fresh parsley leaves
- 2 cups plain whole-milk yogurt

1. FOR THE HASHWEH: Place rice in fine-mesh strainer and rinse under cold running water until water runs clear. Place rice in bowl and cover with 2 cups hot water; let stand for 10 minutes. Drain rice in now-empty strainer and return to bowl (do not wash strainer). Add lamb, 1 tablespoon oil, salt, pepper, and cinnamon and mix until rice is well dispersed. Heat remaining 1 tablespoon oil in 12-inch nonstick skillet over medium-high heat until shimmering. Add lamb mixture to skillet (do not wash bowl) and, using heat-resistant spatula, mash to thin layer. Cook, stirring constantly and breaking up meat with side of spatula, until meat is almost cooked through but still slightly pink, 3 to 4 minutes. Transfer mixture to now-empty strainer set over bowl. Return juices and fat to skillet. Transfer lamb mixture to now-empty bowl and, using fork, break up mixture until meat is reduced to pieces no larger than ¼ inch.

2. FOR THE SAUCE: Add oil to juices and fat in skillet and heat over medium-low heat until sizzling. Stir in pepper and cinnamon and cook until just fragrant, about 30 seconds. Add onion and garlic and cook, stirring occasionally, until very soft and light golden, 7 to 9 minutes.

3. Transfer onion mixture to food processor. Add tomatoes, tomato paste, vinegar, and salt to processor and process until smooth, 1½ to 2 minutes. Transfer tomato mixture to now-empty skillet. Bring to boil over medium-high heat. Reduce heat to simmer and cook, uncovered and stirring occasionally, until sauce is thickened and heat-resistant spatula dragged across bottom of skillet leaves trail, 25 to 30 minutes. While sauce cooks, prepare zucchini.

4. FOR THE ZUCCHINI: Remove stem end of 1 zucchini and discard. Holding zucchini with your hand, insert apple corer into stemmed end and press and turn until cutting end of corer is about ½ inch from bottom of zucchini (or as far as corer will go), being careful not to damage walls of zucchini. (If stemmed end is too narrow to accommodate corer without damaging walls, remove additional inch of stemmed end.) Remove corer. Using melon baller or long-handled bar spoon, scoop out any remaining core in pieces until farthest part of hollow is ½ inch from bottom of zucchini. Repeat with remaining zucchini. Rinse hollows and drain zucchini on dish towel.

5. Hold 1 zucchini stemmed side up on counter. Using your hand or small spoon, drop small portions of stuffing into hollow, tapping bottom of zucchini lightly on counter to help stuffing settle, until stuffing is ½ inch from top of zucchini. Do not compact stuffing. Repeat with remaining zucchini and stuffing.

6. Remove sauce from heat. Gently arrange stuffed zucchini in single layer in skillet. Return skillet to medium-high heat and bring to boil. Adjust heat to maintain low simmer, cover, and cook for 20 minutes (small wisps of steam should escape from beneath skillet lid, but sauce should not boil). Turn zucchini over gently. Cover and continue to simmer until rice and meat are fully cooked and zucchini are tender but not mushy, 20 to 25 minutes longer. Drizzle zucchini and sauce with oil; sprinkle with parsley; and serve, passing yogurt separately.

Zucchini-Cucumber Salad with Pine Nuts and Mint

SERVES 4   TOTAL TIME: 40 MINUTES

This recipe was designed to use the squash cores and trimmings from our Kousa Mihshi (Lebanese Stuffed Squash) recipe. If you'd like to make this salad separately from the kousa mihshi, substitute 3 cups of finely chopped zucchini (two small zucchini) for the cores and trimmings. If you can't find Persian cucumbers, substitute half an English cucumber.

- 3 tablespoons extra-virgin olive oil, divided
- ¼ small onion, chopped fine
- 1 garlic clove, minced

Zucchini cores and trimmings from 1 recipe Kousa Mihshi (Lebanese Stuffed Squash), chopped fine
- ¾ teaspoon table salt, divided
- 2 tablespoons lemon juice
- ½ teaspoon pepper
- ¼ teaspoon sumac
- ½ cup fresh mint leaves, divided
- 3 Persian cucumbers, quartered lengthwise, cut into ½-inch pieces, and chilled
- ¼ cup chopped fresh parsley
- 3 tablespoons pine nuts, toasted

Flake sea salt

1. Heat 1 tablespoon oil in 10-inch skillet over medium heat. Add onion and garlic and cook, stirring occasionally, until translucent, about 4 minutes. Add zucchini cores and trimmings and ½ teaspoon table salt and cook, stirring occasionally, until zucchini is slightly softened but skin on trimmings is still vibrant green, 5 to 6 minutes. Transfer mixture to fine-mesh strainer set over bowl. Transfer to refrigerator to drain and cool, at least 10 minutes.

2. Whisk lemon juice, pepper, sumac, remaining 2 tablespoons oil, and remaining ¼ teaspoon table salt together in serving bowl. Chop half of mint. Add chopped mint, zucchini mixture, cucumber, parsley, and pine nuts to dressing and toss gently to combine. Sprinkle with remaining ¼ cup mint leaves and flake sea salt to taste, and serve.

KALBI (KOREAN FLANKEN-STYLE SHORT RIBS)

✔ **WHY THIS RECIPE WORKS** The word "kalbi" literally means "rib" in Korean. The dish is typically made with beef short ribs cut flanken-style, across the bones, ideally ¼ inch thick. You can find this cut at Asian markets, especially ones that specialize in Korean ingredients. Kalbi is most often made with beef, but it can also be made with pork. Kalbi marinade gets its characteristic sweetness from sugar and typically some fruit. Asian pear is often used, but finding a very sweet, juicy Asian pear year-round can be a challenge. Canned pineapple provides a reliable substitute because it's consistently sweet and readily available. Ripe kiwi adds additional sweetness, but its real function was to tenderize the meat: The enzymes found in green kiwi are natural tenderizers. Just be sure not to add too much, or you'll get mushy short ribs. Aside from making sure to marinate the meat for at least 24 hours, the biggest tip for success is to cook the kalbi for longer than you might think (about 6 minutes per side on a charcoal or gas grill). Kalbi shouldn't be quickly seared on the grill like a thin steak. Short ribs are by nature a tough cut, and the last thing you want is rare kalbi. While their thinness certainly speeds up the cooking time, you still need to allow the fat to be rendered and the connective tissues to break down. The result should be tender meat with nice char resulting from the caramelization of the sugars in the marinade. You'll know when the kalbi are done because the bones will pull away cleanly from the meat with just a little bit of resistance.

My mom is a great cook, but like many people with her depth of experience, she never measures anything. By the time I came of age and really wanted to learn how to make some of the nostalgic Korean dishes I ate growing up (and now enjoyed at fancy Korean restaurants), I was living in New York City, nearly 3,000 miles away from home.

This is when I enlisted the help of my older sister, Yong Woo, who lives in Portland, Oregon, near my mom. She, like me, grew up baking, so she appreciates the exactness of a leveled measuring cup and the preciseness of a gram of sugar. When she married into a very traditional Korean family, she suddenly found herself needing to know how to make authentic Korean dishes, including the most iconic of them all, beef kalbi (grilled beef short ribs). During her newlywed years, she often cooked with my mom, took notes, and got feedback from well-traveled Koreans to eventually land on what I think is the best kalbi recipe. It's a crowd-pleaser, and it's certainly better than any version I've had in a restaurant.

I first made a variation of this recipe when I appeared on an episode of *Grill It! with Bobby Flay* on the Food Network back in 2012. At the time, I was working as a pastry chef in fine-dining restaurants, writing for a national food magazine, and half-heartedly pursuing a career in food television. The recipe, which you can still find online, is very good, but it was modified for television. At home—and in this recipe for *Cook's Country*—we puree the solid ingredients for the marinade before combining them with the liquid ingredients, but chopping looks better on camera.

NOTES FROM THE TEST KITCHEN

THE RIGHT RIBS

This recipe calls for flanken-style beef short ribs (pictured below). Unlike English-style short ribs, these ribs are cut thin across the bones. The thin shape means that the fat is rendered and the connective tissue breaks down more quickly, so the ribs get tender enough to eat (the marinade helps here, too; see below) in a shorter amount of time on the grill.

Kalbi marinade gets its characteristic sweetness from sugar and typically some fruit. Asian pear is often used, but finding a very sweet, juicy Asian pear year-round can be a challenge. Canned pineapple serves as a reliable substitute because it's consistently sweet and readily available. Ripe kiwi contributes additional sweetness, but its real function is to tenderize the chewy meat; the enzymes found in green kiwi have natural tenderizing power. Just be sure not to add too much, or you'll get mushy short ribs.

As for the meat, the word "kalbi" literally means "rib" in Korean. The dish is typically made with beef short ribs cut flanken-style, across the bones, ideally ¼ inch thick. You can find this cut at Asian markets, especially ones that specialize in Korean ingredients. Kalbi is most often made with beef, but it can also be made with pork.

Aside from making sure to marinate the meat for at least 24 hours, my next biggest tip for success is to cook the kalbi for longer than you might think. I often see people sear kalbi quickly on the grill, as they would a thin steak. But short ribs are by nature a tough cut— that's why you often see recipes for braised (English-style) short ribs cooked low and slow in the oven. The last thing you want is rare kalbi. Using thin flanken-style ribs certainly speeds up the cooking time, but you still need to allow the fat to be rendered and the connective tissues to break down to achieve tender results. You'll want to maintain a moderately hot grill and cook the ribs for about 6 minutes per side. The result should be tender meat with nice char resulting from the caramelization of the sugars in the marinade. You'll know when the kalbi are done because the bones will pull away cleanly from the meat with just a little bit of resistance.

KALBI (KOREAN GRILLED FLANKEN-STYLE SHORT RIBS)

Beef kalbi is traditionally served with steamed white rice; some pickled vegetables, including kimchi; and an assortment of Korean side dishes and accompaniments known as banchan. Do like Koreans do and snip each rib into thirds with kitchen scissors, which makes them easier to pick up and eat with chopsticks.

This marinade can be easily doubled; you can use half for this recipe and save the rest for another time. It lasts for several weeks in the refrigerator or even longer in the freezer. This kalbi marinade is delicious on any cut of beef that benefits from a marinade. If you don't want to deal with bones, use it to marinate tri-tip, skirt, or flank steak. It's even great with chicken. It might be called kalbi marinade, but it's our go-to, universal meat marinade at home.

—JUDIAANN WOO, *Cook's Country*

Kalbi (Korean Grilled Flanken-Style Short Ribs)

SERVES 4

TOTAL TIME: 1¼ HOURS, PLUS 24 HOURS MARINATING

We call for clear rice wine here; michiu, cheongju, or mirin can be used. This recipe can be easily doubled to accommodate a larger group (you will need to marinate the ribs in two separate dishes, and you may need more charcoal if using a charcoal grill). We don't typically wash our proteins before cooking, but flanken-style short ribs tend to have a fair amount of bone fragments stuck to them because they are cut with a band saw. Rinsing is necessary to remove those fragments. A small, 8-ounce can of pineapple chunks will yield enough for this recipe. Some grocery stores sell yellow kiwi; the flavor of green kiwi is preferred here. Garnish the kalbi with sliced scallions, if desired.

- ¾ **cup packed dark brown sugar**
- ⅔ **cup soy sauce**
- 1 **cup coarsely chopped onion**
- ½ **cup canned pineapple chunks, plus 3 tablespoons juice**
- ½ **green kiwi, peeled**
- 6 **garlic cloves, smashed and peeled**
- ¼ **cup clear rice wine**
- 2 **tablespoons toasted sesame oil**
- 3 **pounds flanken-style beef short ribs, ¼ inch thick, trimmed**

FRUIT IN THE MARINADE

Canned pineapple adds a consistent sweetness to the marinade, while fresh kiwi adds a sweet-tart flavor and, more important, contains enzymes that help tenderize the short ribs.

1. Combine sugar and soy sauce in small saucepan and cook over medium-high heat, stirring occasionally, until sugar is dissolved. Let cool completely off heat.

2. Combine onion, pineapple and juice, kiwi, and garlic in blender and puree until smooth, about 30 seconds. Transfer onion mixture to 13 by 9-inch baking dish; stir in wine, oil, and soy sauce mixture until combined.

3. Line rimmed baking sheet with triple layer of paper towels. Rinse ribs under cold running water to remove any bone fragments, then transfer to prepared sheet. Pat tops of ribs dry with additional paper towels.

4. Working with a few ribs at a time, transfer ribs to marinade, turn gently to coat, and submerge in marinade. Cover dish with plastic wrap and refrigerate for at least 24 hours or up to 2 days.

5A. FOR A CHARCOAL GRILL: Open bottom vent completely. Light large chimney starter three-quarters filled with charcoal briquettes (4½ quarts). When top coals are partially covered with ash, pour evenly over grill. Set cooking grate in place, cover, and open lid vent completely. Heat grill until hot, about 5 minutes.

5B. FOR A GAS GRILL: Turn all burners to high; cover; and heat grill until hot, about 15 minutes. Turn all burners to medium.

6. Clean and oil cooking grate. Grill ribs, uncovered, until evenly browned on first side, about 6 minutes, moving ribs as needed for even cooking and to prevent flare-ups. Flip ribs and continue to grill until evenly browned on second side, about 6 minutes longer. Transfer ribs to platter, tent with aluminum foil, and let rest for 5 minutes. Serve.

STIR-FRIED BEEF AND GAI LAN

✓ **WHY THIS RECIPE WORKS** Our take on this ever-evolving Chinese American standard features gai lan (Chinese broccoli) and filet mignon: The luxe cut is ideal for quick, high-heat cooking; is readily available in small portions; and just needed a brief chill in the freezer to firm up for easy slicing before being coated in a simple mixture of soy sauce, Shaoxing wine, and cornstarch. While the meat chilled, we sliced the gai lan stalks thin on the bias and cut the tender leaves into wide ribbons. We started the stir-fry by cooking the stalks in oil in a hot wok. As they sizzled, the oil smoldered, infusing the dish with smoky wok hei. We then set the stalks aside and stir-fried the leaves with garlic and toasted sesame oil, speeding their cooking with a small but flavorful addition of chicken broth before arranging them on a serving platter. Finally, we stir-fried the marinated beef; returned the stalks to the wok; and stirred in a blend of chicken broth, oyster sauce, soy sauce, Shaoxing wine, toasted sesame oil, and cornstarch. The sauce thickened in less than a minute. We arranged the beef mixture over the leaves, ensuring that each bite was perfectly sauced.

The joys of stir-fried beef and broccoli enhanced with a jolt of dark, saline-sweet oyster sauce can't be overstated. Whether the vegetable is the standard variety or the Chinese type, gai lan, the trio comes together seamlessly, producing a savory, mineral-y synergy that belies its simplicity.

Like many such long-standing favorites, beef and broccoli is thought to have originated in the mid-1800s when Chinese workers migrated from the Pearl River Delta to coastal California. We don't know precisely when the dish emerged or exactly what form it took—documentation of the food these workers prepared is virtually nonexistent—but it presumably followed the trajectory of similar staples: Nascent recipes catered to Chinese tastes but shifted toward the Western palate over time. To wit: A once vegetable-forward stir-fry of gai lan, beef, and oyster sauce has morphed into something that's heavy on beef; features broccoli florets instead of gai lan; may include carrot, bell pepper, or onion; and is napped with a savory-sweet sauce.

But the form all depends on the cook. "Everybody has a different interpretation, a different presentation," explained one of my culinary heroes during a recent phone conversation. Martin Yan isn't just a restaurateur, cookbook author, and global television host. He is also a native of Guangdong and a resident of the San Francisco Bay Area—two geographic regions that were instrumental in shaping Chinese American cuisine. When I pressed him for advice on creating my own interpretation, he encouraged me to do my own thing: "It doesn't matter as long as it pleases your palate."

That's not to say he didn't offer opinions. His take features the gai lan, beef, and oyster sauce that scholars think appeared in early iterations, as well as soy sauce, sesame oil, Shaoxing wine, and fresh garlic and ginger—more ingredients with centuries of history in the Chinese kitchen.

I planned to follow Yan's lead and pay tribute to the three original ingredients while pulling back on the sweetness level that's common in modern versions of the dish.

A pound of gai lan, along with half as much beef, would serve four nicely with rice. Although the brassica is related to broccoli, its taste—delicately nutty, mineral-y, and bitter—and form—wide, succulent leaves and tender stalks—are altogether different, not to mention incredibly delicious.

For the beef, Yan sometimes steps up from the usual flank steak in favor of filet mignon. What a brilliant idea. The ultratender cut is ideal for quick, high-heat cooking and easy to find in pretrimmed, 8-ounce portions. Since I needed only a small steak, it wouldn't break the bank.

NOTES FROM THE TEST KITCHEN

OYSTER SAUCE

Oyster sauce is a viscous, briny-sweet seasoning that's integral to Chinese and Southeast Asian cuisines. The sauce is traditionally made by simmering oysters in water until the broth thickens and caramelizes, but producers these days more typically thicken liquid made from oyster extractives with cornstarch and wheat flour and season it with salt, sugar, and often monosodium glutamate. We sampled two common supermarket products, Lee Kum Kee Panda Brand Oyster Sauce and Lee Kum Kee Premium Oyster Sauce, and an online product, Megachef Oyster Sauce. While these condiments taste of the sea, they don't taste like oysters. Instead, they feature a briny savoriness and a rounded caramel sweetness; the Megachef product also offers a hint of roasted nuttiness that some tasters likened to toasted sesame oil. Tasters found all the samples acceptable, though a few preferred the Lee Kum Kee Premium sauce for its more intense flavor.

STIR-FRIED BEEF AND GAI LAN

Most of the work for a stir-fry happens before you light the stove: I quartered a thick center-cut filet and popped the pieces into the freezer to firm up and make them easy to slice thin. While the beef chilled, I sliced the gai lan leaves into wide ribbons and the stalks thin on the bias.

I cut the wedges of nearly frozen beef into thin slices and then coated them in equal parts soy sauce and Shaoxing wine (the amber alcohol provided acidic depth and a sweet aroma) along with cornstarch to help the liquids grip the meat. After I'd minced garlic and grated ginger, my last task was to stir glossy oyster sauce together with heady sesame oil; chicken broth; and more soy sauce, wine, and cornstarch.

With the components neatly lined up stoveside, I fired up my wok. Garlic and ginger crackled when they hit the hot oil just before I briskly stir-fried the voluminous pile of gai lan. I scooped the vegetable from the wok, cooked the marinated beef, and then tumbled everything together with the sauce.

The filet was meltingly tender and the gai lan stalks wonderfully crisp, but the leaves were sodden, the sauce trapped in their folds. What's more, the overall flavor fell flat, lacking what Yan characterized as "the breath, the aroma, the steam." He was referring to the intangible quality called wok hei—a smoldering, singed-oil essence that "you can smell two blocks away."

Some cooks mitigate saturated, droopy greens by stir-frying the leaves first, heaping them onto a platter, and then cooking the beef and stalks separately with the sauce. It was worth a shot.

I started anew, stir-frying the oblong stalk pieces in oil. Without the leaves to fill and cool the bowl of the wok, the pieces seared beautifully. As I tossed the stalks, they passed through the clouds of steam and smoke that rose from the sizzling-hot carbon steel, taking on the electric, fleeting taste of wok hei. I set aside the pale stalks, now spotted with brown, and tossed the leaves in garlicky oil. A drizzle of sesame oil joined the mix, sending up a toasty fragrance with the charred, vegetal ones. As soon as the emerald strips darkened, I splashed in some chicken broth to steam them tender.

After transferring the wilted (but not gloppy) leaves to a serving dish, I stir-fried the beef until it lost its rosy hue, returned the stalks to the wok, and drizzled in the sauce mixture. Not 60 seconds later, the savory-salty liquid was glossy and thick, so I piled the stalks and beef atop the glistening leaves.

HOW TO SLICE FILET THIN
This supertender, premium cut is optimal for quick, high-heat wok cookery.

1. Cut beef into 4 equal wedges and freeze until very firm, 20 to 25 minutes.

2. Stand each wedge on its side and slice against grain ¼ inch thick.

I'd reached my destination, and it was just as satisfying as the journey: Each bite of lush beef and greens had just the right amount of velvety, savory sauce spiked with garlic, ginger, and hints of smoke.

—LAN LAM, *Cook's Illustrated*

Stir-Fried Beef and Gai Lan

SERVES 4   TOTAL TIME: 55 MINUTES

We developed this recipe for a 14-inch wok, but a 12-inch carbon-steel or cast-iron skillet can be used. If gai lan is unavailable, you can use broccolini, substituting the florets for the gai lan leaves. Do not use standard broccoli. This recipe was developed with Lee Kum Kee oyster sauce. Serve with white rice.

- 1 (8-ounce) center-cut filet mignon, trimmed
- 1 pound gai lan, stalks trimmed
- 5 teaspoons Shaoxing wine or dry sherry, divided
- 1 tablespoon soy sauce, divided
- 2 teaspoons cornstarch, divided
- ¾ cup chicken broth, divided
- 2 tablespoons oyster sauce
- 1½ teaspoons toasted sesame oil, divided
- 2 tablespoons vegetable oil, divided
- 1½ teaspoons grated fresh ginger
- ¾ teaspoon minced garlic, divided

1. Cut beef into 4 equal wedges. Transfer to plate and freeze until very firm, 20 to 25 minutes. While beef freezes, prepare gai lan. Remove leaves, small stems, and florets from stalks; slice leaves crosswise into 1½-inch strips (any florets and stems can go into pile with leaves); and cut stalks on bias into ¼-inch-thick pieces. Set aside. When beef is firm, stand 1 piece on its side and slice against grain ¼ inch thick. Repeat with remaining pieces. Transfer to bowl. Add 1 teaspoon Shaoxing wine, 1 teaspoon soy sauce, and 1 teaspoon cornstarch and toss until beef is evenly coated. Set aside.

2. In second bowl, whisk together ½ cup broth, oyster sauce, ½ teaspoon sesame oil, remaining 4 teaspoons Shaoxing wine, remaining 2 teaspoons soy sauce, and remaining 1 teaspoon cornstarch; set aside. In third bowl, combine 4 teaspoons vegetable oil, ginger, and ¼ teaspoon garlic.

3. Heat 1 teaspoon vegetable oil in wok over high heat until just smoking. Add stalks and cook, stirring slowly but constantly, until spotty brown and crisp-tender, 3 to 4 minutes. Transfer to bowl.

4. Add remaining 1 teaspoon sesame oil, remaining 1 teaspoon vegetable oil, and remaining ½ teaspoon garlic to wok and cook, stirring constantly, until garlic is fragrant, about 15 seconds. Add leaves and cook, stirring frequently, until vibrant green, about 1 minute. Add remaining ¼ cup broth and cook, stirring constantly, until broth evaporates, 2 to 3 minutes. Spread evenly on serving dish.

NOTES FROM THE TEST KITCHEN

AN EARLY CHINESE IMPORT
When Chinese immigrants first set sail from the entrepôt of Hong Kong to San Francisco, labor contractors provided the sojourners with "all kinds of necessities and luxuries," according to Anne Mendelson, author of *Chow Chop Suey: Food and the Chinese American Journey* (2016). Among the bountiful provisions "were seeds for everything that you could grow in both Guangdong and California . . . and I'm sure that gai lan [Chinese broccoli] was among them," she said. Later, as the settlers spread to the suburbs, cooks without access to purveyors of Asian produce swapped broccoli for gai lan. (The two vegetables are different varieties of the same *Brassica oleracea* species.) Gai lan's broad, waxy leaves offer hints of minerality and bitterness and branch from smooth, fleshy stalks (mature specimens may have started to flower) that are prized for their crispness and delicate nuttiness.

5. Add ginger-garlic mixture to wok and cook, stirring constantly, until fragrant, about 30 seconds. Add beef and cook, stirring slowly but constantly, until no longer pink, about 2 minutes. Return stalks to wok and add oyster sauce mixture. Cook, stirring constantly, until sauce thickens, 30 to 60 seconds. Place mixture on top of leaves. Serve.

MEHSHI BAZAL

✓ **WHY THIS RECIPE WORKS** To easily separate the onion layers and render them pliable enough for wrapping around filling, we made partial cuts into whole onions before blanching them; the cuts allowed the boiling water to reach (and soften) the interiors. Some recipes for stuffed vegetables call for raw rice (medium-grain for its binding quality) soaked in water to prevent it from wicking away all the moisture from the meat and turning it tough. In our recipe, we gave the rice a quick dunk in the onion-blanching water for 5 minutes, which was enough to hydrate it and give us a tender filling.

Stuffed vegetables, or mehshi, of all kinds—squash, cabbage, Swiss chard, eggplant, and more—are standards throughout Lebanon, Syria, and Palestine. But it wasn't until speaking with New York–based Syrian Jewish cook Sheila Sutton that I learned of an impressive variant particular to Sephardic Jewish cuisine: mehshi bazal, or stuffed onions. In the Middle East, stuffed vegetables tend to be cooked in a savory tomato-based sauce, but these onions are simmered in pomegranate juice, pomegranate molasses, and Aleppo pepper. This braising medium reduces down to a fruity sweet-sour sauce that's enriched by the juices of a warm-spiced meat (and rice) filling. The sauce lacquers the onions with its ruby-hued shine.

The onions sounded delicious, and I was intrigued by the deviation from the typical (albeit tasty) tomatoey sauces I expected with Middle Eastern stuffed vegetables. I did a little more digging and found that Claudia Roden had written about stuffed onions cooked in a tamarind-based sauce that her Syrian Jewish friends (who now live in Egypt) make. My hunch was that cooking stuffed onions in a pomegranate-based sauce is linked to the Syrian Sephardic Jewish community that used to live in Aleppo. For my version, I wanted

MEHSHI BAZAL

to stay true to the Aleppo version. As Sutton noted, "The use of cherry and pomegranate is key to the cuisine of Aleppo." Onions, pomegranate, Aleppo pepper, and cherries—I had my game plan. It was time to get started.

My first challenge was finding a way to easily separate the onion layers and ensure that they were pliable enough to wrap around filling without tearing. I tried blanching, but the boiling water couldn't reach the interior, so the outside layers were mushy by the time the interiors were ready. Partially cutting the onions through just one side (but not halving them) did the trick. I slipped the whole onions into boiling water, turned them occasionally until the layers began to soften and separate, and then set them aside until they were cool enough to separate. Some of them tore, but that wasn't a problem—I needed only 15 layers.

For the filling, I went with ground beef, spices, and rice. For the meat, you could also use lamb or a mix of lamb and beef. For the spices, I settled on the warm, savory spice blend baharat bolstered with a little cinnamon for warmth. For the rice (medium-grain is best for its binding quality), I followed the traditional method of mixing it in raw, but the filling ended up a bit crunchy. Plus, it wicked away all the moisture from the meat, turning it tough. Instead, I gave the rice a quick dunk in the onion-blanching water for 5 minutes. This was enough time to hydrate the grains and allow the filling to remain tender.

With the filling settled, I turned to the sauce. I kept it all in one skillet to keep it easy and build flavor and whisked together pomegranate juice and pomegranate molasses (a perfect tart-sweet balance). I nestled the stuffed onions into the sauce in the skillet and sprinkled them with Aleppo pepper, which contributed a complex, raisin-like sweetness; tang; and slow-to-build heat with roasty notes. Once the meat-stuffed onions had simmered away for 25 minutes, I flipped them and cooked them uncovered until the glaze thickened and the onions were perfectly soft with a thoroughly cooked, tender interior.

Sprinkled with parsley and fresh pomegranate seeds for a pop of tartness, these sour, sweet, fruity, spicy gems were ready. They were perfect warm, but I liked them even better at room temperature.

—JOSEPH GITTER, *America's Test Kitchen Books*

Mehshi Bazal

SERVES 4 TO 6   TOTAL TIME: 2 HOURS

Look for large onions that are approximately 12 to 16 ounces each. If medium-grain rice is unavailable, short-grain rice can be substituted; do not use long-grain rice here. Serve the onions warm, or let them rest longer in step 5 and serve them at room temperature.

- 3 large red onions (about 1 pound each)
- ⅓ cup medium-grain rice, rinsed
- 12 ounces 85 percent lean ground beef
- ¾ teaspoon Baharat (page 160)
- 1 teaspoon table salt
- Pinch cinnamon
- 2 cups pomegranate juice
- 1 tablespoon pomegranate molasses
- ½ teaspoon ground dried Aleppo pepper
- ½ cup pomegranate seeds
- 2 tablespoons chopped fresh parsley

1. Bring 4 quarts of water to boil in Dutch oven. Trim ends of onions and arrange on cutting board with 1 cut side down. Starting at top of each onion with tip of knife at core, cut through 1 side. (Onion should remain intact; do not halve onion completely.) Add onions to boiling water and cook, turning occasionally, until onion layers begin to soften and separate, about 15 minutes.

2. Using slotted spoon, transfer onions to cutting board. Once cool enough to touch, gently separate first 7 layers from each onion. Some layers may tear slightly; only 15 layers are needed. Reserve remaining onion cores for another use.

3. Meanwhile, add rice to water left in pot and let sit, off heat, for 5 minutes; drain. Using your hands, gently knead rice, beef, baharat, salt, and cinnamon together in bowl until combined. Arrange 1 onion layer on counter with short side facing you. Place 2 tablespoons of rice mixture about ½ inch from bottom and roll up onion to form torpedo shape with tapered ends. Transfer stuffed onion to plate, seam side down. Repeat with 14 more onion layers and remaining rice mixture. (Stuffed onions can be refrigerated for up to 24 hours.)

4. Whisk pomegranate juice and pomegranate molasses together in 12-inch nonstick skillet. Evenly space 12 stuffed onions seam side down around edge of skillet and place three in center. Sprinkle with Aleppo pepper. Bring to vigorous simmer over medium-high heat. Cover, reduce heat to medium-low, and cook for 25 minutes.

5. Using 2 forks, carefully flip onions. Continue to cook, uncovered, until onions are softened and glaze has thickened slightly, 10 to 15 minutes. Off heat, let rest for at least 10 minutes. Gently turn onions to coat with glaze, then transfer to serving platter. Spoon glaze over top and sprinkle with pomegranate seeds and parsley. Serve.

WINE-BRAISED SPARERIBS WITH GARLIC AND ROSEMARY

✓ **WHY THIS RECIPE WORKS** To amp up the flavor, we slathered the ribs with an herb paste and refrigerated the ribs for at least an hour. We covered the ribs and braised them in a little white wine (meat side down) before flipping them and browning them meat side up, creating a crispy crust. We prefer the slightly smaller St. Louis–style ribs (each rack weighing 2½ to 3 pounds), which fit better side by side on a baking sheet for roasting (or on a backyard grill) because the bones and meat from the brisket section have been removed. They cook more quickly and evenly, too.

Italian cooks are masters at creating deeply flavorful food from simple, often humble, ingredients—and that includes ribs. This easy, straightforward recipe for oven-roasted ribs uses seasonings common to Italian pork recipes: garlic, rosemary, fennel seeds, and red pepper flakes. In the spirit of the best Italian cooking practices, these ingredients are artfully employed to enhance, and not cover up, the natural pork flavor of the ribs—it's a lighter (and, dare I say, more elegant) approach than smoky, saucy barbecued ribs. And it's easier and faster, too.

THREE STEPS TO AMAZING INDOOR RIBS

1. Pulse rosemary, olive oil, garlic, and seasonings in food processor to make paste.

2. Rub paste over ribs, arrange ribs meat side down in baking sheet, and refrigerate.

3. Add white wine to baking sheet, cover sheet with foil, and roast (flipping once).

Begin by making a superflavorful paste by buzzing fresh rosemary in the food processor with olive oil, garlic, fennel seeds, red pepper flakes, salt, and pepper: This mixture is your powerhouse marinade. Slather the paste onto two racks of St. Louis–style ribs and refrigerate the ribs for at least an hour so that the flavors can sink in. Then roast the ribs in the oven, meat side down and covered with foil, with some white wine; the wine brings brightness and creates steam to help the ribs cook efficiently. After 45 minutes, uncover the ribs, flip them, and let them roast for another 1¾ hours. During this last stretch of cooking, the ribs become tender and the caramelized garlic-herb paste forms an incredibly tasty crust. Plus, your kitchen smells fantastic!

These ribs do take a little bit of time, but it's mostly hands-off and the tasty reward is well worth it. They are also highly versatile—with white wine and steamed vegetables, they're elegant enough for company, yet they're easy enough to make for a night on the couch with a movie or your favorite television show.

—AMANDA LUCHTEL, *Cook's Country*

WINE-BRAISED SPARERIBS WITH GARLIC AND ROSEMARY

Wine-Braised Spareribs with Garlic and Rosemary

SERVES 4 TO 6

TOTAL TIME: 2¾ HOURS, PLUS 1 HOUR 20 MINUTES MARINATING AND RESTING

One ¾-ounce package of rosemary is enough to yield ½ cup of leaves.

- ½ cup fresh rosemary leaves, chopped coarse
- ⅓ cup extra-virgin olive oil
- 10 garlic cloves, smashed and peeled
- 1 tablespoon table salt
- 1 tablespoon fennel seeds
- 1 teaspoon red pepper flakes
- 1 teaspoon pepper
- 2 (2½- to 3-pound) racks St. Louis–style spareribs, trimmed
- 1 cup dry white wine

1. Combine rosemary, oil, garlic, salt, fennel seeds, pepper flakes, and pepper in food processor. Pulse mixture until finely chopped, 15 to 20 pulses, scraping down sides of bowl as necessary.

2. Rub ribs evenly with paste and place meat side down in rimmed baking sheet. Cover sheet with plastic wrap and refrigerate for at least 1 hour or up to 24 hours.

3. Adjust oven rack to upper-middle position and heat oven to 350 degrees. Add wine to sheet with ribs. Cover sheet tightly with aluminum foil. Roast for 45 minutes. Remove foil and flip ribs meat side up. Continue to roast, uncovered, until meat is tender and well browned, about 1¾ hours longer.

4. Let ribs rest for 20 minutes. Transfer ribs to cutting board and slice racks between ribs. Serve.

NOTES FROM THE TEST KITCHEN

ST. LOUIS–STYLE SPARERIBS

Cut from near the belly of the pig, regular spareribs include the rib bones, the meat between them, and the brisket bone near the pig's chest. We prefer the slightly smaller St. Louis–style ribs (each rack weighs 2½ to 3 pounds), which fit better side by side on a baking sheet for roasting (or on a backyard grill) because the bones and meat from the brisket section have been removed. They cook more quickly and evenly, too.

SISIG WITH GARLIC FRIED RICE

✔ **WHY THIS RECIPE WORKS** Sisig is a traditional Filipino bar snack with sharp flavors and contrasting textures. Marinating slabs of pork belly and pork butt in a mixture of cane vinegar and soy sauce lent brightness to the rich meat. We grilled the pork to add smokiness and light char before chopping it and combining it with a mixture of mayonnaise, chiles, and onions. Finally, a quick stint in a furiously hot cast-iron skillet crisped the bits of pork while the garnish of fresh eggs, chicharrones, and more fresh onion and chile rounded out the dish. To make the garlic rice—a typical Filipino side dish—we gently toasted chopped garlic in oil until it was golden brown. Then we added cold cooked rice to the skillet and stirred to infuse it with the garlic-flavored oil as it heated through and to disperse the chopped garlic throughout.

Bobby Punla gathers his ingredients on a long butcher block table and begins thinly slicing scallions and dicing red onions with perfect precision. Behind him, Jan Dela Paz fans the coals in a hibachi grill to a bright-orange glow. When the coals are just right, he grills slabs of marinated pork belly and butt until they're lightly charred and crisp at the edges. Jan wafts the smoke from the grill up to his face, inhales deeply, and says, "That's what the Philippine streets smell like."

The two men are preparing sisig, a traditional Filipino dish of chopped pork, onions, and chiles made sour with vinegar or calamansi juice and served on a searing-hot cast-iron platter. Sisig is what's known in the Philippines as a pulutan, or bar snack, usually consumed with beer or other alcoholic beverages.

The concept of sisig as a sour salad has existed in the Philippines since the 1700s. Through the years, the dish evolved to use meat from boiled pigs' heads, which in the early 1970s often went unused in the mess halls and commissaries at Clark Air Base in Angeles City, Philippines. By 1974, Lucia Cunanan was serving the now-popular grilled version at Aling Lucing's Sisig in Angeles City, earning her the informal title of the Sisig Queen.

Bobby and Jan met when they were both cooks at Ramen Shop in Oakland, California. The two bonded over their shared Filipino heritage. Bobby is an American-born Filipino, and Jan was born and raised in Manila. Bobby confesses, "It wasn't until I met [Jan] that I realized I didn't know anything about my roots. I knew more about Japanese food, Korean food. I knew how to cook French, Italian. I didn't really know anything about my own culture. All I really knew how to make was, like, adobo and lumpia. It was a depressing realization."

In 2017, with the encouragement and support of the owners of Ramen Shop, the two cooks decided they wanted to spread awareness of Filipino food, and they established Likha as a pop-up restaurant. After a successful start, they eventually landed an 18-month stint cooking their brand of Filipino food, which they describe as California Filipino, at an Oakland sports bar from mid-2018 to December 2019.

"One of the reasons we did sisig at the pop-up was because we knew that no one knew Filipino food at the time, and any time you hear and smell a sizzling plate of pork walk by you, you're gonna look and want to order it. It was our way to flex," says Bobby. He explains that the hot platter actually serves an additional, and more important, purpose of rendering the fat and crisping the bits of pork.

Prior to grilling the meat, Bobby and Jan marinate it in a mixture of cane vinegar, soy sauce, garlic and onion powders, and gochugaru. "The marinade is about 60 percent vinegar to 40 percent soy sauce to give it a nice tang, as opposed to a soy-saucy caramel flavor," Jan says. They use garlic and onion powders in the marinade because fresh garlic and onions would burn on the grill.

Jan makes the garlic fried rice by frying finely chopped garlic until it's golden brown and then quickly straining it through a sieve set over a bowl to reserve the garlic-flavored oil. He tosses cooked jasmine rice in a bowl with some of the garlic oil, a few heaping spoonfuls of the crisp fried garlic, and a hearty pinch of salt. By comparison, the homestyle version of garlic fried rice is made by browning the garlic in a Filipino-style skillet and then adding the rice and stirring to cook it briefly and distribute the garlic.

Bobby combines the chopped pork with homemade mayonnaise, calamansi juice, onions, and chiles. He explains, "There are so many versions of sisig, because, you know, 7,000 [Philippine] islands, 7,000 different ways of making it. Some are just grilled; some they don't use the sizzle platter; some are just the vinegar marinade; some are deep-fried; some are 'wet,' which

we're doing when we cover it in mayonnaise." Jan chimes in to add, "The mayonnaise creates another layer of flavor and helps form a crust."

The two approach the sizzle platter and take turns quickly building the dish with the various ingredients. Their movements seem telepathic as they anticipate what's needed next, where the other is standing, and which way to pass ingredients. One spreads the pork in an even layer on the hot platter as it immediately begins to smoke and hiss. The other begins layering on the onions, scallions, and chiles. Finally, they crack an egg on top—a common addition—and sprinkle the sisig with crumbled chicharrones.

While Likha is currently on hiatus, Bobby and Jan reflect on their run serving Filipino food to the sports bar clientele. In the beginning, the experience pushed them to cook more traditional bar food, such as chicken wings, than they would have preferred. But as the months went on, they found that people were increasingly coming for their Filipino food: their kare-kare (oxtail and peanut stew), their sisig. Bobby says, "In the beginning we weren't that confident how people would receive Filipino food, but they eventually came out searching for it. They wanted it."

—BRYAN ROOF, *Cook's Country*

Sisig

SERVES 4

TOTAL TIME: 1¾ HOURS, PLUS 12 HOURS MARINATING

This recipe was developed with Datu Puti cane vinegar, but you can use distilled or cider vinegar, if desired. Maggi liquid seasoning can be used in place of the Knorr liquid seasoning. When grilling the pork, you should expect flare-ups to occur, so do not walk away

---

NOTES FROM THE TEST KITCHEN

CALAMANSI: SMALL CITRUS WITH BIG FLAVOR

Cherry-size calamansi (aka calamondin) pack a sour punch. They are grown in Florida and California and can be found in some Asian markets.

SISIG WITH GARLIC FRIED RICE

from the grill. Adding the pork to the preheated cast-iron skillet in step 5 will create a decent amount of smoke. Turn on your exhaust fan or crack open a window prior to cooking. This dish is traditionally made with calamansi juice and served with calamansi halves as a garnish. If you're able to find them, use them in place of the lemon juice and lemon wedges. Serve with Garlic Fried Rice (recipe follows).

½ cup cane vinegar

⅓ cup soy sauce

1½ tablespoons Knorr liquid seasoning, divided

4 teaspoons granulated garlic

4 teaspoons onion powder

2 teaspoons gochugaru

2 teaspoons kosher salt

1¼ pounds skinless pork belly, sliced ¼ to ½ inch thick

1 pound boneless pork butt roast, sliced ¼ to ½ inch thick

½ cup diced red onion, divided

6 tablespoons mayonnaise

1 serrano chile, stemmed and sliced into thin rings, divided

1½ tablespoons lemon juice, plus lemon wedges for serving

3 garlic cloves, minced

3 large eggs

3 scallions, sliced thin

½ cup coarsely broken chicharrones (½- to ¾-inch pieces)

1. Whisk vinegar, soy sauce, 1 tablespoon liquid seasoning, granulated garlic, onion powder, gochugaru, and salt together in large bowl. Add pork belly and butt and toss to thoroughly combine. Transfer pork and any excess marinade to large zipper-lock bag; seal bag; and refrigerate for at least 12 hours or up to 2 days, turning occasionally.

2A. FOR A CHARCOAL GRILL: Open bottom vent completely. Light large chimney starter filled with charcoal briquettes (6 quarts). When top coals are partially covered with ash, pour evenly over half of grill. Set cooking grate in place, cover, and open lid vent completely. Heat grill until hot, about 5 minutes. Clean and oil grate.

2B. FOR A GAS GRILL: Turn all burners to high; cover; and heat grill until hot, about 15 minutes. Turn primary burner to medium-high and turn off other burner(s).

3. Clean and oil cooking grate. Working with half of pork, cook over hotter side of grill until browned, lightly charred, and just cooked through, about 4 minutes per side if using charcoal or 6 minutes per side if using gas, moving pork to cooler side of grill as flare-ups occur. Transfer pork to rimmed baking sheet. Repeat with remaining pork.

4. Once pork is cool enough to handle, cut into approximate ¼- to ½-inch pieces. Combine pork, ¼ cup onion, mayonnaise, half of serrano, lemon juice, garlic, and remaining 1½ teaspoons liquid seasoning in bowl. Crack eggs into 3 separate ramekins or small bowls. Heat 12-inch cast-iron skillet over high heat until very hot, about 10 minutes.

5. Working quickly, add pork mixture to hot skillet, spread into even layer, and make 3 shallow wells for eggs. Sprinkle scallions and remaining ¼ cup onion evenly over pork mixture. Add 1 egg to each well. Sprinkle chicharrones and remaining serrano over top. Garnish with lemon wedges. Bring to table while sizzling. Just before serving, stir to incorporate eggs.

Garlic Fried Rice

SERVES 4 TOTAL TIME: 20 MINUTES

One-and-a-half cups of raw jasmine rice cooked with 2¼ cups of water will yield 4½ cups of cooked rice. Make sure that the rice is cold before frying; otherwise, it can turn gummy. We run the cooled rice under water to break up the clumps so that it's easier to manage in the skillet. Be sure to let the excess water drain off the rice for at least 5 minutes before transferring it to the skillet. Serve this with Sisig.

4½ cups cooked jasmine rice, cold

3 tablespoons vegetable oil

8 garlic cloves, chopped fine

1 teaspoon kosher salt

1 scallion, sliced thin

1. Transfer rice to fine-mesh strainer. Place rice under cold running water and break up clumps with your hands. Let drain for 5 minutes.

2. Combine oil and garlic in 12-inch nonstick skillet. Cook over medium heat until garlic turns golden brown, 3 to 5 minutes. Add rice and salt and cook, stirring frequently, until garlic is evenly distributed throughout rice, about 2 minutes. Off heat, season with salt to taste. Transfer to dish, sprinkle with scallion, and serve.

FOUR TASTE MAKERS

These ingredients give this version of sisig its signature flavor.

1. CHICHARRONES These crunchy fried pork skins are great right out of the bag or crumbled atop dishes (such as sisig or mac and cheese) as a garnish.

2. CANE VINEGAR A lightly sweet vinegar made from sugarcane syrup with similar acidity to distilled and cider vinegars. Use it any time you would use those vinegars.

3. KNORR LIQUID SEASONING This supersavory seasoning tastes a bit like sweet, beefy soy sauce and is popular in Filipino cooking. Add it to marinades, soups, and stir-fries, or use it as a condiment for meat, vegetables, or popcorn.

4. GOCHUGARU These relatively mild Korean pepper flakes provide depth and tartness; they are similar to Aleppo pepper flakes and are great anytime you want complex chile flavor without a big burn.

KIMCHI AND HAM STEAK FRIED RICE

WHY THIS RECIPE WORKS There are endless variations of the Korean comfort food kimchi bokkeumbap, but they all showcase kimchi's fermented umami goodness, often using its juices in the sauce. For our take we did just that, rounding it out with sweet and funky gochujang. Leftover rice (arguably the best way to use it up) soaked up the deliciously pungent liquid, and ham steak nuggets added surprise salty, savory bites. We made sure not to stir the rice while it was cooking so that it would crisp up on the bottom.

Developing recipes for our *Five-Ingredient Dinners* cookbook really challenged my creativity. I learned a lot about how to get the most out of a single ingredient and also found multiple ways to utilize a single ingredient (such as adding the juice from a jar of pepperoncini). We also relied on store-bought flavor bombs (Thai curry paste, gochujang, pesto, etc.).

One of my favorite recipes in the book is my Kimchi and Ham Steak Fried Rice. Fried rice is versatile, quick to make, and delicious. While it can also be a great way to clear out the refrigerator—eggs, proteins, and vegetables are all good additions—my goal was to figure out how to make the most of the few ingredients I was able to use.

I started with one of the most valued ingredients in the book—scallions. Their beauty is that they're a two-for-one deal. The whites are more strongly flavored than the greens, so they can be sautéed without falling flat. I used the whites in the base for the rice and threw the greens, which provided both a pop of color and a bite full of mild oniony goodness, in at the end.

Next up was the protein. This recipe was assigned to the "Meaty Meals" chapter, so ingredients such as tofu were out of the question. Chicken, beef, and pork were great options, but they would require additional ingredients to deliver more flavor. So then I thought, "What about ham steak?" It's an incredibly convenient piece of meat when you don't have the time to make an entire ham. I diced it into tiny pieces and fried them up in the skillet. These little crispy, salty, meaty bits sprinkled throughout the fried rice were a delight to eat.

Now it was time to introduce a flavor powerhouse: gochujang. It's savory, spicy, and slightly sweet due to the natural sweetness from the starch of cooked rice, making it the perfect multiple-role-playing ingredient. Besides providing supercharged flavor, it also gave the dish a stunning neon-red hue. A little water helped thin the paste so that it would evenly coat all the other components of the dish.

Finally, the kimchi. Kimchi, a spicy fermented vegetable (I used the cabbage kind), is another ingredient that packed a flavor punch. Not only did it add a briny crunch but it also helped bulk up the dish. And remember when I mentioned cross-utilizing ingredients? The kimchi is a perfect example: A portion of the liquid it's packed in goes into the skillet. Boom.

I'm very proud of this recipe. When combined, its five ingredients taste like 50. I hope you enjoy it as much as I do, especially those crispy ham bits!

—SAMANTHA BLOCK, *America's Test Kitchen Books*

Kimchi and Ham Steak Fried Rice

SERVES 4 TOTAL TIME: 30 MINUTES

Kimchi bokkeumbap is typically made with leftover short-grain white rice (recipe follows), but any kind of leftover rice will do. In our *Five-Ingredient Dinners* cookbook, where this recipe originated, water and pantry staples such as salt, pepper, and oil are not counted as an ingredient.

 2 tablespoons vegetable oil
 1 pound ham steak, cut into ¼-inch pieces
 1¼ cups cabbage kimchi, drained with ¼ cup juice reserved, kimchi cut into 1-inch pieces
 3 tablespoons gochujang paste or sauce
 6 scallions, white and green parts separated and sliced thin on bias
 2 tablespoons water
 ¼ teaspoon pepper
 4 cups cooked rice (preferably short-grain)

1. Heat vegetable oil in 12-inch nonstick skillet over medium-high heat until just smoking. Add ham and cook, stirring frequently, until beginning to brown, 6 to 8 minutes. Stir in kimchi and reserved juice, gochujang, scallion whites, water, and pepper. Fold in rice until well combined.

2. Firmly press into compact, even layer. Cover and cook, without stirring, until rice begins to crisp, about 2 minutes. Uncover; reduce heat to medium; and continue to cook until bottom of rice is golden brown, 4 to 6 minutes. Season with salt and pepper to taste, sprinkle with scallion greens, and serve.

Short-Grain White Rice

SERVES 4 TO 6 (MAKES ABOUT 4 CUPS)

 1½ cups short-grain white rice
 1½ cups water
 ½ teaspoon table salt

Combine all ingredients in medium saucepan and bring to boil over high heat. Reduce heat to low, cover, and simmer for 7 minutes. Let sit off heat for 15 minutes. Serve. (Rice can be refrigerated for up to 3 days.)

HONEY-GLAZED PORK SHOULDER

✔ WHY THIS RECIPE WORKS A Boston butt (or pork butt) was a good starting point for this recipe since it is relatively inexpensive and has plenty of fat and connective tissue that—with low, slow cooking—melt out as the meat becomes tender and silky. Coating the roast in honey before roasting resulted in an overcaramelized (read: burnt) roast, no matter how low of an oven temperature we used. Instead, we stirred together a spiced honey with spicy red pepper flakes and aromatic five-spice powder. We waited to brush this onto the pork until the final half-hour of cooking, which created a juicy roast with a beautiful brown crust and a shiny honey glaze. To make it even better, we topped the finished roast with an extra layer of spiced honey and saved some to drizzle over the sliced meat. This allowed all the pork, even the interior pieces, to be saturated with that bold, sweet honey flavor.

Pork and sugar play well together (think maple bacon, brown sugar–glazed ham, and sticky ribs). As an unapologetic fan of all things swine (it's a bit of a joke among my coworkers), I wanted to enhance a holiday-worthy pork roast with fruity, floral honey.

I started with a roast from the pig's shoulder called a Boston butt (or pork butt), which I think of as the darling of the meat department. It's relatively inexpensive and has plenty of fat and connective tissue that—with low, slow cooking—melt out as the meat becomes tender and silky. It's the cut that most people, including us here in the test kitchen, use for pulled pork.

For the honey, I bought every type I found in local markets: clover, wildflower, orange blossom, buckwheat, and alfalfa. Tasted plain and brushed onto some simple roasted pork, they were all fine here save one: The flavor of the buckwheat honey was too strong and dominant. (I ultimately developed the recipe with clover honey, which is the most common in supermarkets.)

To merge the meat with the sweet, I coated three pork butts with honey at different points: before refrigerating overnight, before roasting, and halfway through cooking. I roasted them in a moderate 325-degree oven to 190 degrees, the sweet spot for ultramoist but still sliceable pork butt (any higher and it shreds). But all the roasts emerged with burnt exteriors. Honey's high sugar content caused it—in this case—to caramelize way too quickly.

The roast with honey brushed on halfway through cooking was the closest to edible, so I forged on with that method. I tried lowering the oven temperature to 250 degrees, but the butt took a solid 8 hours to become tender, and the exterior was still straddling the line between deeply caramelized and burnt. I also tried covering the pork with aluminum foil as it roasted, but it stuck to the honey and made a mess.

And then it struck me: Why not add the honey even later? For my next test, I roasted a pork butt with only salt until it was almost done, which took about 5 hours. Then I brushed it with honey for the final half-hour of cooking. Finally I had a juicy roast with a beautiful brown crust and a shiny honey glaze. Now, onto the last details.

An overnight rub of kosher salt and brown sugar (to double down on the honey's sweetness) seasoned the meat throughout. The rub had the added benefit of drying out the exterior of the roast, which created a clingy surface for the honey to adhere to. To provide depth and complexity to the honey slather, I added red pepper flakes for heat, soy sauce for rich salinity, aromatic five-spice powder to counterbalance the richness of the succulent meat, and red wine vinegar for brightness. These flavors enhanced, rather than overshadowed, the honey's sweetness.

My tasters were fighting over the honey-lacquered, crispy edges of the pork. So for a final test, I doubled the amount of spiced honey, gave the roast a light brush with

it after resting, and saved some to drizzle over the meat after slicing. This allowed all the pork, even the interior pieces, to be saturated with that bold, sweet honey flavor.

—MORGAN BOLLING, *Cook's Country*

Honey-Glazed Pork Shoulder

SERVES 8 TO 10

TOTAL TIME: 5¾ HOURS, PLUS 13 HOURS SALTING AND RESTING

Plan ahead: The roast must be seasoned at least 12 hours before cooking. We developed this recipe with clover honey.

- 3 tablespoons kosher salt
- 3 tablespoons packed light brown sugar
- 1 (6- to 7-pound) bone-in pork butt roast with fat cap
- ½ cup honey
- 1½ tablespoons soy sauce
- 2 teaspoons red wine vinegar
- ¾ teaspoon red pepper flakes
- ¼ teaspoon five-spice powder

1. Combine salt and sugar in bowl. Using sharp knife, cut 1-inch crosshatch pattern about ¼ inch deep in fat cap of roast, being careful not to cut into meat. Place roast on 2 large sheets of plastic wrap and rub salt mixture over entire roast and into slits. Wrap roast tightly with plastic. Place on large plate and refrigerate for 12 to 24 hours.

2. Adjust oven rack to lowest position and heat oven to 325 degrees. Line rimmed baking sheet with aluminum foil and set wire rack in prepared sheet. Unwrap roast and place on rack. Cover sheet tightly with foil. Transfer to oven and cook for 2 hours. Remove foil and continue to cook until meat registers 180 degrees in several places, 2½ to 3½ hours longer.

3. Combine honey, soy sauce, vinegar, pepper flakes, and five-spice powder in bowl. Remove roast from oven. Brush top and sides of roast with ¼ cup honey mixture (set aside remainder). Return roast to oven and continue to cook until meat registers 190 degrees and fork slips easily in and out of meat, 30 to 45 minutes longer. Transfer roast to carving board and let rest for 1 hour.

4. Brush pork with 2 tablespoons reserved honey mixture. Using boning or paring knife, cut around inverted T-shaped bone until it can be pulled free and removed from roast (use clean dish towel to grasp bone if necessary). Using serrated knife, slice roast ½ inch thick. Drizzle with remaining honey mixture and serve.

NOTES FROM THE TEST KITCHEN

BONE REMOVAL

1. CUT AROUND BONE: Using boning knife, carefully separate bone from meat.

2. REMOVE BONE: Grasp bone (with clean dish towel if bone is hot) and pull.

PAN-SEARED THICK-CUT, BONE-IN PORK CHOPS

✓ **WHY THIS RECIPE WORKS** Achieving deeply browned, juicy bone-in pork chops starts with choosing the right chop: We settled on 1½-inch-thick rib chops, which were thick enough to build up a browned exterior before cooking through. We started the chops in a cold (not preheated) nonstick skillet over high heat and flipped them every 2 minutes so that the meat's temperature increased gradually, allowing a crust to build up on the outside without overcooking the interior. Starting the chops in a cold pan helped the meat heat up slowly and evenly, and using a nonstick pan meant that no oil was necessary. Starting over high heat drove off moisture and prevented the chops from steaming, and lowering the heat to medium encouraged browning without smoking. Slicing the chops and sprinkling with coarse or flake sea salt ensured that they were well seasoned.

In 2020, my former colleague Andrew Janjigian developed a recipe that was nothing short of game-changing: splatterless, smokeless, perfectly pan-seared steaks. Unlike the reverse-sear method, his technique doesn't even require an oven: just a dry pan on the stovetop, in which the steaks are flipped frequently during cooking. In minutes, you end up with beautifully browned steaks with rosy interiors and no mess to boot. This "cold-sear" method, as we've come to call it at *Cook's Illustrated*, is so simple yet foolproof that I was eager to apply it to other cuts of meat, and I wondered if it might be particularly beneficial for leaner cuts that are prone to drying out during a traditional sear. Enter: pork chops. Through the cold-sear method, I hoped to achieve chops with even, flavorful browning and juicy, tender interiors, a company-worthy dish that I could enjoy with guests without having to fuss over the mess it left behind on my stovetop.

For this recipe, I quickly settled on bone-in rib chops, which are a tender and flavorful cut that features one large eye of loin muscle surrounded by fat. The bone helps insulate the meat, keeping it juicier (and it contains superflavorful bits to gnaw on). I opted for thicker, 1½-inch chops, which would both make for a more impressive presentation and cook through more slowly than standard 1-inch chops, allowing for more time to build up a browned crust using the cold-sear method. The added heft from the extra-thick chops also helped avoid buckling, or the tightening of the chops' outer band of connective tissue, which can cause the chops to curl and sear unevenly.

The cold sear begins with a dry, nonpreheated 12-inch nonstick (or carbon-steel) skillet. Starting the chops in a cold pan allows them to heat up gradually and evenly, which prevents the meat directly below the surface from overcooking. Using nonstick allowed me to skip adding oil to the pan, which greatly reduces splatter and smoke, and the cold start avoids the safety hazard of overheating nonstick cookware. I placed two large chops (which would be plenty to serve four once sliced) in the skillet, maximizing space by arranging them so that the wider end of one chop was next to the narrower end of the other, and then set the pan over a burner set to high heat. I cooked the chops for 2 minutes on each side, at which point no real browning had taken place, and then adjusted the heat to medium (which kept the skillet hot enough to continue browning but not so hot that the fat smoked) and continued to flip the chops every 2 minutes until they were deeply browned and reached an internal temperature of 140 degrees. Regular flipping is the key to the technique: It evenly heats both sides of the chop at (almost) the same time, cooking the chop faster and more evenly than a traditional uninterrupted sear. And, as long as the pan is hot enough, the protein will still develop a rich, mahogany crust—it just happens gradually, like multiple coats of paint applied to a wall.

I let the chops rest for 5 minutes after cooking and then carved them off the bone, slicing the meat ½ inch thick. The chops' browned crusts and tender, juicy interiors make for an impressive main course when served with just a sprinkle of sea salt, but I also wanted to develop a couple sauces to dress them up even more for entertaining. Using flavors that naturally pair with pork, I devised two options: a sweet, spicy, and creamy apple-mustard sauce and a glossy maple agrodolce. Intensely flavored, viscous enough to cling to the meat, and quick to make, either makes for a dazzling finishing touch.

—ANNIE PETITO, *Cook's Illustrated*

PAN-SEARED THICK-CUT, BONE-IN PORK CHOPS

SHOPPING FOR RIB CHOPS

Bone-in rib chops may be labeled as rib cut, end cut, or center cut. To be sure that you are purchasing the correct chop, look for ones that feature one large eye of loin muscle. Be sure to seek out 1½-inch-thick chops for this recipe; the extra weight allows for longer cooking and better browning.

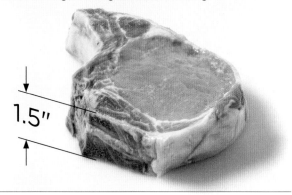

1.5"

Pan-Seared Thick-Cut, Bone-In Pork Chops

SERVES 4   TOTAL TIME: 30 MINUTES

If you have time, salt the chops for at least 1 hour or up to 24 hours before cooking: Sprinkle each chop with 1½ teaspoons of Diamond Crystal Kosher Salt (if using Morton, which is denser, use only 1⅛ teaspoons), refrigerate them, and pat them dry with paper towels before cooking. If the pork is enhanced (injected with a salt solution), do not salt the chops ahead. Make sure to include the bones when serving; they're great for nibbling. The chops can be served plain or with one of our sauces (recipes follow).

- 2 **(14- to 16-ounce) bone-in pork rib chops, 1½ inches thick, trimmed**
- ½ **teaspoon pepper**

1. Pat chops dry with paper towels and sprinkle both sides with pepper. Place chops 1 inch apart in cold 12-inch nonstick or carbon-steel skillet, arranging so narrow part of 1 chop is opposite wider part of second. Place skillet over high heat and cook chops for 2 minutes. Flip chops and continue to cook on second side 2 minutes longer. (Neither side of chops will be browned at this point.)

2. Flip chops; reduce heat to medium; and continue to cook, flipping chops every 2 minutes, until exterior is well browned and meat registers 140 degrees, 10 to 15 minutes longer. (Chops should be sizzling; if not, increase heat slightly. Reduce heat if skillet starts to smoke.)

3. Transfer chops to carving board and let rest for 5 minutes. Carve meat from bone and slice ½ inch thick. (When carving chops, meat at tapered end near bone may retain slightly pink hue despite being cooked.) Season meat with coarse or flake sea salt to taste. Serve with bones.

Creamy Apple-Mustard Sauce

MAKES ABOUT ½ CUP   TOTAL TIME: 10 MINUTES

- ¼ **cup whole-grain mustard**
- 3 **tablespoons unsweetened applesauce**
- 2 **tablespoons Dijon mustard**
- 4 **teaspoons cider vinegar**
- 1 **tablespoon honey**
- 1 **tablespoon minced fresh chives (optional)**
- ¼ **teaspoon table salt**

Stir all ingredients (including chives, if using) in bowl until combined.

Maple Agrodolce

MAKES ABOUT ⅓ CUP   TOTAL TIME: 20 MINUTES

- ¼ **cup balsamic vinegar**
- 2 **tablespoons maple syrup**
- 2 **tablespoons minced shallot**
- 2 **tablespoons chopped golden raisins**
  Pinch red pepper flakes
  Pinch table salt

Bring all ingredients to boil in small saucepan over medium heat. Reduce heat to low and simmer until reduced and slightly thickened, 8 to 10 minutes (sauce will continue to thicken as it cools). Cover to keep warm until ready to serve.

MULTICOOKER ABGOOSHT (PERSIAN LAMB AND CHICKPEA STEW)

✓ **WHY THIS RECIPE WORKS** Dating back centuries, abgoosht is a rustic Persian stew consisting of lamb cooked with chickpeas, potatoes, fresh tomato, and onion. Enhanced with warm spices such as turmeric and cinnamon, abgoosht gets its unique flavor from limu omani. The dried Persian limes deliver sweetness, sourness, and muskiness. Once cooked, the solids are mashed into a savory paste, which is served alongside the tart, meaty broth. The lamb mash is served with bread and adorned with any number of toppings, including fresh herbs, scallions, sliced radishes, and raw onion.

Najmieh Batmanglij smiled and relaxed into her chair when asked about abgoosht. The iconic Iranian American cookbook author and culinary instructor was carried back to her childhood home in old Tehran, where her family had a special custom on the 14th of each month, the time of the ecclesiastical full moon. To honor the day, which they considered ideal for praying, feasting, rituals, and being kind, her parents and volunteer helpers would prepare "a large cauldron" of the wholesome meal—a coarse meat, bean, and vegetable paste and its savory-tart cooking broth; sangak (a type of flatbread); and fragrant herbs—to offer as alms. "[It] was an open house for friends and family," Batmanglij said. "Without invitation, they knew they could come and have a bowl of soup, goosht koobideh [meat paste], bread, and all the trimmings."

Abgoosht has been prepared throughout Iran's mountains and fertile valleys for centuries, with the earliest documentation seen in the work of the 14th-century Persian poet Bos'haq, who penned verses exclusively about food and cooking.

One of the oldest iterations is still widely prepared today. It consists of a fatty, bony cut of lamb—shank and shoulder are common—simmered in water ("ab" translates as "water"; "goosht," "meat") with dried chickpeas, potatoes, onion, fresh tomato, and warm spices. The broth gets a distinctive musky tang from limu omani (dried limes) that are steeped whole in the pot.

Once the lamb is falling off the bone and the chickpeas and vegetables are meltingly soft, the broth is strained off for serving and the solids are pounded to a paste, either by the cook with a potato masher or the back of a large spoon or by diners with individual pestles and bowls. Mashing distributes the flavors throughout the paste and historically was a way to stretch animal protein and ensure that each guest received an equal portion.

The lightly spiced mash is presented with the savory-tart broth and sabzi khordan, the fresh, verdant platter of palate-cleansing herbs and aromatics offered with most Persian meals. Sangak, a stone-baked flatbread, must also be on the table (lavash, which is soft, works well, too): Break some up and stir it into the broth or sip the broth on its own, and then use the sangak as a base for customized mouthfuls of meat paste and herbs. "The idea," said Batmanglij, "is to make your own sandwich with all the goodies."

While the earliest versions of abgoosht bubbled on a hearth for 10 to 15 hours in a ceramic or clay pot called a dizi ("dizi" also refers to modern Iranian teahouses that exclusively serve abgoosht), for decades many home cooks have been relying on the increased speed of a pressure cooker. As the technology continues to advance, a multicooker has become the next logical vessel.

Indeed, America's Test Kitchen cookbook editor Emily Rahravan grew up eating abgoosht prepared by her father Cyroos, who agrees that the tool is ideal for turning the meat, chickpeas, and vegetables tender quickly and at once. His recipe, which we worked from, is as simple as loading all the ingredients into the cooker. Thin lamb shoulder chops quickly soften, and the flavorful, moderately fatty meat is easy to pull off the bone for mashing. Soaked dried chickpeas, peeled and quartered Yukon Gold potatoes, a yellow onion, and fresh tomatoes bolstered with a spoonful of tomato paste also go in, along with a couple limu omani, ground turmeric, and half a cinnamon stick.

After pouring in enough water to cover the ingredients, cook the stew under pressure for just 40 minutes before straining out the solids for mashing. A pinch of saffron gives the steaming, velvety broth—now infused with lime, spices, and meaty richness—an amber glow. Served with stacks of flatbread and an enticing platter of fresh mint, dill, and/or tarragon; grassy sliced scallions; slivers of sharp red onion; and thinly sliced red radishes, you have a delicious spread for the entire family (and then some).

—SARAH EWALD WITH BECKY HAYS, *Cook's Illustrated*

MULTICOOKER ABGOOSHT (PERSIAN LAMB AND CHICKPEA STEW)

Multicooker Abgoosht (Persian Lamb and Chickpea Stew)

SERVES 6   TOTAL TIME: 2 HOURS, PLUS 8 HOURS BRINING

This recipe requires soaking the chickpeas for at least 8 hours. Limu omani, also known as black limes, are dried limes that can be found at Middle Eastern markets or online; if you can't find them, substitute 2 tablespoons of fresh lime juice. This dish can also be cooked in a stovetop pressure cooker. If cooking on the stovetop, place the cooker over medium-high heat when instructed to use the "highest sauté function." Sip the broth on its own or stir in pieces of the bread. Use pieces of the bread to scoop up the meat paste, and top the paste with herbs, scallions, radishes, and onion before eating.

1½   tablespoons table salt for brining
8   ounces (1¼ cups) dried chickpeas, picked over and rinsed
2   pounds lamb shoulder chops (blade or round bone), ¾ to 1 inch thick, trimmed
1   pound Yukon Gold potatoes, peeled and quartered
2   tomatoes, cored and quartered
1   yellow onion, quartered
2   limu omani
1   tablespoon tomato paste
2   garlic cloves, lightly crushed and peeled
2   teaspoons table salt
1   teaspoon pepper
1   teaspoon ground turmeric
½   cinnamon stick
    Pinch saffron threads
3   cups fresh dill, mint, and/or tarragon leaves
4   scallions, sliced thin
8   radishes, trimmed and sliced thin
1   small red onion, halved and sliced thin
    Sangak or lavash

1. Dissolve 1½ tablespoons salt in 2 quarts cold water in large container. Add chickpeas and soak at room temperature for at least 8 hours or up to 24 hours. Drain and rinse well.

2. Add chickpeas, 7 cups water, lamb, potatoes, tomatoes, yellow onion, limu omani, tomato paste, garlic, salt, pepper, turmeric, and cinnamon stick to multicooker. Lock lid into place and close pressure-release valve. Select high pressure-cook function and cook for 40 minutes. Turn off multicooker and let pressure release naturally for 15 minutes. Quick-release any remaining pressure, then carefully remove lid, allowing steam to escape away from you.

3. Using slotted spoon, transfer large pieces of lamb and vegetables to large bowl. Strain broth through fine-mesh strainer into separate large bowl or container; discard bones, limu omani, and cinnamon stick. Transfer strained solids to bowl with lamb and vegetables.

4. Return broth to pot. Using highest sauté function, bring broth to simmer, then turn off multicooker. Stir in saffron and let steep for 5 minutes. Season with salt and pepper to taste.

5. Using potato masher, gently mash lamb mixture until meat is finely shredded and chickpeas and vegetables are mostly smooth. Season with salt and pepper to taste and transfer to shallow serving bowl. Ladle broth into individual serving bowls and serve with lamb mixture, fresh herbs, scallions, radishes, red onion, and sangak.

FISHERMAN'S PIE

CHAPTER 6

POULTRY AND SEAFOOD

TUNISIAN TAJINE WITH WHITE BEANS

TUNISIAN TAJINE WITH WHITE BEANS

Ⓥ WHY THIS RECIPE WORKS Like a frittata or a Spanish tortilla, these eggs are chock-full, prepared with a wide variety of hearty proteins, herbs, and spices. In Tunisia, tajine is now commonly cooked in a baking dish; for our version, we chose a skillet to limit the equipment needed. We included white beans, which became highly flavorful when cooked with spices and tomato paste, and tender pieces of sautéed chicken thighs. We stirred bread crumbs into the eggs to absorb extra moisture and set the tajine's texture. Nuggets of mild Monterey Jack cheese melted into satisfying pools on the surface. We baked the stuffed skillet just until the eggs were set and browned.

The word "tagine"—or "tajine," as spelled in Tunisia—tells a culinary story of history and custom. The classic earthenware vessel used to cook myriad North African dishes, often eponymous stews, has a unique conical shape that creates moist, delicious results. In Tunisia, the word "tajine" is also the name of a specific satiating egg dish that was originally made in the same pot, despite looking nothing like a stew. Similar to a Spanish tortilla or Italian frittata, these eggs are chock-full, prepared with a wide variety of hearty proteins, herbs, and North African spices and sliced into wedges meant to be eaten by hand. Tajine is typically enjoyed as a starter to a larger meal but can be eaten on its own as a tasty anytime snack or light meal.

I'd never cooked or eaten tajine before, so I needed to learn its story before starting on my recipe. In addition to watching videos online of Tunisian home cooks preparing the dish, I explored tajine's historical Berber elements as well as its Arabic, Italian, French, and Spanish influences. I consulted with Tunisian food experts, such as Chef Sami Fgaier; Walid Hachani of El Tounsi Foods, a Toronto-based harissa company; and Sarah Fourti, a friend who lives in Tunis. From my conversations with these chefs, I learned that cooking tajine is a beautiful evolution with incremental additions to its main components.

My research taught me that many of the tajine ingredients are cooked separately before being mixed together and baked. Instead of using a baking dish, I found that an ovensafe skillet allowed me to limit the amount of equipment I needed while focusing on building layers of flavor in that one pan. It also made the transition from stovetop to oven seamless.

The first step was to cook the meat. I chose chicken; a few versions I came across called for lamb, but it's usually reserved for special-occasion tajines. Chicken thighs worked well; they remained moist throughout the cooking process. I browned the chicken in the skillet before adding tomato paste, garlic, and spices (ras el hanout and cayenne brought the heat that is common in Tunisian cuisine).

The next element was the requisite starchy ingredient. Potatoes were an option, but I opted to use a pantry staple: beans. Canned cannellini beans not only served as a creamy binder but also took on a lot of flavor from the other ingredients.

With the protein and starch components set, I turned my attention to the eggs, which were added to the skillet on the stovetop, stirred to form large curds, and baked through in the oven. Panko bread crumbs serve two functions in this recipe. First, they are mixed into the eggs to help them thicken, making the tajine beautifully sliceable when it comes out of the oven. Second, they also act as a garnish; pretoasted, they top the tajine and provide crunchy contrast to the softer elements of the dish.

Cheese is a ubiquitous component of a tajine, so I added some grated Parmesan to the beaten eggs along with some chopped fresh parsley for a savory bite throughout. Traditional recipes call for adding a creamy cheese, and wax-wrapped Laughing Cow mini cheese wheels are often used because they are easy to transport and store. Wanting to avoid calling for a specific brand of cheese, I considered goat cheese or cream cheese, but I found those options too tangy in comparison. Monterey Jack had a similar mild flavor profile, so I nestled small cubes of it into the egg mixture before sprinkling on the panko topping. When the tajine emerged from the oven, it was puffy and golden brown, and the cheese cubes created little pockets of creaminess, melting ever so slightly into satisfying pools on the tajine's surface.

Cut into slices, this tajine is my new favorite snack, but in my house it also functions as a satisfying meal when served with a salad.

—CARMEN DONGO, *America's Test Kitchen Books*

SERVES 4 TO 6   TOTAL TIME: 1 HOUR

When purchasing ras el hanout, be sure that your blend features cumin, coriander, and turmeric. Turmeric will create the distinctive yellowish tone typical of traditional Tunisian tajines.

12	large eggs
½	cup panko bread crumbs, toasted, divided
½	cup minced fresh parsley
1	ounce Parmesan cheese, grated (½ cup)
3	tablespoons water
½	teaspoon table salt, divided
½	teaspoon pepper, divided
3	tablespoons extra-virgin olive oil
1½	pounds boneless, skinless chicken thighs, trimmed and cut into ½-inch pieces
1	tablespoon tomato paste
6	garlic cloves, minced
1	tablespoon ras el hanout
¼	teaspoon cayenne pepper
1	cup canned cannellini beans, rinsed
4	ounces Monterey Jack cheese, cut into ½-inch cubes (1 cup)

1. Adjust oven rack to upper-middle position and heat oven to 350 degrees. Whisk eggs, ¼ cup panko, parsley, Parmesan, water, ¼ teaspoon salt, and ¼ teaspoon pepper together in bowl; set aside.

2. Heat oil in 12-inch ovensafe nonstick skillet over medium-high heat until shimmering. Add chicken, tomato paste, remaining ¼ teaspoon salt, and remaining ¼ teaspoon pepper and cook, stirring occasionally, until chicken is well browned, 6 to 8 minutes. Stir in garlic, ras el hanout, and cayenne and cook until fragrant, about 1 minute. Stir in beans and cook until heated through, about 5 minutes.

3. Reduce heat to medium-low and stir in egg mixture. Cook, using spatula to scrape bottom of skillet, until large curds form but eggs are still very wet, about 2 minutes. Smooth egg mixture into even layer. Nestle Monterey Jack into egg curds and sprinkle top with remaining ¼ cup panko. Transfer skillet to oven and bake until tajine is slightly puffy and surface bounces back when lightly pressed, 10 to 12 minutes. Using oven mitt, remove skillet from oven. Being careful of hot skillet handle, use rubber spatula to loosen tajine from skillet and transfer to cutting board. Let sit for 5 minutes before slicing and serving.

CHICKEN PARMESAN MEATBALLS

✓ **WHY THIS RECIPE WORKS** To flavor the ground chicken meatballs, we chose a mixture of Parmesan cheese, dried oregano, garlic powder, salt, and pepper to perk up the flavor. We then stirred in a mix of crushed Ritz Crackers and egg in place of a panade (a seasoned mix of starch and liquid). This paste added enough structure for us to skip the browning step (which helps meatballs hold together). To keep the sauce simple, we seasoned crushed tomatoes and tomato sauce with a generous amount of fresh garlic, dried oregano, salt, and pepper flakes. After briefly simmering the sauce, we poured it over the meatballs and topped it with mozzarella (for its gooey meltability) prior to baking. When the saucy meatballs emerged from the oven, a sprinkle of savory Parmesan cheese, crunchy panko, and fragrant basil was the crowning touch.

Chicken Parmesan can be time-consuming to make. Traditional recipes call for pounding chicken cutlets, breading using a multistage process, frying, and finally, baking with cheese and homemade sauce. Making meatballs is less complex, but it's still a labor of love (and sticky hands).

We love both chicken Parmesan and meatballs with marinara. So to make things a little easier for the cook—and to eliminate the need to choose between the two—I tinkered with several recipes to capture the best flavors of both dishes while minimizing the effort.

Starting with the meatballs, I chose a flavorful mixture of Parmesan cheese, dried oregano, garlic powder, salt, and pepper to perk up the flavor of mild ground chicken. At this point, most recipes also call for adding a panade, a seasoned mix of starch and liquid (often bread and milk mashed together). Instead, I stirred in crushed Ritz Crackers and a beaten egg. This paste allowed me to skip the browning step (which helps meatballs hold together) and still have meatballs that held their shape and remained tender.

As a bonus, the Ritz Crackers gave the meatballs a rich, buttery flavor. As for the sauce, I kept it simple, seasoning crushed tomatoes and tomato sauce with a generous amount of fresh garlic, dried oregano, salt, and pepper flakes. After a brief simmer, I poured the bright, garlicky tomato sauce over the meatballs and topped the dish with a crown of shredded mozzarella (for its gooey meltability) before baking.

A CRUMB-Y SOLUTION

Place flavorful Ritz Crackers in a zipper-lock bag (to contain the mess) and crush them into crumbs with a rolling pin.

When the saucy meatballs emerged from the oven, sprinkles of savory Parmesan cheese, basil, and crunchy panko bread crumbs imparted that familiar chicken Parmesan vibe.

—LAWMAN JOHNSON, *Cook's Country*

Chicken Parmesan Meatballs

SERVES 4 TO 6   TOTAL TIME: 1½ HOURS, PLUS 15 MINUTES COOLING

Avoid ground chicken labeled "99 percent fat-free," as it tends to yield dry meatballs. Serve with crusty bread.

- 5 tablespoons extra-virgin olive oil, divided
- 5 garlic cloves, sliced thin
- 1 (28-ounce) can crushed tomatoes
- 1 (15-ounce) can tomato sauce
- 2¼ teaspoons dried oregano, divided
- 1½ teaspoons table salt, divided
- ¼ teaspoon red pepper flakes
- 22 Ritz Crackers
- 5 ounces Parmesan cheese, grated (2½ cups), divided
- 1 large egg, lightly beaten
- 2 teaspoons garlic powder
- 1 teaspoon pepper
- 2 pounds ground chicken
- 8 ounces whole-milk block mozzarella cheese, shredded (2 cups)
- 1 cup panko bread crumbs
- ¼ cup torn fresh basil

1. Heat 3 tablespoons oil in large saucepan over medium heat until shimmering. Add sliced garlic and cook until lightly browned, about 1 minute. Stir in crushed tomatoes, tomato sauce, ¼ teaspoon oregano, ¼ teaspoon salt, and pepper flakes. Bring to simmer; reduce heat to medium-low; and cook until slightly thickened, 10 to 15 minutes, stirring occasionally. Remove from heat and cover to keep warm.

2. Adjust oven rack to middle position and heat oven to 350 degrees. Place crackers in large zipper-lock bag, seal bag, and crush crackers fine with rolling pin (you should have about 1 cup crumbs).

3. Combine crumbs, 2 cups Parmesan, egg, garlic powder, pepper, remaining 2 teaspoons oregano, and 1 teaspoon salt in large bowl. Add chicken and mix with your hands until thoroughly combined. Divide mixture into 20 portions (about ¼ cup each). Using your hands, roll each portion into ball, and transfer to 13 by 9-inch baking dish.

4. Pour sauce over meatballs, then sprinkle with mozzarella. Bake until meatballs register at least 160 degrees and mozzarella is melted and beginning to brown, 40 to 45 minutes. Let cool for 15 minutes.

5. Meanwhile, combine panko, remaining 2 tablespoons oil, and remaining ¼ teaspoon salt in bowl. Microwave until panko is light golden brown, 1 to 3 minutes, stirring every 30 seconds.

6. Sprinkle meatballs with panko mixture, remaining ½ cup Parmesan, and basil. Serve.

GRILLED CHICKEN SOUVLAKI

✅ WHY THIS RECIPE WORKS We marinated strips of boneless, skinless chicken breast in a bold mixture of lemon zest, olive oil, oregano, thyme, and other seasonings before threading them onto skewers in an S shape. This threading technique trapped the potent marinade in the folds of the skewered chicken, providing concentrated pops of flavor. After getting some good char on the meat by grilling it over high heat, we drizzled it with a tahini-butter sauce, which cloaked the chicken with an extra layer of richness and allure.

Souvlaki is a dish of marinated meat (or occasionally vegetables) threaded onto skewers or a spit ("souvla" means "spit" in Greek) and cooked over a fire. Back in 2018, our executive food editor, Bryan Roof, had an exemplary version of chicken souvlaki at Johnny's Restaurant in Homewood, Alabama, that he couldn't forget. Inspired by his own Greek heritage, the restaurant's chef, Timothy Hontzas, marinated boneless, skinless chicken breasts in a bold mixture of lemon juice, olive oil, and his proprietary seasoning blend before threading the meat onto skewers. After getting some good char on the meat, he brushed it with a tahini-butter sauce to cloak the chicken with an extra layer of richness and allure. We decided it was time to pay homage to that dish.

Meat for souvlaki is typically cut into chunks. But at Johnny's Restaurant, Hontzas cuts the chicken breasts into long, easy-to-thread strips. Taking a cue from this technique, I sliced boneless, skinless chicken breasts into ½-inch-thick strips and marinated them in a potent mixture of oil, thyme, garlic, lemon zest, oregano, and other seasonings. Since chicken breasts are so mild, marinating them for at least 2 hours was necessary to thoroughly season the meat. I threaded the chicken onto 10-inch skewers and headed to the grill.

Chicken breasts are prone to drying out, and indeed this meat was overcooked by the time it was well browned. Solving this problem was all about adjusting my skewering technique; to create a denser mass of chicken on each skewer that would cook more slowly, I manipulated each strip into an S shape as I threaded it onto the skewer. In addition to providing a safeguard against overcooking, this technique allowed the marinade to get stuck in the folds of the skewered chicken, providing concentrated pops of flavor.

To finish it off, I whipped up a tahini-butter sauce inspired by the one made by Hontzas. The combination of melted butter, creamy tahini, and fresh lemon juice is genius: The sauce is rich, bright, and a little surprising. Now the only decision left to make was whether to eat the deeply flavored chicken directly off the skewer or tucked into a pita with yogurt or tzatziki sauce.

—MORGAN BOLLING, *Cook's Country*

NOTES FROM THE TEST KITCHEN

TAHINI

Tahini, a paste made from toasted sesame seeds, is a core ingredient in hummus and baba ghanoush. It's also often thinned with water or lemon juice and drizzled over falafel, kebabs, pilaf, and roasted or raw vegetables in Middle Eastern recipes.

Grilled Chicken Souvlaki

SERVES 4 TOTAL TIME: 1¼ HOURS, PLUS 2 HOURS MARINATING

You can serve the chicken with lemon wedges, pitas, thinly sliced red onion, tomato, cucumber, torn fresh mint, and/or plain yogurt or tzatziki sauce, if desired. We recommend removing the lemon zest with a vegetable peeler. If you use wooden skewers, be sure to soak them in water for 20 minutes before using them.

CHICKEN

- 2 tablespoons extra-virgin olive oil
- 1 tablespoon chopped fresh thyme
- 3 garlic cloves, minced
- 3 (3-inch) strips lemon zest, chopped
- 2 teaspoons kosher salt
- 1 teaspoon dried oregano
- ½ teaspoon ground coriander
- ¼ teaspoon red pepper flakes
- ¼ teaspoon pepper
- 2 pounds boneless, skinless chicken breasts, trimmed
- 6-8 (10-inch) wooden or metal skewers

TAHINI-BUTTER SAUCE

- 2 tablespoons tahini
- 1½ tablespoons lemon juice
- ½ teaspoon kosher salt
- ¼ teaspoon pepper
- ¼ teaspoon dried oregano
- 4 tablespoons unsalted butter, melted

1. FOR THE CHICKEN: Combine oil, thyme, garlic, lemon zest, salt, oregano, coriander, pepper flakes, and pepper in large bowl.

2. Slice chicken breasts lengthwise into ½-inch-thick strips. Transfer chicken to bowl with oil mixture and toss until chicken is evenly coated. Cover bowl and refrigerate chicken for at least 2 hours or up to 24 hours.

3. Tightly thread chicken strips lengthwise onto skewers in S shape until no more than 1 inch of skewer is exposed on either end, 4 or 5 strips per skewer.

4A. FOR A CHARCOAL GRILL: Open bottom vent completely. Light large chimney starter filled with charcoal briquettes (6 quarts). When top coals are partially covered with ash, pour evenly over half of grill. Set cooking grate in place, cover, and open lid vent completely. Heat grill until hot, about 5 minutes.

GRILLED CHICKEN SOUVLAKI

4B. FOR A GAS GRILL: Turn all burners to high; cover; and heat grill until hot, about 15 minutes. Leave all burners on high.

5. Clean and oil cooking grate. Place kebabs on grill (over coals, if using charcoal) and cook (covered, if using gas) until chicken is lightly charred and registers 160 degrees, 3 to 5 minutes per side. Transfer to serving platter and let rest while preparing tahini-butter sauce.

6. FOR THE TAHINI-BUTTER SAUCE: Whisk tahini, lemon juice, salt, pepper, and oregano in bowl until combined. Slowly whisk in melted butter until emulsified.

7. Drizzle tahini-butter sauce over chicken and serve.

MSAKHAN

✓ **WHY THIS RECIPE WORKS** Because this dish relies on so few ingredients, our version keeps the traditional elements of the dish intact while providing store-bought substitutes and adaptations for the home kitchen when needed. To find a substitute for the taboon bread, we opted to call for supermarket naan. A whole chicken is frequently called for in recipes, but to cut down on cooking time, we relied on chicken pieces, which we cooked atop a layer of chopped onions and a spice mixture that included baharat, a traditional spice blend found in dishes across North Africa and the Middle East. To prevent sogginess and make this dish easier to eat with our hands, we crisped the naans under the broiler before piling on the onion mixture and chicken.

Msakhan, the Palestinian dish of roasted chicken and flatbread served with onions cooked in generous amounts of olive oil and sumac, is a meal to "eat with your hands and with your friends," says Palestinian chef Sami Tamimi in his cookbook *Falastin* (2020). As Palestine's national dish, msakhan's cultural significance runs deep, directly to the olive oil tree that's at the heart of both this dish—it's traditionally made to celebrate the olive harvest and test the quality of the oil—and Palestinian identity itself. Historically, relates Palestinian American educator and chef Awad Awad, olive trees figured into msakhan's every component, from the olive oil–enriched flatbread baked in clay and stone taboon ovens that are fueled by olive wood and dried olive pulp, to the chicken and onions cooked in

generous glugs of olive oil. Awad shares that "a famous Palestinian saying says that a good msakhan should have olive oil dripping from your elbows."

While variations of msakhan exist—for example, "msakhan wraps" where the chicken is shredded and wrapped together with the sumac onions in flatbread—I wanted our version to keep as many of the traditional elements intact as possible. I started by looking at the taboon bread on which the chicken and onions are served. "Taboon" refers to the clay and stone ovens that are used in Palestine to bake bread. The floors of these communal ovens are lined with small stones, so the dough that is laid on top has a characteristic dimpled appearance after it is baked (the better to hold all the delicious juices from the chicken, sumac, and olive oil). As such, replicating this bread at home would be a challenge; so many recipes, as well as Palestinian Americans I spoke with, suggest store-bought substitutes. Indian naan, Afghani bread, and pocketless Greek pita were recommended as the closest in texture to the olive oil–enriched texture of the traditional Palestinian bread and may be more readily available in many grocery stores in the United States.

Traditionally, a whole chicken was roasted (generally in the same communal oven where you brought your bread) and then broken down to serve at the table with the olive oil–simmered sumac onions (cooked separately) and bread. To speed up the process and allow for more even cooking of different chicken parts, I chose to start with chicken pieces. I also wanted to see if cooking the onions and chicken together would work well, thereby cutting down on equipment and allowing the two components' flavors to meld a bit. I started by searing the chicken pieces, skin side down, in olive oil in a skillet. Once the skin was crispy, I removed the pieces and added a generous amount of chopped onions, along with more olive oil, cooking them until just softened. I stirred in some sumac, a lemony spice made from the ground berries of an eastern Mediterranean shrub, and baharat, a spice blend also known as "seven-spice blend" that generally contains black pepper, cumin, cardamom, coriander, cloves, nutmeg, cinnamon, and in Palestine, frequently allspice. Then I placed the chicken pieces on top, skin side up, and put the whole skillet in a hot oven to let the chicken and onions finish cooking together. The result was a lusciously delicious combination of crispy

MSAKHAN

skin, tender meat, and meltingly soft onions, warmly spiced from the baharat but with the richness cut by the acidic tang of the sumac.

The final challenge to tackle was how to serve everything together in a way that facilitated eating with your hands. Most often, the flatbread is first spread with the sumac onions and then the chicken is placed on top. Slathering the naan breads with the olive oil–rich onions led to slightly soggy bread that was hard to pick up under the weight of the onions, but a quick trip under the broiler before filling crisped the bread just enough to avoid this. Cutting the bread into pieces after being topped with the onions also helped "portion" the bread more easily, and an additional sprinkle of sumac added back some pucker that had mellowed in the oven. I spread out the onion-topped breads on a large platter and placed the golden chicken pieces on top. A finishing handful of chopped parsley, some toasted almonds, and a last spoonful of sumac added freshness, crunch, and color. This was a meal that I could not wait to get my hands on, ideally with a bunch of family and friends.

—CAMILA CHAPARRO, *America's Test Kitchen Books*

Msakhan

SERVES 4 TO 6 TOTAL TIME: 1¼ HOURS

Afghan or Indian naan and pocketless Greek pita are close substitutes for taboon bread, but any flatbread can be used. For the best results, use a good-quality, flavorful extra-virgin olive oil. (Palestinian olive oil can be purchased online.)

⅓ cup slivered almonds or pine nuts

5 tablespoons extra-virgin olive oil, divided, plus extra for drizzling

3 pounds bone-in chicken pieces (split breasts cut in half, drumsticks, and/or thighs), trimmed

¾ teaspoon pepper

1½ teaspoons table salt, divided

1½ pounds red onions, chopped

¼ cup sumac, divided

2 teaspoons Baharat (recipe follows)

3 naans

¼ cup chopped fresh parsley

1. Line bowl with double layer of paper towels. Cook almonds and 1 tablespoon oil in 12-inch ovensafe skillet over medium heat, stirring frequently, until almonds are golden brown, 3 to 5 minutes. Using slotted spoon, transfer almonds to prepared bowl; set aside.

2. Adjust 1 oven rack to lower-middle and second rack 6 inches from broiler element. Heat oven to 475 degrees. Pat chicken dry with paper towels and sprinkle with pepper and 1 teaspoon salt. Add 1 tablespoon oil to fat left in skillet and heat over medium-high heat until just smoking. Place chicken skin side down in skillet and cook until skin is well browned and crisp, 8 to 10 minutes. Transfer chicken to large plate.

3. Pour off fat from skillet and wipe skillet clean with paper towels. Add onions, remaining 3 tablespoons oil, and remaining ½ teaspoon salt to now-empty skillet. Cook over medium heat, stirring occasionally and scraping up any browned bits, until onions soften and start to stick to bottom of skillet, 8 to 10 minutes. Off heat, stir in 2 tablespoons sumac and baharat.

4. Arrange chicken skin side up on top of onions and pour in any juices that have accumulated around chicken. Transfer skillet to lower rack in oven and cook until breasts register 160 degrees and drumsticks/thighs register 175 degrees, 15 to 20 minutes.

5. Using pot holder, remove skillet from oven. Being careful of hot skillet handle, transfer chicken to clean plate, tent with aluminum foil, and let rest while preparing naans.

6. Heat broiler. Arrange naans in even layer on rimmed baking sheet (pieces may overlap slightly) and broil on upper rack until lightly toasted, about 2 minutes. Transfer naans to cutting board, spread onions evenly over top, and sprinkle with 1 tablespoon sumac. Cut each naan in quarters and arrange on serving platter. Arrange chicken pieces on top of naan and sprinkle with almonds, parsley, and remaining 1 tablespoon sumac. Drizzle with extra oil and serve.

Baharat

MAKES ABOUT ½ CUP

Baharat, the Arabic word for "spices," is the name of a spice blend found in dishes across North Africa and the Middle East. It's often also called seven-spice blend, and the seven spices featured in our blend are those most commonly found, though there are regional variations. In Palestine, you may find allspice in the blend; in

Turkey, the blend contains dried mint. No matter the combination, the warm blend has an intense profile that benefits meat dishes and roasted vegetables. See page 134 for more information.

3 (3-inch) cinnamon sticks, broken into pieces
4¾ teaspoons cumin seeds
1½ tablespoons coriander seeds
1 tablespoon black peppercorns
2 teaspoons whole cloves
1 tablespoon ground cardamom
2 teaspoons ground nutmeg

Process cinnamon sticks in spice grinder until finely ground, about 30 seconds. Add cumin seeds, coriander seeds, peppercorns, and cloves and process until finely ground, about 30 seconds. Transfer to bowl and stir in cardamom and nutmeg. (Baharat can be stored in airtight container at room temperature for up to 1 month.)

CHICKEN TERIYAKI

WHY THIS RECIPE WORKS Our version of chicken teriyaki started with bone-in chicken thighs, not because we wanted the bones (we promptly removed them), but because we wanted the skin, which protects the meat from the heat of the skillet and adds succulence and meaty flavor. Cutting the thighs into bite-size pieces not only made them easier to eat with chopsticks but also created plenty of surface area for browning and, eventually, for the glaze. A pretreatment with sake boosted savory flavor. Adding cornstarch to the sake had a triple benefit: forming an extra layer of protection around the chicken to keep it supple; providing a surface that "grabbed" the glaze; and thickening the glaze as some of the cornstarch sloughed off. Our glaze has plenty of soy sauce for seasoning, sake for savory depth, sugar for sweetness and luster, and a small amount of ginger for brightness.

I've never passed up a serving of chicken teriyaki, whether it was neatly arranged in a gleaming bento box at a Japanese American restaurant, charred on a backyard grill, or piled atop a disposable plate at a shopping mall food court. Because even when it's not stellar, the salty-sweet, umami-packed chicken manages to hit most of the pleasure centers in my brain. But these versions aren't much like the teriyaki that's made in Japan.

"Teri" means "glaze," and "yaki" means "seared." Due to prohibitions on eating meat, the method was used on fish, not chicken, for most of the dish's history. Japanese cooks would briefly sear yellowtail and then glaze it with a mixture of soy sauce, sake and/or mirin, and sugar. But when the emperor lifted those prohibitions in the second half of the 19th century, chicken teriyaki became an option, at least for those wealthy enough to buy or raise poultry.

During a call from her home in Tokyo, award-winning cookbook author and culinary instructor Elizabeth Andoh explained that cooks in Japan make chicken teriyaki with boneless, skin-on thighs because, unlike the skinless cuts that are often used stateside, they can withstand a thorough sear without drying out or toughening. Sizzling small, chopstick-friendly pieces in a skillet is the norm, whereas in the United States it's common to cut the chicken into pieces after cooking. Finally, Andoh pointed out that "the method of yaki is all about layers of flavor." That means that the interior of the meat should be savory and juicy—pure chicken—while the exterior should be well seasoned but only slightly sweet. Armed with this knowledge, I set about devising a recipe that was reflective of the Japanese approach.

Cutting the thighs into bite-size pieces prior to cooking made sense: It would create more surface area for flavorful browning and for holding glaze. Boneless,

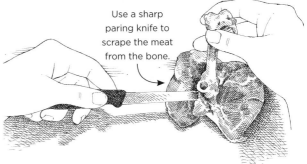

NOTES FROM THE TEST KITCHEN

DEBONING SKIN-ON THIGHS
Traditional chicken teriyaki is made with boneless thighs with the skin still attached; the skin protects the meat and contributes rich, savory flavor. Most supermarkets don't sell this cut, but it's easy to strip out the bones from the thighs yourself. See the recipe for detailed instructions.

Use a sharp paring knife to scrape the meat from the bone.

CHICKEN TERIYAKI

skin-on thighs aren't available in most supermarkets, but they can be easily prepared at home. I removed the bone from 1½ pounds of skin-on thighs and cut the meat into 1½-inch pieces, leaving as much skin attached as possible. I seared the chicken in a nonstick skillet until the pieces were browned on the skin side and then flipped them and cooked them a bit more. Next, I added a placeholder teriyaki sauce—¼ cup of soy sauce, 3 tablespoons of mirin, and just a touch of sugar—and spooned the mixture over the meat until it thickened into a glaze. Andoh was right: The skin-on meat was tender, juicy, and ultra-chicken-y.

Any lingering doubts that I had about using skin-on meat were put to rest when I did a quick test using skinless thighs. The results weren't even close: The chicken was tough and fibrous on the exterior and not nearly as savory.

That said, skin-on thighs did lead to a glaze that was so greasy it didn't cling as well. I'd stick with skin-on chicken, but going forward I'd swab up any excess grease in the skillet before adding the sauce.

I had set aside any recipes that called for marinating the chicken in the soy sauce–mirin mixture because I worried that the sugary mirin would scorch. But I was intrigued when Andoh mentioned that she tosses her chicken in a thick mixture of potato starch and sake shortly before searing it.

Curious to try this myself, I prepared a batch with sake and cornstarch, which is a more common starch in the United States. The cornstarch formed a barely there coating around the pieces of meat, protecting them from the heat of the skillet and making them especially supple. The coating also helped the reduced glaze cling, and some of the coating sloughed off into it, thickening the glaze a bit more. Finally, the chicken tasted more savory than before, as the sake provided a synergistic boost to its umami. Cornstarch and sake were in. Now I just had to dial in the glaze.

My glaze was mostly soy sauce and mirin, with a little bit of sugar. That's not a lot of ingredients, but since I was already using sake to coat the chicken, I wondered if I could swap out the mirin in the glaze for sake. After all, sake is a rice wine like mirin. So I tried a common 3:2:1 ratio (3 tablespoons of soy sauce, 2 tablespoons of sake, and 1 tablespoon of sugar) and microwaved the mixture briefly to dissolve the sugar.

This was very close. With both sake and soy sauce, the glaze had a lot of depth, but it lacked lighter notes. Andoh had mentioned that she sometimes likes to add a small amount of ginger juice, so while my last batch of chicken seared in the skillet, I grated 2 tablespoons of ginger, placed it in a fine-mesh strainer over my glaze mixture, and pressed to release the juice.

When the chicken was cooked through, I transferred it to a plate so that I could degrease the skillet. Then back in went the chicken, followed by the soy sauce mixture. The glaze bubbled and thickened as I stirred the chicken, and after a couple minutes it coated each piece lightly. I transferred the chicken to a serving bowl using a slotted spoon and, before drizzling the glaze over the chicken, I passed it through the strainer for a little extra clarity.

I stand by my assertion that all chicken teriyaki is good chicken teriyaki. But this one? It's my new favorite.

—ANDREA GEARY, *Cook's Illustrated*

NOTES FROM THE TEST KITCHEN

GAMAN IN THE KITCHEN

PATIENCE IS A VIRTUE
Don't flip the chicken until it turns white at the edges.

"Gaman" is a Japanese term of Buddhist origin that means enduring difficult circumstances with patience, perseverance, and dignity. In fact, gaman is considered to be one of the forces that sustained Japan's recovery from the devastating 2011 earthquake and tsunami. The concept touches almost every aspect of Japanese culture: Preschoolers are introduced to it when they learn to share and take turns, and it seems unlikely that Tokyo's Shinjuku train station, which serves 3.5 million passengers per day, could function without it.

Gaman has a role in cooking as well. In our recipe, we practice gaman by leaving the chicken undisturbed in the hot skillet for several minutes, resisting the urge to peek at the underside of the meat until the edges of each piece turn solid white, an indication that cooking is well underway. As Tokyo-based culinary instructor and cookbook author Elizabeth Andoh advised us, "If you're able to engage positively in gaman, you will get that gorgeous sear and glaze." And if you're not able to, she warns, "it's a mess."

Andoh suggested a strategy for those who struggle to practice gaman when cooking: Instead of agonizing, multitask. Distract yourself by tidying up or by chopping vegetables. You'll get a couple small jobs done, and you'll be rewarded with beautifully seared chicken.

SERVES 4 TOTAL TIME: 1 HOUR

It's worth deboning chicken thighs here so that you can retain the skin. Boneless, skin-on thighs are a rare find, but if you do find them, buy 1½ pounds for this recipe; do not use skinless thighs, because they'll be less juicy. Use a Frywall or splatter screen if you have one. Inexpensive sake is fine here; it can often be purchased in small cans. We strain the glaze in step 4 to improve its clarity, but you can skip this process if you prefer. Serve with unseasoned short-grain white rice, peppery greens such as watercress or mizuna, and sliced scallions.

1½–2	**pounds bone-in chicken thighs**
3½	**tablespoons sake, divided**
1	**tablespoon cornstarch**
3	**tablespoons soy sauce**
1	**tablespoon sugar**
2	**tablespoons grated fresh ginger**
2	**teaspoons vegetable oil**

1. Place 1 chicken thigh skin side down on cutting board. Using sharp paring knife, trim excess skin and fat, leaving enough skin to cover meat. Cut slit along length of thigh bone to expose bone. Using tip of knife, cut/scrape meat from bone. Slip knife under bone to separate bone from meat. Discard bone and trim any remaining cartilage from thigh. Keeping thigh skin side down, cut into 1½-inch pieces, leaving as much skin attached as possible. Transfer to medium bowl and repeat with remaining thighs. Add 1½ tablespoons sake and cornstarch and stir gently until chicken is evenly coated.

2. Combine soy sauce, sugar, and remaining 2 tablespoons sake in small bowl. Microwave until sugar is dissolved, about 30 seconds. Place fine-mesh strainer over bowl containing soy sauce mixture. Add ginger to strainer and press to extract juice. Discard solids, but do not wash strainer.

3. Line large plate with paper towels. Heat oil in 12-inch nonstick skillet over medium heat until shimmering. Place chicken skin side down in skillet (skillet may be very full). Increase heat to medium-high; place Frywall or splatter screen, if using, on skillet; and cook, without moving chicken, until all pieces have ¼- to

½-inch perimeter of white, 6 to 8 minutes. Slide skillet off heat and flip chicken. Return skillet to burner and reduce heat to medium. Continue to cook until chicken is just cooked through, 1 to 2 minutes longer.

4. Remove skillet from heat. Using slotted spoon, transfer chicken to prepared plate. Pour off fat, scrape any browned bits out of skillet, and wipe skillet clean with paper towels. Return chicken to skillet. Add soy sauce mixture and cook over medium heat, stirring frequently, until chicken is thinly coated and sauce has consistency of maple syrup, 1 to 2 minutes. Using slotted spoon, transfer chicken to serving bowl. Pour glaze in skillet through now-empty strainer set over small serving bowl. Drizzle 2 tablespoons glaze over chicken and serve, passing remaining glaze (there will be only a few tablespoons, but it is potent) separately.

POLLO A LA BRASA (PERUVIAN GRILL-ROASTED CHICKEN)

✅ **WHY THIS RECIPE WORKS** Our version of this Peruvian dish calls for marinating the chicken in a beer-based marinade that also includes soy sauce for salinity; lime juice and mustard for brightness; and garlic, dried thyme, black pepper, and cumin for earthy, savory depth. Instead of relying on a rotisserie to rotate the bird horizontally, we used a half-empty beer can to prop it up vertically and then positioned the bird in the center of a kettle grill outfitted with a split fire. For remarkably succulent, smoky meat packaged in well-rendered, uniformly mahogany skin, we rotated the chicken a quarter turn every 15 minutes (about five turns total). We developed two sauces to accompany the chicken: one seasoned with garlic, huacatay paste, cilantro, lime, cotija, and jalapeño and another seasoned with garlic, ají amarillo paste, lime, and huacatay paste.

Asociación Peruana de Avicultura (Peruvian Association of Poultry Farming) estimates that more than 155 million pollos a la brasa are consumed annually in Peru. Maestros polleros, or poultry masters, grill-roast the extraordinarily popular birds on rotisseries that spin lazily over crackling wood fires ("brasa" means "ember") to produce meat that's encased in tawny, paper-thin skin and dripping with juices. Served with a pile of crispy

POLLO A LA BRASA (PERUVIAN GRILL-ROASTED CHICKEN)

french fries, a simple green salad, and an array of peppy ají (chile) sauces, the flavor-packed, satisfying dish has been central to the country's dining scene for decades.

It all began in the 1940s when Swiss migrant Roger Schuler needed a way to rescue his bankrupt poultry farm on the outskirts of Lima, Peru. To attract customers, he set up a roadside stand peddling all-you-can-eat chicken that he'd skewered on a thick iron spit rod and roasted over an algarrobina (black carob) fire. The birds were such a hit among Limeños that Schuler recruited Swiss metal worker Franz Ulrich to increase production by engineering a six-spit rotisserie. In 1950, the pair opened a pollería called Granja Azul, and customers flocked to it.

Since then, pollerías have sprung up on nearly every block in most Peruvian cities, providing a go-to option for affordable takeout or dining in. Home cooks prepare these grill-roasted chickens, too. So beloved is the chicken that it's been given its own national holiday, Día del Pollo a la Brasa, celebrated on the third Sunday of every July.

To learn more about this iconic dish, I called Peruvian-born chef Jose Duarte, owner of Tambo 22 restaurant near Boston. He recalled Peru's family-friendly take-out routine: "Instead of cooking dinner one night, you just go and buy one chicken with french fries, and they sell you the sauces in little bags tied in knots . . . and a big bottle of soda."

Duarte feels that a high-quality bird needs only salt, pepper, and licks from wood-fired flames to taste great, but it's now common for Peruvian cooks to ratchet up the flavor via a marinade or wet rub. I came to prefer a beer-based marinade, which seeped into the flesh of the chicken when I loosened the skin covering its breast and leg quarters. Along with half a can of malty beer, I incorporated ingredients that are often used in pollerías today: soy sauce for salinity; lime juice and mustard for brightness; and garlic, dried thyme, black pepper, and cumin for earthy, savory depth.

Since I didn't have a rotisserie to rotate the chicken horizontally, I used the half-empty beer can to prop it up vertically, sliding the cavity onto the vessel to create a sort of tripod with the drumsticks. I positioned the propped-up bird in the center of a kettle grill outfitted with a split fire made by dumping piles of hot coals onto either side of a disposable aluminum pan and nestling a packet of wood chips on one side.

The key was to rotate the chicken a quarter turn every 15 minutes so that at any given moment, two sides would be blasted with heat while the other two sides got a reprieve. While not the constant movement of a rotisserie, about five turns produced remarkably succulent, smoky meat packaged in well-rendered, uniformly mahogany skin.

Zippy ají sauces are mandatory with pollo a la brasa, but they're not just for the chicken: Peruvians also drizzle them onto the salad and fries that share the plate. There are lots of local variations, but most are mayonnaise-based, and all are packed with gutsy seasonings such as garlic, lime, and herbs. After whipping up yellow (ají amarillo) and green (jalapeño) versions—make both if you can swing it—I devoured pollo a la brasa, right in my own backyard.

—DAVID PAZMIÑO, *Cook's Illustrated*

Pollo a la Brasa (Peruvian Grill-Roasted Chicken)

SERVES 4   TOTAL TIME: 2½ HOURS, PLUS 24 HOURS MARINATING

Our gas grill instructions are for a three-burner grill. If using a two-burner grill, turn both burners to high and place the wood chips on the primary burner while the grill heats. When the grill is hot, turn the primary burner to medium and turn the secondary burner off; stand the chicken on the cooler side of the grill, about 4 inches from the primary burner, and proceed with the recipe, adjusting the primary burner as needed to maintain 350 to 375 degrees. A rasp-style grater makes quick work of grating the garlic. Inexpensive beer is fine; avoid those with strong hoppy or bitter flavors. Do not use a 16-ounce can because its height will make the chicken less stable. Serve with french fries and salad and one or both sauces (recipes follow).

1 **(12-ounce) can beer, divided**

2 **tablespoons finely grated garlic**

2 **tablespoons lime juice**

2 **tablespoons soy sauce**

2 **teaspoons table salt**

2 **teaspoons yellow mustard**

1 **teaspoon pepper**

1 **teaspoon dried thyme**

1 **teaspoon ground cumin**

1 **(4- to 4½-pound) whole chicken, giblets discarded**

1 **cup wood chips**

1 **(13 by 9-inch) disposable aluminum roasting pan**

1. Whisk ½ cup beer, garlic, lime juice, soy sauce, salt, mustard, pepper, thyme, and cumin together in liquid measuring cup. Refrigerate remaining beer, still in can, until ready to grill. Using your fingers or handle of wooden spoon, gently loosen skin covering chicken breast and leg quarters. Using paring knife, poke 10 to 15 holes in fat deposits on skin of back. Tuck wingtips underneath chicken.

2. Place chicken in bowl with cavity end facing up. Slowly pour marinade between skin and meat and rub marinade inside cavity, outside skin, and under skin to distribute. Cover and refrigerate for 24 hours, turning chicken halfway through marinating.

3. Using large piece of heavy-duty aluminum foil, wrap wood chips in 8 by 4½-inch foil packet. (Make sure chips do not poke holes in packet.) Cut 2 evenly spaced 2-inch slits in top of packet.

4. Place beer can in large, shallow bowl. Spray can all over with vegetable oil spray. Slide chicken over can so drumsticks reach down to bottom of can and chicken stands upright; set aside at room temperature while preparing grill.

5A. FOR A CHARCOAL GRILL: Open bottom vent fully and place disposable pan in center of grill. Light large chimney starter two-thirds filled with charcoal briquettes (4 quarts). When top coals are partially covered with ash, pour into 2 even piles on either side of disposable pan. Place wood chip packet on 1 pile of coals. Set cooking grate in place, cover, and open lid vent fully. Heat grill until hot and wood chips are smoking, about 5 minutes.

5B. FOR A GAS GRILL: Remove cooking grate and place wood chip packet directly on one of outside burners. Set grate in place; turn all burners to high; cover; and heat grill until hot and wood chips are smoking, about 15 minutes. Turn 2 outside burners to medium and turn off center burner. (Adjust outside burners as needed to

NOTES FROM THE TEST KITCHEN

THE NEXT BEST THING TO A ROTISSERIE
To mimic a wood-fired rotisserie, prop the bird up on a beer can and flank it with smoldering charcoal, placing a packet of wood chips on one side. Rotate the bird 90 degrees every 15 minutes for about five turns. The resulting chicken will be almost indistinguishable from the spit-roasted kind: succulent; imbued with the sweetness of wood smoke; and encased in evenly browned, well-rendered skin.

NOTES FROM THE TEST KITCHEN

TWO PASTES THAT MAKE THE SAUCES
Ají amarillo (yellow chile) and huacatay (an herb that's often called black mint) add spark and depth to many of the sauces that accompany pollo a la brasa. Vibrant ají amarillo gives off fruity, habanero-like vibes with moderate heat. Huacatay, on the other hand, is evocative of vegetables and freshly cut grass with menthol undertones. Both can be hard to find fresh in the United States and are typically sold as jarred pastes.

AJÍ AMARILLO PASTE

HUACATAY PASTE

maintain grill temperature between 350 and 375 degrees.)

6. Scrape cooking grate clean with grill brush. Transfer chicken with can to center of cooking grate with wings facing piles of coals (or outer burners on gas grill) at 3 and 9 o'clock (ends of drumsticks should rest on grate to help steady bird). Cover grill (with top vent open for charcoal grill) and cook for 15 minutes. Using tongs and wad of paper towels, rotate chicken 90 degrees so wings are at 6 and 12 o'clock. Continue cooking and turning chicken at 15-minute intervals until thickest part of thigh registers 170 to 175 degrees, 1 hour to 1¼ hours longer.

7. With large wad of paper towels in each hand, transfer chicken and can to clean bowl, keeping can upright; let rest for 15 minutes (do not discard paper towels). Using wads of paper towels, carefully lift chicken off can and onto cutting board. Discard can. Carve chicken, transfer to platter, and serve.

Ají Verde (Peruvian Green Chile Sauce)

MAKES ABOUT ¾ CUP   TOTAL TIME: 10 MINUTES

You can find huacatay paste in supermarkets or online. If it's unavailable, increase the cilantro to 5 tablespoons.

- ½ **cup mayonnaise**
- 1 **jalapeño chile, stemmed, seeded, and chopped coarse**
- 3 **tablespoons minced fresh cilantro**
- 2 **tablespoons grated cotija cheese**
- 2 **tablespoons lime juice**
- 1 **tablespoon jarred huacatay paste**
- 1 **garlic clove, minced**

Combine all ingredients in blender and process until smooth, about 1 minute. (Sauce can be refrigerated for up to 1 week.)

Ají Amarillo (Peruvian Yellow Chile Sauce)

MAKES ABOUT ⅔ CUP   TOTAL TIME: 10 MINUTES

Ají amarillo paste, made from yellow Peruvian chiles, is available in supermarkets or online. If huacatay paste is unavailable, it can be omitted.

- ½ **cup mayonnaise**
- 2 **tablespoons ají amarillo paste**
- 1 **tablespoon lime juice**
- 1 **garlic clove, minced**
- 1 **teaspoon jarred huacatay paste**

Combine all ingredients in blender and process until smooth, about 1 minute. (Sauce can be refrigerated for up to 1 week.)

CHICKEN FRANCESE

☑ **WHY THIS RECIPE WORKS**   To make chicken Francese, cooks dip cutlets in flour and then beaten egg; shallow-fry them; and sauce them with a lemony, beurre blanc–like reduction that saturates the plush coating. Cutting and pounding each boneless, skinless breast into three ¼-inch cutlets ensured that they cooked through evenly in minutes. Briefly salting the meat seasoned it and helped it retain moisture during cooking. For a tender coating, we diluted the eggs with 2 tablespoons of water to prevent their proteins from coagulating tightly and cooking up tough and rubbery. It was important to fry the chicken in enough oil (⅔ cup for a 12-inch skillet) that it crested just above the sides of the cutlets, which prevented the coating from slipping off before it had time to set. Using a combination of vegetable and olive oils reduced cost while adding just enough of the olive oil's grassy bitterness. We captured complex fruit flavor in the lemony butter sauce by combining juice, zest, and browned lemon slices; the latter also made for a visually striking garnish. Thickening the sauce with flour-dredged cubed butter was simpler than making a proper beurre manié (butter-flour paste), and the dredged fat added lush, silky body.

"Frenching" in the Italian American culinary tradition means to dip a piece of food in flour and beaten egg; shallow-fry it; and sauce it with a lemony, beurre blanc–like reduction that saturates the plush, golden-brown coating. This retro technique, originally devised for veal

but popularized with chicken cutlets, found fame at the Brown Derby restaurant just outside Rochester, New York. Chef James Cianciola's "Chicken French" (or "Francese" in Italian) drew such crowds that the restaurant reportedly switched off its lit sign to discourage the arrival of more patrons. In fact, the dish sold so well that Cianciola started "Frenching" artichokes, eggplant, and seafood, too. Restaurants all over the region, and eventually the country, mimicked the preparation, elevating it to what would become one of Red Sauce America's all-time favorite takes on the sautéed cutlet tradition known as scaloppine.

Francese is timeless with home cooks, too. (In 2018, the *New York Times* food reporter Julia Moskin's version ranked as the paper's most popular recipe of the year.) That bright, satiny sauce and rich, savory egg coating make it feel luxurious, but the everyday ingredients and straightforward method keep it just as grounded as any other cutlet. And like other simple sautés, this dish is flexible and has evolved over time.

My approach starts with pounding: I like very thin cutlets that cook through by the time the coating is golden brown, so I cut and flatten each breast into three ¼-inch-thick pieces and then briefly salt (and pepper) them for flavor and to help them retain moisture during cooking. And I like a relatively thin and tender egg coating—just sturdy enough to hug the meat without tearing—so I shake off extra flour to avoid excess egg from clinging. And I whisk water into the eggs to dilute their proteins; that way, the proteins won't bond too tightly and toughen as they cook.

CHICKEN FRANCESE

The tricky thing about chicken Francese's egg-on-the-outside coating is that it can slip off if the eggs don't set quickly enough. After a few tries, I discovered that oil volume is key: You need enough of it in the pan (⅔ cup for a 12-inch skillet) that the oil just crests the sides of each cutlet, creating a dam of sorts that supports the coating until it's cooked enough to stay put. And given that extra-virgin olive oil (the classic Francese cooking medium) is pricey, I use a 50/50 blend of olive and vegetable oils. The cost of the dish goes down, and the cutlets still benefit from some of the olive oil's fruity bitterness.

As for the sauce, I invest a little extra effort in mine to make the lemon flavor more than just tangy. In fact, I put the whole fruit to work: juice for acid to balance the rich butter; zest for its floral, spicy-sweet fragrance; and skin-on slices that I brown in butter and use as a complex-tasting garnish.

NOTES FROM THE TEST KITCHEN

THE LEMONIEST PAN SAUCE

Bright-tasting lemon juice balances Francese's rich butter sauce, but the fruit has a lot more to offer the dish than just acidity—namely spicy-sweet, floral fragrance from the zest's aromatic oils, and the distinct bitterness that develops in citrus when acid and enzymes in the zest and cottony pith react with one another.

To capture all those flavors, grate the zest from half a lemon; halve the fruit crosswise and juice the zested half; and slice the lemon's unzested half into thin rounds. Wait to add the zest and juice to the sauce until after it has reduced to avoid cooking off their volatile aromatic compounds. And brown the slices in butter: Moderate heat will enhance the fruit's fragrance by forcing oil out of the skin (intact peel can take more heat than grated zest); mellow some of its bitter-tasting limonin by destroying the enzyme that helps create it; and coax out sweet, round nuttiness that will make for an exceptionally complex-tasting garnish.

After sautéing garlic, I pour white wine and chicken broth into the pan and substantially reduce the liquid to concentrate its flavor. Then I add the lemon zest and juice (delayed additions to preserve their volatile flavors), followed by 3 tablespoons of cubed butter that I dredge in flour—a shortcut to the classic French beurre manié butter-flour paste that thickens the sauce just as effectively, enriching it to the consistency of heavy cream.

Spooned over the cutlets, the sauce seeps into the coating so that every bite is bright and aromatic. And thanks to the chemical interplay between the lemon's zest and cottony pith, the browned slices offer a hint of bitter citrus bite that's tempered by the heat into something round, beautifully balanced, and, well, timeless.

—STEVE DUNN, *Cook's Illustrated*

Chicken Francese

SERVES 6   TOTAL TIME: 1½ HOURS

Use a stainless-steel skillet, not cast iron, the seasoning of which can be damaged by the acidic sauce. To ensure that the sauce develops the correct flavor and consistency, transfer the liquid to a heatproof liquid measuring cup once or twice during simmering to monitor the amount. Serve the cutlets with buttered pasta, white rice, potatoes, or crusty bread and a simple steamed vegetable.

4   (6- to 8-ounce) boneless, skinless chicken breasts, trimmed

2   teaspoons table salt

½   teaspoon pepper

1   large lemon

4   tablespoons unsalted butter, divided

¾   cup all-purpose flour, divided

3   large eggs

2   tablespoons water

⅓   cup extra-virgin olive oil for frying

⅓   cup vegetable oil for frying

1   garlic clove, minced

⅓   cup dry white wine

1½   cups chicken broth

2   tablespoons minced fresh parsley

1. Adjust oven rack to middle position and heat oven to 200 degrees. Cut each chicken breast in half crosswise, then cut thick half in half again horizontally, creating 3 cutlets of similar thickness. Place cutlets between sheets of plastic wrap and gently pound to even ¼-inch thickness. Place cutlets in bowl and toss with salt and pepper. Set aside for 15 minutes.

2. Grate peel from 1 end of lemon to yield 1 teaspoon zest. Cut lemon in half crosswise and juice zested lemon half. Measure out 2 tablespoons juice. Slice remaining (unzested) lemon half into four ¼-inch-thick rounds. Discard end. Cut 3 tablespoons butter into ½-inch cubes and transfer to small bowl. Sprinkle cubes with 1 teaspoon flour and toss until cubes are fully coated and no loose flour remains in bowl; refrigerate until needed.

3. Set wire rack in rimmed baking sheet. Spread remaining flour in shallow dish. In medium bowl, whisk eggs with water. Working with 1 cutlet at a time, dredge cutlets in flour, shaking gently to remove excess. Transfer to prepared rack.

4. Heat olive oil and vegetable oil in 12-inch skillet over medium-high heat until shimmering. Working with 1 cutlet at a time, coat 4 cutlets with egg mixture and gently place in skillet. Reduce heat to medium and cook until golden brown on 1 side, about 2 minutes. Using tongs, flip and cook until golden brown on second side, about 2 minutes. Arrange cutlets on serving platter and place in oven. Repeat with remaining cutlets in 2 batches.

5. Discard oil. Gently wipe out skillet with paper towels. Return skillet to medium heat and add lemon slices and remaining 1 tablespoon butter. Cook, flipping slices occasionally, until lightly browned on both sides, about 3 minutes. Transfer lemon slices to cutting board.

6. Add garlic to now-empty skillet and cook, stirring constantly, until fragrant, about 30 seconds. Stir in wine, scraping up any browned bits, and increase heat to medium-high. Bring to rapid simmer and cook until wine is mostly evaporated, 2 to 3 minutes. Stir in broth and continue to simmer, stirring occasionally, until liquid is reduced to ⅔ cup, 6 to 8 minutes longer.

7. Reduce heat to low and stir in reserved lemon zest and juice. Whisk in floured butter cubes, a few at a time, until sauce is thickened to consistency of heavy cream, 1½ to 2 minutes. Off heat, stir in parsley. Season with salt and pepper to taste. Cut browned lemon slices in half and scatter over cutlets. Spoon sauce over cutlets and serve.

BLACKENED CHICKEN

✓ WHY THIS RECIPE WORKS Blackening refers to coating quick-cooking proteins in a robust Cajun spice blend and flashing them in a ripping-hot cast-iron pan until the fat and spices smoke and char but don't completely burn. It's usually smoky business but can be well controlled with a few tweaks. Pounding the cutlets very thin (⅛ inch) helped them cook through quickly, so there was little time for the fat and spices to burn. Arranging them in the pan so that they covered as much of the surface as possible prevented hot spots from forming in the gaps and overheating the fat and juices. Keeping the amount of butter (which smokes readily in a high-heat application like this) to just 3 tablespoons total also kept the smoke to a minimum. For robust spice flavor, we dredged the moist cutlets directly in the spice rub rather than "gluing" the spices to the chicken with melted butter; this helped the spices stick to—rather than melt off—the meat during cooking. Adding smoked paprika to the spice mix enhanced its smoky profile.

During the 1980s, the red drum population along the Gulf Coast was decimated by overfishing. Demand for the fish (also known as redfish) had soared to such unprecedented levels that the National Marine Fisheries Service was forced to ban commercial harvests in federal waters and limit recreational anglers to one fish per person per trip.

Arguably, the surge in demand had little to do with the fish itself, which is mild; firm fleshed; and considered comparable to red snapper, grouper, and black sea bass. The interest was caused by the way locals were cooking it—specifically Paul Prudhomme and his wife, K. Hinrichs, at their acclaimed K-Paul's Louisiana Kitchen in New Orleans. Allegedly riffing on a grilling method that he'd picked up during his childhood, Prudhomme dipped the fillets in melted butter, dredged them in a classic Cajun spice blend, and flashed them in a ripping-hot cast-iron skillet with more melted butter. The fat and spices smoked and charred just enough to give the coating a primal, boundary-pushing savoriness that stopped just short of fully burnt.

"What you do is, you're not burning it, you're blackening it," Prudhomme explained in a 1986 interview for the *San Bernardino County Sun*. "The reason you blacken," he said, "is because it gives you the ultimate taste."

His customers agreed. They went wild for "blackening," and chefs all over the country copied the method—hence the overfished red drum. Soon chefs were blackening all sorts of proteins, including other types of fish and shellfish, chicken cutlets, and steak. Prudhomme even launched a line of retail Cajun spice blends, headlined by Blackened Redfish Magic and Blackened Steak Magic, which became pantry staples for home cooks who aspired to blacken foods in their own kitchens.

But here's the rub: Blackening is a smoky business, the kind of cooking that trips alarms and requires high-powered ventilation. Those side effects have been enough to keep home cooks like me from attempting the method, despite its appeal as a speedy, ultrasimple way to jazz up workaday proteins such as chicken cutlets. So what I really aspired to do was blacken without so much billowing smoke.

I needed to know exactly what about the typical blackening method causes heavy smoke, so I set myself up to try it with chicken cutlets. Besides boneless, skinless breasts, which I pared and pounded myself to guarantee uniformly thick pieces that cooked evenly, I grabbed butter, a slew of dried spices and herbs that appear in a typical blackening blend (paprika, garlic and onion powders, salt, black and cayenne peppers, thyme, and oregano), and a 12-inch cast-iron skillet. I let the pan get good and hot over a high flame, and then I laid a few of the buttered, spice-rubbed cutlets on the surface.

The smoke puffed almost immediately—and very noticeably from portions of the pan not covered by chicken. That made sense, since the chicken cooled the pan where it touched it, but where there was no meat to absorb energy, just fat and juices on bare metal, they heated, bubbled, and smoked heavily. So I made a few adjustments to the chicken itself: First, I pounded the cutlets really thin (about ⅓ inch thick), which created more surface area to blanket the skillet and also helped the chicken cook through faster (just a minute or two on each side) so that there was less time for the fat and spices to burn. A side benefit: More surface area for the meat meant a higher proportion of butter and spices in each bite. Second, I arranged the cutlets (six per batch, cooked in two batches) in the pan like jigsaw puzzle pieces that minimized the negative space and, thus, the smoke.

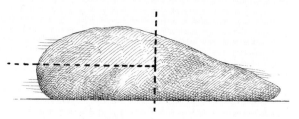
The other major factor behind the smoke was the prodigious amount of butter. When Prudhomme blackened fish fillets, he used about 8 tablespoons per pound of fish, and the fat's abundant milk proteins made for thick plumes. Plus, I noticed in my own tests that much of the butter and spice rub dripped off the cutlets when they hit the hot pan, leaving me with a sooty mess and a spotty spice crust. So I knocked the butter way down to 3 tablespoons for about 2 pounds of chicken—frankly, the dish didn't need more richness than that—and instead of melting it as a coating that would "glue" the spices to the meat, I dredged the chicken in the spices and added the butter directly to the pan. (I also added a teaspoon of oil to the cold skillet as a temperature gauge, knowing that butter would smoke before the pan was sufficiently hot.) The spices clung nicely to the moist chicken, leaving just a thin film that I wiped out of the pan between batches to avoid burning. Along with the milk solids in the butter, the spices took on that deeply rich, toasty, "blackened" character that I amped up even more by adding smoked paprika to the rub.

Collectively, those changes hugely reduced the smoke output from the pan. (Admittedly, some smoke is inevitable with blackening and any searing, so I still made sure to power on the exhaust fan.) Since cooking both batches of chicken took all of 6 minutes and delivered juicy, robustly spiced cutlets, I considered my retooled blackening method a win for all of us home cooks looking for big payoff from our everyday proteins.

—STEVE DUNN, *Cook's Illustrated*

BLACKENED CHICKEN

Blackened Chicken

SERVES 4   TOTAL TIME: 55 MINUTES

We prefer a 12-inch cast-iron skillet here, but a heavy-bottomed stainless-steel or well-seasoned carbon-steel skillet will also work. Avoid nonstick cookware due to the high cooking temperature. This cooking method will produce a modest amount of smoke, so turn on your exhaust fan or crack open a window prior to cooking. If your chicken breasts weigh more than 8 ounces each, add 15 seconds to the cooking time after the cutlets have been flipped. We developed this recipe using Diamond Crystal kosher salt; if using Morton kosher salt, which is denser, use only 2¼ teaspoons. For a less spicy dish, use only ½ teaspoon of cayenne pepper.

- 1 tablespoon smoked paprika
- 1 tablespoon paprika
- 1 tablespoon kosher salt
- 2 teaspoons garlic powder
- 2 teaspoons onion powder
- 1½ teaspoons pepper
- 1½ teaspoons dried oregano
- 1½ teaspoons dried thyme
- ½–1 teaspoon cayenne pepper
- 4 (6- to 8-ounce) boneless, skinless chicken breasts, trimmed
- 1 teaspoon vegetable oil
- 3 tablespoons unsalted butter, cut into ½-tablespoon pieces, divided

1. Combine smoked paprika, paprika, salt, garlic powder, onion powder, pepper, oregano, thyme, and cayenne in wide, shallow bowl. Set wire rack in rimmed baking sheet. Wad up paper towel and place within reach of stove.

2. Working with 1 chicken breast at a time, halve chicken breast crosswise, then cut thicker half in half horizontally, creating 3 cutlets of similar thickness. Place cutlets between sheets of plastic wrap and gently pound to even ⅓-inch thickness.

3. Working with 1 cutlet at a time, dredge thoroughly in spice mixture, pressing to adhere, then shake off excess. Place cutlets in single layer on second rimmed baking sheet.

4. Heat oil in 12-inch cast-iron skillet over high heat until just smoking. Add 1 tablespoon butter to skillet, then tilt skillet or spread butter with flexible spatula until it coats skillet evenly. Add 6 cutlets to skillet, press on each firmly with spatula, and cook undisturbed for 2 minutes. Using tongs, flip cutlets. Press cutlets against skillet with spatula and cook for 1 minute. Slide skillet off heat (leave burner on) and transfer cutlets to prepared wire rack. Grab paper towel with tongs and wipe out skillet to remove any debris.

5. Return skillet to heat. Add remaining 2 tablespoons butter and repeat with remaining cutlets. Let cutlets rest for 3 minutes on rack and serve. (Leftover chicken can be refrigerated for up to 3 days.)

NOTES FROM THE TEST KITCHEN

THE ART (AND SCIENCE) OF BLACKENING

Whether you're searing meat, frying potatoes, baking bread, or caramelizing sugar, color is a pretty good indicator of flavor development, and a rich shade of brown is usually the goal. It's a visual cue that proteins and/or sugars in the food have undergone either Maillardization or caramelization—both complex chemical reactions that break down a food's molecules and cause them to react with each other, creating hundreds of new flavor compounds that smell and taste delightfully complex. Maillard browning boasts savory, meaty, roasty, buttery depth; caramelization can overlap with the roasty, buttery profile, but it skews more bitter and sharp.

By that color spectrum logic, a surface that has merely tanned hasn't reached its full flavor potential, and one that has blackened entirely has overshot the mark and burned. But there's a zone of prized, next-level flavor and complexity as food pushes past the browning phase and elements of charred flavor come into being and coexist with the browned flavors. A crème brûlée's torched sugar crust, the charry edges of barbecued brisket, blistered aromatics in curry paste, and the smoking milk solids and spices that define Prudhomme's blackening technique all live here, and they're thanks to an entirely different set of chemical reactions, called pyrolysis. The term, which is rooted in the Greek words for "fire" and "to break" or "release," refers to decomposition brought on by high temperatures—in essence, burning. When proteins and sugars are heated to temperatures above 350 degrees, the compounds they formed during Maillardization and caramelization break down even further into smaller molecules that taste deeply roasty, tarry, smoky, and bitter, offering a dark allure all their own. The trick to doing it well is restraint: Food can take only a modest dose of pyrolysis before it tastes truly burnt.

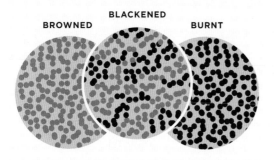

BROWNED   BLACKENED   BURNT

PORCHETTA-STYLE TURKEY BREAST

✓ WHY THIS RECIPE WORKS Turkey porchetta, or turchetta, is a flavor-packed, visually impressive turkey breast preparation that takes its name, shape, and seasonings from the iconic Italian pork roast called porchetta. After deboning a crown roast (better than starting with a boneless turkey breast, since doing the butchery yourself guarantees that the skin and meat are intact), we found it best to toss the breast halves and tenderloins with the herb-spice paste (ground fennel and black peppercorns, rosemary, thyme, sage, garlic, salt, and olive oil) in a bowl rather than spread the mixture on one side of the meat. When we wrapped the meat in the skin into a cylinder, the paste was evenly swirled throughout, lending each slice attractive marbling and loads of flavor. Refrigerating the assembled roast for 8 hours (or up to two days) before cooking allowed the salt in the paste to migrate into the meat, seasoning it and helping it retain its juices during cooking. Starting the roast in a low oven and pulling it out 15 degrees shy of the target temperature (160 degrees) meant that carryover cooking could gradually raise its internal temperature so that it didn't overshoot the mark. Salting the exterior of the roast so that it dried out as it rested in the fridge and brushing melted butter (the milk solids of which encouraged browning) over the surface just before cooking led to rich, flavorful color development. Briefly blasting the roast at 500 degrees deepened its color.

If turkey breast is your holiday centerpiece this year, I've got a proposition for you: Trade the roasted turkey crown and brown gravy for the prettiest, most flavor-packed piece of white-meat poultry you've ever tasted.

I'm talking about turkey porchetta, or turchetta, a preparation that takes its name, shape, and seasonings from the iconic Italian pork roast called porchetta. To make the pork version, home cooks usually slather a boneless loin with a garlicky herb and spice paste; wrap it with the fatty, skin-on belly; and roast the pork low and slow until the skin browns and crisps and the meat is ultratender. Borrowing the approach for turkey breast has become a popular way to deliver bold flavor and an impressive presentation with a typically mild-mannered roast, and it actually offers turkey cookery a few unique advantages. As an all-breast-meat preparation, it skirts the challenge of evenly cooking a whole bird, and this treatment is make-ahead friendly because the bulk of the hands-on work is done well in advance. The boneless, cylindrical roast also cooks evenly from end to end and slices beautifully, and the skin, which essentially swaddles and insulates the lean meat, browns exceptionally well. The garlic-herb paste adds so much flavor that gravy is unnecessary, and the leftovers elevate next-day turkey sandwiches to a whole new level.

Of course, a turkey breast is anatomically unlike pork loin and pork belly, so assembling it in the classic porchetta format requires a completely different approach. Since my first few attempts produced meat that was overcooked and unevenly seasoned, I got strategic with the potent herb-spice paste concentrated in the center of the roll rather than distributed throughout each slice. Wrapping the delicate skin all around the roast proved tricky, too, and the browning was spotty.

I opted to debone a turkey crown myself rather than start with a boneless roast because the quality of the latter tends to vary widely (it often features ragged skin and poorly butchered portions of breast meat), whereas a whole breast guarantees that all parts are intact. After removing the backbone, I peeled away the skin in one piece and set it aside while I cut each breast half off the bone, gently separated the tenderloins from the lobes so that I ultimately had four pieces of boneless meat, and butterflied the plump end of each breast half so that it was evenly thick.

Porchetta seasonings classically include ground fennel seeds and black peppercorns, rosemary, thyme, loads of garlic, and salt. I added fresh sage to steer the profile toward Thanksgiving and buzzed the mixture in a food processor with olive oil to make a loose paste. Then, instead of painting the paste onto one side of the meat as many recipes suggest, I tossed the meat with it in a bowl so that every surface was coated. That way, when I wrapped the skin around the meat into a cylinder (with some creative arranging, all four pieces lined up nicely), the paste was swirled throughout the roast, lending each slice attractive marbling and loads of flavor. Plus, the salt could work its moisture-retention magic throughout the roast rather than just from the exterior.

I tied up the roast and refrigerated it for at least 8 hours so that the salt had time to migrate into the muscle and so that the skin (which I sprinkled with more salt) could dry out, which would help it brown.

On serving day, I brushed the roast with melted butter (its milk solids encourage browning) and used a three-stage cooking approach to ensure that it cooked up juicy and evenly browned. First, I slid the roast into a 275-degree oven and let it cook gently. When it hit 125 degrees—well shy of the 160-degree target—I removed the twine, cranked the heat to 500 degrees, and blasted it for about 15 minutes to brown the surface and raise the turkey's internal temperature to 145 degrees. Finally, I let it sit on the counter for 30 minutes. During that time, carryover cooking raised its temperature the last 15 degrees with zero risk that it would over- or undercook. Simultaneously, the meat rested, so it retained most of its flavorful juices when sliced.

Succulent, marbled with the heady paste, and deeply browned, it was a showstopper—not to mention the friendliest bird I'd ever cooked and carved on Turkey Day.

—STEVE DUNN, *Cook's Illustrated*

Porchetta-Style Turkey Breast

SERVES 6 TO 8   TOTAL TIME: 3½ HOURS, PLUS 8 HOURS SALTING

We prefer a natural turkey breast here; if you're using a self-basting breast (such as Butterball) or kosher breast, omit the 4 teaspoons of salt in the herb paste. This recipe was developed using Diamond Crystal kosher salt; if you're using Morton kosher salt, which is denser, use 1 tablespoon in the herb paste and 1½ teaspoons on the exterior of the roast.

1	tablespoon fennel seeds
2	teaspoons black peppercorns
¼	cup fresh rosemary leaves, chopped
¼	cup fresh sage leaves, chopped
¼	cup fresh thyme leaves
6	garlic cloves, chopped
2	tablespoons kosher salt, divided
3	tablespoons extra-virgin olive oil
1	(7- to 8-pound) bone-in turkey breast
2	tablespoons unsalted butter, melted

1. Grind fennel seeds and peppercorns using spice grinder or mortar and pestle until finely ground. Transfer to food processor and add rosemary, sage, thyme, garlic, and 4 teaspoons salt. Pulse mixture until finely chopped, 15 to 20 pulses, scraping down sides

of bowl as needed. Add oil and process until paste forms, 20 to 30 seconds. Cut seven 16-inch lengths and one 30-inch length of kitchen twine and set aside. Measure out 20-inch piece of aluminum foil and crumple into loose ball. Uncrumple foil and place on rimmed baking sheet (crinkled foil will insulate bottom of sheet and minimize smoking during final roasting step). Spray wire rack with vegetable oil spray and place on prepared sheet.

2. To remove turkey back, place turkey breast skin side down on cutting board. Using kitchen shears, cut through ribs, following vertical lines of fat where breast meets back, from tapered ends of breast to wing joints (A). Using your hands, bend back away from breast to pop shoulder joints out of sockets (B). Using paring knife, cut through joints between bones to separate back from breast (C).

3. Flip breast skin side up. Starting at tapered side of breast and using your fingers to separate skin from meat, peel skin off breast meat and reserve (D). Using tip of chef's knife or boning knife, cut along rib cage to remove each breast half completely (E). Reserve bones for making stock, or discard. Peel tenderloins from underside of each breast (F) and use knife to remove exposed part of white tendon from each tenderloin.

4. Lay 1 breast half on cutting board, smooth side down and with narrow end pointing toward your knife hand. Holding knife parallel to cutting board, slice into breast starting where breast becomes thicker (about halfway along length). Stop ½ inch from edge of breast (G) and open to create 1 long piece of even thickness. Repeat with remaining breast half. Transfer all meat to large bowl. Add herb paste and massage into meat to coat evenly.

5. Pat exterior of skin dry with paper towels and lay flat, exterior side down, on cutting board with long side running parallel to counter. Remove any loose pieces of fat. Lay 1 breast half on 1 side of skin with butterflied end closest to you. Lay second breast half next to first with butterflied end farthest away from you (H). Spread breast halves slightly apart and lay tenderloins between them with their thin ends overlapping in center (I).

6. Using skin as aid, fold up each breast half over tenderloins so skin meets directly over tenderloins. Slip one 16-inch length of twine under roast about 2 inches from 1 end and tie into simple knot, pinching skin closed as you tighten. Repeat tying at opposite end (J).

HOW TO ASSEMBLE TURCHETTA

Almost all the hands-on work for turchetta happens up front—and is worth the effort.

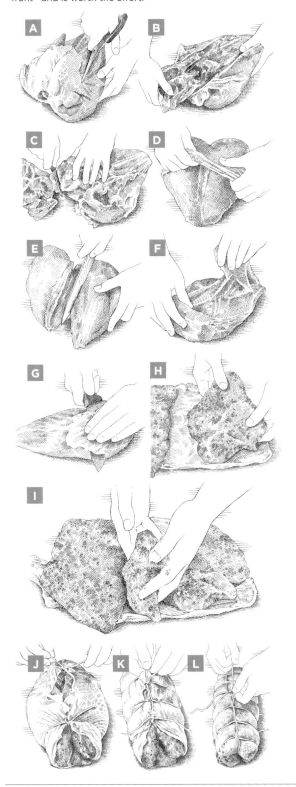

Tie remaining five 16-inch lengths of twine evenly between 2 end pieces. Trim excess twine.

7. Tie 1 end of 30-inch length of twine onto loop farthest from you. Working toward you, loop twine over top and around each successive strand until you get to bottom of roast (K). Flip roast and continue looping to bottom of roast (L). Flip roast again and tie off where you started. Sprinkle roast evenly with remaining 2 teaspoons salt; place on prepared rack; and refrigerate, uncovered, for at least 8 hours or up to 2 days.

8. Adjust oven rack to upper-middle position and heat oven to 275 degrees. Brush roast with melted butter. Cook until thickest part of roast registers 125 degrees, 1½ to 1¾ hours. Remove roast from oven and increase oven temperature to 500 degrees. When oven is up to temperature, remove twine from roast; return roast to oven; and cook until skin is browned and roast registers 145 degrees, 15 to 20 minutes.

9. Transfer roast to cutting board, tent with foil, and let rest for 30 minutes. Slice ½ inch thick and serve.

HOLIDAY SMOKED TURKEY

✔ **WHY THIS RECIPE WORKS**   We started with a spatchcocked turkey (the backbone is removed so that the bird lies flat and cooks more evenly). We developed this recipe on a charcoal grill, so we employed the charcoal snake method, a setup where the coals are arranged in a C shape around the perimeter of the bottom of the grill. Lighting both ends simultaneously meant that the coals would burn slowly, working their way toward the middle, ensuring even heat. Wood chunks added on top of the charcoal provided bursts of smoke throughout cooking. Using a probe thermometer helped us know when the breast hit 160 degrees, at which point we removed the turkey from the grill so that the meat wouldn't dry out and the skin stayed beautifully bronzed and not too dark.

Smoking a turkey for the holidays is a pro move. Why? Since you cook it outside, it's one less dish that has to compete for precious oven space. Slowly smoking the turkey cooks it gently, helping the relatively lean meat stay moist and juicy. The smoke and seasonings add a lot of flavor to the mild bird. And barbecuing is an activity that brings people together as they are drawn to the sights, sounds, and smells of the grill.

HOLIDAY SMOKED TURKEY

Someone who understands the beauty of a smoked turkey better than anyone is James Beard Award–winning pit master and restaurateur Rodney Scott. While Scott's barbecue restaurants in Charleston, South Carolina; Birmingham, Alabama; and Atlanta, Georgia, are famous for whole-hog barbecue, his new book, *Rodney Scott's World of BBQ* (2021), includes a holiday recipe that calls for a spatchcocked turkey (the backbone is removed and the bird is flattened so that it cooks more evenly and is easier to maneuver). In that recipe, which also calls for a ceramic smoker, the turkey is seasoned with a spice mixture and cooked skin side down for 1½ hours before it is brushed with a thin, vinegar-based mop. The turkey is then flipped skin side up; brushed with the mop again; and cooked for another 1½ hours in the smoky, low heat until it's done.

After talking with Scott about his recipe, I decided to adapt it to work on a more common kettle grill, so I turned to a trusted test kitchen technique that transforms a kettle grill into a smoker: a charcoal snake. For this method, charcoal briquettes are arranged in a C shape around the perimeter of the grill bottom. When one side is lit, the briquettes slowly ignite in succession for a nice low, long (upwards of 6 hours) burn without the need to open the grill to add more charcoal. We like to place a disposable aluminum pan filled with water in the center of the C-shaped charcoal snake to help moderate the grill's temperature. We also strategically place wood chunks on top of the briquettes for bursts of smoke throughout cooking.

The first few times I ran through Scott's recipe with a charcoal snake on the kettle grill, the birds cooked unevenly. Since the heat moves in a circular pattern around the turkey, the side of the bird that was originally closest to the burning charcoal was dark and overcooked by the time the second side, which was initially farther from the heat source, was cooked through. Lighting both ends of the charcoal snake at the start resolved the uneven cooking problem but created another problem: too much heat. The turkey's skin turned too dark before the meat was done.

The turkey was positioned at the edge of the grill, with the breast facing away from the arc of the snake. The solution: positioning the water pan toward the edge of the grill as well, not in the center, so that it was directly beneath the turkey. Having the steam from the pan directly under the turkey kept the turkey skin from overbrowning while the meat cooked.

GRILL SETUP
This "two-headed snake" (you light both ends simultaneously) provides hours of heat and smoke to gently cook and flavor the turkey.

WOOD CHUNK PLACEMENT
About 2 inches apart for consistent smoke

SNAKE CONSTRUCTION
Two briquettes wide by two briquettes high

ADD LIT BRIQUETTES TO BOTH ENDS

TURKEY PLACEMENT
Skin side down over water pan, with drumsticks pointing toward arc in charcoal snake

I could now leave the turkey skin side down for longer (until the 2-hour mark) and then let the skin brown when I flipped it. I also used a temperature probe to signal when the turkey breast was cooked to 160 degrees; that way, I could remove the bird from the grill before it could dry out.

I kept Scott's rub, a blend he makes in bulk at his restaurants. And I used his recipe for the mop, too, but I scaled it down. Scott explained that the acidic mop simultaneously adds flavor and tenderizes the meat. In his book, Scott acknowledges that this turkey isn't going to look like one you see on a magazine cover, but it will taste much better. With all respect to the chef, we think this bronzed, smoky, perfectly seasoned turkey is both delicious and gorgeous!

—MORGAN BOLLING, *Cook's Country*

SERVES 10 TO 12   TOTAL TIME: 4¾ HOURS, PLUS 30 MINUTES RESTING

We developed this recipe, which is adapted from Rodney Scott's holiday turkey recipe in his cookbook, *Rodney Scott's World of BBQ* (2021), using a 22-inch kettle charcoal grill. We recommend reading the entire recipe before starting. You can reserve the turkey neck and giblets for making gravy, if desired. You can also ask your butcher to spatchcock the turkey and skip step 3.

MOP

2   **cups distilled white vinegar**

¼   **cup granulated sugar**

2   **thin lemon slices**

1   **tablespoon pepper**

2   **teaspoons cayenne pepper**

½   **teaspoon red pepper flakes**

RUB

2   **tablespoons kosher salt**

1   **tablespoon monosodium glutamate**

1   **tablespoon pepper**

1   **tablespoon paprika**

1   **tablespoon chili powder**

1   **tablespoon packed light brown sugar**

1½ **teaspoons garlic powder**

1½ **teaspoons onion powder**

¼   **teaspoon cayenne pepper**

TURKEY

1   **(12- to 14-pound) turkey, neck and giblets discarded**

4   **(3-inch) wood chunks**

1   **(13 by 9-inch) disposable aluminum pan**

1. FOR THE MOP: Combine all ingredients in medium saucepan and bring to simmer over medium-high heat. Cook until sugar is dissolved, about 2 minutes. Remove from heat and let cool completely. Discard lemon slices. (Mop can be refrigerated in airtight container for up to 2 months.)

2. FOR THE RUB: Combine all ingredients in bowl.

3. FOR THE TURKEY: Place turkey breast side down on cutting board with cavity facing counter edge. Using kitchen shears, cut through bones on either side of backbone, staying as close as possible to backbone. Discard backbone. Flip turkey and press down firmly on breast with heels of your hands to flatten breastbone.

4. Sprinkle rub all over both sides of turkey. Open bottom vent of charcoal grill completely. To make charcoal snake, arrange 50 charcoal briquettes, 2 briquettes wide, around perimeter of grill, overlapping slightly so briquettes are touching and leaving 9-inch gap between ends of snake. Place second layer of 50 briquettes, also 2 briquettes wide, on top of first. (Completed arrangement should be 2 briquettes wide by 2 briquettes high.)

5. Starting 2 inches from each end of charcoal snake, place wood chunks on top of charcoal about 2 inches apart. Slide disposable pan into charcoal gap, running lengthwise into arc of snake and touching grill wall on opposite side of snake. Pour 6 cups water into pan.

6. Light chimney starter filled with 20 briquettes (pile briquettes on 1 side of chimney so they catch). When coals are partially covered with ash, use tongs to pile 10 coals on each end of charcoal snake, where briquettes meet water pan, so both ends of snake ignite.

7. Set cooking grate in place, then clean and oil grate. Position turkey, skin side down, over water pan with drumsticks pointing toward arc in charcoal snake. Cover grill, position lid vent over turkey, and open lid vent completely. Cook, undisturbed, for 2 hours.

8. Using small barbecue mop or basting brush, baste turkey liberally with mop. Using oven mitts or grill mitts, flip turkey skin side up, again positioning it over water pan with drumsticks pointing toward arc in charcoal snake. Baste skin side liberally with more mop (you may not need all of it; discard any extra).

9. Insert temperature probe into thickest part of breast. Cover grill and cook until breast registers 160 degrees (check temperature of both sides of breast) and thighs register 175 degrees, about 1 hour.

10. Transfer turkey to rimmed baking sheet. Let rest for 30 to 40 minutes. Carve turkey and transfer to serving platter. Serve.

DUCK BREASTS WITH PORT WINE–FIG SAUCE

✔ **WHY THIS RECIPE WORKS**   We developed this recipe using boneless breasts from White Pekin ducks for their balanced meat-to-fat ratio. White Pekins are also the most popular breed raised in the United States, so they're easier to find in grocery stores, and the breasts are typically more consistent in size. To help render fat and ensure the crispest skin, we trimmed away excess fat and any gristly bits while also checking for bone fragments and then scored the skin in a crosshatch pattern. To help the breasts retain moisture and achieve deep flavor, we salted and then refrigerated them, wrapped, for at least 6 hours. Starting the breasts skin side down in a cold skillet and then cooking them over medium heat was an efficient way to render the fat, crisp the skin, and cook the meat gently. After flipping the breasts and lowering the heat, we finished cooking them to the desired temperature on the stovetop (we prefer medium-rare or medium). A simple sauce made of port wine, dried figs, vinegar, and sugar cut through the fat and paired perfectly with the duck.

Duck is a special-occasion restaurant dish that is also a great choice to cook at home. To love duck is to embrace its uniqueness: This game bird is hunted wild, but it's also commonly farm raised and can be purchased in supermarkets. Duck is often eaten rare (like beef). Because it flies, its muscles are firmer and pinker, more similar to red meat. Most important, with a little know-how, you can have restaurant-quality duck at home. My goals are to get you to share my love of duck and to make you confident in cooking it.

I developed this recipe using boneless breasts from White Pekin ducks, which tend to have a more balanced meat-to-fat ratio than the breasts of moulard, Muscovy, and mallard breeds. Also, since White Pekin is the most popular breed raised in the United States, it's easier to find in grocery stores, and the breasts are typically more consistent in size. Sourcing the duck might actually be the hardest part of this recipe.

Let's begin. Too much duck fat can be too much of a good thing, so trim away excess fat and any gristly bits, and then double-check for bone fragments. Score the skin in a crosshatch pattern to help the subcutaneous fat render and the skin crisp. Salt the breasts and refrigerate

NOTES FROM THE TEST KITCHEN

CROSSHATCH WITH CAUTION

When crosshatching the skin, be sure not to cut all the way through it to the meat.

them, wrapped in plastic wrap, for at least 6 hours so that they firm up, retain moisture, and become deeply seasoned. Place the breasts skin side down in a cold skillet, and then turn the heat to medium; this "cold start" technique is an efficient way to render the fat, crisp the skin, and cook the meat gently. Once the fat is rendered and the skin is browned (after about 20 minutes of hands-off cooking), flip the breasts, lower the heat, and finish cooking them to your desired temperature on the stovetop—this part takes only a few minutes more.

The duck is perfectly cooked, so now what? A sauce! Our choice is a simple affair of port wine and dried figs (duck goes very well with fruit) that cooks in about 15 minutes.

It's true, you might have to seek out a source for your duck, but with a little preparation ahead of time and a hands-off cooking method, this recipe is the perfect introduction to cooking duck. Time to celebrate!

—MARK HUXSOLL, *Cook's Country*

Duck Breasts with Port Wine–Fig Sauce

SERVES 4   TOTAL TIME: 50 MINUTES, PLUS 6 HOURS SALTING

This recipe was developed with duck breasts weighing 7 to 8 ounces each. However, if you can find only larger duck breasts that weigh 10 to 12 ounces each, they will also work here. They tend to come with more excess fat; once it's trimmed away, the breasts will weigh closer to 8 or 9 ounces. You may need to cook these larger duck breasts about 1 minute longer on the second side to reach the desired temperature. We prefer duck cooked to medium-rare or medium.

DUCK

    4 (7- to 8-ounce) boneless duck breasts
    2 teaspoons kosher salt
  1½ teaspoons pepper

SAUCE

    ½ cup ruby port
    ¼ cup dried Black Mission figs, halved through stem
    ¼ cup red wine vinegar
    3 tablespoons sugar

1. FOR THE DUCK: Pat duck breasts dry with paper towels. Place breasts skin side down on cutting board. Using sharp knife, trim away excess fat around edges of breasts, then remove any visible silver skin attached to meat.

2. Flip breasts and cut ½-inch crosshatch pattern in skin, being careful not to cut into meat. Sprinkle all over with salt and pepper. Place duck on large plate skin side up, cover tightly with plastic wrap, and refrigerate for at least 6 hours or up to 24 hours.

3. FOR THE SAUCE: Meanwhile, combine all ingredients in small saucepan. Bring to boil over medium heat. Cook until reduced to about ½ cup, about 15 minutes; set aside off heat. Sauce will thicken to syrupy consistency as it cools. (Cooled sauce can be stored in airtight container for up to 3 days or refrigerated for up to 2 weeks.)

4. Place breasts skin side down in cold 12-inch nonstick skillet. Cook over medium heat until copious amount of fat has rendered and skin is well browned and crispy, 17 to 20 minutes.

5. Flip breasts skin side up and reduce heat to medium-low. Cook until centers of breasts register 125 to 130 degrees (for medium-rare), 1 to 2 minutes; 130 to 135 degrees (for medium), 3 to 4 minutes; 135 to 140 degrees (for medium-well), 4 to 5 minutes; or 145 to 150 degrees (for well-done), 7 to 8 minutes.

6. Transfer breasts to wire rack set in rimmed baking sheet. Tent with aluminum foil and let rest for 10 minutes.

7. Transfer duck to carving board and slice ¼ inch thick. Serve with sauce.

NOTES FROM THE TEST KITCHEN

LIQUID GOLD

Rendered duck fat is one of the most flavorful fats you can cook with. To save duck fat after making this recipe, pour it through a fine-mesh strainer into a Mason jar (or similar container). Once the fat is cool, cover the jar and refrigerate the fat for up to one month or freeze it for up to six months.

Once you have duck fat at the ready, you can use it to make duck or chicken leg confit, croutons, or french fries; add fat to gravy; sauté vegetables; roast potatoes; or fry eggs.

SALMON PEPERONATA

✓ **WHY THIS RECIPE WORKS** Made from sweet bell pepper, onion, garlic, and tomato stewed in extra-virgin olive oil until meltingly soft, peperonata can be served in myriad ways. In this recipe, we paired it with rich, quick-cooking skinless salmon fillets. Two bell peppers, one onion, six garlic cloves, and a can of diced tomatoes gave us enough sauce for a 2-pound salmon fillet. Using different-colored bell peppers gave the dish an extra dimension of visual appeal. Red pepper flakes provided just a hint of spice. Cooking the salmon fillets on top of the peperonata allowed the flavors of the two to mingle. Lemon juice perked up the dish, and a sprinkle of basil added freshness. More pepper flakes brought on a little extra heat, and a drizzle of olive oil rounded out the flavors.

Peperonata is a quiet hero of Italian cuisine. Sweet bell peppers, stewed in extra-virgin olive oil until meltingly soft, play the starring role with onion, garlic, and tomato as supporting players. The mixture is served at room temperature as part of an antipasto platter or warm as a condiment for different meats. It is equally fantastic on salads, with eggs, spread on slices of crusty bread, or layered into sandwiches.

We wanted to pair this mild, sweet vegetable mélange with rich, quick-cooking skinless salmon fillets for an easy weeknight supper. To make the peperonata, slice up two bell peppers and an onion, crush six garlic cloves, and add them all to a skillet with lots of olive oil plus some salt. Cover and cook, stirring occasionally, until the peppers and onion are soft, about 10 minutes. Stir in a can of diced tomatoes (including the juice), some capers and a little of their brine, and red pepper flakes and cook until the sauce is thickened. Then turn down the heat and nestle the salmon fillets into the peperonata. Cover and cook until the salmon is done, about 15 minutes more.

This last bit of cooking is where the magic in this dish happens. The flavors of the peperonata and salmon mingle, with the peperonata gaining richness from the salmon and the salmon picking up a subtle sweetness from the vegetables. A drizzling of lemon juice perks up the flavors of both the peperonata and the salmon, a sprinkle of basil adds freshness to the dish while more pepper flakes add heat, and an extra drizzle of olive oil is the perfect finishing touch.

—MARK HUXSOLL, *Cook's Country*

SALMON PEPERONATA

Salmon Peperonata

SERVES 4   TOTAL TIME: 55 MINUTES

To ensure uniform pieces, we prefer to purchase a whole center-cut salmon fillet and cut it into four equal pieces. Alternatively, you could purchase four 6- to 8-ounce skinless fillets of similar thickness. The most accurate way to assess the doneness of the salmon is with an instant-read thermometer.

1   (2-pound) skinless center-cut salmon fillet,
     1 to 1½ inches thick
1   teaspoon pepper
1¾   teaspoons table salt, divided
¼   cup extra-virgin olive oil, plus extra for drizzling
1   red bell pepper, stemmed, seeded, and cut into
     ¼-inch-wide strips
1   yellow bell pepper, stemmed, seeded, and cut into
     ¼-inch-wide strips
1   onion, halved and sliced ¼ inch thick
6   garlic cloves, crushed and peeled
1   (14.5-ounce) can diced tomatoes
2   tablespoons capers, rinsed, plus 4 teaspoons brine
¼   teaspoon red pepper flakes, plus extra for sprinkling
1½   teaspoons lemon juice
¼   cup chopped fresh basil

1. Cut salmon crosswise into 4 equal fillets. Pat salmon dry with paper towels and sprinkle with pepper and ¾ teaspoon salt.

2. Heat oil in 12-inch nonstick skillet over medium-high heat until just smoking. Add bell peppers, onion, garlic, and remaining 1 teaspoon salt. Cover and cook, stirring occasionally, until vegetables are soft, about 10 minutes.

NOTES FROM THE TEST KITCHEN

SKINNED SIDE
Many of our salmon recipes—including this one—reference the skinned side of skinless salmon. That simply means the side from which the skin has been removed; with salmon fillets, the skinned side is typically grayer.

The side that looks slightly gray is the skinned side.

3. Stir in tomatoes and their juice, capers and brine, and pepper flakes. Continue to cook, uncovered, until slightly thickened, about 5 minutes longer. Season with salt and pepper to taste.

4. Reduce heat to medium-low. Nestle salmon into peperonata, skinned side down. Cover and cook until centers of fillets are still translucent when checked with tip of paring knife and register 125 degrees (for medium-rare), 10 to 15 minutes.

5. Drizzle lemon juice over salmon. Sprinkle with basil and extra pepper flakes. Serve, drizzled with extra oil.

POKE

✓ **WHY THIS RECIPE WORKS**   We created two versions of our poke ("poh-KAY")—a Hawaiian raw fish salad that's become increasingly popular across the rest of the United States. For both, we relied on the freshest fish we could find: dense, meaty, clean-tasting yellowfin tuna and rich, clean-tasting salmon. We dressed the tuna with a simple, savory mix of soy sauce and sesame oil. Sweet onion, scallions, pepper flakes, ginger, and garlic added pungency, spice, and texture. We dressed the salmon in a microwaved mix of soy sauce, mirin, sugar, garlic, and ginger. Toasted sesame oil added roasty depth while scallions, diced cucumber, and Fresno chile added pungency, texture, and spice. Finishing both versions with a garnish of furikake (a Japanese seasoning blend of dried seaweed, bonito flakes, and sesame seeds) layered on texture and gave us an easy, all-in-one ingredient for boosting the umami.

The poke (pronounced "poh-KAY") scene hasn't always looked the way it does today, with bowl shops in shopping centers all over the country offering every imaginable ingredient—miso-lemon mayonnaise, crispy beet chips, zucchini noodles, etc.—to accompany the base of diced raw fish. Positioned as a healthy alternative to your average fast-food option, the poke bowl has never been trendier. But it can be traced back to a traditional Hawaiian version, which pares down the extras and focuses on good, fresh fish.

As food writer Martha Cheng explains in *The Poke Cookbook: The Freshest Way to Eat Fish* (2017), the earliest Hawaiian version of poke dates back to before Captain James Cook and other Westerners arrived on the islands. These early iterations of poke (the word means "to cut or slice into pieces") were ultrasimple: just raw, shallow-water fish pulled straight from the ocean and tossed with sea salt, seaweed, and ground roasted kukui nuts. This preparation endures, and you can still find a similar style, called Hawaiian-style poke, sold alongside more modern variations on the islands today (although the fish is more likely to be ahi tuna than shallow-water fish).

Ahi shoyu poke, the modern version that's become Hawaii's most popular in the last half century or so, is almost as simple as the original. Heavily influenced by Japanese sushi culture, this mix of ahi (yellowfin) tuna, soy sauce, sesame oil, sweet onion, scallion, and sometimes chiles is probably the quintessential poke, the foundation upon which every fast-casual chain slinging myriad variations of seafood salads is ultimately built.

And it is a solid foundation. Fresh fish is the bedrock of the recipe, and once you've procured it, little else is needed to make your own ultradelicious poke. Rich, dense, meaty, and clean-tasting, raw yellowfin tuna (and even richer salmon in the case of our salmon teriyaki variation) makes a deeply satisfying base. To that, you need only to add a dressing of soy sauce (for seasoning and complex umami), vegetable oil, and toasted sesame oil (for roasty depth); crisp, pungent sweet onion and scallion; and a touch of heat from fresh ginger, garlic, and pepper flakes. The macadamia nuts and furikake (optional) in our recipe are delicious additions inspired by the seaweed and kukui nuts from the traditional Hawaiian version. Try it and see for yourself. There's no simpler way to create a meal that satisfies so deeply and leaves such a lasting impression.

—MATTHEW FAIRMAN, *Cook's Country*

Tuna Poke

SERVES 4   TOTAL TIME: 25 MINUTES

See "Poke Fish Primer" for information on buying the tuna. Vidalia, Maui, or Walla Walla sweet onions will all work here. If you can't find sweet onions, you can substitute a yellow onion by soaking the thinly sliced onion in ice water for 20 minutes and then draining and patting it dry. Serve this poke as a snack or an appetizer, or make it a meal by serving it over warm rice.

1   **pound skinless yellowfin tuna, cut into ¾-inch cubes**

¼   **cup thinly sliced sweet onion (halved and sliced through root end)**

⅓   **cup finely chopped salted dry-roasted macadamia nuts**

POKE FISH PRIMER

Freshness is key when serving fish raw. The raw tuna and salmon flesh should appear moist and shiny; feel firm (the flesh should spring right back when pressed); and smell clean, not fishy. Ask your fishmonger to slice tuna steaks to order, ideally those that have little to no connective tissue, which can be too chewy raw. Similarly, ask to have salmon cut to order from a center-cut fillet that has little to none of the thin belly attached, as it can be tough and fatty when eaten raw.

SALMON —
You may need to remove pinbones

TUNA
Best when sliced to order

- When possible, research to **find a purveyor that supplies local sushi or poke restaurants**. Some wholesale purveyors like these will sell directly to individuals.

- You can also **inquire at sushi or poke restaurants to see if they will order extra fish for you to pick up**.

- Otherwise, **look for a busy fish market/counter with a good reputation**. The more customers they have, the faster they will need to replenish their stock and the fresher the fish will be.

- **Call ahead to notify your fishmonger** that you're looking for fish to serve raw and to inquire about when fresh fish is delivered.

- **We call for farm-raised salmon because wild-caught salmon can be prone to parasites**; it must be commercially frozen to the Food and Drug Administration's standards to be safe for raw consumption.

- **If buying frozen tuna or salmon, plan ahead.** Thawing the fish slowly in the refrigerator (which can take 24 hours or longer) is the superior method for preserving its texture.

3   **scallions, white and green parts separated and sliced thin on bias**

3   **tablespoons soy sauce**

2   **tablespoons vegetable oil**

2   **teaspoons toasted sesame oil**

2   **teaspoons grated fresh ginger**

1   **garlic clove, minced**

¾   **teaspoon red pepper flakes**

Furikake (optional)

Gently combine tuna, onion, macadamia nuts, scallion whites, soy sauce, vegetable oil, sesame oil, ginger, garlic, and pepper flakes in large bowl using rubber spatula. Season with salt to taste. Serve, sprinkled with furikake, if using, and scallion greens. (Poke can be refrigerated for up to 24 hours.)

SALMON TERIYAKI POKE AND TUNA POKE

FURIKAKE

Furikake is a multitextured Japanese seasoning blend that comes in many styles. We recommend using a blend containing dried seaweed (nori and/or kombu), bonito flakes, and sesame seeds. Look for it at an Asian market, in the Asian section of the grocery store, or online. It's great sprinkled over rice, eggs, and popcorn.

Salmon Teriyaki Poke

SERVES 4   TOTAL TIME: 40 MINUTES

This recipe was inspired by the Teriyaki Salmon and Avocado in Martha Cheng's *The Poke Cookbook: The Freshest Way to Eat Fish* (2017). See "Poke Fish Primer" (page 185) for information on buying the salmon. You can serve this poke as a snack or an appetizer, or you can make it a meal by serving it over warm rice.

- 3 tablespoons soy sauce
- 1 tablespoon mirin
- 2 teaspoons sugar
- 2 teaspoons grated fresh ginger
- 1 garlic clove, minced
- 1 pound skinless farm-raised salmon, cut into ¾-inch cubes
- 1 small avocado, halved, pitted, and cut into ½-inch pieces
- ¼ English cucumber, cut into ½-inch pieces (½ cup)
- 3 scallions, white and green parts separated and sliced thin on bias
- 1 Fresno chile, stemmed, halved, seeded, and sliced thin
- 2 teaspoons toasted sesame oil
- 1 teaspoon kosher salt
  Furikake (optional)

1. Microwave soy sauce, mirin, sugar, ginger, and garlic in bowl until steaming, 30 to 60 seconds. Stir to dissolve sugar. Refrigerate until no longer warm, about 15 minutes.

2. Gently combine salmon, avocado, cucumber, scallion whites, Fresno chile, oil, salt, and soy sauce mixture in large bowl using rubber spatula. Serve, sprinkled with furikake, if using, and scallion greens. (Poke can be refrigerated for up to 24 hours.)

FISHERMAN'S PIE

✔ **WHY THIS RECIPE WORKS**   We hewed close to tradition when selecting the seafood for our Fisherman's Pie, landing on a trio that offers a variety of flavors and textures: flaky, white-fleshed cod; delicate cold-smoked salmon; and snappy jumbo shrimp. A roux-thickened mixture of heavy cream, clam juice, and white wine produced a light, elegant sauce. We kept the flavorings simple, using just leek, thyme, and parsley so as not to overwhelm the delicate fish. Gently simmering the seafood in the sauce on the stovetop before topping it with fluffy mashed potatoes ensured that the seafood would be perfectly cooked.

The way Brits describe their fish pie is a lot like the way Texans talk about brisket or New Yorkers explain a properly chewy bagel—which is to say, with great conviction and affection. *The Guardian* columnist Felicity Cloake has compared the beloved casserole to a cozy pair of slippers or a Sunday-afternoon film with a mug of tea, and Manchester-based journalist Tony Naylor dubbed it "elbows-on-the-table, fork-in-one-hand, glass-in-the-other eating." "Fish pie," he wrote in his own *Guardian* account, "should be a dish of seamless comfort-troffing."

Unequivocally snug, substantive fare that likely evolved as a Lenten dish made with seafood scraps, the dish is the surf equivalent of shepherd's or cottage pie. It's typically a mixture of fresh and smoked finfish such as cod, haddock, and salmon and shellfish such as shrimp, which is all napped with a creamy, roux-based sauce flavored with stock, wine, and aromatics; sealed with a lid of mashed potatoes; and baked or broiled until the crust is craggy and lightly bronzed. The result is as comforting as it is luxurious, ideal cold-weather fare for family or company.

THE BOOZY HISTORY OF CLAM JUICE

If you woke with a hangover in the early 1900s, you may have downed aspirin with an iced clam juice chaser to cure your ailments. In the same era, the briny blend—made by filtering the salted water used to steam clams—also became popular as a mixer for hot soda-fountain drinks such as the clam and ginger and the malted clamette. Since then, the bivalve-based brew is mainly used to add marine savoriness to seafood soups and stews, though its role in drinks persists in cocktails such as the bloody Caesar. –Rebecca Hays

HOW TO SPREAD THE SPUDS

To neatly spread the thick topping over the loose filling, start by applying spoonfuls of mashed potato around the edges of the baking dish and then arrange the remainder in the center of the dish. Smooth the potato topping with a rubber spatula, making sure to seal the edges so that no seafood or sauce is exposed.

For my own recipe, I opted to use cod fillets (widely available both fresh and frozen) as well as smoked salmon in place of the smoked haddock that is traditionally used in the UK but rarely available in the United States. Four ounces of cold-smoked fillets added vivid color and rich flavor to the stew, and I preferred their silkier texture to the drier, flakier fillets of hot-smoked salmon (though the latter made a perfectly acceptable substitute). Jumbo shrimp added briny sweetness and snappy bite, especially after I tossed them with salt and a bit of baking soda before cooking. Even though the shrimp are cooked a bit longer than usual in this dish, they stayed moist and springy since baking soda raises the shrimp's pH and helps them retain moisture.

Sautéed aromatics (leek instead of onion for its milder allium flavor, plus fresh thyme) were the flavor base for my creamy sauce, which I thickened to a chowder-like consistency by whisking in flour and bottled clam juice. The latter delivered the clean, briny flavor of the sea without the extra effort of making a seafood stock. Then came the dairy: Heavy cream got the nod over milk for the lush richness it added.

There are two common routes for cooking the seafood: combining it raw with the sauce in a gratin dish, topping it with mashed potatoes, and then baking the assembly until the fish is cooked through, or parcooking it in the sauce on the stove before smoothing the potatoes over the filling and broiling the pie to color and crisp the topping. I preferred the latter because it was much faster, and it also allowed for close monitoring of the seafood as it simmered, ensuring moist, tender results every time. But regardless of the method, there was potential for the sauce to break, since the exuded seafood jus and cream don't readily mix.

The solution was to frequently stir the seafood and sauce while they gently bubbled together on the stovetop to ensure that juices given off by the seafood were fully incorporated.

To finish up, I adapted our Shepherd's Pie potato topping for this pie, swapping cream for the milk (as I was already using cream in the filling) and eliminating the scallions. I kept the egg yolk to help the russets soufflé. Its protein and fat—along with a drizzle of butter—also encouraged browning on top of this seafood pie that I hope will earn plenty of fans on this side of the pond.

—STEVE DUNN, *Cook's Illustrated*

Fisherman's Pie

SERVES 4 TO 6   TOTAL TIME: 1¾ HOURS

We use an 8-inch square broiler-safe baking dish for this recipe, but any broiler-safe dish that holds 2 quarts will work here. At the end of step 3, the base for the pie should look quite thick; it will loosen to the perfect consistency as the seafood cooks. We prefer cold-smoked salmon here because it's less likely to overcook, but you can substitute hot-smoked salmon if you prefer it. Making a pattern on the topping not only looks attractive but also provides textural contrast when the pie is broiled.

TOPPING

- 2 **pounds russet potatoes, peeled and cut into 1-inch chunks**
- 1 **tablespoon table salt for cooking potatoes**
- 3 **tablespoons unsalted butter, cut into 3 pieces**
- ⅓ **cup heavy cream**
- 1 **large egg yolk**

FILLING

- 12 **ounces jumbo shrimp (16 to 20 per pound), peeled, deveined, tails removed, and cut in half crosswise**
- ¾ **teaspoon table salt, divided**
- ⅛ **teaspoon baking soda**
- 4 **tablespoons unsalted butter, divided**
- 1 **leek, white and light-green parts only, halved lengthwise, sliced thin, and washed thoroughly**
- 1 **teaspoon minced fresh thyme**
- ⅓ **cup dry white wine or dry vermouth**
- 3 **tablespoons all-purpose flour**

2   (8-ounce) bottles clam juice

⅔   cup heavy cream

¼   teaspoon pepper

1   pound skinless cod fillets, cut into 1-inch chunks

4   ounces cold-smoked salmon, cut into ½-inch pieces

½   cup fresh parsley leaves, minced

1. FOR THE TOPPING: Place potatoes in large saucepan and add water to just cover. Add salt and bring to boil over high heat. Reduce heat to maintain simmer and cook until tip of paring knife inserted into potato meets no resistance, 8 to 10 minutes. Drain potatoes and return to saucepan over low heat. Cook, shaking saucepan occasionally, until any surface moisture on potatoes has evaporated, about 1 minute. Off heat, mash potatoes well. Stir in butter until melted. Whisk cream and egg yolk together in bowl; stir into potatoes. Season with salt and pepper to taste. Cover to keep warm and set aside.

2. FOR THE FILLING: Set 8-inch square broiler-safe baking dish on rimmed baking sheet. Sprinkle shrimp with ¼ teaspoon salt and baking soda in bowl and toss to combine. Refrigerate until needed.

3. Melt 3 tablespoons butter in medium saucepan over medium-low heat. Add leek and thyme and cook, stirring occasionally, until leek is softened, 6 to 7 minutes. Add wine and cook, stirring occasionally, until wine has evaporated, about 5 minutes. Add flour and cook, stirring constantly, for 1 minute. Add clam juice and stir until mixture is smooth. Stir in cream, pepper, and remaining ½ teaspoon salt. Increase heat to medium-high and bring to simmer. Lower heat to maintain simmer and cook, stirring frequently, until mixture resembles thick chowder, 10 to 13 minutes.

4. Stir cod, salmon, and shrimp into sauce and return to simmer. Cover and cook, stirring every 2 minutes and adjusting heat if needed to maintain simmer, until shrimp are opaque and just cooked through, 4 to 6 minutes. Off heat, stir in parsley. Transfer filling to prepared dish.

5. Adjust oven rack 8 inches from broiler element and heat broiler. Spoon topping over filling, starting at edges and working toward center. Smooth with rubber spatula, making sure to seal around edges of dish so no seafood or sauce is exposed. Using back of spoon or tines of fork, make pattern on topping. Melt remaining 1 tablespoon butter and drizzle over topping. Broil pie, still on sheet, until topping is golden brown and crusty and filling is bubbly, 6 to 7 minutes (watch closely). Let cool for 10 minutes before serving.

GARLICKY BROILED SHRIMP

✓ **WHY THIS RECIPE WORKS** The broiler's direct, intense heat is great for browning, but shrimp are so small that it's hard to get color on them before they overcook. We started by lightly salting the shrimp so that they retained moisture even as they were cooked under high heat. A coating of butter and honey added richness, boosted browning, and underscored the shrimp's sweetness. To cook, we arranged the shrimp in a single layer on a wire rack set in a rimmed baking sheet to allow for airflow, which promotes even cooking. Setting the oven rack 4 inches from the broiler ensured that the shrimp had enough distance to cook evenly and brown quickly without needing to be turned. Garlic and red pepper flakes were stirred directly into the honey-butter mixture before cooking, giving the shrimp a scampi-like profile.

The broiler is an unsung hero in the kitchen: It preheats quickly, transfers heat more efficiently than the ambient waves of the oven's bake setting, and in certain applications requires less babysitting than the stovetop. Take shrimp, for example, which cook so rapidly in a hot pan that they must be constantly monitored. Spreading them out on a baking sheet and broiling them, I hoped, would be a more hands-off way to "sear" the pieces, since I could strategically distance them from the broiler's fierce element. If I found that sweet spot, I could achieve a tray of snappy, lightly charred shrimp to top rice, noodles, or salads or swipe through cocktail sauce.

When shopping for shrimp, I gravitate toward the extra-large size—they're meaty but conveniently bite-size, perfect for everyday applications. After peeling and deveining them, I salted them for 15 minutes so that they'd be thoroughly seasoned and hang on to their moisture during cooking. Then I thoroughly blotted them dry, hoping that would allow their surfaces to brown.

But no matter where I positioned the oven rack—within 2 inches or as far as 8 inches from the broiler element—the shrimp cooked through before taking on any attractive, flavorful char. The problem wasn't the broiler itself; the rack positions offered plenty of range for harnessing its radiant heat, which is focused and intense at close range and more diffuse with distance. The problem was that shrimp cook quickly and lack sufficient fat to undergo rapid browning.

GARLICKY BROILED SHRIMP

So I zeroed in on the setup that produced the plumpest, most succulent shrimp—4 inches below the element, elevated on a wire rack in the baking sheet so that the heat could circulate around each piece—and tried coating the pieces with various sources of fat and sugar in hopes of boosting browning. Melted butter was a great start—and a better option than oil—thanks to its quick-browning milk solids. A sprinkle of sugar nudged the browning a little further but not nearly as much as honey. The latter's reducing sugars catalyzed the color development almost instantly. I incorporated a tablespoon into the butter and then coated the shrimp thoroughly in the mixture, especially in and along the crevices where they'd been deveined so that those ridges would char attractively.

Briny-sweet and juicy, with toasty bits of char, the shrimp were a treat straight off the pan. And the formula was easy to dress up with bold seasonings: Loads of garlic and red pepper flakes paid tribute to scampi, while smoked paprika, cumin, and coriander made for a smoky spice blend, freshened up with a shower of cilantro. Suffice it to say, the broiler finally got its due.

—ANNIE PETITO, *Cook's Illustrated*

Garlicky Broiled Shrimp

SERVES 4 AS A MAIN COURSE OR 6 AS AN APPETIZER

TOTAL TIME: 30 MINUTES

We prefer untreated shrimp; if yours are treated with salt or additives such as sodium tripolyphosphate, skip the salting in step 1. This recipe was developed with Diamond Crystal kosher salt. If you're using Morton, which is denser, use a little less than ½ teaspoon. A rasp-style grater makes quick work of turning the garlic into a paste. For a simpler flavor profile suitable for serving with cocktail sauce or adding to salad or pasta, omit the garlic and red pepper flakes.

1½	pounds extra-large shrimp (21 to 25 per pound), peeled and deveined, tails left on
½	teaspoon kosher salt
4	tablespoons unsalted butter
1	tablespoon honey
6	garlic cloves, minced to paste
½–¾	teaspoon red pepper flakes
	Lemon wedges

1. Toss shrimp and salt together in bowl; set aside and let sit for 15 to 30 minutes.

2. Combine butter and honey in small bowl. Cover and microwave until butter is melted, 30 to 60 seconds. Add garlic and pepper flakes and stir to combine. Let cool slightly, about 5 minutes. While mixture cools, adjust oven rack 4 inches from broiler element and heat broiler. Line rimmed baking sheet with aluminum foil and set wire rack in sheet.

3. Spread out shrimp on large plate or cutting board and pat dry with paper towels. Return to bowl and pour butter mixture over shrimp. Toss until shrimp are thoroughly and evenly coated, including where they are split from deveining (it's OK if butter starts to solidify). Arrange shrimp in single layer on prepared rack.

4. Broil until shrimp are opaque throughout and beginning to lightly char in spots, 3 to 5 minutes. Transfer shrimp to serving platter and serve, passing lemon wedges separately.

VARIATIONS

Hot Honey Broiled Shrimp

Omit garlic and pepper flakes. Increase honey to 2 tablespoons. Stir ¾ teaspoon chili powder and ¼ teaspoon cayenne pepper into warm honey-butter mixture before cooling. Sprinkle cooked shrimp with 2 thinly sliced scallions.

Smoky, Spiced Broiled Shrimp

Omit garlic and pepper flakes. Stir 1½ teaspoons smoked paprika, 1 teaspoon ground cumin, and 1 teaspoon ground coriander into warm honey-butter mixture before cooling. Sprinkle cooked shrimp with 2 tablespoons chopped fresh cilantro.

OMELET WITH CHEDDAR AND CHIVES

ÇILBIR (TURKISH POACHED EGGS WITH YOGURT AND SPICED BUTTER)

✓ **WHY THIS RECIPE WORKS** To make çılbır, we started with a base of thick, creamy whole-milk strained yogurt that would stand up to a poached egg being placed on top. We added grated garlic, which is potent but mixed seamlessly with the yogurt, and a bit of salt. Letting the yogurt sit at room temperature took the chill off. For perfect poached eggs, we drained the loose whites before dropping the eggs into water seasoned with salt and vinegar, which helped the whites set up quickly, ensuring that the yolks would still be liquid, as did gently cooking the eggs off the heat. For the finishing touch, we melted butter until it started to sizzle and turn nutty before adding fruity pul biber, which turned the butter bright red. A pinch of dried mint brightened the dish.

As I spooned sizzling, red-tinged butter over my awaiting plate of yogurt and a wobbly poached egg, painting rusty swirls across the stark white canvas, the voice of Turkish culinary expert Filiz Hösükoğlu echoed in my head. "When you see the colors yellow, white, and red, it looks so simple," Hösükoğlu told me when I asked her to describe çılbır (pronounced "CHILL-burr"), a hot meze and light meal cooked in homes all over Turkey. "But when you eat, the result is not so simple."

The moment I broke into the egg, allowing its golden yolk to ooze across the plate, and then scooped and took a bite, I understood exactly what Hösükoğlu meant. Çılbır is a beloved, homey dish Turkish cooks turn to when they need a quick, ultrasatisfying meal, thanks to its succinct ingredient list of yogurt, eggs, butter, and the red pepper flakes pul biber. At the same time, the dish is so thrilling to eat and to behold—the creamy, garlicky yogurt and golden yolk are luscious; the butter is toasty, fruity, and warm from the spice—that it's no wonder that the dish was once served to Ottoman royalty.

But nailing a pitch-perfect iteration of this dish was no small feat. While the assembly of çılbır is quick and straightforward—spread yogurt on a plate, top it with a poached egg, drizzle the plate with sizzling and nutty spiced butter—the dish hinges upon a precise balance of flavors. Hösükoğlu told me that in an ideal çılbır, "No ingredient dominates the others. Rather than jumping and saying, 'I am here,' each ingredient takes its turn

to come and please you." I made it my goal to master this flavor and textural harmony as I developed my own version of the dish.

Traditionally, the yogurt base of çılbır is thick and creamy, and when I plated a few yogurts, I immediately knew I'd be sticking with this customary choice. Whole-milk strained yogurt had enough structure to provide a plush, creamy bed for the poached egg, while the runniness of unstrained yogurt didn't provide enough textural contrast with the liquid-y egg yolk.

To give the yogurt a savory edge, I incorporated garlic, as some cooks like to do, grating it into a paste so that it melded seamlessly into the smooth yogurt. Most recipes don't call for adding salt to the yogurt, but I found that a small amount brought the flavors into focus. I divided the seasoned mixture among four serving plates; spread the dollops into even layers; and then followed the traditional step of leaving the plates on the counter for a few minutes so that the yogurt could warm up, ensuring that it wouldn't be too cold against the hot egg and butter.

When I spoke with Aysenur Altan, a Turkish food writer, content creator, and YouTuber, about çılbır, she told me that palace chefs in the Ottoman Empire had to audition by making an egg dish before they could take on high positions in the royal kitchens. It's easy to understand why: There are a lot of ways that poached eggs, the most common preparation for çılbır, can go wrong. A perfectly poached egg has a tender, fully set white with no raw bits; a fluid but thickened yolk; and no ragged edges. Thankfully, a few years ago my former *Cook's Illustrated* colleague Andrew Janjigian mastered a foolproof poached egg method, which I was happy to adopt here. First, I briefly strained four eggs in a colander, which allowed the looser parts of the white to slip away before cooking, ensuring tidy edges in the cooked egg. I seasoned the water with salt and vinegar, two ingredients that help the whites set up more quickly, to ensure that the faster-cooking yolk would still be liquid by the time the whites were firm and cooked through. When the water came to a boil, I took the pot off the heat and then gently slipped the eggs in and let them cook in the residual heat for just a few minutes. I removed the poached eggs with a slotted spoon, gently patting them dry before laying them atop their yogurt beds.

The last component was the spiced butter, a nuanced finishing touch that graces dishes throughout Turkish cuisine, from countless soups to manti (Turkish

ÇILBIR (TURKISH POACHED EGGS WITH YOGURT AND SPICED BUTTER)

dumplings stuffed with spiced meat). Making this condiment is, according to Hösükoğlu, "an art"—the butter is melted and then taken just a whisper further, the milk solids taking on a hint of browning and nuttiness as moisture is driven off. "It is something you want to hear," Altan explained to me, referencing the foaming and sizzling that occurs during the process. That sizzling also signals that the butter is hot enough to rapidly absorb the pigment of the pul biber, taking on the pepper's brilliant red-orange hue.

In a small saucepan (instead of a skillet, to catch some of the sputtering), I heated a couple tablespoons of unsalted butter over medium heat for a few minutes. Once the butter began to sputter and just smell nutty, I added a teaspoon of pul biber and then quickly removed the saucepan from the heat so that I didn't risk burning the spice. As I swirled in the pul biber, I watched as the butter took on an incredible red color and then spooned it over each plate.

The dish can then be enjoyed as is, but some add a final garnish of fresh herbs, such as parsley, dill, or mint, or dried herbs, such as sage or mint. Dried mint is my favorite: Though its grassy, vegetal flavors dissipate during drying, the dried herb's characteristic menthol flavors, which come from a class of compounds known as terpenes, are far more stable and potent than in the fresh leaves. Dried mint also boasts an earthy depth that you don't get from fresh.

INGREDIENT SPOTLIGHT

THE RIGHT YOGURT FOR ÇILBIR
Yogurts run the gamut in consistency, ranging from thin and liquid-y to thick and spreadable, depending on how much whey has been drained away. The yogurt in çılbır should be thick and strained to support the poached egg and provide contrast with its runny yolk. However, the yogurt should still contain enough moisture to be scooped up with bread—labneh is too thick.

UNSTRAINED YOGURT	STRAINED YOGURT	LABNEH
Too thin	Just right	Too thick

I knew I had finally constructed a palace-worthy plate of çılbır—strikingly simple yet beguilingly complex—and that it certainly wouldn't be my last. Whether I'm in the mood for something luxurious, comforting, or just quick, at breakfast, lunch, or dinner alike, çılbır fits the bill. I understand now why Hösükoğlu personifies the dish the way she does. "It's like a good friend," she said. "It fits all days."

—ANNIE PETITO, *Cook's Illustrated*

Çılbır (Turkish Poached Eggs with Yogurt and Spiced Butter)

SERVES 4   TOTAL TIME: 40 MINUTES

Strained yogurt has had some of the whey removed so that it's thicker than regular yogurt. Turkish strained yogurt is ideal for çılbır, but if you can't find it, Greek yogurt works well, too; do not use labneh, which is too thick for this recipe. A rasp-style grater makes quick work of turning the garlic into a paste. We strongly recommend seeking out the mild Turkish red pepper flakes pul biber or Aleppo pepper; however, ½ teaspoon of paprika can be substituted. For the tidiest presentation, use the freshest eggs possible. Çılbır can be eaten at any time of day; we like to pair it with a salad when serving it for lunch or dinner.

- 1 **cup plain whole-milk strained yogurt**
- ½ **teaspoon garlic, minced to paste**
- ⅛ **teaspoon table salt, plus salt for cooking eggs**
- 4 **large eggs**
- 1 **tablespoon distilled white vinegar**
- 2 **tablespoons unsalted butter**
- 1 **teaspoon pul biber or ground dried Aleppo pepper**
- ¼ **teaspoon dried mint (optional)**
  Pita, flatbread, or crusty bread

1. Stir yogurt, garlic, and salt in medium bowl until just combined. Divide yogurt mixture evenly among 4 serving plates or shallow bowls, spreading each portion with small spatula or back of spoon to make flat bed large enough to hold 1 poached egg. Set aside plates and allow yogurt to warm up while you prepare eggs.

2. Bring 1½ quarts water to boil in Dutch oven over high heat. Meanwhile, crack eggs, one at a time, into colander. Let stand until loose, watery parts of whites drain away from eggs, 20 to 30 seconds. Gently transfer eggs to 2-cup liquid measuring cup.

3. Add vinegar and 1 teaspoon salt to boiling water. Remove pot from heat. With lip of measuring cup just above surface of water, gently tip eggs into water, one at a time, leaving space between them. Cover pot and let stand until whites closest to yolks are just set and opaque, about 3 minutes. If after 3 minutes whites are not set, let stand in water, checking every 30 seconds, until eggs reach desired doneness.

4. While eggs cook, heat butter in small saucepan over medium heat until it sputters, 2 to 3 minutes. Stir in pepper flakes (butter will foam) and remove from heat.

5. Using slotted spoon, carefully lift and drain 1 egg over pot. Pat bottom of spoon dry with paper towel and gently place egg on yogurt bed. Repeat with remaining eggs. Drizzle butter evenly over eggs. Sprinkle each serving with pinch dried mint, if using, and season with salt and pepper to taste. Serve immediately, passing pita separately.

OMELET WITH CHEDDAR AND CHIVES

✓ **WHY THIS RECIPE WORKS** To make an easy, elegant cheese omelet, we started by cooking three beaten eggs in an 8-inch nonstick skillet; this yielded an omelet that was delicate but strong enough to support the filling. Stirring constantly as the eggs cooked broke up the curds so that the texture of the finished omelet was even and fine. Once a small amount (about 10 percent) of liquid egg remained, it helped to smooth this "glue" over the curds off the heat so that the whole thing held together in a cohesive round. The filling must be at serving temperature before being rolled into the omelet; briefly microwaving shredded cheddar cheese on a plate melted it just enough. Shaping the cheese filling into a 2-inch-wide strip and centering it in the omelet perpendicular to the handle made it easy to roll the egg around the filling and out of the skillet. We briefly covered the skillet off the heat after adding the filling to trap steam that helped the bottom of the eggs set enough to withstand rolling. (It also kept the filling warm.) We used a rubber spatula to slide the eggs to the far side of the skillet and folded them partway over the filling to start the rolling process. Switching our grip so that we could tilt the skillet forward allowed us to fully invert the omelet onto a plate below.

For a year and a half during my early 30s, I worked the brunch shift at Craigie on Main, a French-inspired restaurant in Cambridge, Massachusetts. My charge was the egg station, where I turned out the kitchen's variant of a classic French omelet featuring tender, butter-yellow curds cushioned around substantial fillings such as mushrooms, crabmeat, and asparagus. Early on, it was a trial-by-fire gig: As I acquainted myself with the stove's heat zones, I would shuffle the skillets—three to five at a time—around the broad steel cooktop, trying to pinpoint just the right spot to preheat the pan, and also gauge how to quickly compensate if I added the eggs when the skillet was too hot or too cold. At the same time, I was learning when to stop cooking the eggs before smoothing them into an even layer; how much filling to add so that the omelet would be plump but not bloated; and how thoroughly to precook any watery ingredients, lest they ooze juices and mar the presentation. More than anything, I sweated "the dismount"—that final step of rolling the eggs around the filling and out of the skillet in a single motion so that the omelet landed seam side down in a tidy log. Doing it well requires at least as much faith as it does skill, and if I inverted it with trepidation, the whole package would fall apart on the way down and I'd have to start over.

But I got better fast, because making a great omelet is actually easy to do. The learning curve is really just practicing the motions so that you can operate on muscle memory and recognize the visual cues. Once you can do that, the process—which takes all of 4 minutes—becomes smooth and fun, and the burst of satisfaction you feel when that tight, uniformly golden cylinder hits the plate never gets old, whether you're running through it for the first time or the thousandth. To this day, I can't think of another dish that's as quick, meditative, and gratifying. Read on for a breakdown of my method, and then grab a skillet and give it a whirl.

—LAN LAM, *Cook's Illustrated*

Omelet with Cheddar and Chives

MAKES 1 OMELET   TOTAL TIME: 10 MINUTES

Read the recipe carefully and have your ingredients and equipment ready before you begin. To ensure success, work at a steady pace. For the best results, cook the omelet in a nonstick skillet that's in good

THE METHOD

The cooking goes very quickly and requires your full attention, so read through these steps before you start to ensure that you understand the process. Don't be discouraged if your first few omelets aren't perfect; you will get better with practice.

COOK EGGS

Stir constantly so that the texture of the finished omelet is fine and uniform. Stop cooking once a small amount (about 10 percent) of liquid egg remains; smooth this "glue" over the curds so that the whole thing holds together in a cohesive round.

ADD CHEESE

Shape the warmed cheese filling (microwaved first to jump-start melting) into a 2-inch-wide strip and center it in the omelet perpendicular to the handle; this will allow you to easily roll the egg around the filling and out of the skillet.

Cook, stirring constantly and scraping bits of egg from sides of skillet into middle.

Remove from heat; scrape eggs from sides and smooth into even layer.

Place cheese filling in center of eggs, perpendicular to handle.

Cover for 1 minute.

LOOSEN AND FOLD

The omelet should be set enough to easily slide the spatula underneath and scooch it to the far side of the skillet.

CHANGE GRIP AND TILT

Move with purpose so that the momentum of falling from the skillet helps shape the log. Tilting too slowly may cause the cheese to fall ahead of the eggs.

Loosen omelet and slide to rim opposite handle.

Fold eggs partway over filling.

Grasp handle with nondominant hand; hold skillet over plate at 45-degree angle.

Slowly tilt skillet toward yourself while using spatula to roll omelet onto plate.

condition (not scratched or worn). To serve two, make two three-egg omelets instead of a single six-egg omelet. Omelets can be held for 10 minutes in an oven set to the lowest temperature.

3 large eggs

Pinch table salt

1 ounce extra-sharp cheddar cheese, shredded (¼ cup)

1½ teaspoons unsalted butter

1½ teaspoons chopped fresh chives

1. Beat eggs and salt in bowl until few streaks of white remain.

2. Sprinkle cheddar in even layer on small plate. Microwave at 50 percent power until cheese is just melted, 30 to 60 seconds. Set aside.

3. Melt butter in 8-inch nonstick skillet over medium heat, swirling skillet to distribute butter across skillet bottom. When butter sizzles evenly across skillet bottom, add eggs. Cook, stirring constantly with rubber spatula and breaking up large curds, until eggs are mass of small to medium curds surrounded by small amount of liquid egg. Immediately remove skillet from heat.

4. Working quickly, scrape eggs from sides of skillet, then smooth into even layer. Using fork, fold cheese into 2-inch-wide strip and transfer to center of eggs, perpendicular to handle. Cover for 1 minute. Remove lid and run spatula underneath perimeter of eggs to loosen omelet. Gently ease spatula under eggs and slide omelet toward edge of skillet opposite handle until edge of omelet is even with lip of skillet. Using spatula, fold egg on handle side of skillet over filling. With your nondominant hand, grasp handle with underhand grip and hold skillet at 45-degree angle over top half of plate. Slowly tilt skillet toward yourself while using spatula to gently roll omelet onto plate. Sprinkle chives over omelet and serve.

ASPARAGUS, LEEK, AND GOAT CHEESE QUICHE

✓ **WHY THIS RECIPE WORKS** For a light, bright springtime quiche, we filled our luscious egg custard with crisp-tender asparagus; buttery leek; a bit of fresh lemon zest; and vibrant, creamy goat cheese. We partially baked the pie crust with plenty of pie weights to ensure that it didn't slump and baked up crisp from edge to center. We sautéed the leek and asparagus briefly so that the leek would melt into the filling and the asparagus would retain a bit of its crispness. We saved the raw asparagus tips for a decorative element on top of the quiche.

This asparagus, leek, and goat cheese quiche is fresh, vibrant, and full of green vegetables, making it the perfect springtime lunch or light dinner.

Some crucial techniques made this recipe failproof. Chilling the pie dough between forming, rolling, and blind-baking it not only ensured that it was a breeze to work with but also guaranteed that the butter in the dough remained in distinct pieces, creating a flaky pastry crust. Baking the crust before filling it—first lined with parchment paper and weighted to set its shape, and then uncovered and baked until the sides and bottom were fully set—guarded against the dreaded soggy bottom.

Sautéing the sliced leek in butter for a few minutes before adding the sliced asparagus spears (and cooking them together only briefly) ensured that both vegetables

were perfectly cooked when the quiche emerged from the oven—the sweet, creamy leek melded with the egg filling and the still-bright, juicy asparagus retained some crispness. A bit of cornstarch in the custard kept the eggs from curdling, and layering in the filling ingredients in stages before pouring over the custard ensured that the cheese, vegetables, and seasonings were evenly distributed throughout. Reserving the tender, beautiful asparagus tips for the top of the quiche kept them from becoming mushy and added a decorative element to the top.

—MATTHEW FAIRMAN, *Cook's Country*

Asparagus, Leek, and Goat Cheese Quiche

SERVES 6 TO 8

TOTAL TIME: 2½ HOURS, PLUS 3¼ HOURS CHILLING AND COOLING

To prevent the crust from sagging, make sure that the crimped edge overhangs the edge of the pie plate slightly in step 4 and use plenty of pie weights (3 to 4 cups) in step 5. Do not use asparagus that is thinner than ½ inch in diameter. Shred the Parmesan on the large holes of a box grater. To keep from overfilling the quiche, be sure to use the volume measurements given for the leek and asparagus spears.

NOTES FROM THE TEST KITCHEN

ASPARAGUS PREP

The spears are sliced ½ inch thick and sautéed with a sliced leek until they're just softened; they go right in with the custard and cheese. We save the tender tips—uncooked before the quiche bakes—for the very top.

ASPARAGUS, LEEK, AND GOAT CHEESE QUICHE

CRUST

- 3 tablespoons ice water
- 2 tablespoons sour cream
- 1¼ cups (6¼ ounces) all-purpose flour
- 1½ teaspoons sugar
- ½ teaspoon table salt
- 8 tablespoons unsalted butter, cut into ½-inch pieces and chilled

FILLING

- 1 pound asparagus, trimmed
- 2 tablespoons unsalted butter
- 1 leek, white and light-green parts only, halved lengthwise, sliced thin, and washed thoroughly (about 1½ cups)
- ¾ teaspoon table salt, divided
- ¾ teaspoon pepper, divided
- ¾ cup heavy cream, divided
- 2 teaspoons cornstarch
- 4 large eggs
- 2 teaspoons grated lemon zest
- 2 garlic cloves, minced
- 4 ounces goat cheese, crumbled (1 cup), divided
- 1 ounce Parmesan cheese, shredded (⅓ cup)

1. FOR THE CRUST: Combine ice water and sour cream in bowl. Process flour, sugar, and salt in food processor until combined, about 5 seconds. Scatter butter over top and pulse until butter pieces are no larger than peas, about 10 pulses. Add ice water mixture and pulse until dough forms clumps and no dry flour remains, about 12 pulses, scraping down sides of bowl as needed.

2. Transfer dough to counter and knead briefly until it comes together. Form into 5-inch disk, pressing any cracked edges back together. Wrap in plastic wrap and refrigerate for 1 hour. (Wrapped dough can be refrigerated for up to 2 days or frozen for up to 1 month. If frozen, let dough thaw completely on counter before rolling.)

3. Adjust oven rack to middle position and heat oven to 350 degrees. Let chilled dough sit on counter to soften slightly, about 10 minutes, before rolling. Roll dough into 12-inch circle on lightly floured counter. Loosely roll dough around rolling pin and gently unroll it onto 9-inch pie plate, letting excess dough hang over edge. Ease dough into plate by gently lifting edge of dough with your hand while pressing into plate bottom with your other hand.

4. Trim overhang to ½ inch beyond lip of plate. Tuck overhang under itself; folded edge should be flush with edge of plate. Crimp dough evenly around edge of plate using your fingers. Push protruding crimped edge so it slightly overhangs edge of plate. Wrap dough-lined plate loosely in plastic and freeze until dough is firm, about 15 minutes.

5. Place chilled pie shell on rimmed baking sheet. Line shell with double layer of parchment paper, covering edges to prevent burning, and fill with pie weights. Bake until edges are light golden brown, about 20 minutes. Remove parchment and weights; rotate plate; and bake until crust bottom dries out and turns light golden brown, about 20 minutes. If crust begins to puff, pierce gently with tip of paring knife. Set aside. (Crust needn't cool completely before adding filling.)

6. FOR THE FILLING: Meanwhile, cut tips from asparagus; set aside. Slice asparagus spears ½ inch thick. (You should have 1¾ cups ½-inch asparagus spear slices; reserve any extra for another use.) Melt butter in 12-inch nonstick skillet over medium heat. Add leek, ¼ teaspoon salt, and ¼ teaspoon pepper and cook until leek is softened, 3 to 5 minutes. Stir in sliced asparagus spears and cook until asparagus is bright green and crisp-tender, about 3 minutes. Set aside to cool slightly.

7. Whisk ¼ cup cream and cornstarch in large bowl until cornstarch dissolves. Whisk in eggs, lemon zest, garlic, remaining ½ teaspoon salt, remaining ½ teaspoon pepper, and remaining ½ cup cream until mixture is smooth.

8. Sprinkle ½ cup goat cheese evenly over crust followed by asparagus-leek mixture, spreading into even layer. Slowly pour custard evenly over top. Sprinkle remaining ½ cup goat cheese evenly over top. Arrange asparagus tips in single layer on top of custard. Press tips gently to submerge partially in custard. Sprinkle evenly with Parmesan.

9. Bake on baking sheet until top of quiche is lightly browned and center registers 170 degrees, 40 to 50 minutes, rotating sheet halfway through baking. Transfer to wire rack and let rest until cool to touch, about 2 hours. Slice and serve. (Quiche can be refrigerated for up to 3 days.)

MATZO BREI

✔ **WHY THIS RECIPE WORKS** Matzo brei (Yiddish for "fried matzo") is an Ashkenazi dish of eggs, matzo (unleavened flatbread made from flour and water), and fat that's eaten during Passover, the Jewish holiday during which observers avoid eating leavened food. To make a scrambled version with hearty egg presence, we used three eggs for two sheets of matzo; that way, the cooked dish was cohesive and boasted tender pockets of egg. Soaking the broken matzo pieces in the whisked eggs cut out the usual separate step of soaking them in water or milk before cooking. Frying the egg-matzo mixture, as well as plenty of chopped onion, in flavorful fat such as butter or schmaltz suffused the dish with rich flavor that worked well as a backdrop for a range of toppings and seasonings. Liberally seasoning the dish with salt and pepper made it ultrasavory.

If you've ever wanted another way to harness the transformative power of butter or schmaltz, you should make matzo brei. If you're always on the lookout for quick, comforting meals, you should make matzo brei. If you've ever eaten scrambled eggs and thought, "These could be better," you should make matzo brei. If you think anything made with matzo tastes bland and lean, you should make matzo brei.

I'll stop there, since there are as many reasons to make matzo brei as there are ways to make it.

"Matzo brei" is Yiddish for "fried matzo." (The "brei" conveniently rhymes with "fry.") This simple Ashkenazi dish of eggs, matzo (unleavened flatbread made from flour and water), and fat is eaten during Passover, the Jewish holiday during which observers avoid eating leavened food. The requisite steps go something like this: Break sheets of matzo into pieces, soften them in liquid (water or milk), mix them with eggs, and then scramble everything in fat. Those details in between? They all depend on what you grew up with and what you're used to.

"Matzo brei is a blank canvas," said Jake Cohen, author of *Jew-ish: Reinvented Recipes from a Modern Mensch* (2021). "For many people, it could be the thing that changes their minds about matzo."

The first brei I had was cooked on a hot plate in my friend's college dorm room. She had sautéed some onion in butter before adding the egg-matzo mixture to the pan and folding it all together for a minute or two. The result was deeply savory, and its texture—with its tender pockets of egg-coated matzo—was more substantial and satisfying than any plate of scrambled eggs I'd ever eaten.

In the 20 years since then, I've made matzo brei countless times—always during Passover but also any time I've had a box of matzo to use up or wanted a heartier, more dynamic plate of eggs. Because one of the best things about fried matzo is that it's infinitely customizable. You can cook it like a pancake in a single layer or stir it up like a scramble. You can make it sweet or savory and zhuzh it up with just about any condiment: hot sauce, maple syrup, jam, applesauce, sour cream, or ketchup. And the flavor is neutral, so it can easily be the foundation for more elaborate riffs. When I talked to legendary Jewish cookbook author Joan Nathan, the conversation turned into a brainstorm of possible mix-ins.

"I happen to really love chicken livers, so I would put them in," Nathan said. "And then, of course, if you're going to do chicken livers, you might as well do green and red onions with them."

Other ideas for spiffing up the scramble that arose from my conversations with Nathan and Cohen: sautéed mushrooms, crispy pastrami, peanut butter and bananas, and stewed rhubarb.

But you can't have great matzo brei without nailing the building blocks, starting with the egg-to-matzo ratio. You can use as little as one egg per sheet, which sufficiently binds up the matzo shards, but I prefer my fried matzo to have a more substantial scrambled egg presence. Three eggs per two sheets, I found, is enough to thoroughly coat the matzo pieces without overwhelming them. As for the soaking liquid, water (many cooks rinse matzo under the faucet) and milk work perfectly well, but I realized that I could do without either one if I simply dunked the broken pieces right into the whisked eggs. It saves a step, and as long as I let them hydrate in the eggs for a few minutes, the matzo softens without turning soggy.

Meanwhile, matzo brei's flavor is largely bound up in the fat and additional seasonings, which is why I always use nutty-tasting butter for a sweet scramble or schmaltz when I'm going for savory. And I'm generous with it—both for the flavor it delivers and to pay off the "brei" that the name promises.

Onions are the other key to matzo brei with a savory backbone, so I usually start by chopping and sautéing a big handful in the fat until it's soft and just shy of

MATZO BREI

browned. (Alternatively, you can use caramelized onions.) Then I pour in the egg-matzo mixture, gently stirring and folding everything together over medium heat until the eggs are just cooked through and most of the scramble sets up into rustic, tender, two-bite clumps. That's all there is to it, save for liberal doses of salt and pepper and sometimes a last-minute handful of fresh herbs (I like dill and chives). Be generous with the seasonings—the main ingredient in matzo brei is still matzo, after all.

—MARI LEVINE, *Cook's Illustrated*

Matzo Brei

SERVES 2   TOTAL TIME: 20 MINUTES

The brittleness of matzo makes it challenging to break into uniform pieces; don't worry if yours are slightly irregular. Different brands of matzo hydrate at slightly different rates; start checking for softness at the beginning of the time range in step 2. Matzo brei can be served with condiments such as sour cream, crème fraîche, yogurt, hot sauce, applesauce, or ketchup.

2½   tablespoons unsalted butter or schmaltz
⅔   cup chopped onion
½   teaspoon pepper, divided
¼   teaspoon table salt, divided
3   large eggs
2   sheets plain, unsalted matzo (about 2 ounces), broken into approximate 1½-inch pieces

1. Melt butter in 10-inch nonstick skillet over medium heat. Add onion, ¼ teaspoon pepper, and ⅛ teaspoon salt and cook, stirring occasionally, until onion has softened and started to brown, 6 to 8 minutes.

2. While onion cooks, whisk eggs, remaining ¼ teaspoon pepper, and remaining ⅛ teaspoon salt in medium bowl until no streaks of white remain. Add matzo pieces to egg mixture. Stir and fold until matzo is thoroughly coated with egg and pieces have softened (they should maintain their shape, but you should be able to break them easily with spatula), 2 to 4 minutes.

3. Add matzo mixture to skillet and gently but constantly stir and fold mixture onto itself, scraping along bottom and sides of skillet as needed until eggs are soft and just set, about 2 minutes. Serve immediately, seasoning with salt and pepper to taste.

VARIATIONS

Matzo Brei with Cinnamon and Sugar

Omit onion and pepper. Add 1 teaspoon ground cinnamon and 1 teaspoon sugar to eggs. Cook in butter. Serve with maple syrup.

Matzo Brei with Mushrooms and Chives

Substitute ⅔ cup chopped white mushrooms for onion. Transfer to serving dish and sprinkle with 2 tablespoons minced fresh chives; pass crème fraîche separately.

Matzo Brei with Smoked Salmon and Dill

Transfer to serving dish; top with 1 ounce smoked salmon, torn into ½-inch strips; and sprinkle with 1 tablespoon chopped fresh dill. Pass crème fraîche separately.

BREAKFAST BURRITOS WITH CHORIZO AND CRISPY POTATOES

☑ **WHY THIS RECIPE WORKS** Breakfast burritos first appeared on a menu in 1975 at Tia Sophia's in Santa Fe, New Mexico, but now they're beloved around the United States as a handheld, hearty, and customizable morning meal. For our version, we wanted potatoes that stayed extra-crispy. Frozen Tater Tots, thawed and then smashed flat in the skillet, did the trick. Along with the Tater Tots, we added fluffy scrambled eggs; sharp cheddar cheese; and Mexican-style chorizo, which imbued the rest of the burrito with its savory garlic and paprika seasonings. A potent chipotle sour cream sauce provided tang and heat without adding excess moisture, keeping the burritos neat and portable. Browning the rolled burritos in a hot skillet right before serving produced a crispy golden exterior and helped them stay sealed.

Who doesn't like breakfast burritos? From austere wraps containing only eggs and potatoes to ample fork-and-knife affairs draped in chile sauce and molten cheese, they seem to have universal appeal. When I make breakfast burritos at home, I like them to fall squarely in the middle of this spectrum: a full, hearty meal packed with contrasting flavors and textures but compact and contained enough to be handheld and portable for mornings on the go.

BREAKFAST BURRITOS WITH POBLANO, BEANS, CORN, AND CRISPY POTATOES

But first, what exactly is a breakfast burrito? Arguably, any burrito eaten for breakfast could be considered a breakfast burrito, though ingredients typically include eggs; potatoes; cheese; and a breakfast meat such as sausage, bacon, or ham. (You'll find similar ingredients in Texan breakfast tacos, but they're encased in smaller tortillas.)

Which brings us back to my quest for great breakfast burritos at home. While the versatility of the breakfast burrito makes it a great utilitarian tool for repurposing leftovers, I wanted a solid recipe to satisfy my craving for a balanced mix of fluffy eggs; crispy potatoes; creamy cheese; and savory, spicy sausage.

For me, the crispy potatoes were the critical element, and the one that's elusive in restaurant versions: Even the crispiest fried potatoes tend to turn soggy when wrapped in a steaming-hot tortilla with eggs and gooey cheese. I decided to start with a favorite potato product: Tater Tots. The nubby, craggy exterior of these potato morsels takes on a wonderfully crispy texture (and, as a bonus, using a frozen convenience food that did not require peeling and cutting potatoes made the burritos weekday friendly). To up the crunch factor, I shallow-fried the tots in a skillet (after thawing and patting them dry to avoid angry splattering) and pressed them flat for an even crispier exterior. The resulting spuds were almost too crunchy when eaten alone, but once wrapped in their warm tortilla blanket? Perfect.

Chorizo was my meat of choice, its garlic and paprika seasonings imbuing the rest of the burrito with knock-out flavor. Scrambled eggs and sharp cheddar cheese rounded out the cast of characters. I steamed a stack of tortillas to keep them tender and pliable throughout the assembly process and then crisped the assembled burritos in a hot skillet right before serving.

The resulting burrito was sublime, but I kept reaching for sour cream and hot sauce to cut the richness. Since I was after portability, I wanted to add a sauce inside the burrito, one potent enough to offset heavy fillings without adding moisture and making a soggy mess. I started with sour cream for tang and added a hefty dollop of minced chipotle chile in adobo for smoky heat, which I bolstered with cayenne pepper. Minced garlic and lime juice added sharpness and vibrancy. The sauce was bracing—nearly overwhelming—on its own, but a thin layer within the burrito was just the counterbalance I sought.

NOTES FROM THE TEST KITCHEN

FILL, ROLL, AND CRISP
Here's how to burrito like a pro.

1. Cook thawed and smashed Tater Tots in oil until crispy and golden brown.

2. Divide filling among tortillas, then fold sides of tortillas over filling.

3. Fold up bottom and roll tightly.

4. Arrange burritos seam side down in skillet and cook until crisp and golden.

Happy with my finished product, I developed two variations: one with crispy bacon, pepper Jack, and scallions and a vegetarian option with sautéed poblano chile, frozen corn, and pinto beans. But don't let these recipes limit you—the beauty of these burritos is they work great with whatever meat, vegetables, or cheese you have on hand. I do urge you to try adding the crispy tots at least once, though—if you're anything like me, you'll never go back!

—JESSICA RUDOLPH, *Cook's Country*

Breakfast Burritos with Chorizo and Crispy Potatoes

SERVES 4   TOTAL TIME: 55 MINUTES

Use fresh Mexican-style chorizo here, not the dry-cured Spanish version. If you are spice averse, omit the cayenne pepper and reduce the chipotle chile to 1 tablespoon. To thaw frozen Tater Tots, either let them sit in the refrigerator for 24 hours or arrange them on a paper towel–lined plate and microwave them for 1½ minutes. It's important to follow the visual cues when making the eggs, as your skillet's thickness will affect the cooking time. If you're using an electric stovetop, heat a second burner on low and move the skillet to it when it's time to adjust the heat for the eggs. You can serve the burritos right after they're rolled, if you prefer, but we like the crispy texture the tortillas get from browning them in step 5.

CHIPOTLE SOUR CREAM

¼   **cup sour cream**

2   **tablespoons minced canned chipotle chile in adobo sauce**

2   **teaspoons lime juice**

1   **garlic clove, minced**

¼   **teaspoon cayenne pepper**

¼   **teaspoon table salt**

BURRITOS

¼   **cup vegetable oil, divided**

2   **cups frozen Tater Tots, thawed and patted dry**

8   **ounces Mexican-style chorizo sausage, casings removed**

8   **large eggs, beaten**

3   **ounces sharp cheddar cheese, shredded (¾ cup)**

4   **(10-inch) flour tortillas**

1. FOR THE CHIPOTLE SOUR CREAM: Stir all ingredients together in bowl; set aside.

2. FOR THE BURRITOS: Heat 3 tablespoons oil in 12-inch nonstick skillet over medium-high heat until shimmering. Add Tater Tots to skillet and press with spatula or underside of dry measuring cup to flatten slightly. Cook until crispy and deep golden brown, about 4 minutes per side. Transfer Tater Tots to paper towel–lined plate and set aside. Wipe skillet clean with paper towels.

3. Cook chorizo in now-empty skillet over medium heat, breaking up meat with wooden spoon, until well browned, 6 to 8 minutes. Add eggs and, using heat-resistant rubber spatula, constantly and firmly scrape along bottom and sides of skillet until eggs begin to clump and spatula leaves trail on bottom of skillet, about 2 minutes. Reduce heat to low and add cheddar. Gently but constantly fold eggs until clumped and slightly wet, 30 to 60 seconds. Remove from heat and cover to keep warm.

4. Wrap tortillas in damp dish towel and microwave until warm and pliable, about 1 minute. Arrange tortillas on counter. Spread about 1½ tablespoons chipotle sour cream across bottom third of each tortilla, leaving 1-inch border. Divide Tater Tots and eggs evenly over chipotle sour cream. Working with 1 burrito at a time, fold sides of tortilla over filling, then fold up bottom of tortilla and roll tightly around filling.

5. Wipe skillet clean with paper towels. Heat remaining 1 tablespoon oil in now-empty skillet over medium heat until shimmering. Arrange burritos in skillet seam side down and cook until crisp and golden, about 1 minute per side. Serve.

VARIATIONS

Breakfast Burritos with Bacon and Crispy Potatoes

Substitute 8 slices bacon, cut into ½-inch pieces, for chorizo. In step 3, cook bacon in skillet over medium heat until crispy, 8 to 10 minutes. Pour off all but 2 tablespoons fat from skillet (leaving bacon in skillet) before adding eggs. Substitute pepper Jack for cheddar. Add 2 thinly sliced scallions with pepper Jack.

Breakfast Burritos with Poblano, Beans, Corn, and Crispy Potatoes

Omit chorizo. In step 3, heat 2 tablespoons vegetable oil in skillet over medium heat until shimmering. Add 1 stemmed, seeded, and chopped poblano chile; ½ cup canned pinto beans, rinsed; ½ cup frozen corn; ¼ cup chopped onion; 1 teaspoon chili powder; and ½ teaspoon table salt and cook until vegetables are softened, 6 to 8 minutes, before adding eggs.

ALU PARATHAS (PUNJABI POTATO-STUFFED GRIDDLE BREADS)

ALU PARATHAS (PUNJABI POTATO-STUFFED GRIDDLE BREADS)

✔ **WHY THIS RECIPE WORKS** These potato-stuffed flatbreads hail from Punjab and are a staple across the northern part of the Indian subcontinent and in big cities such as Mumbai and New Delhi. Alu parathas are made by wrapping circles of dough around a boldly spiced potato stuffing, rolling the stuffed balls into slim disks, and browning the disks (brushed with ghee) until crisp brown patches develop. The steamy, pliable breads are typically enjoyed as the center of a meal, and frankly, there is no more satisfying breakfast, lunch, or dinner than a stack of piping hot alu parathas. We started by making a compact, flavorful potato stuffing of mashed russets, aromatics, and a bold mix of spices and seeds: amchoor, cumin, kalonji, and ajwain. Next, we mixed a quick dough in the food processor, letting it rest for 30 minutes to allow the gluten to relax. After stuffing the potato balls into rounds of dough, we rolled the packages thin and griddled them in a cast-iron skillet using plenty of nutty ghee. Flipping the breads only a few times ensured that they stayed pliable while still developing lots of crisp brown spots.

My mother, Meera Marathe, is the most accomplished Indian bread maker I know. No one's chapatis, puris, or sweet stuffed griddled breads such as puran poli and gulachi poli are as good as hers. And her alu parathas? They're exceptional. These potato-stuffed flatbreads hail from Punjab and are a staple across the northern part of the Indian subcontinent.

Alu parathas are made by wrapping circles of dough around a boldly spiced potato stuffing, rolling the stuffed balls into slim disks, and browning the disks (brushed with ghee) until crisp brown patches develop. The steamy, pliable breads are typically enjoyed as the center of a meal rather than as an accompaniment, and frankly, there is no more satisfying breakfast, lunch, or dinner than a stack of piping hot alu parathas served with spicy-sweet mango pickle, cooling raita, or a refreshing tomato salad.

Acclaimed cookbook author Meera Sodha whole-heartedly agrees. After reading in her column in *The Guardian* that alu paratha is one of her "all-time favorite dishes," I reached out. She doubled down on her affinity for the breads, proclaiming them "one of the most delicious foods a human could eat." The mother of two young children has a habit of packing alu parathas as an on-the-go breakfast for family jaunts: "We take [them] wrapped up in foil to our local forest, where we go walking with the dog most weekends," she said.

Although my experience with Indian food runs deep—I authored *The Essential Marathi Cookbook* (2009) and owned a catering company specializing in Indian cookery—I'd never made alu parathas myself. Mom's were so good that there was never a need, and they're not part of the cuisine in my native state, Maharashtra.

So when I was asked to develop a recipe for *Cook's Illustrated*, I promptly phoned Mom. She explained that while there's nothing particularly hard about making the breads, they involve multiple steps, the dough can be tricky to roll, and cooking the rounds efficiently takes practice. But after she talked me through her technique, I felt ready to embark on an alu paratha adventure.

Mom uses a floury Indian potato for her stuffing, and I suspected that russets would be a good stand-in. I peeled, chopped, and boiled a pound and then mashed and cooled them before incorporating the blend of herbs, aromatics, and spices that she assembled from fond memories of the alu parathas her own mother used to cook. A fresh, fragrant trio—cilantro, ginger, and chile—starts things off. Then comes sweet-tart amchoor (dried mango powder); oniony kalonji (nigella seeds); earthy cumin; ajwain (carum seeds) to aid in digestion; and, of course, salt. Even though Mom had done her best to give me exact measurements, I needed to tweak the amounts to produce the flavor I remembered. As I divided the stuffing into eight portions, I knew she would be pleased—the high-starch mixture held together in neat balls and tasted wonderfully complex.

It was time to make the dough. Many cooks pick atta, a stone-ground whole-wheat flour, but Mom's choice is maida, a refined white flour. I found that dough made from all-purpose flour, which I think of as American maida, produced parathas with a subtle nuttiness just like Mom's.

Indian cooks have kneaded dough by hand for centuries, so when colleagues suggested that I use a food processor, I balked. Still, I decided to experiment, pulsing the flour with touches of sugar, salt, and oil and then drizzling in cold water. I was quickly won over: In mere seconds, the machine produced a satiny, pliable dough. I finished kneading by hand so that I could appreciate its silky feel while ensuring that it was perfectly smooth, and then I set it aside and let it rest for 30 minutes (as Mom suggested) to allow the gluten to relax. After dividing the dough into eight pieces, I went one step beyond my mom's recommendation and let the individual balls rest again, this time for just 15 minutes. This second rest let the dough become more slack so that it was a breeze to roll it out into 4-inch circles.

Now I stuffed the parathas by placing a round of dough on the counter and centering a potato ball on top. From there, it was easy to bring the sides of the dough up and around the potato mixture and seal its edges together. I sprinkled flour on the counter and set the ball seam side down.

As I prepared to roll the parathas, I reflected on Mom's ability to produce remarkably thin, delicate, and pliable breads, useful for those who eat with their hands. I took her advice and rolled the dough slowly and gently to avoid tearing and exposing the stuffing, producing parathas that were about 8 inches in diameter and ⅛ inch thick. It requires patience, but there's no need to fret if the round isn't perfect. As Sodha soothingly noted, "The brilliant thing about making filled parathas is that there's always another one to roll and you get a little better every time."

Mom cooks her parathas on a traditional Indian tava, a thin, round pan that's flat or concave and made of cast iron or aluminum. Brushing the breads with ghee as she goes, she flips them several times until they are mottled brown. I tried her approach using a cast-iron skillet, and there was no discernible difference in the end result. The skillet was just a little thicker than a tava, so it took longer to heat.

The last way my paratha recipe differs from Mom's is due to her expertise. While she nimbly griddles one paratha while stuffing and rolling the next, I chose to assemble all the parathas before starting to cook. This way, I had to focus only on browning the breads instead of ping-ponging between the tasks of stuffing, rolling, and griddling.

When all the parathas were golden brown, I sat down to enjoy them with bowls of vibrant condiments. I can't wait until Mom visits next. I know just what I'm going to make for dinner.

—KAUMUDI MARATHÉ, *Cook's Illustrated*

NOTES FROM THE TEST KITCHEN

ALU PARATHAS, STEP BY STEP
Rolling the alu parathas thin is crucial; to prevent the edges from tearing, take your time and press gently as you roll. Cooking the flatbreads only twice on each side ensures that they stay pliable.

1. Roll dough to 4-inch round.

2. Place stuffing in center of dough.

3. Pinch edges tightly to seal. Turn ball seam side down.

4. Roll stuffed dough to ⅛-inch-thick, 8-inch round.

5. Place in skillet, being careful not to stretch paratha.

6. Flip when large bubbles start to form on surface.

7. Brush surface of paratha with ghee.

8. Press any puffed edges to ensure even contact with skillet.

9. Flip, then repeat brushing, pressing, cooking, and flipping.

10. Cover loosely with towel after letting paratha cool slightly.

Alu Parathas (Punjabi Potato-Stuffed Griddle Breads)

SERVES 4 (MAKES 8 PARATHAS)

TOTAL TIME: 1½ HOURS, PLUS 1 HOUR 5 MINUTES COOLING AND RESTING

Ghee, kalonji, ajwain, and amchoor can all be purchased at a South Asian market or online. Ajwain has an oregano-like flavor and is often added to fried Indian food to aid digestion; if you can't find it, it's OK to leave it out. If preferred, you can substitute ¼ teaspoon of cayenne pepper for the Thai chile in the stuffing. We strongly recommend weighing the flour for this recipe. Serve the parathas as an entrée with raita, prepared mango pickle, or our Tamatya-Kandyachi Koshimbir (Tomato-Onion Salad) (page 212) for breakfast, lunch, or dinner.

POTATO STUFFING

- 1 pound russet potatoes, peeled and cut into 1-inch pieces
- 2 tablespoons minced fresh cilantro
- 1 tablespoon grated fresh ginger
- 1½ teaspoons amchoor
- 1 teaspoon ground cumin
- ¾ teaspoon table salt
- 1 Thai chile, stemmed and minced
- ¼ teaspoon kalonji
- ¼ teaspoon ajwain

DOUGH

- 1⅔ cups (8⅓ ounces) all-purpose flour
- ½ teaspoon table salt
- ½ teaspoon sugar
- 2 tablespoons vegetable oil
- ½ cup plus 1 tablespoon cold water
- ¼ cup ghee, melted

1. FOR THE POTATO STUFFING: Place potatoes in large saucepan, add cold water to cover by 1 inch, and bring to boil over high heat. Reduce heat to maintain simmer and cook until potatoes are very tender, about 16 minutes. Drain well and process through ricer or mash with potato masher until completely smooth. Set aside and let partially cool, about 20 minutes.

2. Stir cilantro, ginger, amchoor, cumin, salt, Thai chile, kalonji, and ajwain into potatoes. Season with salt to taste. Cover and set aside. (Potato stuffing can be refrigerated for up to 24 hours; let come to room temperature before using.)

3. FOR THE DOUGH: Pulse flour, salt, and sugar in food processor until combined, about 5 pulses. Add oil and pulse until incorporated, about 5 pulses. With processor running, slowly add cold water and process until dough is combined and no dry flour remains, about 30 seconds. Transfer dough to clean counter and knead by hand to form smooth, round ball, about 30 seconds; transfer to bowl, cover with plastic wrap, and let rest for 30 minutes.

4. Divide potato stuffing into 8 equal portions and roll into balls (they will be about 1½ inches wide); cover with plastic. Divide dough into 8 equal pieces, about 1¾ ounces each, and cover loosely with plastic. Working with 1 piece of dough at a time, form dough pieces into smooth, taut balls. (To round, set piece of dough on unfloured counter. Loosely cup your hand around dough and, without applying pressure to dough, move your hand in small circular motions. Tackiness of dough against counter and circular motion should work dough into smooth ball.) Let dough balls rest, covered, for 15 minutes. While dough balls rest, line rimmed baking sheet with parchment paper.

5. Roll 1 dough ball into 4-inch disk on lightly floured counter. Place 1 stuffing ball in center of dough disk. Gather edges of dough around stuffing to enclose completely; pinch to seal. Place seam side down on lightly floured counter, gently flatten, and lightly and gently roll to even ⅛-inch-thick round (about 8 inches wide). Transfer to prepared sheet and cover loosely with plastic. Repeat with remaining dough balls, stacking parathas between layers of parchment.

6. Heat 10-inch cast-iron skillet over medium heat for 5 minutes, then reduce heat to low. Brush any remaining flour from both sides of 1 paratha, then gently place in hot skillet, being careful not to stretch paratha. Cook until large bubbles begin to form on surface, underside of paratha is light blond, and paratha moves freely in skillet, 30 to 60 seconds. (Paratha may puff.) Using metal spatula, flip paratha; brush with ghee. Cook until underside is spotty brown and moves freely in skillet, 20 to 60 seconds, pressing any puffed edges firmly onto skillet with spatula to ensure even contact.

7. Flip paratha back onto first side. Repeat brushing with ghee, pressing, cooking, and flipping once more until paratha is even more spotty brown on both sides and no longer looks raw, about 30 seconds per side. Transfer cooked paratha to second rimmed baking sheet, let cool slightly, then cover loosely with dish towel.

A SALAD THAT TURNS BREAD INTO A MEAL

Alu paratha differs from many other Indian breads in that it is typically served as an entrée rather than as an accompaniment. This refreshing, lightly spiced salad is one of my favorite ways to complete the meal. –Kaumudi Marathé

Tamatya-Kandyachi Koshimbir (Tomato-Onion Salad)

SERVES 4   TOTAL TIME: 15 MINUTES

If you are not fond of raw onion, substitute ¼ cup of crushed peanuts.

    4   large, firm tomatoes, cored and cut into ¼-inch dice
    ½   teaspoon table salt
    1   Thai green chile, sliced
        Pinch sugar
    1   large onion, chopped fine
    ¼   teaspoon ground cumin
    2   tablespoons grated fresh coconut (optional)
    2   tablespoons finely chopped fresh cilantro (optional)

Stir tomatoes, salt, Thai chile, and sugar together in bowl. Let sit for 5 minutes to allow flavors to meld. Stir in onion and cumin. Serve, garnishing with coconut and cilantro, if using.

---

8. Repeat with remaining parathas, wiping out skillet with paper towels between each paratha and briefly removing skillet from heat if it begins to smoke or if paratha browns too quickly. Serve hot. (Parathas can be stacked between layers of parchment paper, placed in zipper-lock bag, and refrigerated for up to 2 days; to refresh, heat 10-inch cast-iron skillet over medium heat for 5 minutes, then reduce heat to low. Cook paratha until warmed through, flipping 3 times, 10 to 15 seconds per side.)

KESRA RAKHSIS (SEMOLINA FLATBREAD)

✔ **WHY THIS RECIPE WORKS**   Kesra rakhsis (also often called "rek-sas") is an Algerian flatbread that comes together relatively quickly and makes a great snack, side, or vessel for dips. Our recipe is adapted from a version by Wafa Bahloul, chef and co-owner of Kayma, a restaurant serving Algerian food in the La Cocina Municipal Marketplace in San Francisco. The base of the bread is semolina flour, which is made with whole-grain durum wheat. This flour gives the bread its signature chew and deep flavor that Bahloul enhances with sugar, salt, deeply toasted sesame seeds, chia seeds, nigella seeds, and a hefty dose of olive oil (preferably Algerian olive oil). When she lived in Algeria, Bahloul cooked this bread in a tagine (a sort of clay skillet without a handle) on the stovetop. We call for using a preheated cast-iron skillet on the stovetop to mimic the crisp edges created by the original cooking method.

At home, Wafa Bahloul lets her two children help knead the dough by hand for kesra rakhsis, a traditional Algerian flatbread that she calls rek-sas. But since she and her husband, Mounir, take turns cooking, running their restaurant, and taking care of the children, at work she often does this step alone.

The restaurant is called Kayma; the name comes from an Arabic word for a nomadic dwelling. The couple chose the name because they wanted their restaurant to be as welcoming as their own home, no matter where customers were from. The couple started the restaurant, located in San Francisco's La Cocina Municipal Marketplace, because they missed their homeland and the dishes they grew up eating.

"For my menu, I try to serve Algerian dishes with an American touch," Bahloul says. But when she first moved to the United States, the fusion wasn't an easy transition because the ingredients weren't the same. For example, Kayma sells a popular pistachio baklawa (a pastry similar to baklava); it didn't go well the first time she tried to bake it with American honey. "Here [in the United States] the honey is so sweet," she says. "The first time I did my baklawa it was so sweet you couldn't eat it." She had to adapt her food to American ingredients.

KESRA RAKHSIS (SEMOLINA FLATBREAD)

As for the kesra rakhsis, Bahloul learned how to make it from her mother, an accomplished cook and culinary instructor. For her dough, Bahloul uses traditional semolina flour, which is made from whole-grain durum wheat, the same wheat used to make couscous, the national food of Algeria. Semolina has a higher protein content than all-purpose flour and makes for a chewy bread with deep flavor and a yellow tinge.

To the semolina, Bahloul adds sugar, salt, yeast, and a mix of seeds: deeply toasted sesame seeds, chia seeds ("an American touch"), and what she calls black onion seeds (often labeled as nigella seeds in the United States). They look similar to black sesame seeds, but they have a richer, deeper flavor. She brings the dough together with water (warmed to help jump-start the yeast) and olive oil—preferably Algerian, when she can source it. While most Italian and Californian olive oils are made with green olives, Algerian olive oil is made with black olives, which give the oil a distinct flavor. But any good olive oil will work here.

Traditionally, this thin bread is cooked for just a few minutes on the stovetop in an Algerian tagine (a sort of clay skillet without a handle). But Bahloul bakes hers for the restaurant in the oven, which makes it easier to do larger batches; this is an adaptation that she jokes that her family in Algeria would be skeptical of. She says that she likes it better when it's cooked on the stove. (In our adapted recipe, we chose to cook the dough on the stovetop in a cast-iron skillet.)

The flatbreads are the heart of most Algerian meals. The couple often eat their bread warm with butter or as part of what Bahloul calls "an Algerian picnic" of lots of different dips and spreads. At Kayma, the bread is served alongside soup; it's also cut up, toasted, and used as croutons for salad. "As Algerians, we cannot live without bread," she says.

Bahloul radiates with joy while baking. It makes it easy to forget that she and her husband are the only two employees at Kayma and so must balance the prepping, serving, cleaning, and bookkeeping of a restaurant along with being parents. But their passion seems to outweigh the stress. When asked about running the restaurant, she says, smiling, "I'm practicing my hobbies. You have to have that patience and that love. But for me, today's just another day in paradise."

—MORGAN BOLLING, *Cook's Country*

Kesra Rakhsis (Semolina Flatbread)

SERVES 6 TO 8 (MAKES TWO 8-INCH FLATBREADS)

TOTAL TIME: 1 HOUR, PLUS 1 HOUR RESTING

We adapted this recipe from a recipe by Wafa Bahloul, chef and co-owner of Kayma, a restaurant serving Algerian food in the La Cocina Municipal Marketplace in San Francisco. In her recipe, Bahloul uses Algerian extra-virgin olive oil, which is made with black olives and has a distinct flavor, but you can use any high-quality extra-virgin olive oil here. You can substitute black sesame seeds for the nigella seeds, if desired. Different semolina flours absorb different amounts of water. In our testing, the finer the flour, the sturdier the dough. We had the best results with a very fine semolina flour such as Caputo Durum Wheat Semolina. If your dough is too soft in step 2, add extra flour; the dough's texture should be similar to that of Play-Doh. Serve the bread warm with butter and/or olives or alongside dips or soup.

2	tablespoons sesame seeds
2¾–3	cups (16½ to 18 ounces) fine semolina flour
1¼	teaspoons table salt
1	teaspoon active dry yeast
1	teaspoon sugar
1	teaspoon nigella seeds
1	teaspoon chia seeds (optional)
1	cup warm tap water
½	cup extra-virgin olive oil

NOTES FROM THE TEST KITCHEN

KEY INGREDIENTS

Fine semolina flour, nigella seeds, and Algerian olive oil give this easy flatbread its distinctive flavor.

1. Toast sesame seeds in 8-inch skillet over medium heat until deep golden brown and fragrant, 4 to 6 minutes. Transfer sesame seeds to large bowl. Add 2¾ cups flour; salt; yeast; sugar; nigella seeds; and chia seeds, if using.

2. Stir in warm tap water and oil until fully combined. (Dough should be soft and tacky but still workable. If dough is too wet, stir in additional flour, 1 tablespoon at a time, up to ¼ cup, until dough can hold its shape.) Turn out dough onto clean counter and knead by hand until dough feels less sticky and springs back when pressed lightly with your fingertip (continue kneading if it doesn't), 3 to 5 minutes.

3. Divide dough into 2 equal pieces (about 14 ounces each). Shape each piece into ball. Working with 1 dough ball at a time, place ball seam side down on clean counter and drag in small circles until ball is taut. Cover dough balls loosely with plastic wrap. Let rest for 1 hour.

4. Roll 1 dough ball into 8-inch round. Repeat with remaining dough ball.

5. Heat 12-inch cast-iron skillet over medium-low heat for 10 minutes. Prick 1 dough round all over with fork. Loosely roll dough around rolling pin and gently and carefully unroll it into skillet. Cook until underside is deep golden brown, about 5 minutes, rotating flatbread as needed for even browning. Flip flatbread and continue to cook until second side is deep golden brown, about 4 minutes longer. Transfer to large plate.

6. Repeat pricking and cooking with remaining dough round (you needn't preheat skillet again). Tear or cut into wedges and serve warm.

PAN BOXTY

✅ WHY THIS RECIPE WORKS Pan boxty are densely creamy, buttery, griddled potato pancakes (made either as a single large cake or as several smaller ones) from northwestern Ireland made from a batter of grated and sometimes mashed potatoes, plus flour and perhaps a bit of milk or water. Using a relatively high ratio (2 to 1) of potato shreds to mashed potatoes and minimizing the amount of flour in the batter allowed the spuds' earthy flavor to come through. The raw shreds must be thoroughly cooked, so we covered the skillet during cooking to trap steam that efficiently heated them through. For insurance against overheating the butter, we started it over a low flame and raised the heat to medium only once we added the batter, and we also wiped out the skillet and added fresh butter between batches. The pancakes' earthy, buttery flavor pairs well with almost anything: smoked fish, sausages, rashers, runny eggs, black pudding, corned beef, chicken curry—or just more butter.

Before the Great Famine wiped out Ireland's monocrop in the late 1840s, the average Irishman reportedly ate a dozen or so pounds of potatoes per day—many simply boiled. So it's no wonder that cooks got bored and eventually dreamed up alternative ways to serve them.

In counties such as Fermanagh, Cavan, Roscommon, and Leitrim, where boxty scholar Pádraic Óg Gallagher grew up, the predominant innovation was boxty: a potato "bread" in the broadest sense of the word made from grated spuds and sometimes mashed ones as well, plus flour and perhaps a bit of milk or water. The components were mixed to form a dough or batter and then either baked as a loaf, boiled as dumplings, or griddled as pancakes in butter.

"It's a Northwest peculiarity," said Gallagher, the chef/owner of Gallagher's Boxty House in Dublin who was reared on the dish. "It doesn't exist in other parts of the country."

The griddled version, called pan boxty, is as divine as any potato pancake and remarkably distinct. There's textural complexity, the densely creamy mash threaded with tender shreds and crisp on both sides, and a buttery richness that oil-fried cakes just don't have. Pan boxty tastes pure and earthy—and according to Darina Allen, Ireland's culinary matron, cookbook author, and founder of the Ballymaloe Cookery School in Cork, these potato cakes are "properly delicious" when scented with caraway seeds. And they're a mate for almost anything: smoked fish, sausages, rashers, runny eggs, black pudding, corned beef, chicken curry—or just more butter.

"Butter is the secret to boxty," said Gallagher. "When you fry it up, you've got to have some really good butter to put on top of it."

And yet, boxty is unsung compared with Ireland's more widely established potato dishes such as champ and colcannon. Gallagher means to change that by giving boxty a lift through his restaurant and scholarship (he's part of an effort advocating for boxty's Protected Geographical Indication, or PGI, status). So, I hoped, might I. Because who doesn't love buttery, crispy, creamy potatoes—not

to drain as much liquid as possible. Add shreds to bowl with mashed potatoes. Repeat with remaining shredded potatoes.

3. Add flour; caraway seeds, if using; salt; and pepper to potatoes and mix, breaking up any large mashed potato lumps, until evenly combined. While stirring, add enough milk so mixture is moistened but thick and stiff enough to scoop (you may not need all of milk).

4. Melt 2 tablespoons butter in 12-inch nonstick skillet over low heat. Spoon batter into ¼-cup dry measuring cup and deposit onto skillet. Deposit 3 more portions onto skillet. Using back of measuring cup, press each portion into 3½-inch round. Increase heat to medium. Cover and cook until tops of pancakes are set and bottoms are deeply browned (color will not be uniform), 3 to 5 minutes, adjusting heat as necessary to prevent butter from burning.

5. Carefully uncover (condensation may cause splattering); flip pancakes; and continue to cook, uncovered, until browned on second side, 3 to 4 minutes longer. Transfer pancakes to prepared sheet and place in oven. Wipe out skillet with paper towels and repeat with remaining butter and potato mixture in 2 batches.

6. Season with salt to taste, and serve immediately. (Pancakes can be refrigerated in airtight container for up to 2 days and reheated in dry skillet on stovetop or on rimmed baking sheet in 350-degree oven.)

NOTES FROM THE TEST KITCHEN

PAN BOXTY: BEST-OF-BOTH-WORLDS POTATO CAKES
Mashed potato pancakes are rich and creamy; shredded versions are earthy and crisp. Pan boxty, made from a thick batter that typically contains both forms of potato, combines elements of the two styles. Here's how we prep the spuds.

MASHED: Use leftovers if you've got them. If you don't, cut 1 pound peeled russet potatoes into 1-inch chunks. Cover with water in saucepan and simmer until tender. Drain well and mash or pass through food mill. Stir in ½ teaspoon table salt.

SHREDDED: Grate peeled potatoes on large holes of box grater. Place shreds in clean dish towel and twist tightly over sink to wring out as much liquid as possible.

JALAPEÑO-CHEDDAR SCONES

✓ WHY THIS RECIPE WORKS To get light and flaky scones, we treated the butter in two different ways. First, we processed half the butter until it was fully incorporated into the dough. Then, we added the remaining butter and chopped extra-sharp cheddar cheese and pulsed them until pea-size clumps remained, which would create pockets of steam as the scones baked. A hefty amount of cheese with bits of spicy pickled jalapeños scattered throughout made these scones decidedly savory. The little bit of sugar in the dough balanced the salty cheese and helped with browning and ensuring a crisp exterior. A simple glaze of butter and honey added a nice finish to the scones.

Many bakers and nonbakers alike think of scones as being sweet, but savory scones have become popular around the United States. Here in the test kitchen, the recipe we developed for Mixed Berry Scones makes a great starting point for scones where sweetness isn't the focus. Simply substituting spicy pickled jalapeños and a hefty amount of extra-sharp cheddar cheese for the berries plants these scones solidly in savory territory. The little bit of sugar in the dough stays, as it balances some of the saltiness from the cheese and helps with browning and ensuring a crisp exterior.

To make the scones, start by processing 3 cups of flour and a little baking powder and salt with just half the butter (6 tablespoons) in a food processor so that the butter breaks down and coats the flour. This prevents the flour from absorbing too much liquid later. Then add the remaining butter and some ½-inch pieces of extra-sharp cheddar cheese and pulse until pea-size pieces form. Transfer the flour mixture to a bowl and toss in chopped jalapeños. Then beat 1 cup of milk, an egg, and a yolk together and gently stir the milk mixture into the flour mixture. Knead the dough just a few times to minimize the formation of gluten, which would make the scones tough. Liberally coat the counter with flour. With minimal handling, dust the dough with flour, shape it into a rectangle, and then cut it into triangles. Transfer the scones to a parchment-lined rimmed baking sheet, chill them for at least 30 minutes, and then put them in a 425-degree oven. After they're partially baked, slather the scones with honey butter and continue baking them until they're golden brown.

JALAPEÑO-CHEDDAR SCONES

The sweet-spicy mix of jalapeños, cheddar, and honey makes these scones great as a hearty snack or as an accompaniment to chilis or soups. They also make an outstanding breakfast sandwich with bacon, eggs, and extra cheese!

—AMANDA LUCHTEL, *Cook's Country*

Jalapeño-Cheddar Scones

MAKES 12 SCONES

TOTAL TIME: 30 MINUTES, PLUS 30 MINUTES CHILLING

Work the dough as little as possible, just until it comes together.

SCONES

- 3 cups (15 ounces) all-purpose flour
- 12 tablespoons unsalted butter, cut into ½-inch pieces and chilled, divided
- ¼ cup (1¾ ounces) sugar
- 1 tablespoon baking powder
- 1¼ teaspoons table salt
- 6 ounces extra-sharp cheddar cheese, cut into ½-inch pieces
- ½ cup jarred sliced jalapeño chiles, drained and chopped
- 1 cup whole milk
- 1 large egg plus 1 large yolk

HONEY BUTTER

- 3 tablespoons unsalted butter, melted
- 1½ tablespoons honey

1. FOR THE SCONES: Line rimmed baking sheet with parchment paper. Combine flour, 6 tablespoons butter, sugar, baking powder, and salt in food processor and process until butter is fully incorporated, about 15 seconds. Add cheddar and remaining 6 tablespoons butter and pulse until cheddar and butter are reduced to pea-size pieces, 10 to 12 pulses. Transfer mixture to large bowl. Stir in jalapeños until coated with flour mixture.

2. Beat milk and egg and yolk together in separate bowl. Make well in center of flour mixture and pour in milk mixture. Gently stir mixture with rubber spatula, scraping from edges of bowl and folding inward, until very shaggy dough forms and some bits of dry flour remain. Do not overmix.

3. Turn out dough onto well-floured counter and knead briefly until dough just comes together, about 3 turns. Using your floured hands and bench scraper,

shape dough into 15 by 3-inch rectangle with long side parallel to edge of counter, dusting with extra flour if it begins to stick.

4. Using knife or bench scraper, cut dough crosswise into 6 equal rectangles. Cut each rectangle diagonally into 2 triangles (you should have 12 scones total). Transfer scones to prepared sheet, spacing them about 1 inch apart. Cover sheet with plastic wrap and refrigerate for at least 30 minutes or up to 24 hours. Adjust oven rack to middle position and heat oven to 425 degrees.

5. FOR THE HONEY BUTTER: Meanwhile, combine melted butter and honey in small bowl.

6. Uncover scones and bake until lightly golden on top, 15 to 17 minutes, rotating sheet halfway through baking. Remove scones from oven and brush tops with honey butter. Return scones to oven and continue to bake until golden brown on top, 3 to 5 minutes longer. Transfer scones to wire rack and let cool for at least 10 minutes before serving.

FRESH CORN MUFFINS

✓ **WHY THIS RECIPE WORKS** For a muffin that was tender and full of corn flavor, we microwaved cornmeal with milk until the mixture thickened to a paste-like consistency. This step hydrated and gelled the starch in the cornmeal. It sounds scientific, but it's a simple method that produces a muffin with a tender crumb and plenty of cornmeal flavor. We decided to lean on the sweeter side here by including a cup of sugar to enhance the natural sweetness of the corn. And finally, adding fresh corn to a cornmeal muffin followed the same principles as adding blueberries to a standard muffin. Two cups of fresh corn

NOTES FROM THE TEST KITCHEN

CUTTING KERNELS FROM THE COB

Your chef's knife is the best tool for shearing the kernels from an ear of corn. Here's how we do it: Cut the cobs in half crosswise, and then stand each half on its flat, stable cut side and slice off the kernels using a downward cutting motion.

kernels added nice pops of sweetness in each bite, making for flavorful but not stodgy muffins. These muffins baked up spotty brown with nice domes and were as summery as we'd hoped. To take them over the top, we served them with our Cardamom–Brown Sugar Butter, inspired by Asha Gomez's cardamom cornbread in her cookbook *My Two Souths: Blending the Flavors of India into a Southern Kitchen* (2016). The warm flavor of cardamom and sweet corn made a delicious, distinct pairing.

Fresh sweet corn is one of the best things about summer. And since it's so good on its own, I figured it would be even tastier in buttery, golden corn muffins.

Most corn muffin recipes read similarly to cornbread recipes. And like cornbread recipes, they range dramatically in their ratios of cornmeal to flour, and, of course, there is the question of whether sugar should be added to the batter at all. Baking a few of these existing recipes highlighted the fact that muffins made with more flour were typically more tender but were lacking in corn flavor, while those with a higher proportion of cornmeal had more-pronounced corn flavor but tended to be crumbly and were sometimes dry.

To find a middle ground, I employed a technique that we've used before in the test kitchen and microwaved cornmeal with milk until the mixture thickened to a paste-like texture. This step hydrates and gels the starch in the cornmeal. It sounds scientific, but it's a simple method that produces a muffin with a tender crumb and plenty of cornmeal flavor.

While existing recipes for corn muffins vary as much as cornbread recipes in the amounts of sugar used, I decided to lean on the sweeter side here by including a cup of sugar to enhance the natural sweetness of the corn.

And finally, adding fresh corn to a cornmeal muffin followed the same principles as adding blueberries to a standard muffin. More corn kernels meant more pops of sweetness in each bite, but too much corn weighed down the muffins. Two cups of fresh corn (from three ears) struck the balance, making flavorful but not stodgy muffins.

These muffins baked up spotty brown with nice domes and were as summery as I hoped. To take them over the top, I stirred some cardamom and brown sugar into softened butter, a flavor combination inspired by Asha Gomez's cardamom cornbread in her book *My*

Two Souths: Blending the Flavors of India into a Southern Kitchen (2016). The warm flavor of cardamom and sweet corn made a delicious, distinct pairing.

—MORGAN BOLLING, *Cook's Country*

Fresh Corn Muffins

MAKES 12 MUFFINS

TOTAL TIME: 55 MINUTES, PLUS 20 MINUTES COOLING

We developed this recipe using Quaker Yellow Corn Meal. Yellow or white cornmeal can be used. Three medium ears of corn should yield at least 2 cups of corn kernels. If you don't own a microwave, the cornmeal paste can also be made in a medium saucepan over medium heat. Just be sure to whisk it constantly so that the ingredients don't scorch on the bottom of the saucepan. These corn muffins are great on their own or with our Cardamom–Brown Sugar Butter (recipe follows).

1½ cups (7½ ounces) all-purpose flour

1½ cups (7½ ounces) cornmeal, divided

1 cup (7 ounces) sugar

1½ teaspoons table salt

1½ teaspoons baking powder

1 teaspoon baking soda

1 cup whole milk

½ cup sour cream

8 tablespoons unsalted butter, melted

2 large eggs

2 cups corn kernels

1. Adjust oven rack to middle position and heat oven to 400 degrees. Generously spray 12-cup muffin tin, including top, with vegetable oil spray. Whisk flour, 1 cup cornmeal, sugar, salt, baking powder, and baking soda together in large bowl; set aside.

2. Whisk milk and remaining ½ cup cornmeal together in medium bowl. Microwave until mixture begins to thicken to paste-like consistency, 1 to 3 minutes, whisking frequently. Whisk sour cream and melted butter into cornmeal paste. Whisk in eggs. Stir cornmeal mixture and corn kernels into flour mixture until just combined.

3. Using greased ⅓-cup dry measuring cup or #12 portion scoop, divide batter equally among prepared muffin cups; evenly distribute any remaining batter among cups (cups will be full).

4. Bake until muffins are golden brown and toothpick inserted in center comes out with few crumbs attached, 20 to 24 minutes. Let muffins cool in muffin tin on wire rack for 5 minutes. Remove muffins from muffin tin and let cool on rack for 15 minutes. Serve warm.

Cardamom–Brown Sugar Butter

SERVES 12 (MAKES ABOUT ⅔ CUP)   TOTAL TIME: 20 MINUTES

The butter can be refrigerated in an airtight container for up to one week.

- 8 tablespoons unsalted butter, softened
- ¼ cup packed (1¾ ounces) light brown sugar
- ¾ teaspoon ground cardamom
- ½ teaspoon table salt

Using fork, mash all ingredients in bowl until fully combined.

NOTES FROM THE TEST KITCHEN

CORNMEAL: MODERN VERSUS TRADITIONAL

Cornmeal has changed significantly over the past two centuries. Before the invention of steel grinding rollers around 1900, cornmeal was stone-ground from corn that ripened and dried in the field, so it had a higher natural sugar content and a sweeter taste. Stone grinding also produced cornmeal with variable-sized grains, so each batch would have some fine, powdery pieces and some larger, grittier pieces.

The steel rollers used today are much faster and produce a consistent grind, but they also heat up the cornmeal as they grind it, causing the meal to lose some flavor. Usually the corn is rapidly mechanically dried instead of field-dried, which further saps flavor. Additionally, the germ, one of the most flavorful parts of a corn kernel, is now typically removed before milling. Manufacturers can sell the corn oil they harvest from the germ; plus, that same oil can turn rancid over time, so degerminated cornmeal is more shelf-stable.

We developed this recipe with Quaker Yellow Corn Meal, which is degerminated, since it's the most widely available product in the United States. But if you feel like upping the ante, you can order Anson Mills Fine Yellow Cornmeal. This cornmeal is more akin to traditional cornmeal. Since it is not degerminated, it needs to be refrigerated, but it's incredibly sweet and flavorful.

SHOKUPAN (JAPANESE WHITE BREAD)

✓ WHY THIS RECIPE WORKS For shokupan that's light and fluffy and has a naturally extended shelf life, we started by making yudane, a mixture of equal weights of boiling water and bread flour. We tore the yudane into pieces and mixed them with milk, which both cooled the yudane and warmed the milk, making both more yeast friendly. We rolled out portions of the risen dough to remove all air pockets and then folded and coiled them snugly to build tension, which ensured that our loaf had a fine crumb and straight sides. A lidded Pullman pan kept the loaf confined as it baked, yielding a pleasingly uniform shape.

I considered calling this story "The Conversion of a Former Bread Snob." That's because I've spent the past two years focusing my recreational baking efforts on free-form sourdough boules with crunchy exteriors and holey interiors studded with nubbly whole grains and seeds. If it didn't require a frisky starter and at least 8 hours of engagement to make (and a powerful jaw to chew), I wasn't interested. But I was misguided, and shokupan—Japan's soft, white, feather bed of a loaf—was the source of my enlightenment.

Shokupan is baked in a long, narrow, lidded Pullman pan to create a uniform rectangular shape, all visually crisp edges and smooth, broad planes. The golden crust is thin and pliable, and the interior is plush, though not without resilience, a duality that's described in Japanese as "mochimochi." Shokupan's flavor is mild, so squares of it can be filled with any kind of savory sandwich fixings or decoratively stuffed with fruit and lightly sweetened whipped cream to make the popular Japanese snack known as a fruit sando. Sliced thick, it makes stellar toast.

My first taste at a Japanese bakery threw all my snooty bread notions into question, and I knew I wouldn't fully understand shokupan until I made it myself. Producing an ethereally soft and perfectly rectangular loaf became my baking fixation.

The ingredients are simple: bread flour, a bit of sugar, yeast, and salt. Some bakers use water, while others choose milk, sometimes in the form of reconstituted nonfat dry milk powder. A small amount of butter, lard, or shortening adds a touch of richness, but despite its velvety crumb, shokupan is essentially a lean bread.

SHOKUPAN (JAPANESE WHITE BREAD)

A portion of the flour is often combined with an equal weight of boiling liquid to make a doughy mixture called yudane, which is cooled and then combined with the other ingredients. This pregelatinized flour, which is similar to a Chinese tangzhong (also sometimes used to make shokupan), allows the baker to add more liquid: Because the extra moisture is bound up in a gel, the dough doesn't feel wet and is easy to handle.

After a primary rise comes an unusual shaping method (I'll explain in a moment). When the dough has risen nearly to the top of the pan, you slide the lid closed and bake. Honestly, letting the warm, soft loaf cool before slicing seemed like the most challenging part of all.

Though not all shokupan recipes call for pregelatinized flour, I wanted to use yudane in mine because the supplementary moisture would help the bread stay softer for longer—a natural preservative of sorts. Extra moisture would also produce more steam-powered lift in the oven for an exceptionally fluffy loaf.

Many recipes call for cooling the yudane for a few hours or even overnight, presumably because a hot yudane endangers the yeast, but I simply tore the mixture into pieces and combined them with the milk for my dough. This had the twin benefits of cooling the yudane and warming the fridge-cold milk, making both tepid and yeast friendly.

Those who say that shokupan must contain milk may be confusing it with Hokkaido milk bread, a type of shokupan that is more milk forward, acting as a showcase for the premium dairy that's produced in Japan's Hokkaido prefecture. Made exclusively with milk, Hokkaido milk bread tends to be sweeter; richer; and, well, milkier than shokupan, which limits its utility. But many shokupan recipes call for some amount of milk, and I wanted to know what worked best.

Without the browning power of lactose, an all-water loaf was pale and flat-tasting. On the other hand, an all-milk version turned the requisite "fox brown," as described by Hiroyuki Horie on a call from his bakery Oyatsupan Bakers in Beaverton, Oregon—but the dairy notes dominated. I compromised, using water in the yudane and milk in the dough, for a tawny crust and unobtrusive dairy flavor.

Back to the shaping procedure: Divide the dough into equal pieces, flatten each one, fold it into thirds, and roll it into a spiral before loading the bundles into the

NOTES FROM THE TEST KITCHEN

CARAMELLY BROWN SUGAR TOAST

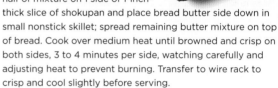

A fluffy slice of shokupan is a pleasure in its own right, but if you want to amp it up, try this crisp, caramelly toast.

Here's how: Mix together 1 tablespoon softened salted butter and 1 tablespoon packed dark brown sugar; evenly spread half of mixture on 1 side of 1-inch-thick slice of shokupan and place bread butter side down in small nonstick skillet; spread remaining butter mixture on top of bread. Cook over medium heat until browned and crisp on both sides, 3 to 4 minutes per side, watching carefully and adjusting heat to prevent burning. Transfer to wire rack to crisp and cool slightly before serving.

long pan for a second rise. It wasn't difficult, and it left charming swirls imprinted on the sides of the bread. But was it necessary?

I tried simply patting the dough into a large rectangle and rolling it into a single cylinder before baking it. When I turned the bread onto a rack, it looked almost like my previous loaves, without side swirls. But as it cooled, the walls contracted, leaving them concave instead of straight and blocky. I'd stick with the established method. Not only was it fun but also the four tight spirals pushed against each other as they rose, creating tension that led to a more stately loaf.

When it comes to soft, pillowy white loaves, consider me a convert.

—ANDREA GEARY, *Cook's Illustrated*

Shokupan (Japanese White Bread)

MAKES ONE 13-INCH LOAF

TOTAL TIME: 1¾ HOURS, PLUS 5½ HOURS RESTING, RISING, AND COOLING

We strongly recommend weighing the flour. For an accurate measurement of boiling water, bring a kettle of water to a boil and then measure out the desired amount. If your dough clears the sides of the bowl before the time stated in step 3, continue mixing for at least the minimum time to ensure the proper structure. If using our favorite Pullman pan, the USA Pan 13 by 4-inch Pullman Loaf Pan & Cover, there's no need to grease it; for other pans, check the manufacturer's instructions.

YUDANE

¾ cup (4⅛ ounces) bread flour

½ cup boiling water

DOUGH

1¼ cups milk

2⅔ cups (14⅔ ounces) bread flour

2 teaspoons instant or rapid-rise yeast

2 tablespoons sugar

1½ teaspoons table salt

2 tablespoons unsalted butter, softened

1. FOR THE YUDANE: Mix flour and boiling water in bowl of stand mixer to form rough but uniform dough. When dough is cool enough to handle, lightly grease your hands and tear yudane into approximate 1-inch pieces.

2. FOR THE DOUGH: Add milk to yudane in mixer bowl and stir to combine (mixture will remain lumpy). Add flour and yeast. Fit mixer with dough hook and mix on low speed until all flour is moistened, 1 to 2 minutes. Let stand for 15 minutes.

3. Add sugar and salt and mix on medium-low speed for 10 minutes, scraping down bowl and dough hook halfway through mixing. With mixer running, add butter. Continue to mix on medium-low speed, scraping down bowl and dough hook if necessary, until dough clears sides of bowl, 5 to 10 minutes longer. Transfer dough to lightly oiled counter. Knead briefly to form ball and transfer, seam side down, to lightly greased bowl; cover and let rise until almost doubled in volume, about 1 hour.

4. Divide dough into 4 equal portions. Shape portions into balls and place seam side down on counter. Cover and let rest for 15 minutes.

5. Lightly oil counter, your hands, and rolling pin. Turn 1 dough ball seam side up on counter and press and pat to 5-inch square. Using rolling pin, roll into 7-inch square, taking care to press out all air bubbles (stretch dough into shape with your hands, using tackiness of dough to hold it in shape). Fold dough lengthwise into thirds to form 7-inch strip. Roll into 9 by 3-inch strip. Starting on short side, roll dough to form snug cylinder and pinch seam to seal. Place seam side down on counter. Repeat with remaining dough balls.

6. Spray 13 by 4 by 4-inch Pullman pan and lid with vegetable oil spray. Place 1 dough cylinder seam side down in 1 end of prepared pan with spirals facing long sides of pan. Repeat with remaining dough cylinders,

NOTES FROM THE TEST KITCHEN

SHAPING SHOKUPAN

Start by dividing the dough into four balls, and then form each one into a tight spiral and arrange them in the pan as follows.

1. Press and pat 1 ball to 5-inch square. Roll into 7-inch square.

2. Fold 7-inch square lengthwise into thirds.

3. Roll into 9 by 3-inch strip.

4. Roll strip from short end. Repeat steps 1 through 4 with remaining balls.

5. Evenly space cylinders, seam side down, in pan.

6. Close lid, leaving 1 inch open to monitor rise; cover with plastic wrap.

spacing cylinders evenly in pan. Slide lid into place, leaving last inch of dough exposed to monitor rise. Cover gap with plastic wrap. Let rise until dough is ½ inch from top edge of pan, 1 to 1¼ hours.

7. Remove plastic and slide lid closed. Adjust oven rack to middle position and heat oven to 375 degrees. (Loaf will continue to rise while oven heats.) Bake until bread registers 195 to 200 degrees, 30 to 35 minutes.

8. Remove lid and invert bread onto wire rack. Reinvert loaf. Let cool completely, at least 3 hours. Slice with serrated bread knife, sawing gently and using very little downward pressure. Serve. (Loaf can be wrapped and stored at room temperature for up to 3 days.)

KANELBULLAR (SWEDISH CINNAMON BUNS)

✓ **WHY THIS RECIPE WORKS** Swedish cinnamon buns are modest in terms of sweetness, richness, and size, but they're lavishly spiced; not only are they swirled with an assertive cinnamon filling, but the dough itself is studded with crushed cardamom seeds, which gives the buns the sweet, almost menthol-like flavor that's foundational in Swedish baking. We incorporated a cooked flour-and-milk paste, called tangzhong, into our dough. It trapped moisture, so the high-hydration dough wasn't sticky or difficult to work with. The water in the dough converted to steam during baking, which made the buns fluffy and light. Refrigerating the dough for an hour allowed the flour to fully absorb moisture and the butter to firm up, making the dough easier to handle, and preshaping it in a baking pan made it easier to roll out later. Starting with a long strip of dough was important when shaping each bun, but stretching the strips strengthened the gluten, which caused the buns to snap back when baked. Instead of stretching, we cut each strip almost in half and then opened it up to a 2-foot length. Shaping the buns loosely gave them the space to expand during baking without becoming misshapen. Swedish pearl sugar, sprinkled on the buns before baking, provided a bit more sweetness and some crunch.

On October 4, 2019, I ate my first Swedish cinnamon bun at a London location of Fabrique, a Stockholm-based bakery chain. The bun was beautiful: a browned swirl of soft, fluffy, lightly sweetened bread infused with cardamom, filled with a buttery cinnamon sugar mixture, and sprinkled with white sugar pearls. I remember the date because October 4 is National Cinnamon Bun Day in Sweden, and it's celebrated by Swedes worldwide, so the atmosphere was especially convivial.

But Swedes don't confine their consumption of cinnamon buns, called kanelbullar, to a single day. They're a favorite feature of the daily (even twice- or thrice-daily) social ritual known as fika, which consists of coffee and a snack enjoyed with friends, family, or colleagues. To call it a mere coffee break is to ignore the Swedes' reverence and affection for the concept. As coauthors Anna Brones and Johanna Kindvall explain in their book *Fika* (2015), "To truly fika" (it's both a noun and a verb) "requires a commitment to making time for a break in your day, the creation of a magical moment in the midst of the routine and the mundane."

Amen to that. My first fika experience was so enjoyable that I was eager to make my own kanelbullar—and to incorporate the habit into my life.

The dough is made with white flour; milk; softened butter; and a bit of sugar, yeast, and cardamom. It's then rolled out and spread with a mixture of sugar, butter, and plenty of cinnamon. Swedish bakers either roll up the dough into a log and cut it into pieces, which they stand on their cut ends like American cinnamon buns, or cut it into strips and wind each one into the intricate knot shape I'd had in London. They brush the risen buns with beaten egg, top them with pearl sugar, and bake them hot and fast so that the outside gets deeply browned before the inside dries out.

Some of the doughs I tried were wet and hard to shape, though they made fluffy, moist buns; others were easier to handle but baked up drier and firmer. And though I'd added a hefty amount of ground cardamom, my kanelbullar lacked the distinctive flavor that I remembered.

Kindvall provided assistance on the flavor: Instead of using commercial ground cardamom, which is typically made by pulverizing whole green pods, it's better to pluck the more robustly flavored seeds from their pods and coarsely grind them so that the pieces are crushed between your teeth as you enjoy the bun, releasing hits of menthol and lemon. "You really want that crunchy bit here and there," she explained.

The solution for the dough was one I've called on before: incorporating a tangzhong, a cooked pudding-like mixture of flour and liquid. Doing so enabled me to add more liquid, but because that extra moisture was bound up in the gel, the dough didn't feel wet and was easy to handle.

A tangzhong also extends the shelf life of bread, so I'd be able to make the buns up to two days ahead, or even freeze them, without them drying out. In many Swedish families, keeping buns at the ready is a tradition. Kindvall's mother, for example, used to stash

KANELBULLAR (SWEDISH CINNAMON BUNS)

batches in the freezer; she would transfer a few buns to a plate and thaw them on the radiator so that they'd be warmed through in time for cozy after-school fikas.

To make my next dough even more workable, I let it rest in the fridge so that the soft butter could firm up. Then I created the layers: I rolled out the dough, spread on the filling, and then folded it and rolled it out again. Next, I cut the layered dough into strips, which I stretched long enough to wind into elaborate knots. As the knots rested, though, the dough protested my rough treatment by snapping back, leaving the buns misshapen.

Unfortunate appearance aside, this batch was a big improvement on my previous one: moister and softer (if a little dense). Even during the room-temperature, postshaping rest, the dough hadn't expanded much, though I'd used my standard ratio of yeast. It turns out that cardamom has antifungal properties that inhibit yeast activity. So I increased the yeast, unworried about excessive yeast flavor because I knew the lavish spicing would hide it. Now to fix the shape.

For my next batch, instead of stretching the dough strips, which caused the gluten to rebel, I cut each strip almost in half lengthwise, gently opened it up to a 2-foot length, wrapped it loosely around my fingers a few times, and looped the last of the strand across the middle of the knot, resulting in a form that resembled a neatly bundled electrical cord. I let the buns rest for an hour and then painted the lightly puffed swirls with egg wash, adorned them with sugar, and baked them.

These kanelbullar were beautifully perfumed with spices, fluffy, and exquisitely shaped. I ate one—and then another—before stashing the remainder in the freezer, looking forward to warming them, perhaps on the radiator, for fikas to come.

—ANDREA GEARY, *Cook's Illustrated*

Kanelbullar (Swedish Cinnamon Buns)

MAKES 12 BUNS

TOTAL TIME: 2 HOURS, PLUS 2 HOURS CHILLING AND RISING

We strongly recommend using a scale to measure the flour. It's well worth seeking out cardamom seeds at a South Asian market or online. Alternatively, crack open whole green cardamom pods and remove the seeds yourself. Coarsely grind the seeds using a spice grinder or mortar and pestle. Swedish pearl sugar is available online; you can substitute turbinado sugar (sometimes sold as Sugar in the Raw) if you prefer, though it may soften on the buns during storage.

FLOUR PASTE

- ¾ cup milk
- ¼ cup (1⅓ ounces) bread flour

DOUGH

- ½ cup milk, chilled
- 2 cups (11 ounces) bread flour
- 1 tablespoon instant or rapid-rise yeast
- ¼ cup (1¾ ounces) granulated sugar
- 1 teaspoon table salt
- 6 tablespoons unsalted butter, cut into 6 pieces and softened
- 2 teaspoons cardamom seeds, ground coarse

FILLING

- ¾ cup (5¼ ounces) granulated sugar
- 6 tablespoons unsalted butter, softened
- 2 tablespoons ground cinnamon
- 1 tablespoon bread flour
- ¼ teaspoon table salt

- 1 large egg beaten with 1 tablespoon water and pinch table salt
- ¼ cup Swedish pearl sugar

NOTES FROM THE TEST KITCHEN

SWEDISH PEARL SUGAR

Swedish pearl sugar is made by compressing sugar crystals to form round particles that are then polished to create a glossy finish. (Don't confuse it with Belgian pearl sugar, which is used almost exclusively in Liège waffles and is larger.) The snow-white pearls won't melt in the oven or draw moisture out of foods, making them ideal for topping baked goods.

SHAPING KANELBULLAR

This takes a bit of practice, but don't fret: An imperfect, jumbled appearance is part of the charm of kanelbullar.

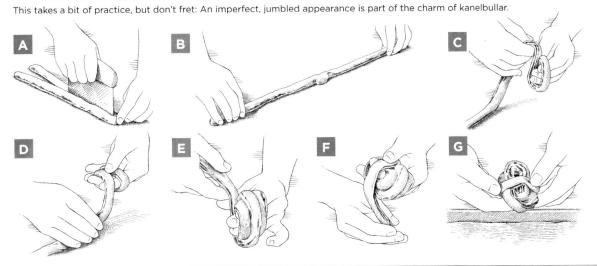

1. FOR THE FLOUR PASTE: Whisk milk and flour in small bowl until no lumps remain. Microwave, whisking every 20 seconds, until mixture has thick, stiff consistency, 1 to 2 minutes.

2. FOR THE DOUGH: In bowl of stand mixer, whisk flour paste and milk until smooth. Add flour and yeast. Fit mixer with dough hook and mix on low speed until all flour is moistened, 1 to 2 minutes (dough will look quite dry). Let stand for 15 minutes. Add sugar and salt and mix on medium-low speed for 5 minutes. Stop mixer and add butter and cardamom. Continue to mix on medium-low speed 5 minutes longer, scraping down dough hook and sides of bowl halfway through mixing (dough may stick to bottom of bowl but should clear sides).

3. Lightly grease 13 by 9-inch baking pan. Transfer dough to prepared pan (scrape bowl but do not wash). Flip dough, then press and stretch dough until it reaches edges of pan. Cover with plastic wrap and refrigerate for 1 hour. While dough chills, make filling.

4. FOR THE FILLING: Add all ingredients to now-empty mixer bowl. Fit mixer with paddle and mix on low speed until fully combined, about 1 minute.

5. Line 18 by 13-inch rimmed baking sheet with parchment paper. Transfer dough to well-floured counter. Roll dough into 18 by 10-inch rectangle, with shorter side parallel to edge of counter. Using offset spatula, spread filling over lower two-thirds of rectangle, going all the way to edges (if filling is too stiff to spread, transfer to smaller bowl and microwave for 5 to 10 seconds). Fold upper third of dough over middle third. Fold lower third over middle third to create 6 by 10-inch rectangle. Roll into 12-inch square.

6. Cut dough into twelve 1-inch strips. Cut each strip in half lengthwise, leaving it attached at very top (each strip will look like a pair of legs) (A). Extend 1 strip to 24-inch length, but do not stretch (B). Starting at 1 end, wrap strip around tips of your first 3 fingers (C), loosely coiling strands side by side along length of your fingers (D). Continue to wrap loosely until you have just 4 to 6 inches left (E). Use your thumb to pin dough to side of bundle closest to you, then loop remaining strip over bundle (F). Transfer to prepared sheet, tucking end of strip under bun (G). Repeat with remaining strips. Cover sheet with plastic or damp dish towel. Let sit until slightly puffed, about 1 hour.

7. About 15 minutes before baking, adjust oven rack to middle position and heat oven to 425 degrees. Brush buns with egg mixture (you won't need all of it) and sprinkle 1 teaspoon pearl sugar on top of each bun. Bake until buns are golden brown and register at least 200 degrees, 13 to 17 minutes, rotating sheet halfway through baking. Transfer buns, still on sheet, to wire rack and let sit for 5 minutes. Use spatula to transfer buns to wire rack (some filling may leak out and form crisp frill around bun). Let cool for at least 10 minutes before serving. (Buns can be cooled completely and stored in zipper-lock bag at room temperature for up to 2 days or frozen for up to 2 weeks.)

BLUEBERRY CREAM PIE

DESSERTS

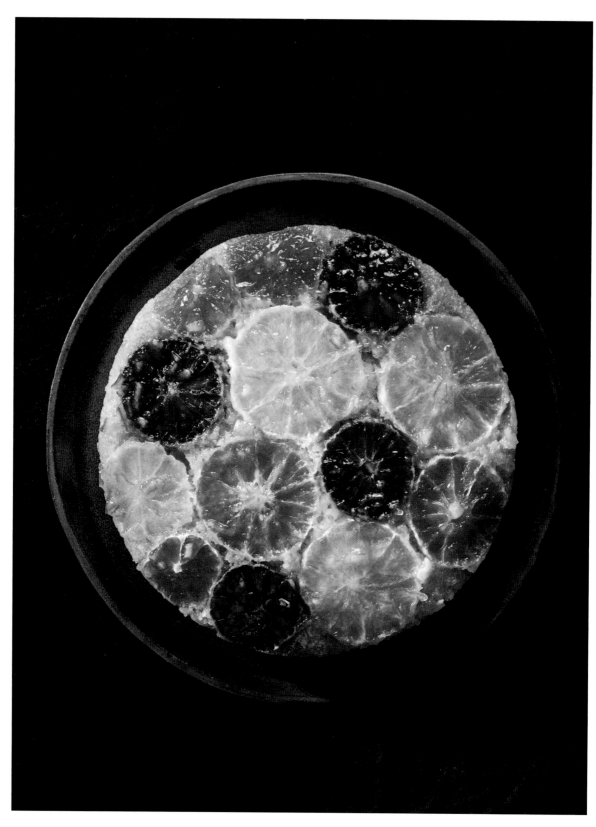

ORANGE UPSIDE-DOWN CAKE

ORANGE UPSIDE-DOWN CAKE

✔ **WHY THIS RECIPE WORKS** We were after a sturdy, buttery cake crowned with jewellike rounds of fresh citrus fruit swathed in a sticky glaze. Peeling the oranges by hand (instead of cutting away the peel and pith with a knife) ensured perfectly round slices. We used white sugar in the fruit layer (instead of commonly used brown sugar or a caramel) for a cleaner taste that didn't obstruct the subtle floral flavor of the oranges. Cornstarch helped trap the excess juices and prevent a soggy cake. A thin layer of orange marmalade brushed over the cooled cake made for an extra-shiny and extra-citrusy finish.

To some readers, the phrase "upside-down cake" likely elicits visions of golden pineapple rings and ruby cherries swathed in sticky caramel. Yes, the pineapple version is ubiquitous, but other renditions of this topsy-turvy cake actually predate it. In the mid-19th century, cooks baked skillet cakes in cast-iron skillets, often with a layer of seasonal fruit such as apples, berries, or stone fruit sitting beneath the batter. However, the popularity of these cakes skyrocketed in the 1920s with the rise in popularity of canned pineapple rings, helping give pineapple upside-down cake the iconic status it enjoys today.

These days, nearly every fruit (and even some vegetables) has been layered with sugar, baked under a buttery cake, and turned out for a showstopping presentation. Orange versions are particularly trendy, likely due to the beautiful stained-glass look mixed varieties can provide.

Adapting the classic recipe isn't as simple as swapping one sliced fruit for another, though: Modifications are necessary to accommodate the unique flavor and delicate texture of oranges. The traditional brown sugar or caramel topping overshadows the bright flavor of oranges, but cleaner-tasting white sugar allows it to shine through. Citrus fruits are also extra-juicy; some cornstarch in the topping helps gel that extra moisture so that the cake doesn't turn soggy. A standard stir-together butter cake (enriched with sour cream for moisture and tang) provides a plush, sturdy base for the fruit, and a little orange zest in the batter underlines the floral citrus flavor throughout the cake.

As tasty as the cake is, the wow factor lies in its stunning look. Using Cara Cara, navel, and blood oranges creates a mix of sunset hues; using only one variety still makes a beautiful, though understated, cake. Peeling the fruit by hand, as opposed to cutting away the peel with a knife, helps ensure picture-perfect round slices. And a finishing brush of orange marmalade adds sheen and bolsters the orange flavor. The end result? A cake that looks as cheerful as it tastes.

—JESSICA RUDOLPH, *Cook's Country*

Orange Upside-Down Cake

SERVES 8

TOTAL TIME: 1½ HOURS, PLUS 1 HOUR 20 MINUTES COOLING

For the most striking visual, we like to use a combination of navel oranges, blood oranges, and Cara Cara oranges. Look for oranges no larger than a tennis ball; you'll be able to use more slices and cover a greater area. Peel the oranges by hand instead of with a knife: Leaving the exterior membrane intact helps maintain a circular shape. We recommend using a serrated knife to slice this cake to get clean slices. Serve the cake with whipped cream, if desired.

- 1 pound small navel oranges, blood oranges, Cara Cara oranges, or a combination (2 to 3 oranges), divided
- 10 tablespoons unsalted butter, melted, divided
- 1½ cups (10½ ounces) sugar, divided
- 1 teaspoon cornstarch
- ⅛ teaspoon plus ½ teaspoon table salt, divided
- 1 cup (5 ounces) all-purpose flour
- 1 teaspoon baking powder
- ½ cup sour cream
- 2 large eggs
- 1 teaspoon vanilla extract
- 2 tablespoons orange marmalade

1. Adjust oven rack to middle position and heat oven to 350 degrees. Grease 9-inch round cake pan, line with parchment paper, then grease parchment. Grate 2 teaspoons zest from 1 orange; set aside. Using your hands, peel oranges. Using sharp chef's knife or serrated knife, trim ends and slice oranges crosswise ¼ inch thick, removing any seeds.

2. Pour 4 tablespoons melted butter over bottom of prepared pan and swirl to evenly coat. Whisk ½ cup sugar, cornstarch, and ⅛ teaspoon salt together in bowl, then sprinkle evenly over melted butter in pan. Arrange orange slices in single layer over sugar mixture, nestling slices snugly together and pressing them flat (you may have fruit left over).

THE MANY SHADES OF ORANGES
While this cake looks beautiful with a single variety of orange, to give it the most stunning appearance, we like to use a mix of three types: blood oranges, Cara Cara oranges, and navel oranges. Blood oranges are a winter citrus standout with their crimson-colored flesh. Cara Cara oranges have a light pinkish-red flesh, similar to that of grapefruit. And navel oranges offer the traditional, well, orange color. The three together are reminiscent of a sunset or stained glass and make for a showstopper of a cake. If you can find only one variety, the cake will still have vibrant color and be sure to impress.

3. Whisk flour, baking powder, and remaining ½ teaspoon salt together in large bowl. Whisk sour cream, eggs, vanilla, orange zest, and remaining 1 cup sugar in second large bowl until smooth, about 1 minute. Whisk remaining 6 tablespoons melted butter into sour cream mixture until combined. Add flour mixture and whisk until just combined.

4. Pour batter over oranges in pan and smooth top with rubber spatula. Bake until deep golden brown and toothpick inserted in center comes out clean, 50 to 55 minutes.

5. Let cake cool in pan on wire rack for 20 minutes. Run knife around edge of pan to loosen cake, then invert cake onto serving platter. Discard parchment. Let cake cool for at least 1 hour.

6. Microwave marmalade in bowl until fluid, about 20 seconds. Using pastry brush, brush marmalade over top of cake. Serve.

ICE CREAM CAKE

✓ **WHY THIS RECIPE WORKS** Building the cake upside down (the ice cream went in first but was ultimately the top layer) in a springform pan made it as compact as possible so that it held together when it was inverted for serving. Any ice cream (smooth or chunky, dense or fluffy) worked as long as we tempered it in the refrigerator, where it could soften evenly so that it was easy to layer with inclusions and press into the pan. When flattening the ice cream in the pan (greased and parchment lined to ease unmolding), it helped to place a sheet of plastic wrap and a clean dish towel over the scoops to buffer it from the heat of our hands. We didn't worry if the ice cream layer wasn't perfectly flat; the fudge sauce filled in any gaps. For the sauce, ample sugar prevented the sauce from freezing solid, and butter made it rich and silky. Chiffon cake was ideal for the base layer: It contains loads of tiny air bubbles that effectively insulated the ice cream, and its oil-based crumb stayed softer when frozen compared with cakes made with solid fat.

Ice cream cakes were part of my childhood birthday party experience, but my first memorable ones weren't until I was in my 30s and working at a restaurant in Cambridge, Massachusetts. Any time there was a staff birthday, I'd pick one up at Toscanini's, a nearby scoop shop that makes (according to the *New York Times*) "the best ice cream in the world," just before family meal. I'd inscribe "Happy Birthday" across the top in chocolate; add candles; and whisk it into the dining room, where the whole crew would sing loudly and off-key.

Those few minutes of goofy joy became a special ritual for a serious bunch like us, who spent our shifts laser-focused on shaping perfect agnolotti and nailing the sear on scallops. And the flamboyance and alluring contrast of those cakes set the tone: layers of cold, rich ice cream strewn with crunchy cookies or candy; gooey fudge; and plush cake, all wrapped up in a smooth coat of vanilla-scented whipped cream.

Fast-forward a decade or so, and I'm still charmed by those triple-decker cakes—only this time I decided to make my own for even more memorable festiveness. In full-circle good fortune, I got to talk shop with Gus and Mimi Rancatore, the brother-sister team behind Toscanini's, and their cake maker, Karen Ross, who shared their approach and their philosophy about the dessert's universal appeal. Its celebratory vibe is a big part of it, they said, as is customization.

"You could colloquially say all God's children eat ice cream cakes, but some want kulfi and some want cookies and cream," said Gus, speaking to the potential for personal modifications. "There are all sorts of pockets of interest and fascination."

In fact, any ice cream works—smooth or chunky, dense or fluffy. And the dessert is naturally make-ahead since each element must be made in advance. Put them

ICE CREAM CAKE

all together, and you've got an impressive, eminently doable project. Here's my version.

Baked cake isn't always part of ice cream cake, but there are a few good reasons to include it. First, it insulates the ice cream, significantly slowing melting after the assembled cake leaves the freezer; it also absorbs some of the ice cream's moisture when it starts to soften, helping the cake stay intact.

"If you don't have cake, everything will just start to fall apart," said Mimi, noting that a cake-free package has very little staying power once it's out of the freezer.

Cake also provides contrast—both textural and thermal. Not only does the tender crumb complement the creamy ice cream and chewy fudge, but it also feels less cold in your mouth than ice cream does (even when frozen to the same temperature) because cake absorbs less heat from your tongue.

I chose chiffon: Its fine, even crumb is full of tiny air bubbles that insulate effectively; it's oil-based and stays softer when frozen compared with cakes made with solid fat, such as butter; its neutral vanilla profile works with any ice cream flavor; and it's easy to make. Whisk together cake flour, sugar, baking powder, salt, a whole egg and egg yolks, oil, water, and vanilla; whip egg whites with more sugar until stiff peaks form; fold the components together; and bake.

Mine is soft when frozen because I boosted the amounts of oil and sugar and the number of yolks; the extra fat improved tenderness while the hygroscopic sugar formed a syrup with the batter's water that prevented the liquid from turning icy. Then I pour the batter into a 9-inch springform pan—the easiest vessel for building and unmolding the ice cream cake—and bake it in a 300-degree oven. The first few I made domed and collapsed as they cooled, leaving the sides sunken enough that the surface required leveling. So I reduced the leavener to minimize expansion and left the sides of the springform ungreased, which meant that the chiffon would grip the pan (instead of caving in on the sides) and rise and fall evenly. Voilà, flat chiffon.

Once the chiffon is cool, I remove it from the springform so that I can use the pan to build the cake upside down, which makes the assembled dessert as compact as possible. Then I invert it for serving, so the ice cream will ultimately be the top layer.

Good fudge sauce packs chocolate oomph and gooey chew, but its ice cream cake party trick is that it simplifies assembly. Spread over the flattened ice cream, the sauce

THE UPSIDE-DOWN WAY TO ASSEMBLE THE CAKE

Built upside down in a springform pan, the triple-layer cake is easily released and inverted once frozen. Start with the ice cream, followed by the fudge sauce and chiffon cake.

FOURTH Invert chiffon on top of fudge and gently press chiffon into fudge.

THIRD Remove dish towel and plastic. Spread fudge sauce evenly over ice cream.

SECOND Place sheet of plastic wrap over ice cream and cover with dish towel. Press firmly with your hands to flatten ice cream into even layer.

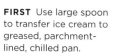

FIRST Use large spoon to transfer ice cream to greased, parchment-lined, chilled pan.

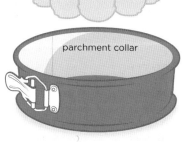

parchment collar

settles into a smooth surface that evens out any nooks and crannies. The key ingredients: cocoa powder and unsweetened chocolate for maximum cacao content and controlled sweetness, ample sugar to prevent the sauce from freezing solid, and butter to make it rich and silky.

The only tricks to the ice cream are tempering it and pressing it into the pan strategically. Give it 20 minutes or so to soften gradually and evenly in the refrigerator—not on the counter, where the outer portion will melt quickly and turn icy when it's refrozen with the assembled cake. It'll be just soft enough to scoop and layer in the pan with inclusions (the industry term for the foods mixed into ice cream), if you want them. Then, when flattening the ice cream in the pan (greased and parchment lined to ease unmolding), buffer it from the heat of your hands by placing a sheet of plastic wrap and a clean dish towel over the scoops. Since the fudge sauce will fill in any gaps, don't worry if the ice cream layer isn't perfectly flat.

Whipped cream complements ice cream cake like it does a sundae, and the air it contains makes it a great insulator—like a down jacket for cake. Ross said she shoots for a ¼-inch-thick layer and applies it quickly because the whipped cream will freeze solid within minutes and become impossible to smooth.

I did the same, using a pastry bag to pipe bands of lightly sweetened whipped cream around and on top of the cake and smoothing it all into place with an offset spatula. Then I briefly froze the cake to set the frosting, fitted the pastry bag with a flat petal tip and filled it with more chilled whipped cream, and edged the top in a decorative border. The cake was even prettier when I added sprinkles to the top and sides.

—LAN LAM, *Cook's Illustrated*

Ice Cream Cake

SERVES 10

TOTAL TIME: 2¼ HOURS, PLUS 8 HOURS 10 MINUTES COOLING AND CHILLING

You'll need a hand mixer, metal springform pan, and pastry bag with a ½-inch flat petal tip or ½-inch round tip. Use your favorite ice cream, chunky or smooth. If your ice cream is too firm to scoop after tempering for 20 minutes in step 6, refrigerate it for another 5 to 10 minutes; do not let it soften on the counter or the ice cream in your cake will be icy. To incorporate inclusions, use 1 cup of the item total. Scoop a quarter of the ice cream into the prepared pan and drizzle or sprinkle it with ⅓ cup of the item. Repeat, alternating layers of ice cream and inclusions. Press the ice cream into an even layer. Decorate the frosted cake with sprinkles, if desired.

FUDGE SAUCE

- 1¼ cups (8¾ ounces) sugar, divided
- 7 tablespoons unsalted butter, cut into ½-inch pieces
- ⅓ cup milk
- ½ cup (1½ ounces) unsweetened cocoa powder
- ⅓ cup heavy cream
- ¼ teaspoon table salt
- 2½ ounces unsweetened chocolate, chopped fine
- 1 teaspoon vanilla extract

CHIFFON

- ⅔ cup (2⅔ ounces) cake flour
- ½ cup (3½ ounces) sugar, divided
- ½ teaspoon baking powder
- ⅛ teaspoon table salt
- 3 large eggs (1 whole, 2 separated)
- 3 tablespoons vegetable oil
- 2 tablespoons water
- 1 teaspoon vanilla extract
  Pinch cream of tartar

CAKE

- 3 pints ice cream
- 1½ cups heavy cream
- 2 tablespoons sugar
- 1 teaspoon vanilla extract

1. FOR THE FUDGE SAUCE: Combine 1 cup sugar, butter, and milk in small saucepan. Bring to gentle simmer over medium-low heat and simmer, stirring occasionally, for 3 minutes. Meanwhile, stir cocoa, cream, salt, and remaining ¼ cup sugar in bowl until no lumps of cocoa remain. Reduce heat to low and whisk cocoa mixture into sugar-butter mixture in saucepan. Cook, stirring occasionally, until sugar dissolves, about 5 minutes.

2. Off heat, add chocolate and stir until well combined. Stir in vanilla. Transfer sauce to bowl and let cool completely, about 1¼ hours. (Sauce can be refrigerated for up to 1 week. Let sit at room temperature for at least 1 hour before using.)

3. FOR THE CHIFFON: Adjust oven rack to middle position and heat oven to 300 degrees. Lightly grease bottom only of 9-inch springform pan and line bottom with parchment paper. Secure collar to bottom of pan. Whisk flour, 6 tablespoons sugar, baking powder, and salt in bowl until well combined. Add whole egg and yolks, oil, water, and vanilla and whisk until smooth batter forms.

4. Using hand mixer, whip egg whites and cream of tartar on medium-low speed in separate bowl until foamy, 30 to 60 seconds. Sprinkle remaining 2 tablespoons sugar over whites. Increase speed to medium and whip whites until glossy, stiff peaks form, 1 to 2 minutes. Transfer one-third of whites to batter; gently whisk until few streaks of white remain. Using rubber spatula, fold remaining whites into batter.

5. Transfer batter to prepared pan and bake until toothpick inserted in center comes out clean, 20 to 25 minutes. Transfer to wire rack and let chiffon cool completely in pan, about 45 minutes. Run thin knife between chiffon and side of pan; remove side of pan. Invert chiffon onto wire rack and remove parchment. Reinvert chiffon. (Cooled chiffon can be stored in airtight container at room temperature for up to 12 hours or frozen for up to 1 month.)

6. FOR THE CAKE: Twenty minutes before assembling cake, place ice cream in refrigerator to soften. While ice cream softens, prepare your work station. Lightly grease 9-inch springform pan; line bottom with parchment; line sides with overlapping 3-inch-wide strips of parchment; and place pan in freezer. Measure out ¾ cup fudge sauce and place large spoon, clean dish towel, 12-inch length of plastic wrap, and chiffon nearby.

7. Working quickly, use large spoon to transfer ice cream to prepared pan. Place sheet of plastic directly over ice cream. Cover plastic with dish towel. Press firmly with your hands to flatten ice cream into even layer. Remove dish towel and plastic. Spread reserved fudge sauce evenly over ice cream. Invert chiffon on top of fudge and gently press chiffon into fudge. Wrap tightly with plastic and freeze for at least 4 hours or up to 1 week.

8. Freeze serving platter for at least 20 minutes. Whip cream, sugar, and vanilla in bowl until stiff peaks form, 3 to 5 minutes. Transfer two-thirds of cream to pastry bag fitted with ½-inch flat petal tip or ½-inch round tip and refrigerate remaining cream. Unwrap cake and remove side of pan. Remove parchment strips. Invert serving platter on top of cake. Invert cake onto platter; remove bottom of pan and parchment.

9. Working quickly, pipe whipped cream evenly onto sides and top of cake. (It's OK if there are small gaps between bands of whipped cream.) Using offset spatula, smooth whipped cream into even layer. Freeze cake until whipped cream at bottom edge of cake is firm, about 20 minutes (bottom edge will be last place to harden). Transfer remaining whipped cream to pastry bag. Pipe decorative border along top edge of cake. Freeze until cake is completely hardened, at least 1 hour or up to 24 hours.

10. TO SERVE: Thirty minutes before serving, transfer cake to refrigerator. Microwave remaining fudge sauce at 50 percent power until fluid, about 1 minute, stirring halfway through microwaving. Slice cake, wiping blade between cuts, and serve, passing remaining fudge sauce separately.

PÂTE SUCRÉE TART SHELL

✓ **WHY THIS RECIPE WORKS** Pat-in-the-pan tart crusts are quick and convenient, but they're thick, so they don't leave a lot of room for filling. A slimmer, more traditional pâte sucrée crust has a greater capacity, but it can be tricky to make. Instead of chilling the dough after mixing, we sped up the usual process by rolling out the just-mixed dough between layers of parchment until it was very thin and then freezing it, so it was ready to shape after only 30 minutes. Cutting the dough into one large round and a few strips allowed us to assemble the tart shell quickly and neatly. Milk chocolate that's been blended with custard instead of cream formed the base of our crémeux filling, a perfect match for our thin, cookie-like pâte sucrée tart shell. Butter enhanced the filling's silky, sliceable texture.

For those daunted by pie and tart dough, a pat-in-the-pan crust can be a saving grace. The method, which involves pressing crumbly dough into the base and sides of the pan, is both simple and ultraforgiving, allowing novice bakers to commit a multitude of sins. But the technique has its limits: Pat-in-the-pan crusts are nearly impossible to distribute in an even layer, so they always bake up a bit chunky, leaving less room for the contents. This means that either the filling must be assertively flavored or you have to build above the edge of the tart, as you would for a classic fruit tart. For a truly elegant, slim crust that can cradle the maximum amount of filling, the training wheels have to come off: You must graduate to a classic rolled-out crust.

Now, before you panic: You needn't be a professional pâtissier to attain such a shell. While many methods for this type of crust are intimidatingly fussy, involving repeated chilling, precise rolling, and careful shaping, I managed to find a way to simplify and streamline the process such that it's just as foolproof as, and only a bit more involved than, patting a dough into the pan.

MILK CHOCOLATE CRÉMEUX TART

Traditional French pastry doughs range from flaky and savory to shortbread-like and sweet. For an all-purpose dessert shell, I opted for a dough firmly on the sweeter side: pâte sucrée. This pastry typically contains more sugar than pâte brisée (the French equivalent of American pie dough), but more important, the butter is incorporated differently, getting thoroughly worked into the flour rather than being left in small chunks. This results in a finer, shorter crumb.

I had only a couple small quibbles with the classic ingredients for the dough. In addition to flour, butter, confectioners' sugar, and flavorings such as salt and vanilla, the formula often calls for an egg yolk instead of a whole egg and about 1 tablespoon of heavy cream. I'm fine with separating eggs, but I'd rather not buy a container of cream to use such a small amount, especially because the butter already provides plenty of richness. So I omitted the cream and added the whole egg, knowing the egg white would replace the cream's

NOTES FROM THE TEST KITCHEN

EASIER ROUTE TO AN ULTRASLIM TART CRUST
We simplified the usual approach of fitting a large, delicate disk of dough into the bottom and sides of a pan.

1. Using the tart pan like a giant cookie cutter, cut out a fluted base and fit it into the bottom of the pan.

2. Fit the excess strips of dough along the sides of the pan to create thin, elegant sides.

3. Trim the top to force the dough into the flutes for a pretty and clean edge.

moisture and its protein would provide a structural boost. The ingredients came together quickly in the food processor, forming a soft, uniform mixture that resembled cookie dough.

The shaping and baking steps were where I was really hoping to make some updates to the classic method. The process most home bakers typically follow goes something like this: Chill the dough for at least an hour; roll it out to a big, thin round; carefully transfer the delicate dough to a tart pan; and ease it up the pan's sides, patching the inevitable breaks and cracks before chilling it once more. Suffice it to say, it's a time-consuming and often frustrating method, but as I pulled my dough from the food processor in preparation for that first lengthy chill, I had an idea about how I could shave off some time and toil. Instead of chilling the dough in a disk, waiting for it to soften, and then rolling it out, I could roll it out straight from the food processor with the help of some parchment paper.

I plopped the dough onto a large piece of parchment and placed another on top. I pressed with my hands until the dough was about half an inch thick, and then I picked up my rolling pin. I gently rolled toward the edges of the parchment until the dough was a uniformly thin rectangle—so much easier than struggling with hard, brittle, refrigerated dough. I slid the parchment package onto a baking sheet and popped it in the freezer. In less than 30 minutes, my soft dough had transformed into a rigid plank. Perfect.

While I was at it, I wanted to rework the inelegant step of squishing the dough into the contours of the pan. I couldn't quite picture accomplished pastry chefs doing something so clumsy—and after doing some research, I learned that they don't. Efficiency is a top priority in pastry kitchens, and all that squishing and patching would take too much time. Instead, pastry chefs cut out a crisp disk of chilled dough and position it in the bottom of the tart pan (or, more commonly, in a steel ring set on a baking sheet), and then they build the sides of the tart with neat strips of dough placed around the edge, spliced together in one or two places. As the tart shell bakes, the edges and bottom meld into a tidy, thin crust.

I set my chilled dough plank back on the counter; removed the bottom from my tart pan; inverted the ring over the dough; and pressed, cutting out my tart base like a huge, fluted cookie. I cut the remaining dough into 1-inch-wide strips. I lifted the round from the parchment, fit it snugly into the assembled tart pan, and then fit the strips around the sides. This tidy process took about 5 minutes and produced the neatest tart shell I'd ever formed.

I chilled the shell while the oven heated and then lined the shell with foil, filled it with baking weights, and baked it for 30 minutes. Then I removed the foil and weights and returned the shell to the oven for 10 more minutes to brown.

And there I had it: an ultrathin, crisp crust with sharp right angles and perfect flutes that wouldn't be out of place on a pastry shop counter. And the hardest part of the whole process, arguably, was choosing a filling to go in it—with a picture-perfect tart shell, the possibilities are endless.

—ANDREA GEARY, *Cook's Illustrated*

NOTES FROM THE TEST KITCHEN

CRÉMEUX: THE CREAMIEST CHOCOLATE FILLING

Chocolate crémeux, whose name translates from French as "creamy," is silkier than a ganache yet denser than a mousse. It's a delicate filling that pairs perfectly with a crisp, cookie-like tart shell such as our Pâte Sucrée Tart Shell. Using milk chocolate rather than dark heightens the filling's luxurious creaminess further, and adding a bit of cocoa powder can cut the chocolate's sweetness and lend a sophisticated note to lower-cacao bars.

Our slim pâte sucrée shell can hold an abundance of this luxurious milk chocolate filling.

Pâte Sucrée Tart Shell

SERVES 8 TO 10

TOTAL TIME: 1 HOUR, PLUS 1 HOUR 20 MINUTES FREEZING AND COOLING

You'll need a 9-inch metal tart pan with a removable bottom for this recipe. If you don't have pie weights, dried beans or raw rice make great substitutes. The tart shell can be baked up to two days ahead; let it cool, wrap it tightly, and store it at room temperature.

- 1 large egg
- 1 teaspoon vanilla extract
- 1½ cups (7½ ounces) all-purpose flour
- ⅔ cup (2⅔ ounces) confectioners' sugar
- ¼ teaspoon table salt
- 8 tablespoons unsalted butter, cut into ½-inch pieces and chilled

1. Whisk together egg and vanilla in 1-cup liquid measuring cup; set aside. Pulse flour, sugar, and salt in food processor until combined, 2 pulses. Scatter butter over flour mixture; process until mixture looks like very fine crumbs with no pieces of butter visible, about 20 seconds. With processor running, add egg mixture and continue to process until dough just forms mass, about 18 seconds longer.

2. Transfer dough to center of 18 by 12-inch piece of parchment paper. Place second sheet of parchment on top of dough and press with your hand to ½-inch thickness. Using rolling pin, roll out dough so it nearly reaches edges of parchment. Using your flat hand on parchment, smooth out wrinkles on both sides. Transfer dough with parchment to baking sheet and freeze until firm, about 30 minutes.

3. Place dough and parchment on counter and peel away top layer of parchment. Replace top layer of parchment, flip dough and parchment, and peel away second piece of parchment. Invert 9-inch metal tart ring on left half of dough and press to cut out circle (leave circle on parchment). Using paring knife and ruler, cut right half of dough lengthwise into 1-inch-wide strips. Place removable bottom in tart pan. Lift dough round (if necessary, use thin spatula to loosen) and fit into bottom of tart pan, pressing edges of dough firmly into corners (it's OK if some dough smears up sides of tart pan). Lift strips and fit into sides of pan, overlapping strips only slightly. Trim final strip to fit. (Dough scraps can be sprinkled with sugar and baked as cook's treat.) If at any point dough becomes too soft to manipulate, freeze for 15 minutes.

4. Freeze tart shell until very firm, about 20 minutes. While tart shell chills, adjust oven rack to middle position and heat oven to 350 degrees.

5. Hold paring knife parallel to counter and shave off any excess dough to force dough into flutes for clean edge. Spray large sheet of heavy-duty aluminum foil with vegetable oil spray. Place foil sprayed side down in tart shell and smooth gently along bottom and sides. Fill with pie weights. Bake on rimmed baking sheet until tart shell is golden and set, about 30 minutes, rotating sheet halfway through baking. Remove foil and weights and continue to bake tart shell until fully baked and golden brown, about 10 minutes longer. Transfer sheet to wire rack and let cool completely, about 30 minutes.

Milk Chocolate Crémeux Tart

SERVES 8 TO 10

TOTAL TIME: 30 MINUTES, PLUS 2 HOURS 20 MINUTES COOLING AND CHILLING

This recipe was developed using Endangered Species Smooth + Creamy Milk Chocolate, which has a high cacao content. If you'll be using another brand, consider adding the optional tablespoon of cocoa powder for a darker milk chocolate flavor. Avoid chocolate chips, which sometimes contain additives to hinder melting. If desired, serve with unsweetened whipped cream or fruit.

1 cup half-and-half

4 large egg yolks

1 tablespoon unsweetened cocoa powder (optional)

⅜ teaspoon table salt

12 ounces milk chocolate, chopped fine

1½ teaspoons vanilla extract

10 tablespoons unsalted butter, melted and hot

1 recipe Pâte Sucrée Tart Shell

1. Place fine-mesh strainer over medium bowl. Whisk half-and-half; egg yolks; cocoa, if using; and salt in medium saucepan until combined. Cook mixture over medium-low heat, stirring constantly and scraping bottom of saucepan with heatproof spatula, until mixture is thickened and silky and registers 170 to 175 degrees, 5 to 7 minutes. Remove from heat. Working quickly, whisk in chocolate and vanilla until smooth. Add melted butter and whisk gently until incorporated. Pour mixture into prepared strainer and transfer strained mixture to cooled tart shell. Let cool completely, about 20 minutes, and then refrigerate until filling is set, at least 2 hours or up to 24 hours.

2. Remove outer ring from tart pan. Insert thin metal spatula between crust and pan bottom to loosen tart; slide tart onto serving platter. Cut into wedges and serve. (Leftovers can be wrapped loosely and refrigerated for up to 3 days.)

FRUIT HAND PIES

✔ **WHY THIS RECIPE WORKS** Hand pies treat you to the pleasures of sugar-crusted pastry and vibrant, jewel-toned fruit without tethering you to a plate and fork. The dough needs a little extra structure, so we made rough puff: a type of pastry dough that contains more gluten than most pie pastry and comes together by thoroughly working cold butter into the flour mixture and then rolling out and folding the dough a few times to create flaky layers. Using frozen fruit saved loads of prep work. Plus, it tastes at least as good as most fresh fruit because it's picked and frozen at its peak, and the freeze-thaw process tenderizes the pieces. Crushing a portion of the fruit with the sugar made a pulpy mash that filled in gaps between the chunks and released juice that gelled lightly when cooked with a little cornstarch. We stirred in plenty of lemon (or lime) juice for acidity and oomph. Making square (not round or crescent-shaped) parcels minimized dough waste and maximized efficiency on the assembly line. Rolling, filling, and sealing the dough using the same process we came up with to make hand-cut ravioli produced tidy, airtight packages. We briefly chilled the assembled pies to help them maintain their sharp, clean edges. Trimming the pastry edges with a fluted pastry wheel or decorating them with the tines of a fork or a serrated knife added visual appeal. Cutting distinctive vents—a series of slashes or a simple pattern on the top of the dough—made it easy to identify different fruit fillings. A sprinkle of demerara sugar on the top of each pie added a hint of sweetness and shimmer.

Pie by the slice is neighborly and bighearted, the kind of dessert that invites you to sit and visit for a while. But hand pies are snack-y and fetching and fun: palm-size parcels that treat you to the pleasures of sugar-crusted pastry and vibrant, jewel-toned fruit without tethering you to a plate and fork. Bringing one up to your mouth for a bite feels more intimate and thrilling than using flatware, the way ice cream tastes better from a cone than from a dish. The sealed-up, dough-heavy framework makes it extra-special for crust lovers, since all those crimped edges mean that every bite is crisp and toasty. And that moment when you break through the buttery shell is electric: The ebullient fruit within bursts onto your palate, flaunting its sweet-tart flavor.

CHERRY HAND PIES

MAKE PRETTIER PIES

These simple tweaks will make the pie crust look prettier and more professional.

DECORATIVE TRIM

Cut the edges of the pies with a fluted pastry wheel, or use the tines of a fork or a serrated knife (hold the blade parallel to the counter and press the scalloped edges into the dough) to fringe the border.

DISTINCTIVE VENTS

Make a series of slashes or a simple pattern on the top of the dough using a sharp paring knife or small decorative cutter. Use a different design for each pie flavor to help tell them apart.

SPARKLY CRUST

Sprinkle the top of each pie with demerara or turbinado sugar for an extra hint of sweetness and shimmer.

All that—and they're functional, too. Not just portable but also easy to assemble and freeze weeks before baking. You can stockpile batches of peach, plum, or cherry pies for parties or personal on-demand indulgence, baking them off as casually as you would preportioned cookie dough.

What they're not, however, is a travel-size version of pie that bakes in a plate. Hand pie dough requires a different formula because pastry that's designed to bake up ultratender and flaky in a plate will slump and spread without walls to support it and shed crumbs with every bite. Same goes for the fruit: There isn't much of it, so the flavor and acidity need to pop with Technicolor vividness. And the chunks can't be as big as what you'd spear with a fork, lest they tumble out when you take a bite.

That's a lot of details to get right, but none of them is difficult—and eating pie with your hands is the ultimate reward. Here's a breakdown of my approach.

Dough that bakes in a plate can get away with moderate gluten, since the vessel and filling hold it in place until the heat of the oven sets its starches and proteins. But hand pie dough needs a little extra structure, which is why I opted to make rough puff: a type of pastry that comes together by working cold butter into the flour mixture and then rolling out and folding the dough a few times to create flaky layers. (The "rough" acknowledges that the layers are haphazard rather than perfectly stacked as they are in true puff pastry.)

Rough puff is sturdier than most pie pastry, thanks to its hydration and the mixing method. Water (when combined with flour) encourages gluten development, which is why most pie dough formulas keep hydration to a minimum (around 32 percent), whereas rough puff contains around 50 percent. The mixing method affects gluten development even more: Whereas pie dough is manipulated as little as possible, leaving some of the butter in small but discrete chunks or shreds, mixing, rolling, and folding rough puff builds gluten that helps the dough hold its shape in the oven, stay crisp underneath the filling, and shed few crumbs. It also creates layers that puff during baking, resulting in a flaky, crisp crust.

To make it, I combine butter planks with the flour-sugar-salt mixture in a zipper-lock bag (handy for keeping everything contained) and use a rolling pin to flatten the fat into thin sheets. When the dough is ragged and pale yellow, a visual cue that most of the butter is incorporated, I transfer the mixture to a bowl and add ice water (its temperature keeps the butter firm as the dough is worked), mix until the dough is tacky, roll it into a large sheet, and then fold it over itself multiple times. The last step is a long (at least 1 hour or up to two days), cold rest: During that time, starch in the flour continues to hydrate so that the dough is pliable, not tacky, and its gluten relaxes so that the pastry doesn't contract when it's rolled and cut.

Tender, bright-tasting, gently bound fruit is always the goal for pie filling, and that cohesiveness is especially important when you're going to be eating the pie with your hands. Fresh fruit is always an option, but my testing really got me to appreciate the benefits of using frozen fruit in pie. It's picked and frozen at its peak, so its flavor is potentially better than fresh fruit that's picked before it's ripe, and it's sold peeled and/or pitted, saving the cook loads of tedious work.

I like to start with ½-inch chunks of peaches, cherries, or pineapple: consistently available options that are sturdy, moderately juicy, and boast similar levels of sweetness and acidity. The trick is to crush a portion of the fruit with sugar: Doing so makes a pulpy mash that fills in gaps between the chunks and releases juice that gels lightly when cooked with a little cornstarch—a two-pronged way to make the filling more cohesive. Stirring in plenty of lemon (or lime) juice gives the fruit's acidity real oomph.

Egg wash is an unsung hero of pastry work. It's the glue that adheres one piece of dough to another and the sugar to its surface for that postbake sweetness and sparkle, and it's the gloss that makes a baked crust shine. And it does each of these tasks more effectively than water or liquid dairy, thanks to its rich protein and fat contents. When I brushed a thin coat around the perimeter of the pastry and let it dry briefly while I placed the filling in the center of each pie, the protein in the wash made it slightly sticky—ideal for fastening the top crust to the bottom so that the package was leakproof. Fat from the yolk gave the coating I applied to the top crust real luster.

Sturdy enough to tote on a stroll or pass around at a picnic or bake sale, make-ahead friendly, and endlessly customizable, these pies are brimming with practical perks—not to mention sweet-tart fruit, butter, and charm.

—LAN LAM, *Cook's Illustrated*

Fruit Hand Pies

MAKES 8 HAND PIES

TOTAL TIME: 1¼ HOURS, PLUS 1 HOUR 35 MINUTES CHILLING AND COOLING

Be sure to have the filling ready before you start this recipe. We strongly recommend weighing the flour here. If you're baking only one sheet of hand pies, adjust the oven rack to the middle position.

2½	cups (12½ ounces) all-purpose flour
2	tablespoons granulated sugar
1	teaspoon plus pinch table salt, divided
20	tablespoons (2½ sticks) unsalted butter, halved lengthwise and chilled
¾	cup ice water
1	large egg
1	recipe hand pie filling (pages 246–247)
2	tablespoons demerara or turbinado sugar (optional)

1. Place flour, granulated sugar, and 1 teaspoon salt in 1-gallon, heavy-duty zipper-lock bag. Seal and shake well to combine. Add butter to bag and shake to coat with flour mixture. Seal bag, pressing out as much air as possible. Set rolling pin over lowest portion of bag and, using rocking motion, flatten butter beneath pin into large flakes. Working in sections, move pin up bag and flatten remaining butter. Shake bag to mix. Roll over bag with pin, shaking bag occasionally to mix, until flour

ASSEMBLE HAND PIES LIKE RAVIOLI
Our strategy for rolling, filling, and sealing the dough, based on the process we came up with to make hand-cut ravioli, is efficient and produces tidy, airtight packages with minimal waste.

1. Roll dough into 17 by 9-inch rectangle. Brush 4 squares onto bottom of dough with egg wash.

2. Add 2 tablespoons filling to each square, spreading up to (but not on) grid lines.

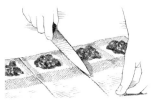

3. Cut dough between filling to create 4 even pieces.

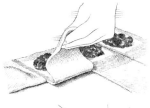

4. Fold 1 piece of dough over itself, aligning top and bottom edges.

5. Seal edges with your fingers, pressing out as much air as possible. Repeat with remaining 3 pieces.

6. Trim ¼ inch from ragged and folded sides of pies. Repeat steps 1 through 5 with remaining dough and filling.

becomes very pale yellow and almost all of butter is incorporated. Transfer mixture to large bowl (use rubber spatula or bench scraper to scrape any remaining butter and flour mixture from bag). Add ice water and toss with rubber spatula until just combined (mixture will be tacky). Transfer dough to floured counter. With your floured hands, press dough into rough 8-inch square.

2. Roll dough into 15 by 10-inch rectangle with short side parallel to edge of counter, flouring counter and dough as needed. Starting at top of dough, fold into thirds like business letter, using bench scraper or metal spatula to release dough from counter. Turn dough 90 degrees and repeat rolling and folding. Divide dough in half crosswise. Wrap each half tightly in plastic wrap and refrigerate for at least 1 hour or up to 2 days.

3. Adjust oven racks to upper-middle and lower-middle positions and heat oven to 400 degrees. In small bowl, beat egg and remaining pinch salt until well combined. Line 2 rimmed baking sheets with parchment paper.

4. On lightly floured counter, roll 1 piece of dough into 17 by 9-inch rectangle with short side parallel to edge of counter. Roll dough loosely around rolling pin, turn 90 degrees, and arrange on counter so long side is parallel to edge of counter. If dough has contracted, roll again briefly to achieve 17 by 9-inch dimensions. Using pastry brush, apply 1-inch-wide band of egg wash horizontally across center of dough. Apply 1-inch-wide strip of egg wash to edges of lower half of dough. Apply 1-inch-wide bands of egg wash vertically to divide bottom half of dough into 4 equal squares.

5. Place 2 tablespoons filling into each square, being careful to keep filling clear of egg wash. Using spoon, shape filling into rough squares. Using pizza cutter or sharp knife, cut dough at center points between filling to create 4 pieces. Leaving pieces in place but working with 1 piece at a time, gently fold dough over, aligning top edge with bottom edge. Use your fingers to gently press dough layers together, working out as much air as possible. Trim ¼ inch of dough from ragged and folded sides of each pie. Arrange pies on prepared sheet, leaving at least ¾ inch between them.

6. Repeat steps 4 and 5 with remaining dough and filling. Cut 1-inch vent on top of each pie. Transfer pies to refrigerator to chill for 15 minutes. (Pies can be frozen on baking sheets until solid, at least 4 hours, and then transferred to airtight container and frozen for up to 6 weeks. Transfer to parchment paper–lined rimmed baking sheets and thaw in refrigerator for 2 hours before proceeding with step 7.)

7. Brush tops of pies with egg wash and sprinkle with demerara sugar, if using. Bake until dark golden brown, 20 to 25 minutes, switching and rotating sheets halfway through baking. Let cool for 20 minutes; serve warm.

NOTES FROM THE TEST KITCHEN

MAKE AN EASY, FLAVOR-PACKED FRUIT FILLING
Frozen fruit and interchangeable seasonings make for lots of filling options.

GO FOR FROZEN
Peeled and/or pitted frozen fruit requires little prep, and most is picked at its peak and individually quick frozen (IQF: blasted with supercold air before packaging). The pieces retain structural integrity when they defrost and are easy to select and weigh, so you get exactly what you need.

SEASON TO TASTE
Feel free to mix and match citrus zest, spices, and extracts with the fruits. Be sure to wait until the fruit has cooked before adding the seasonings, all of which contain volatile compounds that will dissipate if heated.

Zest (lemon, lime): ¼–½ teaspoon
Ground Spices (pepper, cardamom, cinnamon, star anise): ¼–½ teaspoon
Extracts (vanilla, almond): ⅛–¼ teaspoon

All fillings can be made with 10 ounces (2 cups) of fresh fruit instead of frozen and can be covered and refrigerated for up to two days. Don't use canned fruit. Feel free to substitute nectarines, plums, or apricots for the peaches. The cherry filling works well with both sweet and sour varieties.

Cherry Hand Pie Filling
MAKES 1¼ CUPS
TOTAL TIME: 15 MINUTES, PLUS 1½ HOURS CHILLING

- 10 ounces frozen cherries, thawed, juice reserved, cut into approximate ½-inch pieces
- ⅓ cup (2⅓ ounces) sugar
- ⅛ teaspoon table salt
- 2 tablespoons lemon juice
- 4 teaspoons cornstarch
- ⅛ teaspoon almond extract

1. Combine cherries and reserved juice, sugar, and salt in medium saucepan. Using potato masher, crush one-third of cherries. Cook over medium heat, stirring occasionally, until sugar is dissolved, about 5 minutes.

2. Stir lemon juice and cornstarch in small bowl until well combined. Add mixture to saucepan and cook, stirring constantly, until mixture comes to simmer and juice thickens, 30 to 60 seconds. Transfer to bowl and refrigerate until fully cooled, about 1½ hours. Stir in almond extract.

Peach Hand Pie Filling

MAKES 1¼ CUPS

TOTAL TIME: 15 MINUTES, PLUS 1½ HOURS CHILLING

10	ounces frozen sliced peaches, thawed, juice reserved, cut into approximate ½-inch pieces
⅓	cup (2⅓ ounces) sugar
⅛	teaspoon table salt
¼	teaspoon grated lemon zest plus 2 tablespoons juice
4	teaspoons cornstarch

1. Combine peaches and reserved juice, sugar, and salt in medium saucepan. Using potato masher, crush one-third of peaches. Cook over medium heat, stirring occasionally, until sugar is dissolved, about 5 minutes.

2. Stir lemon juice and cornstarch in small bowl until well combined. Add mixture to saucepan and cook, stirring constantly, until mixture comes to simmer and juice thickens, 30 to 60 seconds. Transfer to bowl and refrigerate until fully cooled, about 1½ hours. Stir in lemon zest.

Pineapple Hand Pie Filling

MAKES 1¼ CUPS

TOTAL TIME: 15 MINUTES, PLUS 1½ HOURS CHILLING

10	ounces frozen pineapple chunks, thawed, juice reserved, cut into approximately ½-inch pieces
⅓	cup (2⅓ ounces) sugar
⅛	teaspoon table salt
2	tablespoons lime juice
4	teaspoons cornstarch
¼	teaspoon ground cinnamon

1. Combine pineapple and reserved juice, sugar, and salt in medium saucepan. Using potato masher, crush one-third of pineapple. Cook over medium heat, stirring occasionally, until sugar is dissolved, about 5 minutes.

2. Stir lime juice and cornstarch in small bowl until well combined. Add mixture to saucepan and cook, stirring constantly, until mixture comes to simmer and juice thickens, 30 to 60 seconds. Transfer to bowl and refrigerate until fully cooled, about 1½ hours. Stir in cinnamon.

BLUEBERRY CREAM PIE

✔ **WHY THIS RECIPE WORKS** For a pie that showcased all the nuanced flavors of ripe summer blueberries, we used a combination of raw and cooked berries in the filling. Raw blueberries added juicy pops of tartness, and the cooked puree held them together in a cohesive layer while adding jammy sweetness. We piled the filling into an easy graham cracker crust and swirled on a decorative topping: Whipped sweetened cream cheese was more substantial than whipped cream alone, providing a cheesecake-like richness that perfectly complemented the fruit.

Ripe, farm-fresh blueberries are plump, juicy, and sweet with balancing tartness and have underlying floral and spicy flavors. This pie is a celebration of such berries.

Why? A traditional baked blueberry pie is delicious, but the oven serves as an equalizer for all manner of blueberries: A little heat and some sugar can coax flavor out of even the blandest berries, but it can erase the nuanced flavors and juicy pops of exceptional berries. So the next time you find yourself with a haul of excellent blueberries, try this.

Make a simple graham cracker crust (its warm, nutty flavor complements the berries so well). Blitz some berries into a puree; strain it; and cook it down with sugar, salt, and cornstarch. Once it's thickened, stir in the rest of the raw blueberries and pour it all into the crust. The resulting filling is a beautiful mix of sweet-sour bursts of fresh berries held together by a deeper-flavored cooked berry puree: the best of both worlds.

The pie is great as is, but it gets even better with a whipped cream cheese topping—it tastes like a cheesecake, but it's so much faster to make. Apply the topping with some easier-than-it-appears swirled piping, and you've got a pie that looks (almost) as good as it tastes.

—JESSICA RUDOLPH, *Cook's Country*

Blueberry Cream Pie

SERVES 8 TO 10   TOTAL TIME: 1 HOUR, PLUS 4 HOURS CHILLING

This pie highlights the flavor and texture of fresh blueberries, so use high-quality berries that you enjoy eating by themselves. Do not use frozen blueberries. We prefer Honey Maid Honey Graham Crackers for this crust. The finished pie will look best on the day it's made; it will still taste delicious the next day, but the topping might not look as fresh.

SIMPLE STEPS TO PRETTY PIPING

1. Fit large pastry bag with large closed star tip. Using small spatula, apply 3 vertical stripes of reserved blueberry puree up sides of pastry bag.

2. Fill pastry bag with cream cheese topping. Twist bag shut and apply pressure to push cream cheese topping to tip.

3. For rosettes (left): Pipe straight down, then shift to outside (maintaining pressure) and pipe circle around center. For stars: Hold bag upright and pipe straight down, then pull bag away.

CRUST

- **12** whole graham crackers, broken into pieces (6½ ounces)
- **2** tablespoons sugar
-   Pinch table salt
- **6** tablespoons unsalted butter, melted

FILLING

- **½** cup (3½ ounces) sugar
- **4** teaspoons cornstarch
- **¼** teaspoon table salt
- **1½** ounces (about 4¾ cups) blueberries, divided
- **1** tablespoon lemon juice

TOPPING

- **8** ounces cream cheese, softened
- **¼** cup (1¾ ounces) sugar
- **1** teaspoon vanilla extract
- **1** cup heavy cream, chilled

1. FOR THE CRUST: Adjust oven rack to middle position and heat oven to 325 degrees. Process cracker pieces in food processor until finely ground, about 30 seconds. Add sugar and salt and pulse to combine, about 3 pulses. Add melted butter and pulse until combined, about 8 pulses. Transfer crumbs to 9-inch pie plate. Using bottom of dry measuring cup, press crumbs into bottom and up sides of plate. Bake until crust is fragrant and beginning to brown, 16 to 18 minutes. Transfer plate to wire rack.

2. FOR THE FILLING: Meanwhile, whisk sugar, cornstarch, and salt in medium saucepan until no lumps of cornstarch remain. Process 2 cups blueberries in clean, dry workbowl until smooth, about 2 minutes, scraping down sides of bowl as needed. Strain puree through fine-mesh strainer into sugar mixture in saucepan, pressing on solids to extract as much liquid as possible; discard solids. Whisk puree into sugar mixture until combined.

3. Bring puree mixture to simmer over medium heat, whisking frequently. Continue to cook, whisking constantly, until whisk leaves trail that slowly fills in, about 1 minute longer. Off heat, whisk in lemon juice. Reserve 2 tablespoons puree for piping. Stir remaining blueberries into remaining puree in saucepan. Spread filling evenly over bottom of pie crust (crust needn't be completely cool).

4. FOR THE TOPPING: Using stand mixer fitted with whisk attachment, whip cream cheese, sugar, and vanilla on medium-high speed until very smooth, about 2 minutes, scraping down bowl as needed. With mixer running, slowly pour in cream and whip until stiff peaks form, 1 to 3 minutes, scraping down bowl as needed.

5. Fit large pastry bag with large closed star tip. Using small spatula, apply 3 vertical stripes of reserved puree up sides of pastry bag. Fill pastry bag with topping. Pipe rosettes (spiraling from inside out) in concentric circles over surface of pie, covering filling. Pipe stars in any gaps between rosettes. Refrigerate pie for at least 4 hours or up to 24 hours. Serve.

APPLE-BLACKBERRY BETTY

✔ **WHY THIS RECIPE WORKS** An apple Betty is like an apple crisp, but instead of a crumbly butter/sugar/flour topping, it has slightly sweetened bread crumbs both above and below the apples. A combination of Granny Smith and Golden Delicious apples mixed with just ⅓ cup

APPLE-BLACKBERRY BETTY

of brown sugar in the filling gave our Betty a sweet-tart flavor, and a teaspoon of vanilla and a touch of nutmeg added subtle depth. Two tablespoons of water mixed into the apples created steam in the oven to jump-start the cooking, ensuring that the apples would be luxuriously soft. Bread crumbs made from white sandwich bread, enriched with butter and brown sugar and pressed into the bottom of the baking dish, accommodated any excess moisture shed by the apples as they cooked, while those on the top turned crisp and brown.

When I found myself nearing the end of an autumn cycling vacation with too many apples to cram into my saddlebags, Betty came to my rescue. I was only vaguely familiar with the retro apple dessert—my aunt Kathy may have served me one once—but I had a sense that it was simply fruit baked with buttered, lightly sweetened bread crumbs and that it offered all the coziness of pie, crisp, and crumble with only a fraction of the effort. Just the thing to cobble together in my tiny rental kitchen.

I chopped a partial loaf of sourdough into crumbs; mixed the crumbs with melted butter; and tossed most of them in a baking dish with chunks of apples (a mix of sweet and tart heirloom varieties) that I'd sweetened with sugar pilfered from the coffee station, my last handful of blackberries for bursts of wine-like acidity, and a dash of salt. After scattering the remaining crumbs over the top, I covered the dish with foil and popped it in the oven; about an hour later, I removed the foil so that the top could crisp.

The tender, tangy fruit topped with its craggy roof of crumbs was bright and buttery—and worth repeating, with a few tweaks. Back home in my fully stocked kitchen, I tried it again with Granny Smith (tart) and Golden Delicious (sweet) apples as well as light brown (instead of granulated) sugar, vanilla, and a dash of nutmeg. The new additions contributed hints of warmth and complexity without distracting from the dessert's clean, simple character. I also reconsidered the type of bread, since rustic sourdough must be trimmed of its hard crust, and that offended my (and arguably Betty's) frugal sensibilities. Whizzing slices of soft white sandwich bread in the food processor not only avoided waste but also allowed me to produce evenly buttered, sweetened crumbs in seconds by adding some sugar, salt, and melted butter to the processor bowl.

NOTES FROM THE TEST KITCHEN

ONE MIXTURE, TWO TEXTURES

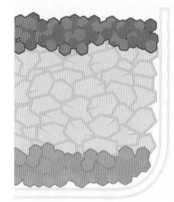

The two layers of buttered, lightly sweetened bread crumbs sandwiching the fruit are the same, but during baking they take on two different textures. The bottom layer captures the exuded fruit juices, plumping and caramelizing in the oven floor's heat, while the top layer crisps and browns during the final segment of uncovered baking.

The bread crumbs soaked up the exuded fruit juices during baking, but they didn't do much to enhance the dessert's flavor or texture until I found a more strategic way to incorporate them. Rather than simply tossing them with the fruit, I pressed a thick layer of crumbs into the bottom of the baking dish, which coalesced into a softly chewy, caramelized "floor." Adding a bit more sugar and moving the baking dish onto a lower rack made the layer even more cohesive, like the absorbent bottom crust of a fruit pie. When I uncovered the Betty, I moved it closer to the top of the oven so that the rest of the crumbs, which I'd sprinkled on top of the apples, could crisp.

Reformatted into a triple-decker dessert with tangy fruit sandwiched between layers of texturally distinct crumbs, Betty was back—and better than ever.

—ANDREA GEARY, *Cook's Illustrated*

Apple-Blackberry Betty
SERVES 6 TO 8

TOTAL TIME: 1½ HOURS, PLUS 20 MINUTES COOLING

You can substitute another soft, enriched bread such as challah or brioche for the sandwich bread; be sure to use 10 ounces. We call for a mix of Golden Delicious and Granny Smith apples here, but feel free to substitute a sweet variety and a tart variety of your choice. You can substitute raspberries or blueberries for the blackberries, and it's fine to use frozen berries; alternatively, you can omit the berries. We like the flavor of nutmeg here, but substitute ½ teaspoon of ground cinnamon if you prefer it. This dessert is best served freshly baked and warm, but you can cover any leftovers tightly with foil and refrigerate them for up to two days; warm before serving.

10 ounces (about 7 slices) hearty white sandwich bread, cut into 1-inch pieces

½ cup packed (3½ ounces) plus ⅓ cup packed (2⅓ ounces) light brown sugar, divided

¾ teaspoon table salt, divided

6 tablespoons unsalted butter, melted

1½ pounds Golden Delicious apples, peeled, cored, and cut into ½-inch pieces

1 pound Granny Smith apples, peeled, cored, and cut into ½-inch pieces

2 tablespoons water

1 teaspoon vanilla extract

¼ teaspoon ground nutmeg

3¾ ounces (¾ cup) blackberries, berries larger than ¾ inch cut in half crosswise

Vanilla ice cream or sweetened whipped cream

1. Adjust oven racks to upper-middle and lower-middle positions and heat oven to 375 degrees. Pulse bread in food processor until coarsely ground, about 15 pulses. Add ½ cup sugar and ½ teaspoon salt and pulse to combine, about 5 pulses. Drizzle with melted butter and pulse until evenly distributed, about 5 pulses. Scatter 2½ cups bread crumb mixture in 8-inch square baking dish. Press gently to create even layer.

2. Combine apples, water, vanilla, nutmeg, remaining ⅓ cup sugar, and remaining ¼ teaspoon salt in bowl. Pile apple mixture atop bread crumb mixture in dish and spread and press into even layer. Sprinkle blackberries over apples (dish will be very full). Distribute remaining bread crumb mixture evenly over blackberries, and press lightly to form uniform layer. Cover tightly with aluminum foil. (Uncooked Betty can be refrigerated for up to 2 days.) Place on rimmed baking sheet and bake on lower rack until apples are soft, 1 hour to 1 hour 10 minutes.

3. Remove foil and transfer dish to upper rack. Bake until crumbs on top are crisp and well browned, about 15 minutes. Transfer to wire rack and let cool for at least 20 minutes. Serve with ice cream.

PEAR CRISP WITH MISO AND ALMONDS

✔ **WHY THIS RECIPE WORKS** This simple, no-fuss pear crisp recipe boasts some upgrades that make it uniquely and surprisingly satisfying. The warm filling of juicy pears and sweet-tart cherries is lavishly draped in a gooey caramel-like blanket of cream, brown sugar, and butter. But that's not all. Top that off with a luxurious crust of rich, salty-sweet miso-almond crumble, and this pear crisp becomes something really irresistible. Adding a small amount of miso to the crumble topping animated all the other ingredients in the dish and brought their flavors into focus. Bosc pears that were just shy of ripe worked best here because their firm, dense flesh retained its shape after baking. Dried cherries, lemon zest and juice, almond extract, and chopped sliced almonds rounded out, complemented, and amplified the sweet floral flavor of the pears. Cooking the filling briefly on the stovetop to coax out and thicken the fruit juices before baking made this recipe failproof, ensuring that the filling would never turn out soupy.

NOTES FROM THE TEST KITCHEN

WHITE MISO

White (shiro) miso is a salty, lightly sweet fermented soybean paste. We use it in the test kitchen to add complex, savory flavor to a wide variety of dishes.

Our favorite, Hikari Organic White Miso, is perfectly balanced and isn't overwhelmingly salty.

BOSC PEARS

We've found that Bosc pears stay sweet and complex once cooked, while other varieties end up bland. Bosc pears develop sweetness earlier in the ripening process, so firm, slightly underripe ones, like the ones we call for here, already have plenty of flavor. They're also firmer, so they don't become mushy, as other varieties would.

PEAR CRISP WITH MISO AND ALMONDS

Fruit crumbles became popular in Britain when ingredients such as flour, butter, and sugar were being strictly rationed during the World Wars. I imagine they caught on and still persist for two reasons: They're absolutely scrumptious, and compared with other desserts such as pies or cakes, they're very easy to prepare. This simple, fuss-free recipe has roots in those first recipes but also boasts some upgrades that make it uniquely and surprisingly satisfying.

For starters, the warm filling of juicy pears and sweet-tart cherries is lavishly draped in a gooey caramel-like blanket of cream, brown sugar, and butter. But that's not even the half of it. Top that off with a luxurious crust of rich, salty-sweet miso-almond crumble, and this pear crisp becomes something really irresistible.

Bosc pears that are just shy of ripe work best here because their firm, dense flesh retains its shape after baking. Dried cherries, lemon zest and juice, almond extract, and chopped sliced almonds round out, complement, and amplify the sweet floral flavor of the pears. Cooking the filling briefly on the stovetop to coax out and thicken the fruit juices before baking makes this recipe failproof, ensuring that the filling will never turn out soupy.

As for the crumble, I'd understand if you'd never considered including miso in this classic dessert. But I strongly recommend trying it out. The Japanese paste, which is made from fermented soybeans, is a powerful, versatile ingredient with countless uses, from soups, stews, and marinades to, yes, even sweets. Adding a small amount of miso to the crumble topping in this pear crisp is akin to adding salt to caramel or sprinkling flake sea salt on top of brownies. It doesn't intrude or announce itself but rather animates all the other ingredients in the dish and brings their flavors into focus on the palate. When you take the first bite, you won't taste miso, but it's the reason that the pears taste more like pears and the lemon, almonds, and cherries are all themselves distinct. You won't be able to resist taking another bite.

—MATTHEW FAIRMAN, *Cook's Country*

Pear Crisp with Miso and Almonds

SERVES 6 TOTAL TIME: 1¼ HOURS

Serve with vanilla ice cream. Be sure to use white (shiro) miso—which is relatively mellow and sweet—in this recipe. If you can't find it, you can substitute ½ teaspoon of table salt. Dried cranberries can be substituted for the cherries.

TOPPING

- ¾ cup (3¾ ounces) all-purpose flour
- ½ cup panko bread crumbs
- ⅓ cup sliced almonds, toasted and chopped coarse
- ¼ cup packed (1¾ ounces) light brown sugar
- 1 teaspoon grated lemon zest
- ¼ teaspoon ground cinnamon
- 6 tablespoons unsalted butter, melted
- 1 tablespoon white miso
- ¼ teaspoon almond extract

FILLING

- 2 pounds slightly underripe Bosc pears, peeled, quartered lengthwise, cored, and sliced crosswise ½ inch thick
- ¾ cup packed (5¼ ounces) light brown sugar
- ⅓ cup dried cherries
- ¼ cup heavy cream
- 1 tablespoon cornstarch
- 1 tablespoon lemon juice
- ¼ teaspoon table salt
- 2 tablespoons unsalted butter

1. **FOR THE TOPPING:** Adjust oven rack to middle position and heat oven to 375 degrees. Whisk flour, panko, almonds, sugar, lemon zest, and cinnamon together in bowl. Whisk melted butter, miso, and almond extract in second bowl until miso is dissolved. Stir butter mixture into flour mixture until no dry spots of flour remain and mixture forms clumps. Refrigerate until ready to use (topping can be covered and refrigerated for up to 24 hours).

2. **FOR THE FILLING:** Toss pears, sugar, cherries, cream, cornstarch, lemon juice, and salt in large bowl until thoroughly combined. Melt butter in 10-inch ovensafe skillet over medium-high heat. Add pear mixture and cook, stirring frequently, until pears have released enough liquid to be mostly submerged and juices have thickened and turned glossy, 6 to 8 minutes. Off heat, stir to ensure cherries are evenly distributed throughout mixture.

3. Squeeze topping into large clumps with your hands. Crumble topping into pea-size pieces over filling. Bake until topping is browned and filling is bubbling around sides of skillet, 20 to 25 minutes. Let cool for 15 minutes. Serve.

PEANUT BUTTER–STUFFED CHOCOLATE COOKIES

PEANUT BUTTER–STUFFED CHOCOLATE COOKIES

✓ **WHY THIS RECIPE WORKS** For fudgy, drop-dead delicious cookies that pack all the lovable flavors of a peanut butter cup, we started by creating a double-chocolate cookie dough that was so easy to work with that stuffing it with a Reese's-like filling was a breeze. Adding chopped and melted bittersweet chocolate as well as Dutch-processed cocoa powder to the cookie dough layered in potent chocolate flavor. The relatively high-fat cocoa powder helped keep the cookies rich and fudgy rather than dry and crumbly. Increasing the standard ratio of flour to sugar, fat, and egg kept the dough from becoming sticky, making it easy to portion and flatten dough balls to be stuffed with a simple mixture of chilled peanut butter, confectioners' sugar, and salt. Finally, rolling the stuffed dough balls in granulated sugar and more confectioners' sugar made the baked cookies crackly, crinkly, and stunningly beautiful.

Chocolate and peanut butter were made for each other. So when you take a filling inspired by the creamy core of a peanut butter cup and bake it inside double-chocolate cookie dough, you get the absolutely mouthwatering combination of a fudgy, crackly, slightly chewy, intensely chocolaty cookie and a satisfying peanutty center. Making stuffed cookies sounds like a

lot more work than unwrapping a peanut butter cup, but it's easier than you'd think, and the reward is worth it.

For the cookie dough, including both unsweetened cocoa powder and bittersweet chocolate, plus a good dose of salt, maximizes the dough's chocolaty complexity and balances out the cookies' sweetness. Dutch-processed cocoa powder, which tends to be high in fat and low in starch, not only helps keep the cookies moist and fudgy (rather than dry and crumbly) but also supplies deeper, earthier chocolate notes than natural cocoa powder (which is fruitier and more acidic). Melting a portion of the chopped chocolate for the dough and then folding in the remaining pieces creates luscious molten pockets in the finished cookies. Using both baking soda and baking powder ensures that the cookies will puff and spread just enough to crackle on top, and a combination of vegetable oil and butter creates the perfect amount of chew.

Once stirred together, the dough is easy to work with, not sticky or messy, so it molds effortlessly around the filling, a simple stir-together mixture of peanut butter, confectioners' sugar, and salt. Briefly freezing the filling while making the dough firms it up, ensuring that stuffing the cookies is fun instead of messy or frustrating. A final roll in granulated and confectioners' sugars coats the dark cookies in a bright-white crust, endowing them with the stunning visual contrast of crinkle cookies and adding a crunchy texture to their exteriors. Very gently flattening the coated dough balls just before baking ensures that each cookie spreads uniformly and consistently, making them pleasingly disk-shaped rather than inconsistently domed and round. Now when you've got chocolate and peanut butter on your mind, you can whip up a batch of these cookies and enjoy their complex notes of bittersweet chocolate and Dutch cocoa and their salty-sweet peanut butter filling.

—MATTHEW FAIRMAN, *Cook's Country*

NOTES FROM THE TEST KITCHEN

DOUBLE CHOCOLATE PUNCH

We wanted these cookies to shout chocolate from the rooftops, so we packed them with both cocoa powder and bittersweet chocolate. We call for Dutch-processed cocoa powder instead of natural cocoa powder for the deep chocolate notes it contributes. Dutch-processed cocoa powder also tends to be high in fat, which makes for moister cookies. Our favorite Dutch-processed cocoa powder is Droste Cacao. Then we add bittersweet chocolate in two ways. Six ounces of the chopped chocolate gets melted and mixed into the dough, while the remaining 4 ounces are folded in to ensure melty, chocolaty bits in every bite. Ghirardelli 60% Cacao Bittersweet Chocolate Premium Baking Bar is our favorite bittersweet chocolate bar.

Peanut Butter–Stuffed Chocolate Cookies

MAKES 16 COOKIES

TOTAL TIME: 1½ HOURS, PLUS 30 MINUTES COOLING

Once baked and cooled, these cookies are best stored in the refrigerator. We developed this recipe using Ghirardelli 60% Cacao Bittersweet Chocolate Premium Baking Bars and Droste Cacao Dutch-processed cocoa powder.

FILLING

½ cup creamy peanut butter

½ cup (2 ounces) confectioners' sugar

¼ teaspoon table salt

DOUGH

1½ cups (7½ ounces) all-purpose flour

¼ cup (¾ ounce) Dutch-processed cocoa powder

1 teaspoon baking powder

¼ teaspoon baking soda

¾ teaspoon table salt

10 ounces bittersweet chocolate, chopped fine, divided

3 tablespoons vegetable oil

1 tablespoon unsalted butter

1 tablespoon vanilla extract

1 cup (7 ounces) granulated sugar, plus ⅓ cup for rolling

2 large eggs

½ cup confectioners' sugar for rolling

1. FOR THE FILLING: Combine peanut butter, sugar, and salt in bowl. Using fork or your hands, stir and mash mixture until thoroughly combined and no dry pockets of sugar remain. Divide filling into 16 equal portions (about 2 teaspoons each). Roll each portion into ball and place on large plate. Freeze until firm, about 30 minutes.

2. FOR THE DOUGH: Meanwhile, adjust oven racks to upper-middle and lower-middle positions and heat oven to 300 degrees. Line 2 rimmed baking sheets with parchment paper.

3. Whisk flour, cocoa, baking powder, baking soda, and salt together in medium bowl. Microwave 6 ounces chocolate, oil, and butter in second medium bowl at 50 percent power, stirring occasionally, until melted, about 3 minutes. Whisk vanilla into melted chocolate mixture until combined.

4. Whisk 1 cup granulated sugar and eggs in large bowl until thoroughly combined. Add melted chocolate mixture and whisk until uniform. Using rubber spatula, fold in flour mixture until combined. Fold in remaining 4 ounces chocolate.

5. Divide dough into 16 equal portions, about scant 3 tablespoons (1⅞ ounces) each; divide any remaining dough evenly among portions. Use your fingers to flatten 1 dough portion into disk with roughly 3-inch diameter. Place 1 ball of filling in center of disk. Wrap edges of dough up and around filling, seal dough, and shape into smooth ball. Repeat with remaining dough portions and filling.

HERE'S HOW TO STUFF AND SHAPE 'EM

1. Use your fingers to flatten 1 dough portion into disk with roughly 3-inch diameter.

2. Place 1 ball of chilled filling in center of disk.

3. Wrap edges of dough up and around filling, seal dough, shape into smooth ball, and roll in sugar.

4. Flatten dough balls into 2-inch-wide disks using bottom of drinking glass. Seal any cracks where filling shows through.

6. Place confectioners' sugar and remaining ⅓ cup granulated sugar in 2 separate shallow dishes. Working in batches, roll dough balls first in granulated sugar, then in confectioners' sugar, to coat. Evenly space dough balls on prepared sheets, 8 dough balls per sheet.

7. Using bottom of drinking glass, flatten dough balls into 2-inch-wide disks. (Dough balls will crack at edges; this is OK. If filling shows through any large cracks, pinch dough together to seal cracks.) Bake until cookies are puffed, edges are just set, and cookies no longer look raw between cracks, about 22 minutes, switching and rotating sheets halfway through baking.

8. Let cookies cool completely on sheets, about 30 minutes. Serve.

ALFAJORES DE MAICENA (DULCE DE LECHE SANDWICH COOKIES)

✔ **WHY THIS RECIPE WORKS** Beloved across Latin America, alfajores de maicena are buttery sandwich cookies that are often filled with the region's caramelized milk jam, dulce de leche. In this iconic version, cornstarch in the dough leads to the characteristically crumbly, melt-in-the-mouth texture. Some recipes call for cornstarch alone, but we found the resulting cookies too fragile. Instead, we used slightly more cornstarch than flour by volume in our dough for powdery-soft cookies with enough structure to hold together when we filled them. Plenty of butter contributed additional tenderness and rich flavor. We opted for yolks instead of whole eggs, since the proteins in the whites can bind the dough and make the cookies less delicate. To provide contrast to the sweetness of the dulce de leche filling, we used a modest amount of sugar in the dough. For the filling, we took a common shortcut and turned to the commercial kind. Nestlé La Lechera Dulce de Leche is thickened with agar-agar, so it was thick enough to keep its shape rather than immediately oozing out from between the cookies. Doctoring it with a little vanilla and salt enhanced its complexity.

One of the best ways I know to enjoy the butterscotch-y goodness of the caramelized milk jam dulce de leche (page 261) is between a pair of buttery, citrus-scented cookies in the Latin American confection called alfajores de maicena. Named for the cornstarch (maicena) in the dough, the cookies are so delicate that they crumble as you eat them, their buttery flavor melding with the rich toffee notes of the dulce de leche. I fell hard for these treats when I first encountered them at Uruguayan American Valery Ketenjian's bakery Alfa Alfajores in San Diego. Now I can't get enough of them.

The name "alfajor" comes from a Hispano-Arabic word for "stuffed" and is an umbrella term for a wide variety of sandwich cookies hugely popular across Latin America and particularly in Argentina, where a billion of these treats are consumed annually. Besides the iconic dulce de leche–filled version, store shelves in that country teem with other styles showcasing different cookie types, fillings, coatings, and flavorings.

"Typically, you pick the one that fits your personality, and you don't veer," said Argentine American cookbook

author Josephine Caminos Oría, whose works include *Dulce de Leche: Recipes, Stories, and Sweet Traditions* (2017).

Whether stuffed with dulce de leche, fruit paste, or peanut butter; rimmed in coconut; or coated in chocolate or meringue, such is the pull of alfajores, said Caminos Oría, that even Argentines living abroad never lose their passion for these treats, always carting at least a few boxes of their favorites back home after visits.

"One of my major marital fights was when we bought three dozen boxes," she said, "and my husband left the duty-free bag on the airplane."

I was set on making the classic cornstarch-based treats and wanted my cookies to be just like Ketenjian's: rich, buttery, and so tender that they'd practically dissolve when you took a bite. "When you're eating it," Ketenjian told me, "it has to all melt in your mouth." Naturally, the filling should delight with luscious complexity, but it would also need to stay neatly in place.

Following the lead of most recipes, I began by creaming butter and sugar. Two sticks of butter for 24 cookies ensured tenderness and plenty of richness. But I kept the sugar in the dough at a modest ½ cup to contrast with the sweetness of the dulce de leche. Putting the flavorings on hold, I slipped in a few egg yolks, which recipes seemed to prefer not only because their fat contributes to a short texture but also because the proteins in the whites can strengthen the dough, making

ALFAJORES DE MAICENA (DULCE DE LECHE SANDWICH COOKIES)

the cookies less delicate. The next step—incorporating the dry ingredients (cornstarch, flour, salt, and leavener)—was where things got a little trickier.

Cornstarch plays a key role in these cookies' powdery-soft texture in a couple ways: It lacks the gluten-forming proteins in flour, and its starch also absorbs some of the moisture in the dough, limiting the flour's ability to form gluten. But if you use too much, the cookies fall apart.

I began cautiously, adding half as much cornstarch as flour by volume to the mixer with the baking powder and salt, but my prudence didn't pay: The cookies were cakey, not crumbly. Next, I switched from all-purpose flour to cake flour, thinking its lower protein content might provide less structure. Still the cookies didn't have that meltingly tender quality of Ketenjian's. Returning to regular flour, I flipped the proportions, this time using one and a half times as much cornstarch as flour. Now the cookies shattered in my fingers before I even got them into my mouth. After a few more tests, I nailed it: Using just a little more cornstarch than flour by volume produced alfajores that were pleasingly fragile but still relatively sturdy.

As for flavorings, aromatic enhancements such as lemon zest and vanilla are typical in alfajores de maicena, and so is a splash of a spirit. I went for all three, choosing brandy as the spirit. The salt brought their flavors into focus.

Typically the dough is chilled to firm it up before rolling, but I streamlined the process with a test kitchen technique: rolling it between two sheets of parchment and then freezing it for 30 minutes. I baked the alfajores in a 350-degree oven just until they were lightly browned on the bottoms but their tops were still elegantly pale.

For the filling, cooks in Latin America often turn to a commercially made confectionary version called dulce de leche repostero that's been shored up with thickeners. Luckily, in the United States there's an equally good option: Nestlé La Lechera Dulce de Leche, which is bolstered with agar-agar. And though the jam tasted rich and butterscotch-y straight from the can, stirring in a little vanilla and salt gave it even more complexity. To help it firm up even more, I chilled the mixture while I made the dough.

It was assembly time. I had two goals: to keep the cookies intact and to spread the filling just to—and not beyond—their edges, where it could easily capture the shredded coconut that I planned for embellishment. I found that it worked best to dollop the filling in the centers of half the cookies, pick them up one by one, place a second cookie on top, and gently press down with my fingers until the filling was flush with the rim.

Buttery and crumbly, bristling with flecks of coconut, and gooey with dulce de leche, these cookies are a perfect accompaniment to coffee and special enough to serve for dessert. They hold well in the refrigerator for five days—if they ever last that long.

—SANDRA WU, *Cook's Illustrated*

Alfajores de Maicena (Dulce de Leche Sandwich Cookies)

MAKES 24 COOKIES   TOTAL TIME: 2 HOURS, PLUS 1 HOUR CHILLING

It's essential to buy the Nestlé La Lechera brand of canned dulce de leche, or the filling won't have the right consistency. Look for it near the sweetened condensed milk in your supermarket. You can also make your own filling by following the multicooker instructions in our recipe for Dulce de Leche (page 261). The brandy complements the flavors of the vanilla and lemon zest, but you can omit it, if preferred. Alfajores are fragile, so we've designed this recipe to make a few extra cookies in case some break. Coconut is a customary garnish, but you can also simply sift confectioners' sugar over the cookies before serving. Refrigerate any leftover dulce de leche in an airtight container for up to one month.

NOTES FROM THE TEST KITCHEN

A FILLING THAT STAYS PUT
Professional bakers fill alfajores with dulce de leche repostero, a thick confectionary version of the beloved milk jam. In my recipe, canned Nestlé La Lechera Dulce de Leche works equally well since it's bolstered with agar-agar. But you can easily make your own filling from scratch with a couple cans of sweetened condensed milk and a multicooker. Heated under pressure in a water bath, the syrupy milk cooks at about 240 degrees, which causes its proteins to denature and gel into a mixture that's much thicker than typical dulce de leche. See the recipe on page 261.

FILLING

2 (13.4-ounce) cans Nestlé La Lechera Dulce de Leche

1 teaspoon vanilla extract

¼ teaspoon table salt

COOKIES

1½ cups (6 ounces) cornstarch

1⅓ cups (6⅔ ounces) all-purpose flour

1 teaspoon baking powder

¼ teaspoon table salt

16 tablespoons unsalted butter, softened

½ cup (3½ ounces) sugar

3 large egg yolks

1 tablespoon brandy (optional)

1 teaspoon grated lemon zest

1 teaspoon vanilla extract

1 cup (3 ounces) unsweetened shredded coconut

1. FOR THE FILLING: Transfer dulce de leche to medium bowl. Stir in vanilla and salt until thoroughly incorporated. Cover and refrigerate until mixture is completely chilled, at least 2 hours.

2. FOR THE COOKIES: While filling chills, in medium bowl, whisk together cornstarch, flour, baking powder, and salt. Using stand mixer fitted with paddle, beat butter and sugar on medium-high speed until pale and fluffy, 2 to 3 minutes. Add egg yolks; brandy, if using; lemon zest; and vanilla and beat until combined. Add cornstarch mixture; reduce speed to low; and mix until dough is smooth, scraping down bowl as needed.

3. Divide dough in half. Place 1 piece of dough in center of large sheet of parchment paper and press with your hand to ½-inch thickness. Place second large sheet of parchment over dough and roll dough to ¼-inch thickness. Using your flat hand on parchment, smooth out wrinkles on both sides. Transfer dough with parchment to rimmed baking sheet. Repeat pressing, rolling, and smoothing second piece of dough, then stack on top of first piece on sheet. Freeze until dough is firm, about 30 minutes.

4. Adjust oven racks to upper-middle and lower-middle positions and heat oven to 350 degrees. Transfer 1 piece of dough to counter. Peel off top layer of parchment and replace loosely. Flip dough and parchment. Peel away second piece of parchment and place on rimmed baking sheet. Using 2-inch round cutter, cut dough into rounds. Transfer rounds to prepared sheet, about ½ inch apart. Repeat with remaining dough and second

rimmed baking sheet. Reroll, chill, and cut scraps until you have 26 rounds on each sheet.

5. Bake until tops are set but still pale and bottoms are light golden, 10 to 12 minutes, switching and rotating sheets halfway through baking. Let cookies cool on sheets for 5 minutes, then carefully transfer to wire rack to cool completely.

6. To assemble, place half of cookies upside down on counter. Place about 2 teaspoons filling on each upside-down cookie. Hold 1 topped cookie on fingers of 1 hand. Place second, untopped cookie on top of filling, right side up, and press gently with fingers of your other hand until filling spreads to edges. Repeat with remaining cookies.

7. Place coconut in small bowl. Working with 1 cookie at a time, roll sides of cookies in coconut, pressing gently to help coconut adhere to exposed filling. Serve immediately or refrigerate in airtight container for up to 5 days. Allow refrigerated cookies to sit out at room temperature for 10 minutes before serving.

DULCE DE LECHE

✓ **WHY THIS RECIPE WORKS** The easiest way to make a batch of dulce de leche is to slowly heat sweetened condensed milk in a water bath set in the oven or in a multicooker. Oven-cooked jam is thick but pourable; multicooker jam is stiffer and ideal for filling pastries and cookies. For the oven method, we transferred the milk to a 13 by 9-inch baking pan so that it spread into a thin layer that was mostly submerged in the water bath and cooked evenly from top to bottom; for the multicooker method, we set the milk into a bowl that we suspended on a rack so that the heat circulated evenly around it. Omitting the baking soda that many recipes call for also helped prevent overcooking, since the alkaline agent raises the pH of the milk, catalyzing the browning reactions at a rate that caused the dulce de leche to easily overcook. Straining the jam ensured that it was silky-smooth, and stirring in a touch of vanilla extract and salt added depth and balanced the sweetness.

Prolonged, steady heat is responsible for some really spectacular culinary alchemy, not the least of which is the glossy, coffee-colored milk jam made throughout Latin America. In Argentina, Uruguay, and Paraguay, where it's referred to as dulce de leche (similar preparations go by different names in other countries), cooks reduce sweetened milk (and often baking soda) until the dairy's proteins and sugars react and transform the mixture into a gooey, butterscotch-y jam that finds its way into almost every kitchen pantry.

"It really is everywhere," said Josephine Caminos Oría, Argentine American author of *Dulce de Leche: Recipes, Stories, and Sweet Traditions* (2017). Tubs of commercial dulce de leche line supermarket shelves throughout Latin America like peanut butter does in the United States—but the milk jam is arguably more pervasive.

"If you're diabetic in Argentina," she said, "you can get a prescription for a dulce de leche with stevia that your insurance company will cover at the pharmacy."

There are myriad styles, too. Dulce de leche tradicional is a schmear for toast, a sweetener for everything from coffee to vinaigrette, and a topping for pancakes; thicker repostero is a confectioners' product used to fill pastries and cookies such as alfajores (page 259); and heladero is a dark-amber base for ice cream.

Caminos Oría spoke lyrically about the lush flavor and consistency of from-scratch versions made by meditatively stirring a pot of fresh milk and sugar for hours. But she also acknowledged that most modern cooks who make the jam usually start with sweetened condensed milk—which is essentially parcooked dulce de leche. Heated further, the viscous, ivory liquid thickens enough to sit up on a spoon, tans deeply, and takes on toffee-like depth.

Cooking the canned milk is simple—the only real effort is time. But it must be done carefully, the milk heated in a water bath so that it cooks gently and evenly. Read on for the methods that I found work best plus details about how a long cooking time transforms the runny, sweetened milk into a luscious, complex-tasting jam.

—SANDRA WU, *Cook's Illustrated*

Dulce de Leche

SERVES 24 (MAKES ABOUT 3⅓ CUPS)

TOTAL TIME: 2½ HOURS (OVEN), 1¼ HOURS (MULTICOOKER)

This recipe can be made in the oven or in a multicooker to produce slightly different consistencies. Dulce de leche cooked in the oven will be thick but pourable when warm—perfect for drizzling over pancakes, waffles, or ice cream or as a milky sweetener for coffee. Made in a multicooker, it will be thick enough to fill cookies (such as our alfajores on page 259) or cakes or to spread on toast; note that you'll need a rack that fits inside your multicooker model.

THE GOOEY SCIENCE BEHIND HOW MILK TURNS TO JAM

Cream-colored, simply sweetened condensed milk will develop a deep butterscotch tone and complexity when it undergoes caramelization as well as the Maillard reaction, the heat-induced interplay between sugars and proteins that causes foods to brown and take on rich, toasty flavor. But the dramatic shift in its consistency—from treacly fluid to jammy goo—is due to a separate change to the milk's proteins. Given ample heat (starting around 170 degrees) and time (an hour or more), they denature and form a gel that gives dulce de leche its semisolid body.

Surprisingly, evaporation plays a minimal role here; most of the milk's water is removed during the condensing process, and much of what's left is bound up in the mixture's high concentration (about 50 percent by weight) of sugar. In fact, the thickest dulce de leche is made when there's no evaporation at all: in a multicooker's pressurized chamber, where the milk reaches 240 degrees and forms an exceptionally stiff gel. In the oven, water in the milk can't rise above its natural boiling point, so its proteins link up less thoroughly, and the jam is a little looser.

It's important that these reactions occur steadily, lest the milk brown unevenly or curdle. (I omitted the dash of baking soda that many recipes call for, since the alkaline agent raises the pH of the milk, catalyzing the browning reactions at a rate that caused my dulce de leche to easily overcook.) The steam-filled multicooker heats evenly, while using a water bath in the oven steadies the milk's temperature so that it cooks consistently.

---

2 **(14-ounce) cans sweetened condensed milk**

1 **teaspoon vanilla extract**

¼ **teaspoon table salt**

1A. FOR THE OVEN: Adjust oven rack to middle position and heat oven to 350 degrees. Pour condensed milk into 13 by 9-inch baking pan. Cover pan tightly with aluminum foil. Pour 1 inch boiling water into large roasting pan and carefully set baking pan inside (water should come about halfway up sides of baking pan). Bake, topping up roasting pan with boiling water every 45 minutes, until condensed milk is brown and has jiggly, flan-like consistency, 2¼ to 2½ hours.

1B. FOR THE MULTICOOKER: Set rack into 6- or 8-quart multicooker and add 8 cups water. Pour condensed milk into 8-inch-diameter stainless-steel bowl. Cover tightly with foil; set on rack. Lock lid into place and close pressure-release valve. Select high pressure-cook function and cook for 1 hour. Turn off multicooker and quick-release pressure. Carefully remove lid, allowing steam to escape away from you.

STRUFFOLI (NEAPOLITAN HONEY BALLS)

2. Carefully transfer cooked condensed milk (it will look broken and grainy) to fine-mesh strainer set over bowl. Stir and press solids with back of small ladle or spoon. Stir in vanilla and salt. Transfer to airtight container. (Jam can be refrigerated for up to 2 weeks.)

STRUFFOLI (NEAPOLITAN HONEY BALLS)

✔ **WHY THIS RECIPE WORKS** Struffoli, a classic Neapolitan treat that's traditionally served at Christmas, Easter, and other festive occasions, consists of chickpea-size deep-fried dough balls that have been drenched in warm honey, piled onto a platter, and topped with multicolored nonpareils and sometimes other embellishments. Making the soft, malleable dough with melted (rather than softened) butter meant that it could be quickly mixed together by hand. Portioning hundreds of tiny, uniform dough balls usually involves rolling ropes, cutting them into small pieces, and rolling each one by hand into a chickpea-size ball, but it was much more efficient to flatten hunks of dough into rectangles and make evenly spaced perpendicular cuts like a grid. Even the ball-rolling step was unnecessary, since the tiny dough pieces puffed into rounds when fried. Briefly simmering the cooled fried dough balls in honey married the two components and thickened the honey a bit so that it clung well. Nonpareils were a must for the toppings, but incorporating candied orange peel and cherries and toasted almonds added complex flavor and texture as well as festive appeal.

Most years, my family spends Christmas Day on Long Island. My aunt Pauline, one of the best cooks I know, prepares a feast that begins with arancini and glazed ham and culminates in a fleet of desserts: bowls of nuts and fruit; trays of colorful Italian butter cookies and cream-filled pastries; and the centerpiece, a platter of struffoli.

Also known as honey balls, struffoli are chickpea-size fried dough balls that have been drenched in warm honey; piled onto a platter or shaped into more elaborate configurations such as a pyramid, cone, or wreath; and embellished with multicolored nonpareils and sometimes confectioners' sugar, nuts, dried or candied fruit, or cucuzzata (candied pumpkin). A classic Neapolitan treat with Greek roots that's traditionally served at Christmas, Easter, and other festive occasions,

it's arguably one of the most distinctive, whimsical sweets in the Italian canon.

"I've never really had anything that's like it," Jack Bishop, America's Test Kitchen's chief creative officer, said affectionately of the struffoli his grandmother Katherine Pizzarello made. "The dough is not sweet because there's a ridiculous amount of sweetness from the honey. The nonpareils are just fantastic and also odd, because there are very few homemade things where you then go and throw candy on them."

Struffoli's snack-y quality is my favorite part. As kids, we'd come and go from the table, casually plucking the tiny treats from the mound and popping them into our mouths as the adults sat and reminisced.

It's also a labor of love, the kind of all-hands-on-deck holiday project that can bring everyone together, and something I've always wanted to try. My aunt graciously walked me through her process, which generally sounded straightforward. But even she acknowledged that she's built up her struffoli-making skills over the years, and I could tell that certain details—recognizing when the dough's consistency is just right, knowing how many pieces to fry per batch, heating the honey just enough—take time to master. Ideally, I'd clarify and maybe even streamline the process for myself and anyone else who wanted to learn.

The first step is to make a malleable dough from flour, baking powder, eggs, softened butter, lemon juice, sugar, and vanilla. Next, shape it by cutting the dough into chunks, rolling the chunks into ropes, cutting the ropes into hundreds of pieces (that aren't "even an inch," Aunt Pauline said), rolling the pieces into balls, and spacing the balls out on a tray so that they don't stick together. Then, deep-fry the balls in batches until they're golden, slightly puffed, and crisp-tender—like a cookie. (Struffoli isn't pillowy like other forms of fried dough.) Let them drain and cool in a paper towel–lined baking pan.

Because the honey is so sweet, I cut back on the sugar in the dough and added salt, which I noticed is absent from most recipes. I also switched from softened butter to melted butter so that I could stir the dough together in a bowl rather than use a stand mixer. (Struffoli dough doesn't need lots of air beaten into it; the eggs and baking powder do an ample job of leavening.) You can perfume the dough with citrus zest and/or liqueurs, but I followed my aunt's lead and stuck with vanilla: Its soft, floral sweetness allowed the dough to function as a neutral canvas for the honey and toppings. However, I found the lemon juice in her recipe too subtle to taste, so I dropped it.

I kneaded the slightly tacky mass and shaped it into a ball before strategizing ways to streamline the cutting and rolling process. My inclination was to create a "portion grid" of the dough by forming it into a square and making evenly spaced cuts in perpendicular directions—an approach coined by my colleague Steve Dunn for his baci di dama, the petite Italian sandwich cookies. But it's tricky to cut hundreds of tiny dough bits from one large grid, so instead I made a few smaller grids. I divided the dough into six pieces, flattened each piece into a rectangle, and cut the rectangle into 60 half-inch morsels—big enough to be adequately tender when fried but still fittingly petite.

As it turned out, the grid system was the first of two time-saving strategies I'd work into my recipe. I stumbled upon the second one when I was testing the frying temperature of the oil. I'd planned to roll each piece into a ball while the oil heated, but when I dropped a few unrolled bits of dough into the pot to check for browning, they puffed so uniformly that it was clear I could skip the rolling step, too.

Once the oil hit 350 degrees, I submerged 25 or so dough bits in the oil. It took only a couple minutes for them to puff and turn golden, at which point I fished them out and let them drain and cool in a paper towel–lined baking pan while I warmed the honey.

Bishop still remembers the scent of the warm honey from decades ago: "a little burnt almost, but in a good way." Most cooks warm the honey to make it fluid, drop in the fried dough balls, and stir them so that they're thoroughly coated. But when I tried this and plated the honey-drenched balls, most of the honey didn't cling well, so the balls were barely coated. So instead I cooked the fried spheres in the honey, which reduced and thickened a bit so that it really clung. As it heated, the honey took on a delicate fragrance—not burnt, but nutty—and a richer bronze tint. (To avoid overreducing the honey, which causes it to set up rock-hard, I kept the heat relatively low.)

I let the struffoli cool briefly before stirring in the nonpareils—add them when it's still hot, and you get rainbow swirls instead of discrete beads of color—as well as candied orange peel and toasted sliced almonds, which balanced the overall sweetness and introduced pleasant chew and crunch. Then I piled the lustrous

PORTION HUNDREDS OF PIECES IN MINUTES

Rather than cutting and rolling hundreds of dough bits, make "portion grids" by dividing the dough into six pieces, flattening each piece into a 5 by 3-inch rectangle with the shorter side facing you, and making perpendicular cuts. Each grid will yield 60 uniform pieces that will puff into balls as soon as you submerge them in the hot oil.

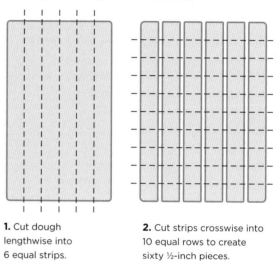

1. Cut dough lengthwise into 6 equal strips.

2. Cut strips crosswise into 10 equal rows to create sixty ½-inch pieces.

pieces onto a lightly greased serving platter, sprinkled the mound with more nonpareils so that the colors really stood out, and—for maximum festiveness—dotted candied cherries around the pile.

Once the struffoli had cooled completely, I popped a few pieces into my mouth the way I always have, appreciating the familiar tackiness of the honey on my fingers and the way the nonpareils cracked like microbursts with each bite. But this time, there was even more going on: The treacly honey was offset by the faintly bitter citrus and toasty nuts. For a moment it felt like Christmas, and it would tide me over until I could make it home for the holiday.

—ANNIE PETITO, *Cook's Illustrated*

Struffoli (Neapolitan Honey Balls)

SERVES 6 TO 8 (MAKES 4½ CUPS)

TOTAL TIME: 2 HOURS, PLUS 20 MINUTES COOLING

We strongly recommend weighing the flour. Use a Dutch oven that holds 6 quarts or more. Make sure that all your equipment is in place before you start frying. For an impressively tall mound of struffoli, use a serving plate that's 10 to 11 inches across.

2 **cups (10 ounces) all-purpose flour**

¼ **cup (1¾ ounces) sugar**

½ **teaspoon table salt**

¼ **teaspoon baking powder**

3 **large eggs, lightly beaten**

4 **tablespoons unsalted butter, melted and cooled slightly**

2 **teaspoons vanilla extract**

2 **quarts vegetable oil for frying**

1 **cup honey**

2 **tablespoons multicolored nonpareils, plus extra for garnish**

¼ **cup sliced almonds, toasted (optional)**

2 **tablespoons candied orange peel, chopped fine (optional)**

8 **candied cherries (optional)**

1. Line 2 rimmed baking sheets with parchment paper. Whisk flour, sugar, salt, and baking powder together in large bowl. Add eggs, melted butter, and vanilla and stir with rubber spatula until soft dough forms. Transfer dough to counter and knead briefly to bring together into ball, about 30 seconds. Dough will be slightly tacky. (Dough can be wrapped in plastic wrap and refrigerated for up to 24 hours.)

2. Add oil to large Dutch oven until it measures about 1½ inches deep and heat over medium heat to 350 degrees. While oil heats, divide dough into 6 equal pieces, about 3 ounces each. Flatten 1 piece of dough into 5 by 3-inch rectangle, with shorter side facing you (lightly grease your hands and counter if dough sticks). Using bench scraper or sharp knife, cut dough lengthwise into 6 equal strips. Cut strips crosswise into 10 equal rows to create sixty ½-inch pieces. Separate dough pieces and place on prepared sheets, keeping pieces from touching (pieces needn't be spherical). Repeat with remaining dough.

3. Line 13 by 9-inch baking pan with triple layer of paper towels. Place 25 to 30 struffoli in slotted spoon or spider skimmer (it's OK if they touch). Gently submerge spoon in oil to transfer struffoli to pot (oil may foam slightly). Cook, stirring frequently, until struffoli are crisp and golden brown, 2 to 3 minutes.

4. Transfer struffoli to prepared pan. Repeat with remaining dough (spoon may be hot), adjusting burner, if necessary, to maintain oil temperature between 350 and 365 degrees. Let struffoli cool completely, about 15 minutes (cooled struffoli can be stored in airtight container at room temperature for up to

3 days or frozen in zipper-lock bag for up to 1 month).

5. Heat honey in large saucepan over medium-low heat until small bubbles break constantly and rapidly across surface. Off heat, add struffoli and stir until evenly coated. Return to heat and continue to cook, stirring occasionally, 4 minutes longer. Remove from heat and let struffoli cool in saucepan for 5 minutes. While struffoli cool, spray serving platter lightly with vegetable oil spray and wipe with paper towel, leaving thin film.

6. Add nonpareils to saucepan and stir to coat evenly. Stir in almonds and orange peel, if using. Using slotted spoon, lift struffoli from saucepan and transfer to prepared platter, piling into mound. Garnish with candied cherries, if using, and extra nonpareils. Let cool completely, about 20 minutes (cooled struffoli can be covered with waxed paper or parchment paper and wrapped tightly in plastic wrap for up to 3 days). Use 2 spoons to transfer individual servings to plates or allow guests to pluck pieces from platter.

BRETON KOUIGN AMANN

✓ WHY THIS RECIPE WORKS A lean yeasted dough made with all-purpose flour offered the best combination of strength and workability. Embedding the sugar (along with a little extra salt, for pronounced salinity) into the butter block by paddling the ingredients together in a stand mixer limited contact between the sugar and dough, thus preventing the sugar from drawing moisture out of the dough and making it unworkably sticky; it also limited abrasion during rolling, which would otherwise tear the dough. It helped to enclose and shape the butter mixture in a parchment paper "envelope." The parchment kept the mixture contained so that we ended up with a thin, even rectangle that perfectly fit the dimensions of the dough and was easy to roll during lamination. Piercing the shaped kouign amann before baking provided escape routes for any trapped air that would otherwise cause the pastry to balloon in the oven, distorting the beautiful layers.

According to legend, about 160 years ago in Douarnenez, a small seaside town in the northwest corner of France, Yves René Scordia ran out of goods to sell in his bakery. The resourceful baker looked around his shop and spotted lean bread dough, sugar, and sea-salty Breton butter. He tucked a slab of the butter and a hefty amount

BRETON KOUIGN AMANN

of sugar inside the dough, rolled it out, folded it, and repeated the process before plopping the mass into a round pan, scoring the top, and sliding it into the oven.

As it baked, some of the butter and sugar leaked out of the dough and pooled at the bottom of the pan, where it cooked down into a subtly salty caramel. The butter that remained in the folds created steam that caused the layers to puff and separate into thin sheets that were soaked in butter and melted sugar. Scordia turned his creation out of the pan, cut it into wedges, and the kouign amann (the Breton name for "butter cake," pronounced "KWEE-nyah-MAHN") was born.

Rustic yet refined and distinctly salty and sweet, the pastry remains a hyper-regional specialty that celebrates the exceptional butter and salt produced along north-western France's hilly coastline. But its appeal is universal: Each bite reads like a mash-up of a crois-sant's striated structure and a lacquered version of the caramel-like goo you might find coating a sticky bun. Traditional recipes also call for scoring an elegant dia-mond pattern into the surface of the dough, brushing it with milk, and showering it with sugar before baking, which renders the top attractively golden and crunchy.

Before I studied up on how to make my own, I fig-ured I was in for a day's worth of intricate pastry work. So imagine my delight when I watched some YouTube footage of Douarnenez bakers at work and realized that kouign amann also happens to be one of the simplest, fastest forms of layered pastry that you can make. Not only did they accomplish the series of turns (a baker's term for the repeated rolling and folding sequence) in a single session rather than resting and refrigerating the dough between turns as you would to create a croissant's ultradelicate structure, but shaping the dough into a single large round was clearly much sim-pler than cutting, rolling, and resting triangles of dough to create individual pastries. This was an afternoon project that impressed like an all-day affair, and I couldn't wait to get rolling.

Enclosing a thick slab (or "block," as bakers call it) of butter in lean, yeasted dough and repeatedly folding and rolling the package into thin sheets is called lam-ination, and it's the fundamental process behind layered pastries such as kouign amann and croissants. Pro bakers make it look easy, but it can be tricky for the average home cook to do because the butter is prone to cracking and breaking into chunks, especially if the dough and fat are not equally firm.

My solve is to start with a thinner butter block that I make by enclosing 8 ounces of salted butter in an "enve-lope" that I fashion from parchment paper and roll into a slim rectangle. The envelope helps contain the butter so that it's just the right shape to fit the dough and thin enough that there's less risk of it breaking up when I roll it out. I also make sure that the butter block and dough are equally malleable by chilling both components before rolling. After mixing up a basic lean dough (all-purpose flour, water, salt, and a modicum of yeast for flavor and just a bit of lift) and forming the butter block, I refrig-erate both for about an hour. Of course, cold butter is much firmer than cold dough, so when I'm ready to start laminating, I let the chilled block soften on the counter for a few minutes while I superchill the cold dough in the freezer to firm it up even more.

Those tactics gave me a solid start with my kouign amann lamination, but I underestimated how challeng-ing it would be to incorporate sugar into the folds as well. Watching the Douarnenez bakers deftly work fistfuls of it into the dough along with the butter block, I figured I would easily do the same. But as soon as I scattered sugar over the butter, enclosed it all, and started to roll, my inexperience showed. The sugar shifted unevenly, and as I folded the package into thirds, turned it, and rolled and folded it again into thin-ner sheets, the abrasive particles tore gaping holes in the dough. It also pulled moisture from the dough, and that moisture dissolved more sugar, which made the whole package sticky and difficult to handle. As the pastry baked, butter flowed out of the large holes before the layers set, so the dough melded into a squat cake-like structure that fried in the buttery flood.

Clearly, I'd have to come up with a more foolproof approach for managing the sugar. Decreasing it wasn't an option; I needed at least ¾ cup for sufficient sweet-ness, and I also wanted to add a little extra salt to match the pronounced salinity of Breton butter. But I could try changing the way I incorporated those ingredients. I transferred my next batch of dough from the mixer bowl to a plate, put it in the fridge to relax, and then—breaking tradition—used the mixer to combine the butter with the sugar and a little salt just until the mixture was uniform. Then I proceeded to wrap, roll, and chill my butter block before laminating the dough.

My experiment was a breakthrough. Embedding the sugar in the butter limited contact between it and the dough, thus minimizing the stickiness caused by

MAKE A BUTTER BLOCK "ENVELOPE"

To form the butter block itself, it helps to enclose and shape the butter mixture in a parchment paper "envelope." The parchment keeps the mixture contained, so you end up with a thin, even rectangle that perfectly fits the dimensions of the dough and is easy to roll during lamination.

1. Fold 18-inch length of parchment in half to create rectangle.

2. Fold over 3 open sides of rectangle to form 6 by 9-inch rectangle with enclosed sides. Crease folds firmly.

3. Open parchment packet and place butter mixture in center.

4. Fold parchment over mixture and press to ½-inch thickness. Refold parchment at creases to enclose mixture.

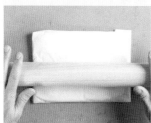

5. Turn packet over so flaps are underneath and roll until butter fills packet, taking care to achieve even thickness.

---

excess moisture and the tears caused by abrasion. The only downside was that without holes in the dough, there were no escape routes for trapped air, and the kouign amann ballooned in the oven, distorting the lovely layers I'd built. But I had another unorthodox fix: air vents, which I poked into my next batch of dough after scoring it. Going forward, I also generously floured my work surface and moved quickly through the folding steps to avoid any potential sticking.

Here, finally, was a kouign amann that boasted all the trappings of well-made laminated pastry—uniformly puffed structure, distinct inner layers, unapologetic butteriness—along with the slightly chewy, salted, caramelly bottom and delectably crunchy top that make this Breton sweet a standout. And it was on the table in a matter of hours. Layered pastry newbies, this one's for you.

—ANDREA GEARY, *Cook's Illustrated*

Breton Kouign Amann

SERVES 8 TO 10

TOTAL TIME: 2 HOURS, PLUS 1¾ HOURS RESTING AND COOLING

We strongly recommend weighing the flour for this recipe. The butter block should be cool but malleable at the beginning of step 4; if your kitchen is cooler than 70 degrees, you may need to leave the butter block on the counter for up to 20 minutes (it's OK to leave the dough in the freezer for the extended time). Once you begin rolling and folding the dough, you'll want to move swiftly and without interruption, so have your ingredients and equipment in place before you start. Keeping plenty of flour under the dough while rolling will help prevent the layers from tearing; brushing away excess flour on top of the dough before folding will help the dough adhere to itself.

- 2¼ cups (11¼ ounces) all-purpose flour
- 1¼ teaspoons table salt, divided
- ½ teaspoon instant or rapid-rise yeast
- 1 cup water, room temperature
- 16 tablespoons salted butter, softened
- ¾ cup (5¼ ounces) plus 1 tablespoon sugar, divided
- 1 tablespoon milk

1. Using rubber spatula, stir together flour, ¾ teaspoon salt, and yeast in bowl of stand mixer. Add water and mix until most flour is moistened. Attach dough hook and knead on low speed until cohesive dough forms, about 1 minute. Increase speed to medium-low and knead until dough is smooth and elastic, about 5 minutes. Shape dough into ball (scrape out mixer bowl but do not wash). Flatten into rough 5-inch square and transfer to lightly greased plate. Cover dough and refrigerate for at least 1 hour or up to 24 hours. While dough rests, make butter packet.

2. Fold 18-inch length of parchment in half to create rectangle. Fold over 3 open sides of rectangle to form 6 by 9-inch rectangle with enclosed sides. Crease folds firmly. Open parchment packet and set aside. Combine butter, ¾ cup sugar, and remaining ½ teaspoon salt in now-empty mixer bowl. Using paddle, mix on low speed until thoroughly combined, about 1 minute. Transfer butter mixture to prepared parchment rectangle, fold parchment over mixture, and press to ½-inch thickness. Refold parchment at creases to enclose mixture. Turn packet over so flaps are underneath and roll gently until butter mixture fills packet, taking care to achieve even thickness. Refrigerate for at least 45 minutes or up to 24 hours.

3. Transfer butter block to counter. Transfer dough to freezer and freeze for 10 minutes. Meanwhile, adjust oven rack to middle position and heat oven to 375 degrees. Lightly grease 9-inch round cake pan and line with 12-inch parchment square, pleating parchment so it lines bottom and sides of pan (A).

4. Transfer dough to well-floured counter and roll into 18 by 6½-inch rectangle with short side parallel to counter edge. Unwrap butter block and place in center of dough (B). Fold upper and lower sections of dough over butter so they meet in center (it's OK to gently stretch dough). Press center seam and side seams closed (C). Dust counter with more flour if necessary. Place rolling pin at top edge of dough and press gently to make slight depression across top. Lift pin, move it 1 inch closer to you, and press again. Continue pressing and lifting to bottom edge (D). Turn rolling pin 90 degrees and make similar depressions across width of dough (E). Roll dough out lengthwise into 21 by 7-inch rectangle (it's OK if it becomes slightly wider) (F). Pop any bubbles that form. Using dry pastry brush, dust off any flour clinging to surface of dough (G). Starting at bottom of dough, fold into thirds like business letter to form 7-inch square (H). Turn square 90 degrees. Dust counter with more flour if necessary. Roll out lengthwise into 21 by 7-inch rectangle, and pop any bubbles (I). Using dry pastry brush, dust off any flour clinging to surface of dough, and fold into thirds (J).

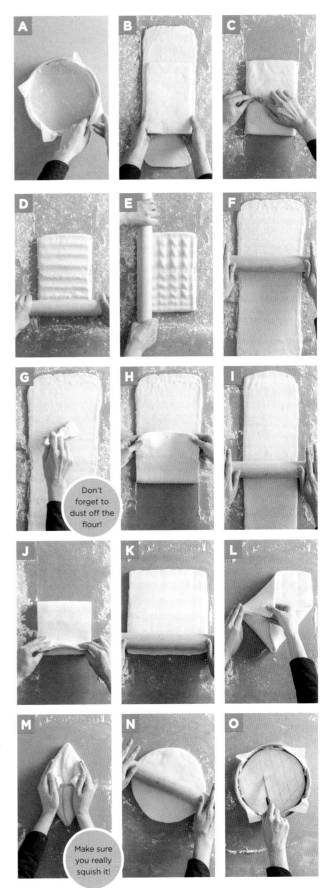

KOUIGNETTES: NOT JUST MINI KOUIGN AMANN

If you're familiar with the term kouign amann ("KWEE-nyah-MAHN"), you might think it refers to the flaky, cupcake-size confections that show up occasionally in American and Parisian bakeries. But this diminutive style is actually a kouignette: a riff on the robust Breton original that features a more delicate structure (the result of more involved lamination); less sugar; and sometimes embellishments such as chocolate, fruit, or nuts swirled into the pastry. In fact, kouignettes bear a stronger resemblance to lightly sweetened croissants than they do to their namesake.

5. Dust counter with more flour if necessary. Roll dough into 11-inch square (K). Fold each corner to center, overlapping slightly, and press to adhere (L). Push right and left corners toward center, and then push top and bottom corners toward center to form rough, crumpled round (M). Press top to compress. Flip dough so smoother side is facing up, then tuck edges under to form round. Flatten gently with your hands, then roll dough into 9½-inch round (N). Transfer to prepared pan (it's OK if dough is slightly sticky), squishing edges to fit.

6. Brush top with milk. Using sharp paring knife, score top of pastry in diamond pattern (O). Sprinkle evenly with remaining 1 tablespoon sugar. Using paring knife, pierce dough all the way down to pan surface in 4 places to create air vents. Bake until pastry is deeply browned and crisp, 50 minutes to 1 hour. Let cool in pan on wire rack for 10 minutes. Invert, remove parchment, and reinvert. Let cool for at least 30 minutes before serving. (Kouign amann is best eaten on the day it's made, but leftovers can be wrapped well and stored at room temperature for up to 3 days. Warm leftovers gently in oven before serving.)

VEGAN CHOCOLATE MOUSSE

✔ **WHY THIS RECIPE WORKS** Dairy and eggs are the cornerstones of conventional mousse. But when you take them out, the result is a whole new standard for what this dessert can be: gossamer light, with profound chocolate flavor. An added perk: This mousse comes together in just 20 minutes from pantry ingredients. For an ethereal texture, we turned to aquafaba, the viscous liquid in a can of chickpeas that has a keen ability to whip to a stiff, snowy-white foam, just like egg whites. Vegetable oil added to the chocolate base contributed richness and, unlike the coconut oil often found in vegan mousse, didn't give the dessert a grainy mouthfeel. For deep, complex chocolate flavor, we used both solid chocolate and cocoa powder. And without the dulling effects of dairy, every nuance of chocolate flavor came shining through.

I've long been a plant-forward cook at home, but when I opened a café called the Farmer's Hand in the Corktown neighborhood of Detroit in 2016, I brought that sensibility to my work as well. Determined to support the local farming community at every turn, I let the seasons dictate the menu and drew a loyal following of vegan and nonvegan diners alike who showed up for items such as quinoa burgers and avocado toast with beet hummus.

So when *Cook's Illustrated* approached me to develop a vegan chocolate mousse that anyone would love, it felt right in my wheelhouse, and I knew it would be a fun challenge. Dairy and eggs are core to the dessert, and when you take them out, all that's left is the chocolate and sugar. Once upon a time, that might have meant relying on products such as commercial egg replacers that nonvegans wouldn't necessarily have in their kitchens. But plant-based cooking has come a long way, making use of everyday ingredients in innovative ways. And even dishes modeled on conventional classics can be so pleasing in their own right that you don't miss the traditional components.

It would take some teasing out, but I was confident that I could produce a showstopping mousse to rival the original—plush and billowy, with profound chocolate flavor—and thrill diners of all stripes.

A traditional chocolate mousse works like this: Solid chocolate provides flavor as well as structure from the cocoa butter, egg yolks and butter contribute more structure as well as richness, and whipped egg whites and/or whipped cream sweetened with sugar add lift. Typically you melt the chocolate, whisk in the yolks and butter, fold in the aerator(s), and then chill the mousse until it's set.

I struck out with vegan approaches that replaced the eggs and butter with either tofu or avocado, simply buzzing one or the other in a blender with the chocolate and sugar. Silken tofu made a smoothie-like mixture

VEGAN CHOCOLATE MOUSSE

that never fully set up, and firm tofu produced a dense concoction that wasn't remotely airy. Avocado was the worst, leaving me with a thick chocolate paste that tasted unmistakably vegetal.

Far more promising were the methods that called for aquafaba, the cooking liquid in a can of chickpeas that has a keen ability to whip to a stiff, snowy-white foam. These recipes also included fat in the form of coconut oil or coconut cream—go-tos in vegan baking and dessert making for their ability to mimic butter's richness. I gave a version with coconut cream a whirl first, melting it with bittersweet chocolate and folding in aquafaba that I'd whipped to soft peaks with sugar. To my delight, the mousse was gossamer light—even airier than the conventional kind since there were no eggs providing bulk. Aquafaba was definitely in. But I wasn't wild about the way the coconut cream's tropical notes muted the chocolate flavor, and strangely, the dessert was marred by a faint but distinct graininess. I'd save the coconut cream to whip into a topping, where it wouldn't directly interfere with the chocolate, and go with neutral-tasting refined coconut oil, figuring out the graininess issue as I went along.

It was time to home in on the chocolate. For a vegan recipe, I'd need to use a vegan chocolate, but many bars fall short of that classification because they contain small amounts of dairy and/or they're sweetened with conventional granulated sugar, which is sometimes processed with bone char to bleach the crystals white (see "Don't Assume All Dark Chocolate Is Vegan"). I chose a bittersweet vegan chocolate with 70 percent cacao (a nonvegan chocolate with 60 to 70 percent cacao will also work), which would give me rich, well-rounded chocolate flavor. For a recipe serving four, I chopped 4 ounces of the chocolate and measured out 3 tablespoons of coconut oil—enough to ensure that I had plenty of liquefied base for folding the foam into. I melted both ingredients in the microwave, and as the mixture cooled, I whipped ½ cup of chickpea liquid with sugar, a pinch of salt, and cream of tartar (acidic ingredients improve aquafaba's whipping ability). I then folded the aquafaba gently into the chocolate mixture. The mousse was so light that it was like spooning up clouds of chocolate, and without dairy (or coconut cream) dulling flavor, I could taste every nuance. But the dessert still had that mysterious subtle graininess.

I realized the problem: My mousse had two forms of saturated fat—the coconut oil as well as the cocoa butter in the chocolate. When chilled, these fats formed tiny solid flecks detectable on the tongue. In traditional mousse, the cream and eggs minimize the formation of these solid fat crystals so that they aren't noticeable.

The obvious solution was to replace the bar chocolate with cocoa powder, which contains minimal cocoa butter, and swap the coconut oil for vegetable oil.

These adjustments did the trick, and my mousse was now silky smooth. But I had a new problem: Since vegetable oil remains a liquid even when it's chilled, it couldn't shore up the structure, and the dessert was prone to slumping. It occurred to me that if I added back a modest amount of solid chocolate, it might have just enough cocoa butter to bolster the mousse's structure but not enough to impact texture, and its rounder flavor would bring even more chocolaty dimension to the mousse. Keeping the amount of cocoa powder at ¼ cup, I was able to incorporate 1½ ounces of bittersweet chocolate without reintroducing graininess.

The final results, if I may say so, were magnificent. With two forms of chocolate and none of the dulling effects of dairy, the mousse boasted seriously bold, complex chocolate flavor. And with its velvety, ethereal texture, each spoonful tasted luxe but not cloyingly decadent. It was truly a mousse in a class of its own.

—KIKI LOUYA, *Cook's Illustrated*

NOTES FROM THE TEST KITCHEN

DON'T ASSUME ALL DARK CHOCOLATE IS VEGAN

You may not realize it without examining the label, but some dark chocolates contain small amounts of milk products such as whey, casein, or milk solids. Furthermore, they may be sweetened with conventional granulated sugar, which is sometimes processed with bone char. To be sure that a dark chocolate is truly plant-based, look for "vegan" on the label.

TRULY VEGAN

DAIRY-FREE BUT NOT VEGAN

AQUAFABA: THE EGG-FREE MIRACLE WHIP

The discovery that an ethereal foam can be created by simply whipping the viscous liquid from a can of chickpeas wasn't made by a food scientist or even a professional chef. Instead, credit goes to an American software engineer named Goose Wohlt. In 2015, inspired by the experiments other scrappy vegan home cooks had shared online, Wohlt successfully turned the whipped cooking water into meringue. He promptly dubbed the liquid "aquafaba" ("aqua" is Latin for "water"; "faba," "bean") and began posting about its properties on Facebook. The magic is in the viscous liquid's proteins and soluble fiber, which, when beaten, link together to trap air bubbles and form a foam, just as egg whites do. Word spread like wildfire, and soon vegans around the globe were using it in all sorts of applications, from angel food cake to mayonnaise to mousse. –Amanda Agee

FROM THIS
Drain canned chickpea liquid.

TO THIS
Whip to peaks just like egg whites.

Vegan Chocolate Mousse

SERVES 4 (MAKES 2 CUPS)

TOTAL TIME: 20 MINUTES, PLUS 3 HOURS CHILLING

Use a chocolate with 60 to 70 percent cacao here. For a plant-based mousse, use organic sugar (conventional sugar is sometimes processed with bone char) and chocolate labeled "vegan" or made with organic sugar and no dairy (some dark chocolates contain small amounts). If avoiding dairy is your only concern, Lindt Excellence 70% Cocoa is a good option. Do not use the aquafaba from Progresso-brand chickpeas or from home-cooked chickpeas; it won't whip as well. Top the mousse with Whipped Coconut Cream (recipe follows) and shaved chocolate.

- ¼ **cup vegetable oil**
- 1½ **ounces bittersweet chocolate, chopped fine**
- ¼ **cup (¾ ounce) unsweetened cocoa powder**
- ½ **teaspoon vanilla extract**
- ½ **cup aquafaba**
- ⅓ **cup (2⅓ ounces) sugar**
- ¼ **teaspoon cream of tartar**
-   **Pinch table salt**

1. Microwave oil and chocolate in large bowl until chocolate is just melted, 30 to 60 seconds. Add cocoa and vanilla and whisk until very smooth. Set aside and let cool.

2. While chocolate mixture cools, combine aquafaba, sugar, cream of tartar, and salt in stand mixer fitted with whisk attachment. Whip on medium-high speed until mixture is slightly glossy and soft peaks form, 4 to 7 minutes.

3. Whisk one-third of aquafaba mixture into chocolate mixture until fully combined. Using rubber spatula, gently fold in remaining aquafaba mixture, making sure to scrape up any chocolate from bottom of bowl, until no streaks remain. Spoon mousse into 4 serving dishes. Cover and refrigerate until set, 3 to 4 hours. (Mousse can be refrigerated for up to 24 hours.) Serve.

Whipped Coconut Cream

SERVES 4 TO 6 (MAKES 1 CUP)

TOTAL TIME: 10 MINUTES, PLUS 24 HOURS CHILLING

To ensure that the cream whips properly, be sure to use full-fat coconut milk here. Refrigerate unopened cans of coconut milk for at least 24 hours to ensure 2 distinct layers form.

- 2 **(14-ounce) cans coconut milk**
- 1 **tablespoon sugar**
- 1 **teaspoon vanilla extract**

Skim top layer of coconut cream from each can and measure out 1 cup (save any extra cream and milky liquid for another use). Using stand mixer fitted with whisk attachment, whip coconut cream, sugar, and vanilla on low speed until well combined, about 30 seconds. Increase speed to high and whip until mixture thickens and soft peaks form, about 2 minutes. (Whipped coconut cream can be refrigerated for up to 4 days.)

TEST KITCHEN RESOURCES

* Not all products we tested are listed in these pages. Web subscribers can find complete listings and information on all products tested and reviewed at AmericasTestKitchen.com.

BEST KITCHEN QUICK TIPS

BEAT EGGS WITH EASE

When they need to beat eggs, John and Denise Goodman of Oak Park, Calif., turn not to a whisk but to a handheld milk frother. The tool buzzes the eggs into an airy, uniform mixture with minimal effort.

SALT IN A DUTCH OVEN TO SAVE SPACE

When refrigerating a salted roast or poultry, KJ Iribe of Alexandria, Va., places the meat inside a Dutch oven and sets a wire rack over the pot to provide a "shelf" for storage and ample airflow for the meat.

PAT IN THE PAN WITH A PAN

When she is making a recipe that requires a 13 by 9-inch pat-in-the-pan crust (such as our Millionaire's Shortbread, November/December 2016), Michelle Chun of Alhambra, Calif., uses an 8 by 8-inch baking pan to evenly distribute the dough in the bottom of the larger pan. The large, flat surface covers the dough more efficiently and provides more-even coverage than a smaller tool can.

GET ALL THE FROSTING OUT OF A PASTRY BAG

If the frosting in her pastry bag is unevenly distributed and not extruding smoothly, Kate Sutcliffe of Amherst, Mass., lays the bag on the counter and uses a rolling pin to push the frosting toward the tip.

BLIND-BAKE THE REUSABLE WAY

In an effort to reduce waste when she's blind-baking pie pastry, Robin Conley of Fort Collins, Colo., trades the usual aluminum foil or parchment paper for a silicone bowl cover. The cover neatly contains her pie weights, and as a bonus, the silicone wrapper is big enough to cover any pie leftovers.

LABEL YOUR ALARMS

When Kathryn Dundon of Lake Zurich, Ill., is cooking several dishes at once, she sets multiple alarms on her phone and labels each one with the name of the corresponding dish. That way, when an alarm goes off, she immediately knows which dish she needs to check on.

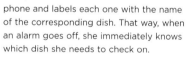

REUSABLE CUTTING BOARD STABILIZER

Many cooks like to steady their cutting board with a damp paper towel or dish cloth. Instead, Randy Andrews of Henderson, Nev., reaches for a silicone baking mat or trivet so that there's nothing to waste or wash.

SEPARATE COFFEE FILTERS WITH EASE

Chuck Weinrick of Marquette, Mich., struggled to separate individual coffee filters from the stack when brewing coffee. He solved the problem by sticking a loop of masking tape to the side of the tin of filters. Every morning, he removes the tape from the tin and sticks it to the filter on the top of the stack, pulling it away from the others with ease.

BROTH BOX TURNED ICE PACK

When Dawn Fleming of Lansing, Mich., finishes a box of store-bought broth, she doesn't discard the container—she turns it into an ice pack. After giving the box a shake with soap and water to rinse it out, she refills it with water (leaving an inch of room at the top) and places it in the freezer. The boxes stack nicely, making them perfect for use in a cooler.

MAKE CRUMB CRUSTS WITH A POTATO MASHER

When making a dessert with a cookie or graham cracker crust, Timothy Haasken of Blacksburg, Va., covers the head of his flat-plate potato masher with heavy-duty foil and uses it as a tamping tool to evenly distribute the crumbs and press them into the bottom of the pie plate. (This method also works for pat-in-the-pan crusts.)

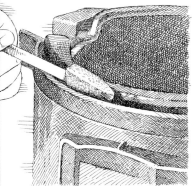

A CRAFTY MINISPONGE

Christine Hill of La Conner, Wash., uses a small foam paintbrush as a miniature sponge to clean hard-to-reach areas on kitchen tools (such as her Instant Pot's rim). She dampens the brush and adds a drop of dish soap to help scrub away messes, and then she rinses the brush and swipes the area again to finish the job.

SOAK POTS AND PANS ON THE STOVE

Because her sink is not big enough to hold large pots and pans, Tiffany Miller of Akron, Ohio, adds soap and water to the cookware; puts on their lids; and places them back on the stove, setting them over low heat. After a few minutes, the hot water and steam loosen any stuck-on residue with no hard scrubbing necessary.

SEPARATE BACON STRIPS WITH EASE

Abe Pendleton of Dublin, Ohio, has a clever trick for separating bacon strips. Before he opens the package, he grabs the short ends and twists them in opposite directions to loosen the stuck-together slices. When he opens the package, it's easy to pull the strips apart.

DON'T TOSS PARCHMENT TRIMMINGS

After trimming parchment paper to fit her baking sheet, Lynn Mangan of Dyer, Ind., doesn't throw away the excess. When she's baking bread, she places one of the long, wide strips across the bottom and up the sides of her loaf pan and uses it as a sling to lift the loaf out.

A NO-SMEAR BRIE SLICER

When Mary Wardley of Bedford, Mass., found that a chef's knife smeared soft cheeses such as Brie, she switched to a pizza cutter. The tool is particularly handy for cutting large, neat pieces for sandwiches.

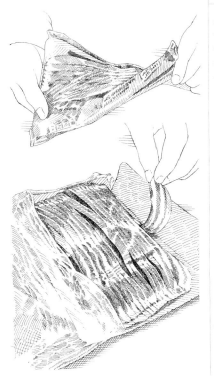

GRIND AND FREEZE FRESH TURMERIC AND GINGER

Judy Brown of Rancho Santa Fe, Calif., frequently cooks with fresh turmeric and ginger, but grating them can be a chore. To save time and money, she buys these roots in bulk, peels them, finely chops them in her food processor, and then freezes them in zipper-lock bags or silicone ice cube trays. When it's time to cook, she breaks off pieces or pops out cubes as needed.

BEST KITCHEN QUICK TIPS

A CLEANER WAY TO BOTTLE USED FRYING OIL

Returning cooled frying oil to its original bottle makes for easy storage or disposal, but the process can get messy. Alex Barunas of Boston, Mass., has found that a funnel and a toothpick make an efficient system: He simply slides the toothpick between the rim of the bottle and the funnel. This creates a gap that provides extra airflow, allowing the oil to flow through the funnel more quickly and smoothly.

CATCH-ALL CAKE FLIPPER

After allowing her cake to cool in the pan, Anne Kampes of Parkton, Md., inverts the cake onto a splatter screen, then uses the screen to flip the cake back onto a cooling rack. The screen helpfully contains any nuts or toppings that fall off of the cake during inversion.

REUSE YOUR CEREAL BAGS

Helen Stowe of Wallingford, Conn., has found that the liner bags from cereal boxes are great for food storage. She uses large ones to hold greens in the fridge and smaller ones to pack sandwiches or snacks. They are easy to rinse out and sturdy enough to reuse several times.

SMASHED BURGERS FOR A CROWD

Camille Wheatley of Salt Lake City, Utah, loves making our recipe for smashed burgers. To simultaneously smash enough patties for her family of six, she arranges the balls of meat on an electric griddle and then presses them thin with an aluminum foil–wrapped baking sheet.

THE BEST TOOL FOR RELEASING HOT MUFFINS

To remove muffins and cupcakes from their tins without burning her hands, Amy Lewanda of Olney, Md., employs two soupspoons. She slips one spoon in next to the baked good, pulling it away from the edge of the tin, and then slips the second spoon underneath to lift the treat out.

THE CLEANEST, MOST EFFICIENT AT-HOME WAFFLE STATION

Maggie and Ben Browder of Reno, Nev., have perfected their waffle-making routine: They place a waffle iron on one side of a rimmed baking sheet and a small wire rack on the other side. The baking sheet catches any batter drips, and the rack prevents the waffles from getting soggy after they are removed from the iron.

KEEP A STASH OF PASTA WATER

After boiling pasta, J. McAuliffe of Grand Blanc, Mich., reduces the cooking water to concentrate the starch and then freezes the water into cubes. The starchy ice is perfect for adding body to sauces and soups—and for the occasions when he forgets to reserve the pasta cooking water while preparing a pasta recipe.

SECURING A POT LID FOR TRANSPORT

When Maggie Moore of Hartland, Vt., brings a pot of food to a gathering, she wraps a dish towel around the lid's handle and pulls the towel's ends through the pot's handles to ensure that the lid stays secure during transport.

THE BEST WAY TO CLEAN YOUR PEANUT BUTTER JAR

Mary Kaszyca of Trumansburg, N.Y., has found that the chain-mail scrubbers sold for cleaning cast-iron cookware are also great for cleaning out empty jars of peanut butter. She places the scrubber in the jar, adds a bit of water, replaces the lid, and shakes and swirls the jar to get the remaining peanut butter out before tossing the jar into the recycling bin. Afterward, she just places the scrubber in the utensil basket of her dishwasher to get it clean.

NO-SLIP RAMEKINS

When Annette Locke of Brockport, N.Y., makes panna cotta, crème brûlée, or other individually portioned chilled desserts, she places the ramekins on a cutting board stabilizer or rubber shelf liner set in a baking sheet. This ensures that the ramekins don't slide around as she places the sheet in the refrigerator.

AN ALTERNATIVE TO MASON JAR LIDS

Ann and Joe Tropea of Baltimore, Md., can never find enough metal lids for their Mason jars—however, they recently discovered that plastic lids from some nut butter jars fit wide-mouthed Mason jars, so they always wash and save them.

A SPACE-SAVING WAY TO FREEZE GROUND MEAT

When Martha Askins of Madison, Wis., freezes ground meat, she shapes it into flattened 1-pound portions. This way, the bags of meat stack neatly and take up less freezer space; plus, they thaw more quickly.

PREVENT SCRATCHES WITH PADDED ENVELOPES

Deb Wilson Vandenberg of Salinas, Calif., offers a clever way to reuse padded shipping envelopes: She slits them in half horizontally to expose the padding and places them between nonstick skillets and delicate china when stacking to prevent scratches and chips.

SHOP FOR INGREDIENTS AT THE ANTIPASTO BAR

When she is making a recipe that calls for only a spoonful of capers or a few olives, Marsha Coleman of Milwaukee, Wisc., heads to the grocery store's antipasto bar. That way, she can purchase only the amount that she needs.

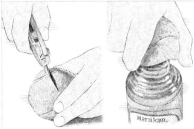

A TENNIS-INSPIRED TWIST-OFF TOOL

Jon Tillman of Mt. Olive, W.Va., discovered the perfect implement for twisting off tight jar lids: a tennis ball cut in half with a utility knife. The ball's rubber interior grips firmly onto lids, and the soft exterior is easy to grasp.

THE GENTLEST WAY TO FREE A STUCK CAKE

When a cake sticks to the bottom of his springform pan, Brian Yoo of North Baldwin, N.Y., slides a piece of unflavored dental floss under the cake and gently saws it free. This way, he doesn't risk scratching the pan with a metal spatula.

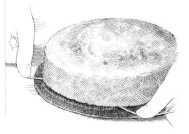

MAKE QUICK PICKLES PART OF YOUR ROUTINE

Got produce, salt, and vinegar? You're minutes away from a tangy, crunchy condiment.

We should all be making more pickles. They're the ultimate pick-me-up for a sleepy sandwich or braise, and the quick kind can be dashed off on a whim while you're cooking something else. Unlike lacto-fermented pickles, which require carefully calibrated salinity and temperature and days or weeks for wild bacteria to develop the acidity that both fends off harmful microbes for long-term storage and supplies their complex tang, quick versions are preserved and flavored by a vinegar brine and refrigeration. They're also a thrifty, low-lift way to get extra mileage out of surplus produce; a bulb of fennel or bunch of radishes will net a small jar's worth of pickles, so you don't have to pickle in bulk to make it worth the effort.

KEY INGREDIENTS

VINEGAR

Vinegar is the main source of flavor in quick pickles, and it also provides acidity that helps preserve them. Distilled white and cider vinegars are the most common types for pickling; both usually contain moderate acid levels (about 5 percent). Wine and unseasoned rice vinegars are great options, too, though their acid levels vary more widely from brand to brand (from 4 to 8 percent). If your vinegar's acidity level is on the low or high end of the spectrum, you may want to add less or more sugar to the brine, respectively. (Do not confuse unseasoned and seasoned rice vinegars; the latter contains added sugar and salt.)

UNSEASONED RICE
ACIDITY: 4–5%
Mellow, sweet

DISTILLED WHITE
ACIDITY: about 5%
Clean, neutral, sharp

CIDER
ACIDITY: about 5%
Sharp with round, pronounced fruitiness

WHITE WINE
ACIDITY: 5–7%
Bright, delicately floral

RED WINE
ACIDITY: 5–8%
Tart, richly fruity

SALT

Brines include salt for seasoning. Use any type of additive-free salt, such as Diamond Crystal kosher salt (Morton kosher salt is not ideal because it contains an anticaking ingredient), or seek out canning and pickling salt, often called preserving salt, a fine-grained product that dissolves easily.

PICKLE CRISP

A granulated form of the firming agent calcium chloride, Ball Pickle Crisp helps relatively soft, porous produce retain some crunch by reinforcing its natural pectin. Add ⅛ teaspoon per pint with the brine if you plan to store your pickles for more than a week. There's no need to use it for sturdier produce or for pickles you plan to eat within a few days.

THREE CLASSICS

Nothing completes a burger, a pile of pulled pork, or pita-swaddled falafel like these timeless standards. We developed these three recipes with Diamond Crystal kosher salt. If using canning and pickling salt, halve the volume (e.g., from 2 teaspoons to 1 teaspoon). These recipes can be scaled up or down. Let the pickles cool completely before covering and refrigerating them.

Dill Pickle Chips

PICKLE	STORE	YIELD
1 day	3 months	2 pints

GO GREAT WITH: burgers · deli salads · Cuban sandwiches · barbecue

1¼ pounds pickling cucumbers, ends trimmed, sliced ¼ inch thick

1. Toss cucumbers with 2 tablespoons kosher salt in bowl and refrigerate for 3 hours. Drain cucumbers in colander (do not rinse), then pat dry with paper towels.

2. Bundle 1 cup chopped fresh dill in cheesecloth and secure with kitchen twine. Bring dill sachet, 1½ cups cider vinegar, 1½ cups water, 2 tablespoons sugar, 1½ teaspoons yellow mustard seeds, and 1 teaspoon dill seeds to boil in large saucepan over medium-high heat. Cover and let steep off heat for 15 minutes; discard sachet.

3. Rinse two 1-pint jars under hot running water until heated through, 1 to 2 minutes; shake dry. Add ⅛ teaspoon Ball Pickle Crisp to each jar, then pack tightly with 2 large fresh dill sprigs, 2 peeled and quartered garlic cloves, and drained cucumbers.

4. Return brine to brief boil. Ladle hot brine over cucumbers to cover, distributing spices evenly.

FOR DILL PICKLE SPEARS: After trimming both ends, quarter cucumbers lengthwise and cut into 4-inch spears. Pack spears vertically into jars.

DON'T FORGET TO PICKLE FRUIT!

Vegetables get most of the glory, but pickled fruits are a pleasure all their own. The fragrant sweetness of peaches and mangos; wine-like nuances of plums and cherries; and complex aroma and crunch of apples, pears, and quince complement

APPLE SLICES

vinegar's vibrant acidity. Dried fruits (such as apricots, currants, and golden raisins) make great pickles, too, plumping up in the brine to deliver bursts of tangy sweetness. And just as with pickled vegetables, adding citrus zest, warm spices, and herbs to the mix can weave in subtle background notes. Any of these can upgrade a seared pork chop, green salad, or bowl of yogurt, not to mention turn your cheese or charcuterie board into a showstopping spread.

HOW TO QUICK-PICKLE ANYTHING

Recipes are great when you're aiming for a particular flavor profile, but the beauty of quick pickling is its flexibility. With the following basic brine formula and method, you can turn just about any produce—in any amount—into a punchy condiment. Feel free to add seasonings as you like.

1. PREP PRODUCE: Trim and cut 1 pound vegetables or fruit into evenly thick pieces for uniform pickling. Depending on porosity of produce and length of pickling, thicker slices might retain a sturdy crunch, while thinner pieces will likely wilt.

2. MIX AND BOIL BRINE: Combine 1½ cups vinegar; 1½ cups water; 3 tablespoons sugar; 2½ tablespoons kosher salt; and seasonings (e.g., citrus zest, spices, aromatics, herbs), if using, in medium saucepan. Bring mixture to boil over medium-high heat. If using seasonings, cover mixture and let steep off heat for 10 minutes, then return brine to brief boil.

3. TEMPER JARS: Rinse jars under hot running water until heated through, 1 to 2 minutes; shake dry. Tempering glass helps prevent it from cracking when hot brine is added. You can use any heatproof container with a tight-fitting lid.

4. MARRY BRINE WITH PREPARED PRODUCE: Tightly pack produce into jars. Ladle boiling brine over produce to cover (a funnel will help contain brine but is not essential), distributing any aromatics and spices evenly among jars.

5. COOL, COVER, WAIT: Let jars cool completely, cover with lids, and refrigerate until pickles are evenly flavorful. Pickling times will depend on thickness and porosity of produce pieces: Thin-sliced onions and radishes are ready when cool; cucumber chips can take 24 hours; root vegetables might take days.

THREE CLASSICS *(continued)*

Dilly Beans

PICKLE	STORE	YIELD
1 day	3 months	2 pints

GO GREAT WITH: cheese plates • sandwiches

1 pound green beans, trimmed and cut into 4-inch lengths

1. Fill large bowl halfway with ice and water. Bring 3 quarts water and 1 tablespoon kosher salt to boil in large saucepan over high heat. Add beans and

cook until crisp-tender but still crunchy at core, about 1 minute. Transfer beans to ice bath and let cool for 2 minutes; drain well, discard ice, and pat dry with paper towels.

2. Bundle 1 cup chopped fresh dill in cheesecloth; secure with kitchen twine. Bring dill sachet, 1½ cups distilled white vinegar, 1½ cups water, 3 tablespoons sugar, 3 tablespoons kosher salt, and 1½ teaspoons black peppercorns to boil in large saucepan over medium-high heat. Cover and let steep off heat for 15 minutes; discard sachet.

3. Rinse two 1-pint jars under hot running water until heated through, 1 to 2 minutes; shake dry. Distribute 3 peeled and quartered garlic cloves evenly between jars, then pack tightly with beans.

4. Return brine to brief boil. Ladle hot brine over beans to cover, distributing peppercorns evenly.

Pink Pickled Turnips

PICKLE	STORE	YIELD
2 days	1 month	2 pints

GO GREAT WITH: falafel • shawarma

1 pound turnips, peeled and cut into 2 by ½-inch sticks

1 small beet, trimmed, peeled, and cut into 1-inch pieces

1. Bring 1¼ cups white wine vinegar, 1¼ cups water, 3 tablespoons kosher salt, 2½ tablespoons sugar, 3 peeled and smashed garlic cloves, ¾ teaspoon whole allspice berries, and ¾ teaspoon black peppercorns to boil in medium saucepan over medium-high heat. Cover and let steep off heat for 10 minutes. Strain brine through fine-mesh strainer, then return to saucepan.

2. Rinse two 1-pint jars under hot running water until heated through, 1 to 2 minutes; shake dry. Pack turnips vertically into hot jars with beet pieces evenly distributed throughout.

3. Return brine to brief boil. Ladle hot brine over vegetables to cover.

QUICK AND EASY EDIBLE GIFTS

These festive sweets can be whipped up on the fly and keep for weeks if not months.

Spicy Caramel Popcorn

SERVES 12 (MAKES ABOUT 3½ QUARTS)
TOTAL TIME: 45 MINUTES

STORE IN: Airtight containers

KEEPS FOR: Two months

If you're using salted popcorn, decrease the salt to ¼ teaspoon. For spicier popcorn, use the greater amount of cayenne pepper. Salted roasted almonds can be used in place of the salted smoked almonds, if desired.

- 10 cups popped popcorn
- 1¼ cups (8¾ ounces) sugar
- ½ cup water
- ⅓ cup light corn syrup
- 6 tablespoons unsalted butter
- ½ teaspoon table salt
- ⅛–¼ teaspoon cayenne pepper
- ½ teaspoon baking soda
- ⅔ cup salted smoked almonds, chopped coarse

1. Lightly spray large bowl and rimmed baking sheet with vegetable oil spray. Place popcorn in prepared bowl. Bring sugar, water, and corn syrup to boil in medium heavy-bottomed saucepan over medium-high heat. Cook, without stirring, until mixture is straw-colored, 6 to 8 minutes. Reduce heat to medium-low and continue to cook, swirling saucepan occasionally, until mixture is dark amber and registers between 365 and 375 degrees, 2 to 5 minutes longer.

2. Off heat, quickly but carefully add butter, salt, and cayenne; stir until fully combined (mixture will bubble and steam). Return saucepan to low heat; stir in baking soda; and cook, stirring constantly, until mixture is uniform in color. Pour caramel over popcorn and, working quickly, stir until well coated. (Use dish towel or oven mitt to hold bowl, and avoid touching hot caramel.) Stir in almonds. Transfer mixture to prepared sheet and spread into even layer. Let cool for 15 minutes. Break cooled popcorn into pieces of desired size and transfer to airtight containers.

ULTIMATE CARAMEL CORN

We turned our best caramel sauce—perfectly bittersweet, easy, and reliable—into a glossy, complex coating for popcorn by adding cayenne pepper, salt, and baking soda. The latter reacts with the acidic caramel and produces tiny air bubbles that make the caramel easy to toss with the popcorn and the final product delicately crisp, not hard.

Dark Chocolate—Peanut Butter Fudge Sauce

SERVES 10 TO 12 (MAKES 2 CUPS)
TOTAL TIME: 25 MINUTES

STORE IN: Wide-mouthed canning jars

KEEPS FOR: One month in refrigerator

Wide-mouthed canning jars are ideal for packaging because their squat shape allows the sauce to spread out and reheat evenly. Dutch-processed cocoa powder (our favorite is from Droste) works best here, but any type will work. To double the recipe, use a large saucepan and extend the cooking time to 8 to 10 minutes. To reheat, microwave the sauce gently (do not let it exceed 110 degrees), stirring every 10 seconds, until it's just warmed and pourable.

- 1¼ cups (8¾ ounces) sugar
- ⅔ cup whole or 2 percent low-fat milk
- ½ teaspoon table salt
- ⅓ cup (1 ounce) unsweetened cocoa powder, sifted
- 3 ounces unsweetened chocolate, chopped fine
- 4 tablespoons unsalted butter, cut into 8 pieces and chilled
- ¼ cup creamy peanut butter
- 1 teaspoon vanilla extract

1. Heat sugar, milk, and salt in medium saucepan over medium-low heat, whisking gently, until sugar has dissolved and liquid starts to bubble around edges of saucepan, 5 to 6 minutes. Reduce heat to low, add cocoa, and whisk until smooth.

2. Off heat, stir in chocolate and let stand for 3 minutes. Whisk sauce until smooth and chocolate is fully melted. Add butter and whisk until fully incorporated and sauce thickens slightly. Whisk in peanut butter until fully incorporated. Whisk in vanilla and transfer to jars.

LIKE A LIQUID REESE'S PEANUT BUTTER CUP

This sauce is perfect for spooning over ice cream or as a dip for cookies or graham crackers. Its lush, rich body and shine are the result of swirling cold butter into the chocolate mixture off the heat, just as you would to thicken a savory pan sauce.

Hot Chocolate Mix

SERVES 12 (MAKES 3 CUPS)
TOTAL TIME: 10 MINUTES

STORE IN:
Canning jars

KEEPS FOR:
Two months

The mix can easily be halved or doubled and comes together with the push of a button. To make one serving, heat 1 cup of milk in a saucepan over medium heat until it's steaming. Whisk in ¼ cup of the mix and continue to heat, whisking constantly, until the hot chocolate is simmering, 2 to 3 minutes longer.

- 1 cup (7 ounces) sugar
- 6 ounces unsweetened chocolate, chopped fine
- 1 cup (3 ounces) unsweetened cocoa powder
- ½ cup (1½ ounces) nonfat dry milk powder
- 5 teaspoons cornstarch
- 1 teaspoon vanilla extract
- ¾ teaspoon kosher salt

Process all ingredients in food processor until ground to powder, 30 to 60 seconds. Transfer to jars.

BETTER THAN BOXED MIX

Whisked into hot milk, this mix boasts the deeply chocolaty flavor and luxurious body of European sipping chocolate, but its richness is restrained enough that you can easily indulge in a full mug's worth. The key is supplementing the cocoa powder (any type works) and bar chocolate with a combination of nonfat dry milk powder and cornstarch: Both add creamy body, and the milk powder helps mask any chalkiness from the cocoa powder.

Brigadeiros

SERVES 10 TO 15 (MAKES ABOUT 30 CANDIES)
TOTAL TIME: 45 MINUTES, PLUS 30 MINUTES CHILLING

If the mixture sticks to your hands when rolling the balls in step 3, spray your hands with a bit of vegetable oil spray.

STORE IN: Separate paper candy cups packed in a shallow gift box in a single layer

KEEPS FOR: Two weeks in refrigerator (but best enjoyed the day they're made)

- 1 (14-ounce) can sweetened condensed milk
- ½ cup (1½ ounces) unsweetened cocoa powder
- 2 tablespoons unsalted butter
  Sprinkles, colored sugar, and/ or nonpareils

1. Grease 8-inch square baking dish. Cook condensed milk, cocoa, and butter in medium saucepan over low heat, stirring frequently, until mixture is very thick and rubber spatula leaves distinct trail when dragged across bottom of saucepan, 20 to 25 minutes.

2. Pour mixture into prepared dish and refrigerate until firm, at least 30 minutes or up to 24 hours (cover with plastic wrap if chilling overnight).

3. Pinch mixture into approximately 1-tablespoon-size pieces and roll into 1-inch balls. Place desired coatings in small bowls, roll each ball in coating until covered, and package.

FUDGY AND FESTIVE

Many sources suggest that these dense, chocolaty, two-bite confections were popularized by Brazilian air force brigadier Eduardo Gomes's 1945 presidential campaign. Brazilian women, who had recently won the right to vote, reportedly sold the treats at his political rallies.

Orange-Cardamom Spiced Nuts

SERVES 8 TO 10 (MAKES ABOUT 3½ CUPS)
TOTAL TIME: 1 HOUR, PLUS 30 MINUTES COOLING

STORE IN:
Airtight containers

KEEPS FOR:
Three weeks

Almonds and pistachios work well here, but use any type or combination of unsalted nuts that you like.

- ⅔ cup (4⅔ ounces) superfine sugar
- 1 teaspoon ground cardamom
- ½ teaspoon pepper
- 1 large egg white
- 1 tablespoon grated orange zest plus 1 tablespoon juice
- 1 teaspoon table salt
- ¼ teaspoon vanilla extract
- 1 pound raw nuts

1. Adjust oven racks to upper-middle and lower-middle positions and heat oven to 275 degrees. Line 2 rimmed baking sheets with parchment paper. Mix sugar, cardamom, and pepper together in bowl.

2. Whisk egg white, orange zest and juice, salt, and vanilla together in separate bowl. Add nuts and toss to coat. Sprinkle sugar mixture over nuts, toss to coat, then spread evenly over prepared sheets. Bake until nuts are dry and crisp, about 50 minutes, stirring occasionally. Let nuts cool completely on sheets, about 30 minutes. Break nuts apart and package in airtight containers.

SALTY, SWEET, SPICED—AND NOT STICKY

Everyone loves spiced nuts—except when they're greasy or tacky. Our coating, a mixture of egg white, orange zest and juice, salt, and vanilla, distributes evenly, helps the spices adhere, and dries sheer and delicately crunchy.

FOUR CORE SKILLETS YOU SHOULD OWN

Each of these pans offers unique features; collecting the full arsenal will meet all your sautéing, searing, and shallow-frying needs.

A well-made skillet is arguably the most critical piece of cookware in your kitchen, but no one pan can do it all. Here's a diagnostic breakdown of the four types of pans we use the most plus our favorite model in each category.

FAVORITE
All-Clad D3 Stainless 12" Fry Pan with Lid ($119.95)

> Fully clad construction: The entire body of the pan is composed of three or more layers of different metals—often highly responsive aluminum sandwiched between heat-retaining, slower-transmitting stainless steel.

FULLY CLAD STAINLESS STEEL

WHY WE LOVE IT: Behold, the ultimate kitchen workhorse: durable and low-maintenance and a champ for steady heat and rich, even browning—as long as it boasts fully clad construction. This is the best material for pan sauces and braises because food sticks to it, creating flavorful fond, and because it won't react with acidic items such as tomatoes, vinegar, or wine. The light-colored pan makes it easy to monitor the progress of dark foods such as browned butter, and it can take a beating. Sauté, sear—even blast it under the broiler—and then scrub the heck out of it.

LIMITATIONS: Sticking, which is an asset for fond development, is a liability for delicate, clingy foods such as eggs and fish fillets.

CLEANING UP STUCK-ON FOOD

For stubborn messes, including any stains that appear to be cooked into the pan's interior or exterior, lightly scrub the surface with Bar Keepers Friend or fill the pan with water and bring it to a gentle simmer on the stovetop. The cooked-on food will come right up.

NONSTICK

WHY WE LOVE IT: A nonstick skillet makes cooking feel effortless. Stick-prone items such as eggs and fish fillets practically glide across the slick surface, which is also great for searing steaks and chops when you don't want a flavorful fond for building a sauce. (When searing, we use our cold-start method to avoid overheating the nonstick coating; for more information, see our recipes for Pan-Seared Thick-Cut, Bone-In Pork Chops [page 146].)

LIMITATIONS: The coating wears out with use, especially over high heat (above 500 degrees, it can break down and release dangerous fumes), or if scrubbed too hard or scratched with metal tools. Given that, it pays to buy relatively inexpensive pans from a reputable manufacturer that can be replaced regularly.

FAVORITE
OXO Good Grips Non-Stick Pro 12" Open Frypan ($42.49)

SEASONING KEEPS NONSTICK SUPERSLICK

Many manufacturers suggest seasoning their nonstick skillets—much like we do cast iron—by warming them, rubbing a little oil into the surface, and then wiping out the excess. Do this when you purchase a new pan and anytime you notice that your nonstick skillet is getting a little sticky.

> Lightweight aluminum base
> Superslick coating primarily composed of PTFE

FAVORITE CERAMIC
GreenPan Valencia Pro Hard Anodized Nonstick Frypan ($79.99)

TRADITIONAL NONSTICK VERSUS CERAMIC NONSTICK: Ceramic pans get their nonstick properties from a form of silica (also found in beach sand). Their surfaces are more brittle than nonstick surfaces composed of polytetrafluoroethylene (PTFE), so they can develop microscopic cracks that can cause food to stick. Pure ceramic pans can be used at high temperatures with no risk of dangerous fumes, but shop carefully, since many ceramic coatings contain PTFE (our winning ceramic pan is PTFE-free). Like all nonstick cookware, these pans will eventually need to be replaced.

CARBON STEEL

FAVORITE
Matfer Bourgeat Black Steel Round Frying Pan, 11⅞″ ($44.38)

WHY WE LOVE IT: It's a jack of almost all trades and a master of many. Carbon steel is thick and sturdy enough to sear nearly as well as cast iron, but it's much lighter and more agile, so it maneuvers almost as nimbly as fully clad stainless steel. And assuming it's well seasoned, it's as slick as nonstick—but naturally so, boasting a supersmooth patina that improves (instead of degrades) with use. The price is right, too. Bar none, it's the most high-value pan in the test kitchen.

LIMITATIONS: Unlike most cast-iron pans, carbon-steel pans are sold unseasoned, so you need to start from scratch. A truly slick patina requires many rounds of seasoning and careful maintenance. Acidic foods such as tomato sauce will react with the metal and strip off its coating.

SEASONING CARBON STEEL AND CAST IRON

These surfaces get slicker with use as heated fat molecules link up to form a hard film that bonds to the metal's surface. For seasoning methods, go to CooksIllustrated.com/seasoncastiron and CooksIllustrated.com/seasoncarbonsteel.

➤ Naturally smooth surface captures a comparatively thin, fragile layer of seasoning

➤ Relatively thin, lightweight frame; durable alloy (roughly 99 percent iron and 1 percent carbon)

CAST IRON

BEST BUY
Lodge 12 Inch Cast Iron Skillet ($43.31)

WHY WE LOVE IT: Once it's hot, cast iron holds heat exceptionally well (even when cool food is added), which makes it ideal for frying, searing, and roasting. Its tall, straight sides also make it well suited for shallow frying and deep-dish applications such as cornbread, pan pizza, and even fruit-packed pies. The patina is endlessly renewable and also protects the metal from rust. You can hand down cast-iron pans for generations.

LIMITATIONS: Its relatively high percentage of carbon makes cast iron a brittle alloy; molding it into a thick, hefty frame makes it durable—but a beast to maneuver and notoriously uneven as it heats up. Like carbon steel, its patina requires gradual buildup and careful maintenance and will react with acidic foods.

HOW TO PREHEAT CAST IRON

To ensure that the pan heats thoroughly and evenly, place it on the middle rack of the oven (the oven's convective heat minimizes hot spots) and heat the oven to 500 degrees. When the oven reaches 500 degrees, use pot holders to set the pan over a moderate flame on the stovetop to maintain the heat.

➤ Thick, heavy frame composed of 97 to 98 percent iron and 2 to 3 percent carbon

➤ Pebbly surface with relatively deep nooks and crannies that tightly grip seasoning

➤ High sides

➤ Naturally nonstick patina protects surfaces from rust and releases food readily

WHAT SMALLER SKILLETS CAN DO

If you buy only one skillet of each style, go for the ultraversatile 12-inch model, which is usually roomy enough to prepare at least four portions of vegetables or proteins. But if there's space in your kitchen for a few more pieces, these smaller pans are also worth keeping on hand.

8-INCH NONSTICK: This pan is perfect for making omelets; the narrow confines help the beaten egg spread out just enough and roll into a tidy log. It's also great for frying eggs and toasting bread crumbs, nuts, and spices.

10-INCH NONSTICK OR CARBON STEEL: Scrambling eggs in a smaller pan helps them spread less and cook in a thicker layer that traps more steam and produces heartier curds.

10-INCH CAST IRON: It's a great for-two vessel and also doubles as a cake pan or deep-dish pie plate.

THE STARCHY SECRETS TO COOKING POTATOES

Starch is the key to the fluffy, crispy, creamy textures that make potatoes so good. The trick is harnessing it to your advantage.

There are more than 4,000 varieties of potatoes in the world, all of which contain water and lots of starch. This starch exists as microscopic granules within a potato's cells. The amount of starch in a given variety and the way you manipulate the tuber before, during, and after cooking is largely responsible for a potato's cooked texture.

3 KEY TYPES

These common potatoes span the starch spectrum and can cover a wide range of spud cookery.

RUSSET

STARCH CONTENT:
High (at least 20 percent by weight)

COOKED TEXTURE:
Dry, fluffy

FLAVOR: Earthy, mild

HOW TO COOK:
Bake, roast, mash, fry

YUKON GOLD

STARCH CONTENT:
Medium (16 to 18 percent by weight)

COOKED TEXTURE: Velvety

FLAVOR: Buttery, sweet

HOW TO COOK: Roast, mash, fry

RED

STARCH CONTENT:
Low (about 16 percent by weight)

COOKED TEXTURE: Firm, creamy

FLAVOR: Mineral-y, sweet

HOW TO COOK: Braise; boil for salads, soups, and stews

HOW STARCH CONTENT AFFECTS COOKED TEXTURE

When cooked, the cells of starchier spuds such as russets soak up more cooking water and interstitial moisture, which causes their cells to swell and push each other apart, resulting in a dry, fluffy interior that eagerly soaks up flavorful liquids such as cream and butter. Meanwhile, low-starch varieties such as red potatoes absorb less moisture into their cells and thus contain more free moisture. That water gets absorbed by pectin that's released from the cell walls during cooking and forms a gel that holds the cells together, creating a waxy potato's famously dense, creamy consistency. The moderate starch content and absorption of Yukon Gold potatoes is what makes them so versatile; they cook up neither dry nor dense but velvety instead.

Cooking cubes of each potato type in water dyed deep blue shows the difference in absorption. The dye travels deep into the russets, seeps a little into the Yukon Golds, and forms only a thin line around the exterior of the red potatoes.

RUSSET   YUKON GOLD   RED

WHY TEMP A BAKED POTATO?

When baking a russet potato, our goal is for its starch to soak up so much interstitial water that the potato's cells swell and separate, rendering the interior uniformly dry and fluffy. We found that this happens when the spud's core surpasses 205 degrees, so it's important to check its doneness with a thermometer.

Best Baked Potatoes

SERVES 4 TOTAL TIME: 1½ HOURS

Dipping the potatoes in salty water before baking seasons their skin; brushing them with vegetable oil once they're cooked through and then baking them for another 10 minutes crisps them up so that they crackle. Be sure to open up the potatoes immediately after removing them from the oven in step 3 so that steam can escape; otherwise, that trapped moisture will make the interior gluey.

Table salt for salting potatoes

4 russet potatoes (7 to 9 ounces each), unpeeled, each lightly pricked with fork in 6 places

1 tablespoon vegetable oil

1. Adjust oven rack to middle position and heat oven to 450 degrees. Dissolve 2 tablespoons salt in ½ cup water in large bowl. Place potatoes in bowl and toss so exteriors of potatoes are evenly moistened. Transfer potatoes to wire rack set in rimmed baking sheet and bake until center of largest potato registers 205 degrees, 45 minutes to 1 hour.

2. Remove potatoes from oven and brush tops and sides with oil. Return potatoes to oven and continue to bake 10 minutes longer.

3. Remove potatoes from oven and, using paring knife, make 2 slits, forming X, in each potato. Using clean dish towel, hold ends and squeeze slightly to push flesh up and out. Season with salt and pepper to taste. Serve immediately.

Classic Mashed Potatoes

SERVES 4   TOTAL TIME: 45 MINUTES

We call for starting the potatoes in cold water, since adding them to boiling water will cause their exteriors to overcook and slough off before the interior cooks through. Boiling them until they're just tender—but not falling apart—helps limit the amount of loose starch in the mix, minimizing gumminess.

- 2 pounds russet potatoes, unpeeled
- 8 tablespoons unsalted butter, melted
- 1 cup warm half-and-half
- 1½ teaspoons table salt

1. Place potatoes in large saucepan and cover with 1 inch water. Bring to boil over high heat; reduce heat to medium-low and simmer until potatoes are tender (paring knife can be slipped into and out of center of potatoes with very little resistance), 20 to 30 minutes. Drain.

2. Set ricer or food mill over now-empty saucepan (saucepan should still be warm). Spear 1 potato with dinner fork, then peel back skin with paring knife. Repeat with remaining potatoes. Working in batches, cut peeled potatoes into rough chunks. Using ricer or food mill, rice or process potatoes into saucepan.

3. Stir in melted butter until incorporated; gently stir in half-and-half, salt, and pepper to taste. Serve immediately.

HOW WE MAKE A BETTER MASH

RICE, DON'T MASH: Unlike conventional potato mashers, which require repeated smashing that can burst the spuds' cells and cause them to spill gluey starch, a ricer forces each cooked spud through a perforated disk only once. Thus, fewer cells burst, and the resulting mash is creamy, not gluey.

ADD BUTTER BEFORE LIQUID: Stirring melted butter into cooked potatoes before adding cream coats their starch molecules and blocks them from absorbing water that would otherwise make them gummy.

HOW WAXY SPUDS TURN SILKY

As the red potatoes in our recipe simmer, they soften but remain largely intact because their plump, moist cells nestle closely together, creating a dense, silky-smooth texture. Cooking them long enough that they absorb as much moisture as possible maximizes this effect.

Duck Fat–Roasted Potatoes

SERVES 6   TOTAL TIME: 1¼ HOURS

Animal fat contributes incredibly savory flavor. Duck fat can be found in many supermarket meat sections, or you can substitute chicken fat, lard, or a 50/50 mixture of bacon fat and olive oil.

- 3½ pounds Yukon Gold potatoes, peeled and cut into 1½-inch pieces
- 1 teaspoon kosher salt, plus salt for boiling potatoes
- ½ teaspoon baking soda
- 6 tablespoons duck fat, melted, divided
- 1 tablespoon chopped fresh rosemary

1. Adjust oven rack to top position. Place rimmed baking sheet on rack and heat oven to 475 degrees.

2. Bring 10 cups water to boil in Dutch oven over high heat. Add potatoes, ⅓ cup salt, and baking soda. Return to boil, cook for 1 minute, and drain. Return potatoes to pot and cook over low heat, shaking pot occasionally, until surface moisture has evaporated, about 2 minutes. Off heat, add 5 tablespoons fat and salt; mix with rubber spatula until potatoes are coated with thick paste, about 30 seconds.

3. Remove sheet from oven and add potatoes, spreading into even layer. Roast for 15 minutes.

4. Remove sheet from oven. Using thin metal spatula, turn potatoes. Roast until golden brown, 12 to 15 minutes. While potatoes roast, combine rosemary and remaining 1 tablespoon fat in bowl.

5. Remove sheet from oven. Spoon rosemary mixture over potatoes and turn again. Continue to roast until potatoes are well browned and rosemary is fragrant, 3 to 5 minutes longer. Season with salt and pepper to taste. Serve immediately.

Braised Red Potatoes with Lemon and Chives

SERVES 4 TO 6   TOTAL TIME: 50 MINUTES

Once the water boils away, the butter in the skillet browns the cut sides of the potatoes for a crisp-creamy interplay. Alter the seasonings as you like; try trading the lemon juice and chives for miso and scallions or Dijon and tarragon.

- 1½ pounds small red potatoes, unpeeled, halved
- 2 cups water
- 3 tablespoons unsalted butter
- 3 garlic cloves, peeled
- 3 sprigs fresh thyme
- ¾ teaspoon table salt
- 1 teaspoon lemon juice
- ¼ teaspoon pepper
- 2 tablespoons minced fresh chives

1. Arrange potatoes in single layer, cut side down, in 12-inch nonstick skillet. Add water, butter, garlic, thyme sprigs, and salt and bring to simmer over medium-high heat. Reduce heat to medium; cover; and simmer until potatoes are just tender, about 15 minutes.

2. Remove lid and transfer garlic to cutting board; discard thyme sprigs. Increase heat to medium-high and vigorously simmer, swirling skillet occasionally, until water evaporates and butter starts to sizzle, 15 to 20 minutes. When cool enough to handle, mince garlic to paste. Transfer garlic paste to bowl and stir in lemon juice and pepper.

3. Continue to cook potatoes, swirling skillet frequently, until butter browns and cut sides of potatoes turn spotty brown, 4 to 6 minutes longer. Off heat, add garlic mixture and chives and toss to thoroughly coat. Serve immediately.

CRUDITÉS MAKE A COMEBACK

Best-in-show produce and vibrant dips refresh this retro spread.

Crudités, a haute French import (the French word means "raw"; the culinary term is always plural), surfaced in stateside cookbooks around the mid-20th century, and Americans latched on immediately. Homemakers and restaurant chefs appreciated how easy it was to platter up crisp vegetables with a dip or two and call it hors d'oeuvres. Even James Beard glorified crudités in one of his works, declaring it "the most appetizing dish imaginable."

With the advent of baby carrots in the 1980s and eventually prepackaged relish trays, the concept stopped feeling even remotely glamorous. But it's back on the upswing: Farm-fresh produce has never been more diverse, dips more inspired, and grazing boards more in vogue.

Start with the freshest seasonal vegetables you can get. Beyond that, it's all about treating the produce nicely, whipping up full-bodied dips, and plotting out an eye-catching display.

BUILD A CURATED BOARD

MAKE THE RIGHT AMOUNT: Plan on 4 to 6 ounces of vegetables and ¼ cup of dip per person.

GO FOR LOTS OF COLOR: Choose produce in a spectrum of colors, including rainbow carrots, Easter Egg radishes, and cherry tomato medleys.

MIX UP THE DIPS: Serving multiple dips means that you can offer a range of flavors and consistencies. Garnishing them adds visual contrast; consider fresh herbs, crushed or ground spices, and olive oil.

CONSIDER THE CUTS: Try making long and short cuts on the same item; quartering colorful cauliflower florets to see the gradient; and leaving the tops partially intact on root vegetables.

SIZE UP THE PLATTER: Decide if you prefer the "wall-to-wall" look, where the surface is generously covered, or a more minimalist aesthetic.

MAKE VEGGIES EXTRA-CRISP: While arranging the board, submerge raw vegetables in an ice bath to keep them hydrated and crisp.

ARRANGE THOUGHTFULLY: Place the dips down first and the vegetables around them. If plating on a rectangular surface, flank the perimeter with longer items and cluster smaller pieces in the middle.

MAKE THE BEST OF THE BEST VEGETABLES

These tips will help maximize the vegetables' textures, flavors, and visual appeal.

(A) GO FOR THIN-SKINNED, LESS-SEEDY CUCUMBERS Slender English (also called European or hothouse) and petite Persian cukes boast thin, tender skins that are usually unwaxed and contain fewer bitter-tasting cucurbitacins than slicing cucumbers do. Plus, their tiny seeds go almost unnoticed.

(B) CHOOSE RADISHES ACCORDING TO HEAT TOLERANCE Common round red varieties pack a fiery punch, as do the streaky Purple Ninja kind. The heat in pastel Easter Egg radishes builds progressively as you eat them, and the tapered French Breakfast type are truly mild mannered.

(C) KEEP COLOR IN COLORFUL CAULIFLOWER Blanch purple cauliflower very briefly to prevent its water-soluble anthocyanin compounds from leaching out. As soon as the pieces are crisp-tender (after about 90 seconds), shock them in ice water to stop the cooking and set their color. (The carotenoids in orange cauliflower are not water-soluble and won't leach out; chlorophyll in the green variety will lose its bright color if overcooked but not in a quick blanch.)

(D) PEEL—DON'T SNAP—ASPARAGUS You'll throw away as much as half of each stalk's weight if you snap off the ends at their natural breaking point, and the uneven bunch won't plate nicely. Trimming 1 inch off the base and peeling the lower half of each stalk reduces waste and results in tender, refined spears.

(E) BUY BUNCHED CARROTS, NOT BAGGED Carrots with their feathery tops still attached aren't just prettier than bagged ones; they're fresher and richer-tasting, too—sold within a few weeks of harvest when their greens are still vibrant and their flavor complex.

TAKE A DIP (OR TWO)

Navy Bean and Artichoke Dip

SERVES 8 (MAKES ABOUT 2 CUPS)
TOTAL TIME: 35 MINUTES, PLUS 30 MINUTES RESTING

1. Combine 1 small clove minced garlic with 1 teaspoon grated lemon zest and 2 tablespoons juice in small bowl; set aside for at least 15 minutes. Thaw and pat dry 1 cup frozen artichoke hearts; measure out 2 tablespoons, chop coarse, and set aside for garnish.

2. Drain 1 (15-ounce) can navy beans, reserving liquid. Cut white and light-green parts of 1 scallion into ½-inch pieces and slice green part thin on bias. Rinse beans, then pulse with garlic mixture, 2 tablespoons reserved bean liquid, scallion whites and light greens, ¼ cup fresh parsley leaves, ¾ teaspoon table salt, ¼ teaspoon ground fennel, pinch cayenne pepper, and remaining artichoke hearts in food processor until fully ground, 5 to 10 pulses. Scrape down sides of bowl with rubber spatula. Continue to process until uniform paste forms, about 1 minute longer, scraping down sides of bowl twice. Add ¼ cup plain Greek-style yogurt (whole milk, 2 percent, or 0 percent will work) and continue to process until smooth and homogeneous, about 15 seconds longer, scraping down sides of bowl as needed. Transfer to serving bowl, cover, and let

> Dips can be refrigerated for two to three days; if necessary, loosen with 1 tablespoon of warm water. Add garnishes just before serving.

stand at room temperature for at least 30 minutes.

3. Season with salt to taste. Sprinkle with reserved artichoke hearts and scallion greens. Drizzle with extra-virgin olive oil. Serve.

Creamless Creamy Green Goddess Dip

SERVES 8 (MAKES ABOUT 2 CUPS)
TOTAL TIME: 20 MINUTES, PLUS 1 HOUR RESTING AND CHILLING

1. Using conventional blender, process ¾ cup raw cashews on low speed to consistency of fine gravel mixed with sand, 10 to 15 seconds. Add ¾ cup water, ⅓ cup chopped fresh chives, ⅓ cup chopped fresh parsley, 3 tablespoons lemon juice, 1 tablespoon chopped fresh tarragon, 2 rinsed anchovy fillets, ¾ teaspoon table salt, ¼ teaspoon pepper, and ¼ teaspoon garlic powder and process on low speed until combined, about 5 seconds. Let mixture sit for 15 minutes.

2. Process on low speed until all ingredients are finely chopped and well blended, about 1 minute. Scrape down blender jar. Process on high speed until dip is smooth and creamy, 4 to 5 minutes. Transfer dip to bowl. Cover and refrigerate until cold, about 45 minutes. Serve.

A CASE FOR BLANCHING

Blanching tenderizes tough vegetables and softens their raw bite; it also seasons them and brightens their color. Here are three keys to doing it well.

BLANCH IN SEA-SALTY WATER Supersalty water (½ cup of table salt per 2 quarts of water) not only seasons the vegetables and concentrates their flavors but also quickly softens pectin in their cell walls so that they turn tender before losing their vibrant color.

SHOCK IN ICE-COLD WATER Shocking halts cooking so that the vegetables don't oversoften or lose their bright color. The water bath will warm up quickly if you're blanching in batches, so be sure to add plenty of ice (and replenish as necessary) to keep it really cold.

COOK IN BATCHES Blanching each type of vegetable separately helps avoid overcooking or undercooking. Here's a cheat sheet of suggested cooking times for common produce for crudités, as well as a list of naturally tender items that shouldn't be blanched.

BLANCH	DON'T BLANCH
Asparagus: 30–45 seconds, depending on thickness	Bell Peppers
Broccoli: 30–45 seconds	Cherry Tomatoes
Carrots: 90 seconds	Cucumbers
Cauliflower: 90 seconds	Endive
Green Beans: 30 seconds	Radishes
Snap Peas: 60 seconds	Snow Peas

NEXT-LEVEL PIE CRUST

Give rich, flaky pastry the showstopper treatment.

Buttery pie pastry can be a blank slate for upping your game. The neutral flavor lends itself to countless flavor adjustments, and you can get crafty with the edging and top crust design by stamping out attractive vents, weaving lattices, and crusting the surface in sugar. Read on to learn how easy it is to make a masterpiece.

START WITH PERFECT PASTRY

Our go-to dough is an all-butter formula with a mixing method that makes it tender, flaky, and easy to roll: "Waterproof" a portion of the flour by processing it with butter to prevent it from absorbing water and forming gluten, and then process the remaining flour into that paste. Moisten it just enough with a measured amount of water, and fold in frozen grated butter for extra richness and flakiness.

Foolproof All-Butter Double-Crust Pie Dough

MAKES ENOUGH FOR ONE 9-INCH PIE

Halve this recipe (and any seasonings in "Season to Taste") to make pastry for a single-crust pie.

1. Grate 4 tablespoons chilled unsalted butter on large holes of box grater and place in freezer. Cut 16 tablespoons chilled unsalted butter into ½-inch cubes.

2. Pulse 1½ cups (7½ ounces) all-purpose flour, 2 tablespoons sugar, and 1 teaspoon table salt in food processor until combined, 2 pulses. Add cubed butter and process until homogeneous paste forms, 40 to 50 seconds. Using your hands, carefully break paste into 2-inch chunks and redistribute evenly around processor blade. Add 1 cup (5 ounces) all-purpose flour and pulse until mixture is broken into pieces no larger than 1 inch (most pieces will be much smaller), 4 to 5 pulses. Transfer mixture to bowl. Add grated butter and toss until butter pieces are separated and coated with flour.

3. Sprinkle ¼ cup ice water over mixture. Toss with rubber spatula until mixture is evenly moistened. Sprinkle another

¼ cup ice water over mixture and toss to combine. Press dough with spatula until dough sticks together. Using spatula, divide dough into 2 equal portions. Transfer each portion to sheet of plastic wrap. Working with 1 portion at a time, draw edges of plastic over dough and press firmly on sides and top to form compact, fissure-free mass. Wrap in plastic

and form into 5-inch disk. Refrigerate dough for at least 2 hours or up to 2 days. Let chilled dough sit on counter to soften slightly, about 10 minutes, before rolling. (Wrapped dough can be frozen for up to 1 month. If frozen, let dough thaw completely on counter before rolling.)

SEASON TO TASTE

Whole-grain flours, nuts, herbs, or citrus zest add nuance.

CITRUS: Add 2½ tablespoons grated citrus zest to dry mix.

HERBS: Add 3 tablespoons minced fresh sage or thyme to dry mix.

NUTS: Reduce cubed butter to 12 tablespoons and first addition of flour to ¾ cup. Process 1 cup chopped and frozen untoasted pecans, walnuts, hazelnuts, almonds, or peanuts with dry mix until finely ground, about 30 seconds.

WHOLE-GRAIN FLOUR: Substitute 1½ cups (8¼ ounces) whole-wheat or rye flour for first addition of all-purpose flour.

VENT THE TOP STYLISHLY

A vented top crust allows moisture to evaporate so that juicy fillings, such as blueberry or peach, thicken. An intricate lattice is classic, but these alternatives are equally functional and easy to execute—and they're also visually striking.

FREE-FORM WEDGES

1. Start with 13 by 10½-inch rectangle of chilled dough. Cut into two 10½-inch-long triangles with ½-inch base, two 10½-inch-long triangles with 1-inch base, two 10½-inch-long triangles with 2-inch base, and two 10½-inch-long triangles with 3-inch base. Refrigerate for 30 minutes.

2. Arrange triangles decoratively over filling, with base of each triangle placed at least ½ inch beyond edge of plate (to anchor pieces) and being careful not to overlap more than 2 triangles. Trim overhang to ½ inch beyond lip of plate, then pinch edges of bottom crust and triangles firmly together to seal. Tuck overhang under itself and crimp dough evenly around edge of plate. Brush with egg wash (or water).

BRAIDED STRIPS

1. Start with 13 by 10-inch rectangle of chilled dough. Cut eighteen 13 by ½-inch strips. Refrigerate for 30 minutes. Arrange 3 strips side by side on counter (keep remaining strips refrigerated), then pinch tops to seal.

2. Tightly braid strips, then pinch ends to seal. Refrigerate while braiding remaining strips. Arrange braids over filling, then trim overhang to ½ inch beyond lip of plate. Pinch braids and bottom crust together to seal. Tuck overhang under itself and crimp dough evenly around edge of plate. Brush with egg wash (or water). (You can also place braid around edge of pie, as shown in photo below.)

CUTOUT CRUST GUIDELINES

- For the clearest visual effect, use cutout crusts on fillings that are flat, not mounded.

- Chill the dough before and after cutting to create sharper, sturdier edges.

- Choose a cutter that measures about 1 inch in diameter; any shape will work.

- Remove one-quarter to one-third of the crust, leaving at least ¾ inch between each cutout and a 1-inch border around the edge.

- Occasionally dip the cutters in flour to prevent them from becoming sticky.

OPTIONAL: For more visual appeal, save a few cutouts to decorate intact areas of crust, brushing their undersides with water and pressing gently but firmly to adhere.

DESIGN AN EDGIER EDGE

Embellishing the edge takes the crust—single or double—from simple to spectacular. Chill the dough before edging to make neater marks.

ROPE EDGE: Holding body of ¼-inch-wide round chopstick at 45-degree angle to edge of plate, firmly press chopstick into dough. Repeat pressing chopstick into dough evenly around edge of pie, leaving ½ inch between each mark.

SCALLOPED EDGE: Line tip of inverted spoon up with inside edge of lip of plate, with spoon handle facing out. Press spoon firmly into dough to leave behind indentation. Shift spoon so tip is halfway between inside and outside edge of plate's lip, and press firmly into dough to leave second indentation. Repeat evenly around edge of pie.

MAKE THE CRUST SHINE AND SPARKLE

Brushing the top crust with egg wash (or water) and sprinkling it with sugar gives the pastry lustrous browning and shimmer—and the effect can be really impressive when you liberally apply both. Thoroughly moistening the dough enables it to grasp lots of sugar, which transforms into a candy-like layer with brilliant sheen, crackly crunch, and notable sweetness that pairs particularly well with tart fruit fillings such as rhubarb, apricot, plum, and sour cherry.

FORMULA FOR 9-INCH PIE

WASH: 1 to 2 tablespoons of beaten egg or roughly 2 tablespoons of water. Add a pinch of salt to the egg wash, which loosens the proteins and makes the wash more fluid and easier to brush evenly over the dough.

SUGAR: 3 tablespoons

OAT MILK

Twenty years ago, dairy-free milks were relegated to natural foods stores, but today they're mainstream. Oat milk is one of the fastest growing nondairy milks, according to data from SPINS, a wellness-focused market research company. Its popularity is due to several factors. First, it has a naturally sweet and nutty flavor. Second, it's a welcome alternative to other dairy-free milks for people with tree nut or soy allergies. Finally, it makes less of an environmental impact to produce than many other milks, and it requires significantly less water to produce than cow's milk and almond milk do, according to BBC News. Oat milk comes in many different styles: original, extra-creamy, low-fat, unsweetened, and "barista" blends intended for whipping into foam for lattes or cappuccinos. We chose six nationally available brands, limiting the lineup to original styles that don't list sugar as an ingredient (but that doesn't mean they're sugar-free). We tasted the mix of refrigerated and shelf-stable products plain and then in coffee. We had a slight preference for the thicker oat milks; added stabilizers or thickeners such as oil, phosphates, and gellan gum gave them both body and richness and also ensured that the milks stayed smooth and fully incorporated once packaged. Many tasters liked the slight nuttiness and mild sweetness of some oat milks, but some of the products we tasted were more oat forward than others. And while none of the products listed sugar as an ingredient, some of the milks were sweeter than others. Enzymes, which are added to help break down some of the oats' starch into sugar, are more active at certain temperatures, so the oat milks that contained more sugar per serving were likely cooked longer and/or remained in a more enzyme-active temperature range for longer. Our top three oat milks are listed below in order of preference (prices are what we paid at the time of testing).

RECOMMENDED

CHOBANI Oat Plain
PRICE: $4.49 for 52 fl oz ($0.09 per fl oz)
INGREDIENTS: Organic oat blend (water, organic whole grain oats), contains 2% or less of: organic rapeseed oil (low erucic acid), sea salt, nutrient extract blend (fruit and vegetable sources), calcium carbonate, gellan gum, tricalcium phosphate, dipotassium phosphate
SUGAR: 7 g
REFRIGERATED: Yes
COMMENTS: Tasters loved this mellow oat milk's "very faint nuttiness" and "slight oat" flavor. With 7 grams of sugar per serving, it was "not too sweet." It was "supersmooth in coffee," in part because of the addition of rapeseed oil, gellan gum, and phosphates. It also produced tender, delicious results when we subbed it for coconut milk in vegan biscuits. One taster said it "seems like a pretty unobtrusive replacement for cow's milk," and another said "I'd keep this in my milk rotation."

PLANET OAT Original Oatmilk
PRICE: $3.99 for 52 fl oz ($0.08 per fl oz)
INGREDIENTS: Oatmilk (filtered water, oats), calcium carbonate, dipotassium phosphate (stabilizer), sea salt, gellan gum, vitamin A palmitate, vitamin D_2, riboflavin (vitamin B_2), and vitamin B_{12}
SUGAR: 4 g
REFRIGERATED: Yes
COMMENTS: This oat milk tasted "pleasant," with a "perfectly reasonable sweetness." Tasters liked this milk but found it "a little on the thin side," perhaps because it contains phosphates and gums but not oil. "As an avid milk drinker, I would use this as an alternative," said a taster.

OATLY Original Oatmilk
PRICE: $4.99 for 64 fl oz ($0.08 per fl oz)
INGREDIENTS: Oat base (water, oats). Contains 2% of less of: low erucic acid rapeseed oil, dipotassium phosphate, calcium carbonate, tricalcium phosphate, sea salt, dicalcium phosphate, riboflavin, vitamin A, vitamin D_2, vitamin B_{12}
SUGAR: 7 g
REFRIGERATED: Yes
COMMENTS: Our tasters praised this "smooth," "silky," and "creamy" oat milk, noting that it had "a bit more body" than some other samples and that it "added a nice creaminess to the coffee." As for flavor, it had a "pleasant sweetness on the finish." However, it tasted more strongly of oats than many of the other samples in our lineup, and several tasters said it was "too much oat."

GARLIC POWDER

We love garlic in all its forms, including garlic powder, which we view as its own ingredient rather than as an alternative to fresh garlic. In recipes where it's the only source of garlic, garlic powder adds sweet, warm flavor without the piquant tingle and punch of fresh garlic. We purchased nine, including some mail-order products, and tried them in two of our recipes: Chive Sour Cream, which calls for garlic powder, and Really Good Garlic Bread, which calls for fresh garlic and garlic powder. Before holding two tastings with a broader panel, we fine-tuned the measurements of garlic powder in the dip and garlic bread. In both, the flavor of the garlic powder was very subtle. To help our tasters home in on each garlic powder's flavor, we increased the amounts in both recipes and cut back or eliminated other bold ingredients such as onion powder. Even with these adjustments, many tasters had a hard time telling the samples apart. However, one product stood out slightly: Tasters liked that it was "on the sharper side." While a few garlic powders were especially "sweet" or "floral," our tasters mostly noticed slight variations in strength: Some were mellow, while others were a bit punchier. Tasters liked the mail-order products, but they were no more nuanced or powerful than the supermarket samples in our lineup. All the products we tasted are listed below in order of preference (prices are what we paid at the time of tasting).

RECOMMENDED

MORTON & BASSETT Garlic Powder
PRICE: $9.27 for 2.6 oz ($3.57 per oz)
COMMENTS: This garlic powder had a "really nice nutty, toasty flavor." It was "sweet and spicy" and had a "strong allium aftertaste." Garlic bread made with this powder had "buttery, garlicky goodness," in the words of one taster.

SIMPLY ORGANIC Garlic Powder
PRICE: $5.08 for 3.64 oz ($1.40 per oz)
COMMENTS: Tasters liked this "spicy" and "strong" garlic powder. One taster praised the "pleasantly sweet and nutty" garlic bread made with this sample, saying, "It was truly some of the best garlic bread I've had."

BADIA Garlic Powder
PRICE: $5.99 for 3 oz ($2.00 per oz)
COMMENTS: This garlic powder was "mellow" and "mild at first," but with a "spicy finish." One taster said it made "punchy-delicious" garlic bread. Another taster said, "It had heat that reminded me of fresh garlic."

SPICEOLOGY Imported Garlic Powder
PRICE: $7.99 for 1.8 oz ($4.44 per oz)
COMMENTS: "Mild, mellow, and sweet," this garlic powder allowed the other flavors in the recipes to shine through. "It's light but still has flavor," said one taster. When used on garlic bread, it had a "sweet and slight spiciness" and was "kind of fruity."

FRONTIER Organic Garlic Powder
PRICE: $8.39 for 2.33 oz ($3.60 per oz)
COMMENTS: Tasters liked the "earthy," "toasty, nutty garlic flavor" this garlic powder provided. It was "slightly spicy." In the sour cream dip, this garlic powder had an "almost raw garlic flavor" that tasters said provided "characteristic garlic heat."

RECOMMENDED (continued)

MCCORMICK Garlic Powder
PRICE: $4.19 for 3.12 oz ($1.34 per oz)
COMMENTS: "Sweet and garlicky," the flavor of this garlic powder was "pronounced, but not harsh or overwhelming." Garlic bread made with it was "milder at first but had a garlic heat that kicked in at the end." Some tasters also noted a "faint sweetness and toastiness."

SPICE ISLANDS Garlic Powder
PRICE: $11.75 for 2.25 oz ($5.22 per oz)
COMMENTS: The most expensive garlic powder in the lineup had "just the right amount of garlic flavor." While it was still "milder than others," it provided enough underlying garlic flavor. "I could eat a loaf of this," noted one taster of the garlic bread made with this powder.

BURLAP & BARREL Purple Stripe Garlic Powder
PRICE: $7.99 for 1.8 oz ($4.44 per oz)
COMMENTS: This garlic powder had "just the right kick from the garlic." It had that "sticky-sweet garlic flavor" and was "faintly nutty." One taster praised it for being "not too sharp, not too mild." Another taster agreed that it "still tasted very good but was less garlicky" than other garlic powders in our lineup.

GOYA Garlic Powder
PRICE: $7.20 for 8 oz ($0.90 per oz)
COMMENTS: The least expensive garlic powder in our lineup was "sweet" and "floral." Tasters liked that this "milder" garlic powder was noticeable but "not overpowering." Both the dip and garlic bread made with this powder had a pleasant "hint of garlic" flavor.

LOUISIANA-STYLE HOT SAUCE

The loyalty some people have to specific brands of hot sauce is undeniable. There's a Crystal Hot Sauce fan base that spans generations, a surprising variety of Frank's RedHot merchandise, and the never-ending debate between the champions and critics of Tabasco. These fans and critics have one thing in common: a passion for Louisiana-style hot sauce. To celebrate this beloved condiment, we rounded up 11 Louisiana-style hot sauces from big-name brands and smaller companies. Panels of tasters tried them two ways: plain and on grits. We also had an independent lab analyze their heat levels in Scoville Heat Units (SHU). During our tasting, we found something for everyone. The sauces that were bright, fresh, or citrusy tended to be thinner and more brightly colored. Those with deeper, richer, and smokier qualities were usually less vinegary and thicker. These thicker sauces tasted savory, sweet, or even buttery. Some sauces had more pronounced seasonings. Garlic was especially common. We've sorted them below from mildest to hottest based on the lab's analysis of their heat levels in SHU (prices are what we paid at the time of tasting).

HIGHLY RECOMMENDED

TRAPPEY'S Louisiana Hot Sauce
PRICE: $3.57 for 6 oz ($0.60 per oz)
ORIGIN: New Iberia, Louisiana
SCOVILLE HEAT UNITS: 310
COMMENTS: This "tart, brightly tangy" sauce made with jalapeño chiles had "a lemony overtone."

PANOLA Cajun Hot Sauce
PRICE: $3.00 for 6 oz ($0.50 per oz)
ORIGIN: Lake Providence, Louisiana
SCOVILLE HEAT UNITS: 330
COMMENTS: This summery, reddish-orange sauce was "sparky" and "citrusy."

TEXAS PETE Original Hot Sauce
PRICE: $1.79 for 12 oz ($0.15 per oz)
ORIGIN: Winston-Salem, North Carolina
SCOVILLE HEAT UNITS: 490
COMMENTS: Tasters liked this sauce's "pleasant acidity" and "simpler, pure expression of heat."

CAJUN CHEF Louisiana Hot Sauce
PRICE: $4.99 for 6 oz ($0.83 per oz)
ORIGIN: St. Martinville, Louisiana
SCOVILLE HEAT UNITS: 550
COMMENTS: This sauce had a fruity, sweet, almost floral start that faded into a subtle heat.

CRYSTAL Hot Sauce
PRICE: $5.77 for 6 oz ($0.96 per oz)
ORIGIN: New Orleans, Louisiana
SCOVILLE HEAT UNITS: 670
COMMENTS: This sweeter sauce tasted like red bell peppers or even tomatoes.

FRANK'S REDHOT Original Cayenne Pepper Hot Sauce
PRICE: $3.59 for 12 oz ($0.30 per oz)
ORIGIN: Springfield, Missouri
SCOVILLE HEAT UNITS: 790
COMMENTS: This iconic sauce was savory, garlicky, and tangy.

HIGHLY RECOMMENDED (continued)

POIRIER'S Louisiana Style Hot Sauce
PRICE: $12.00 for 6 oz ($2.00 per oz)
ORIGIN: Thunder Bay, Ontario, Canada
SCOVILLE HEAT UNITS: 1,100
COMMENTS: Tasters found it "rich and meaty-tasting" and praised its "complexity."

LOUISIANA BRAND Original Hot Sauce
PRICE: $3.29 for 12 oz ($0.27 per oz)
ORIGIN: New Iberia, Louisiana
SCOVILLE HEAT UNITS: 1,200
COMMENTS: One of the more savory sauces in our lineup, it tasted pleasantly "buttery" and rich.

SLAP YA MAMA Cajun Hot Sauce
PRICE: $4.15 for 5 oz ($0.83 per oz)
ORIGIN: Ville Platte, Louisiana
SCOVILLE HEAT UNITS: 1,600
COMMENTS: Tasters liked its slight "smokiness" and subtle vinegar flavor.

CAJOHN'S Small Batch Classic Cayenne Pepper Sauce
PRICE: $7.49 for 5 oz ($1.50 per oz)
ORIGIN: Charlotte, North Carolina
SCOVILLE HEAT UNITS: 1,600
COMMENTS: Tasters described "roasted pepper" qualities, notes of "dried pepper," and a "fruity sweetness."

TABASCO BRAND Pepper Sauce
PRICE: $3.59 for 5 oz ($0.72 per oz)
ORIGIN: Avery Island, Louisiana
SCOVILLE HEAT UNITS: 3,700
COMMENTS: This classic sauce is aged in oak and has an astringent and peppery flavor.

INEXPENSIVE BLENDERS

With a good blender, you can easily whip up smoothies, shakes, frozen drinks, sauces, dips, and dressings and even grind nut butters from scratch. While we've found excellent midpriced and high-end blenders, which cost about $200 or more, we wanted to find out if we could match their performance while spending less. Setting a cap of $100 for each, we bought seven blenders and put them to the test, making smoothies, crushing ice, emulsifying mayonnaise, and grinding almonds into nut butter. We measured noise levels and stain and odor retention and rated the blenders' performance, handling, and cleanup. Several factors, including sheer power, impacted performance. Our two highest-rated blenders had high peak wattages of 1,300 and 1,200 watts; the two lowest-rated models had peak wattages of just 746 and 700 watts. Bigger jars also helped—our top blenders were nearly twice as roomy as lower-ranked models, so foods moved more freely. All jars were lined with vertical ribs, but they were bigger in top models, helping direct spinning food down to the blades. Those blades were bigger, too, with wider wingspans, and there were more of them. A few models had the winning combination of powerful motors, sharp blades, and a jar that kept ingredients moving; the rest just kept getting stuck. The top three models are listed below in order of preference (prices are what we paid at the time of testing except for the Instant Ace Plus because its price rose significantly).

HIGHLY RECOMMENDED	PERFORMANCE	TESTERS' COMMENTS

NUTRIBULLET Full Size Blender

MODEL: ZNBF30400Z
PRICE: $99.99
JAR MATERIAL: Plastic
CAPACITY: 8 cups
EXTRAS: Food tamper, 55-page recipe booklet
WATTS: 1,200

BLENDING AND ICE CRUSHING ★★★
MAYONNAISE ★
ALMOND BUTTER ★★★
NOISE LEVEL ★
CLEANING AND HANDLING ★★★
CONTROLS AND OPERATION ★★★

Tall and lightweight, with a generous 8-cup capacity, a comfortable handle, and very basic controls (Low, Medium, High, and Pulse), this powerful blender aced every challenge except for mayonnaise, where its low speed was simply too fast. It was a bit noisy, but it got the job done.

INSTANT Ace Plus Cooking and Beverage Blender

MODEL: AcePlus
PRICE: $149.99
JAR MATERIAL: Glass
CAPACITY: 7 cups cold; 6 cups hot
EXTRAS: Food tamper, nut milk bag, measuring cup, cleaning brush, free recipe app
WATTS: 1,300

BLENDING AND ICE CRUSHING ★★★
MAYONNAISE ★★★
ALMOND BUTTER ★★★
NOISE LEVEL ★★
CLEANING AND HANDLING ★★½
CONTROLS AND OPERATION ★★½

Usually hands-off and with useful preset programs, this excellent blender powered through every task. Its heavy glass jar (which weighs about 5½ pounds) and locking lid are solidly built. The only drawback is that the electronics in the jar base can't be submerged in water. However, the jar and lid were easy to wash by hand. This model also contains a heating element to cook soups, and it can do so without pureeing the ingredients, so you can determine the soup's final texture. You can delay heating for up to 12 hours, and you can keep foods warm for up to 2 hours. Unfortunately, the blender's price rose significantly above $100 after we purchased it, disqualifying it as our winner, but if you see it for less than $100, it's a worthwhile choice.

RECOMMENDED

BLACK + DECKER Quiet Blender with Cyclone Glass Jar

MODEL: BL1400DG-P
PRICE: $59.99 **BEST BUY**
JAR MATERIAL: Glass
CAPACITY: 6 cups
EXTRAS: Single-serve blending jar
WATTS: 900 peak, 500 continuous blending

BLENDING AND ICE CRUSHING ★★
MAYONNAISE ★★
ALMOND BUTTER ★★★
NOISE LEVEL ★
CLEANING AND HANDLING ★★★
CONTROLS AND OPERATION ★★½

Solidly built, with a glass jar, this blender performed acceptably across the board, but it took time and effort because we had to stop and scrape to get results—it wasn't hands-off. Its lowest speed was almost too fast to make mayonnaise, but it did manage. It was powerful enough to grind nut butter with a bit of effort on our part. The controls were slightly complicated but manageable.

PIZZA/BAKING STONES

The blazing-hot oven of a real pizzeria can produce pizza with a flavorful, crisp, deeply browned crust and melty, bubbling cheese all in a matter of minutes. At home, though, pizza rarely reaches those heights. We've learned that heating a good baking stone or steel in a 500-degree oven for an hour turns out pizzas that come closest to restaurant quality. But which stone or steel performs best? We tested seven models, all rectangular or square, which we prefer to round models for their roomier surfaces. Their thicknesses ranged from ¼ inch to more than 1 inch. Some were simple slabs; others had built-in handles or feet. One was a set of four tiles meant to be positioned side by side. Weights ranged from less than 6 pounds to a whopping 16 pounds. We baked pizza and bread, tracking temperatures and evaluating how easy each model was to use. We know that the main use for a baking stone or steel is to make pizza, so that was the factor we weighted most heavily. Happily, every model in our lineup produced very good pizza. However, we did notice one minor, but important, difference in pizzas baked on steels: Their crusts were a bit more airy and moist and perceptibly more tender. Stone-baked crusts were slightly drier, chewier, and even a smidge tougher than ideal. The top four models are listed in order of preference below (prices are what we paid at the time of testing).

HIGHLY RECOMMENDED	PERFORMANCE	TESTERS' COMMENTS
THE ORIGINAL BAKING STEEL **CO-WINNER** **MODEL:** Original **PRICE:** $99.00 **MATERIAL:** Low carbon steel **SIZE:** 16 x 14 x ¼ in **WEIGHT:** 16 lb 	PERFORMANCE ★★★ EASE OF USE ★★½	Pizzas emerged perfectly browned and crisp on the outside, with a tender interior, as if they were baked in a professional pizza oven. The steel also provided excellent oven spring to make our rustic bread loaf rise tall and develop a deeply browned, crackly, chewy crust. While it's a beast to lift, being absolutely flat with no handholds (but also no cutouts that waste space), this steel is tough and will last forever, providing easy cleanup—just keep it dry and oil it lightly after washing, as you would a carbon-steel or cast-iron skillet.
NERD CHEF Steel Stone, **Standard ¼"** **CO-WINNER** **MODEL:** NC-SS25 **PRICE:** $74.99 **MATERIAL:** Low-carbon steel **SIZE:** 16 x 14¼ x ¼ in **WEIGHT:** 16 lb 	PERFORMANCE ★★★ EASE OF USE ★★½	This steel did an excellent job browning our pizza crust uniformly while leaving the interior tender and moist. It's heavy, at 16 pounds, and very flat, so it's hard to pick up and transfer into the oven, though two corners have cutout circles designed to help lift it (or to hang it on the wall), which we didn't find particularly helpful. Otherwise, this tough, unbreakable steel is a great choice for home pizza making or bread baking.

RECOMMENDED	PERFORMANCE	
OUTSET Pizza Grill Stone Tiles, **Set of 4—Model: 76176** **BEST BUY + BEST LIGHTWEIGHT OPTION** **PRICE:** $29.99 **MATERIAL:** Cordierite ceramic **SIZE:** 15 x 15 x ⅜ in (7½ x 7½ x ⅜ in per tile) **WEIGHT:** 5 lb, 10⅝ oz (1 lb, 6⅜ oz per tile) 	PERFORMANCE ★★½ EASE OF USE ★★★	Supereasy to handle, compact to store, and a great boon for those who can't lift heavy objects, these four lightweight 7.5-inch-square ceramic tiles (each weighing less than 1.5 pounds) are also inexpensive. (Note: You don't have to fuss with arranging them. Just push them together on an oven rack; nothing falls between the cracks.) While they lack the mass of a thick ceramic stone, they still produced nicely browned, crisp pizza that was just a shade more chewy than the pizza we got from baking on steel or thick, heavy stone. From our temperature monitoring, we saw that the tiles were fully preheated to 500 degrees in just 30 minutes compared with the full hour it took the rest of the lineup. We liked their versatility: Two tiles would fit in most toaster ovens, or you could set all four in a row to bake long breads in the full-size oven.
HONEY-CAN-DO 14x16-Inch **Cordierite Pizza Stone** **MODEL:** KCH-09011 **PRICE:** $39.99 **MATERIAL:** Cordierite ceramic **SIZE:** 16 x 14 x 0.6 in **WEIGHT:** 8.2 lb 	PERFORMANCE ★★½ EASE OF USE ★★★	This moderately priced ceramic stone produced a beautifully browned pizza crust with bubbly cheese. It was also fairly lightweight, making it easier to handle than most of the other models we tested. Though it lacked raised feet or handles, it provided an uninterrupted flat surface with plenty of room for baking larger pizzas and breads. While the pizza crust it produced was a shade chewier and drier than the crust produced on a steel, the results were still excellent.

GRILL PANS

Grill pans are skillets customized with ridges across the cooking surface to mimic the cooking grates of a grill. When we compared burgers, panini, and salmon made in ordinary skillets with the same foods made in grill pans, the foods made in the ordinary skillets were less visually appealing and lacked the flavorful char marks produced by the grill pans. We use grill pans to make pressed sandwiches and to grill meats and vegetables. The pan's hot ridges sear grill marks onto the surfaces of food while radiant heat cooks the food. Fat drains away from the food to the channels between the ridges. Grill pans can be made from different materials, including heavy cast iron (enameled or plain) or thinner, lighter sheets of nonstick aluminum or steel (and sometimes nonstick cast aluminum). From previous testing, we know that we prefer cast-iron models for their superior heat retention and taller, more distinct ridges that make better grill marks. Thinner nonstick versions are stamped out of a sheet of metal, so the ridge shapes have to be low and rounded to keep the metal from tearing as it's stamped. As a result, their grill marks—the whole point of this kind of pan—are wimpy. Our top six pans are listed below in order of preference (prices are what we paid at the time of testing).

HIGHLY RECOMMENDED	PERFORMANCE	TESTERS' COMMENTS
LODGE Chef Collection 11 Inch Cast Iron Square Grill Pan MODEL: LC11SGP PRICE: $35.99 MATERIAL: Seasoned cast iron WEIGHT: 7 lb, 3 oz COOKING SURFACE: 9 x 9 x ¾ in RIDGE HEIGHT: 7.1 mm	PERFORMANCE ★★★ EASE OF USE ★★★ CLEANUP ★★★	This tray-shaped pan was handsome and easy to use. It arrived with a well-seasoned surface that released food and cleaned up easily and tall, well-defined ridges that produced excellent grill marks. At the end of extensive testing, it still looked new.
BOROUGH Furnace Grill Pan/Braising Lid MODEL: n/a PRICE: $110.00 MATERIAL: Seasoned cast iron WEIGHT: 6 lb, 9 oz COOKING SURFACE: 9 x 9 x 1¾ in RIDGE HEIGHT: 5.1 mm	PERFORMANCE ★★★ EASE OF USE ★★★ CLEANUP ★★★	A handmade pan by a small producer in Owego, New York, this pan is a work of art, and its smooth, power-sanded finish, which is done by hand, and excellent preseasoned patina released food and cleaned up beautifully. The pan's ridges were tall enough to create crisp, defined grill marks, and its low, flared sides let us slide a spatula under food at a comfortable, near-level angle, so even delicate food stayed intact. It doubles as a lid for the company's 12-inch skillet.

RECOMMENDED	PERFORMANCE	
CUISINEL Cast Iron Square Grill Pan - 10.5 Inch MODEL: C10-SG PRICE: $27.99 MATERIAL: Seasoned cast iron WEIGHT: 7 lb COOKING SURFACE: 8½ x 8½ x 1¾ in RIDGE HEIGHT: 5.2 mm	PERFORMANCE ★★½ EASE OF USE ★★½ CLEANUP ★★★	This square pan had moderately tall ridges that left good grill marks. While it arrived with a rough surface that tore lint off paper and cloth towels, it quickly gained a patina of seasoning as we used it, so it got easier to clean and released food more readily over the course of testing. It came with a silicone handle cover and a plastic scraper for cleaning the ridged surface. The handle was useful; the scraper less so.
FINEX Cast Iron 12″ Grill Pan MODEL: G12–10002 PRICE: $245.00 MATERIAL: Seasoned cast iron WEIGHT: 10 lb, 11.25 oz COOKING SURFACE: 10¼ x 10¼ x 1⅞ in RIDGE HEIGHT: 6.25 mm	PERFORMANCE ★★½ EASE OF USE ★★★ CLEANUP ★★	This high-priced, hefty pan, produced by a small company in Portland, Oregon, was nicely roomy and weighed nearly 11 pounds, but the dual handles helped us hoist it around. It cooked food beautifully, with even browning and distinct grill marks from the high, well-defined ridges. Lightly seasoned upon arrival, it began to rust a bit after we washed it, and it took some scrubbing to get clean, but it began acquiring more patina with further use.
LODGE 10.5 Inch Square Cast Iron Grill Pan MODEL: L8SGP3 PRICE: $19.90 MATERIAL: Seasoned cast iron WEIGHT: 6 lb, 10.75 oz COOKING SURFACE: 8½ x 8½ x 1⅞ in RIDGE HEIGHT: 5.5 mm	PERFORMANCE ★★½ EASE OF USE ★★½ CLEANUP ★★½	We liked the tall ridges of this pan, which produced crisp, golden-striped panini and distinct grill marks on fish. The fish stuck a bit when we tried to flip it, and the pan's tall sides made it slightly awkward to get a spatula under the fish without breaking it. The pan's seasoning improved over the course of testing.
LE CREUSET Signature Square Skillet Grill 10.25″ MODEL: LS2021 PRICE: $184.95 MATERIAL: Enameled cast iron WEIGHT: 6 lb, 6.25 oz COOKING SURFACE: 8¼ x 8¼ x 1¾ in RIDGE HEIGHT: 4.8 mm	PERFORMANCE ★★ EASE OF USE ★★★ CLEANUP ★★½	While this handsome enameled pan produced excellent grilled panini, it didn't perform as well with stickier, more delicate salmon, whose char marks stuck in the pan (we patched it up with glaze, but it still didn't look great). We liked the pan's flaring walls, which helped us get a spatula under food at a lower, more comfortable angle, and we were glad that we could use tons of soap on its enameled coating, but we usually had to do a fair amount of scrubbing to get it clean.

SOUS VIDE MACHINES

A sous vide immersion circulator is a sticklike appliance that heats water in a vessel to a desired temperature and then maintains that temperature to cook food immersed in the water bath. The food, which is first sealed in plastic (though not always; you can cook sous vide in glass jars, and eggs can be cooked right in their shells), eventually reaches the same temperature as the water, so it can't overcook. With meat, poultry, and fish, you usually follow up with a quick sear in a skillet for surface browning. The benefits of this cooking technique are perfectly and uniformly cooked food and a process that's quiet, neat, and mostly hands-off. Cleanup is minimal, because you're cooking your food in water. And because they're not cooked directly in the water, vegetables such as carrots and asparagus come out intensely flavorful and stay brightly colored. Sous vide cooking is easy, if you have the right immersion circulator. We tested six models and compared their speed, accuracy, ease of use, and cooking results. Our top four models are listed below in order of preference (prices are what we paid at the time of testing).

HIGHLY RECOMMENDED	PERFORMANCE	TESTERS' COMMENTS
BREVILLE Joule Sous Vide-White Polycarbonate **MODEL:** CS20001 **PRICE:** $199.95 **WATTS:** 1,100 **HEIGHT:** 11 in **ATTACHMENT:** Clip with magnetic base **EXTRAS:** App compatible with iOS and Android	PERFORMANCE ★★★ SPEED ★★★ ACCURACY ★★★ EASE OF USE ★★★ STURDINESS ★★★	This simple, small, sleek model aced every test: It was the most powerful of the lineup at 1,100 watts, making it the fastest to heat water, and it held whatever temperature we set with perfect accuracy, whether we were cooking for 12 minutes or 20 hours. Easy and quick to set and monitor via an extremely user-friendly app (that's compatible with iOS and Android), it's also simple to clip onto any size vessel for cooking (if desired, a strong magnet in the base lets you stand it in metal pots without clipping it). Because it has no display, it isn't harmed when it's dropped in the water, unlike other models. Its small, lightweight, and slim profile makes it a snap to store when you're done cooking. (Note: The only difference between this model and the stainless-steel version—which costs about $50 more—is the trim on the outside of the device, so we recommend this less-expensive polycarbonate model.)

RECOMMENDED	PERFORMANCE	
YEDI HOUSEWARE Infinity Sous Vide Outset **MODEL:** GV024 **PRICE:** $99.95 `BEST BUY` **WATTS:** 1, **HEIGHT:** 14.5 in **ATTACHMENT:** Clip **EXTRAS:** 20 reusable cooking bags, small hand-pumped vacuum sealer, metal clips, 2 bag-sealing clips, recipe book, and cooking time "cheat sheets"	PERFORMANCE ★★★ SPEED ★★★ ACCURACY ★★★ EASE OF USE ★★½ STURDINESS ★★★ 	We loved (almost) everything about this model: its dead-on accuracy; its solid construction; its speed; its powerful water circulation (it beat the rest of the lineup by several seconds in our food-coloring test); its silence; and, most of all, its great cooking results. But one design flaw annoyed us from the start: The control panel display of this 14.5-inch-tall device points straight up, making it nearly impossible for a shorter tester to see, set, and check without standing on a step stool (and there's no app to use instead). It comes with reusable bags and a hand-operated vacuum pump plus four metal clips to attach bagged food to the vessel. We tried the bags and pump to cook spice-rubbed indoor pulled pork for 20 hours, and while the bags became slightly stained and retained a faint scent, they remained in usable condition. However, the pump is small, flimsy, and plastic, so we wouldn't expect great durability, but it's a nice starter kit.
MONOPRICE Strata Home Sous Vide Immersion Cooker **MODEL:** 121594 **PRICE:** $79.99 **WATTS:** 800 **HEIGHT:** 14½ in **ATTACHMENT:** Screw-on, adjustable **EXTRAS:** None	PERFORMANCE ★★★ SPEED ★½ ACCURACY ★★★ EASE OF USE ★★★ STURDINESS ★½	While we appreciated the accuracy of this model's cooking and the unique control wheel that let us zip up and down rapidly to set time and temperature instead of repeatedly pressing and holding buttons, the device itself felt slightly flimsy, particularly when turning that plastic wheel. It's also slightly clunky and top-heavy. The display could be improved: It flashes between the target temperature and the timer in a single small portion of the readout, so we had to linger to read elapsed time (and when the numbers were similar, such as 16 hours to go at 160 degrees, it was momentarily confusing). The upshot: If you can deal with the slightly awkward operation, this device works fine at a relatively inexpensive price.
DASH Digital Chef Series Sous Vide Circulator **MODEL:** DSV250VPBK10 **PRICE:** $99.99 **WATTS:** 800 **HEIGHT:** 15 in **ATTACHMENT:** Screw-on, adjustable **EXTRAS:** 10 reusable cooking bags, small hand-pumped vacuum sealer, recipe book	PERFORMANCE ★★★ SPEED ★½ ACCURACY ★½ EASE OF USE ★★★ STURDINESS ★★★ 	We loved this device's very large, easy-to-read face with controls that were simple to set. While food came out acceptably, the display was dependably off by a full degree during cooking, reading higher than it actually was. If you buy this machine, you may want to check it against another, more reliable thermometer and adjust temperature settings accordingly. The display has a "chill" button for wine, which means that it circulates the water without heating it; to use it, add ice to a cold-water bath and insert the bottle. An adjustable clamp helps it attach to most vessels (though it could only slide so far and the device sat at a slight angle in our Dutch oven). It comes with a small, plastic hand-operated vacuum pump and 10 reusable plastic bags in two sizes, a nice touch—but even the large size was too small (at 9.5 inches by 9.5 inches) to fit our asparagus or pulled pork.

CAST-IRON SKILLETS

In the 19th century, cast-iron skillets were common in the United States and made by many American manufacturers. Sadly, almost none of those companies survived the 20th century. Lodge Manufacturing, however, has produced cast-iron cookware in Tennessee since 1896, making it the longest-operated American cast-iron cookware company. Today, most cast-iron skillets are imports from China, where cast-iron cookware was invented. But recently, artisan makers have sprung up in the United States, many with a goal of re-creating labor-intensive features that disappeared from most modern cast-iron cookware, including smooth, hand-polished interiors (most new pans have a rougher surface that shows the texture of the sand they were cast in) and pans cast to be thinner and more lightweight. We tested some of each type, scrambling eggs, pan-searing flank steak, shallow-frying potato wedges, skillet-roasting cod, and baking cornbread in each pan. In addition to evaluating the food each produced, we considered how easy the pans were to lift, cook in, and transfer to and from the oven, and how easy or difficult they were to scrub clean. Our top four pans are listed below in order of preference (prices are what we paid at the time of testing).

HIGHLY RECOMMENDED	PERFORMANCE	TESTERS' COMMENTS
SMITHEY Ironware No. 12 Cast Iron Skillet MODEL: n/a PRICE: $200.00 WEIGHT: 7 lb, 15⅞ oz COOKING SURFACE: 10 in SIDES: 2¼ in	PERFORMANCE ★★★ EASE OF USE ★★★ CLEANUP ★★★	Silky-smooth from the get-go, this roomy pan didn't let food stick and stayed impressively slick throughout testing. Its heavy weight helped it retain heat, so it seared food evenly and deeply. The pan's bronze color became blotchy as we used it, but it will gradually gain a nice patina with lots of use.
LODGE 12 Inch Cast Iron Skillet MODEL: L10SK3 PRICE: $43.31 **BEST BUY** WEIGHT: 8 lb, ¾ oz COOKING SURFACE: 10 in SIDES: 2¼ in	PERFORMANCE ★★★ EASE OF USE ★★★ CLEANUP ★★★	While this skillet started out with a rougher surface than those of the artisan pans, its gently nubbly texture quickly gained seasoning, and by the end of testing it released food and cleaned up perfectly. At about 8 pounds, it's heavy, but that weight helps with heat retention and browning. Its roomy surface and high sides make it a versatile performer—all at a great price for a pan that will last forever.

RECOMMENDED	PERFORMANCE	TESTERS' COMMENTS
CUISINEL Pre-Seasoned Cast Iron Skillet 12-Inch w/ Handle Cover MODEL: C12612 PRICE: $35.95 WEIGHT: 8 lb, ⅜ oz COOKING SURFACE: 10 in SIDES: 2⅜ in	PERFORMANCE ★★½ EASE OF USE ★★★ CLEANUP ★★★	A heavy, classic cast-iron pan with excellent heat retention, it deeply browned steak, fries, and cornbread. Its fairly rough surface gained seasoning as we used it and released food beautifully by the end of testing, but it still snagged towel lint and stayed a bit oilier and gummier than was ideal. It came with a very handy silicone handle cover that let us skip using pot holders when it was on the stovetop, though it couldn't protect our hands when the pan had been heated to 500 degrees in the oven.
FIELD Cast Iron Skillet No. 10 MODEL: No. 10 PRICE: $160.00 WEIGHT: 5 lb, 11¾ oz COOKING SURFACE: 10 in SIDES: 2⅛ in	PERFORMANCE ★★½ EASE OF USE ★★★ CLEANUP ★★★	We fell in love with the satiny-smooth surface; simple, elegant, spoutless shape; and slightly lighter weight of this artisan pan, which released food perfectly—even fish, the bane of most of our lineup. Rim to rim it's slightly less than 12 inches across, but nearly straight sides mean that it still has 10 inches of cooking space. Because it's more than 2 pounds lighter and a bit thinner than our top-rated pans, it ran a little hot and browned food slightly less evenly.
CALPHALON Pre-Seasoned Cast Iron 12-Inch Skillet MODEL: 2112855 PRICE: $29.99 ASIN: B00L4771OG WEIGHT: 7 lb, 9¼ oz COOKING SURFACE: 10 in SIDES: 2¼ in	PERFORMANCE ★★½ EASE OF USE ★★★ CLEANUP ★★½	We loved the curved sides and graceful shape of this pan, which has a nubbly surface that started out nicely preseasoned but lost a little slickness along the way. A small strip of cornbread stuck to the pan, and some eggs stuck in the final round, though a gentle scrub was all it took to clean up. It took a bit longer than others to gain seasoning, likely because its surface is slightly rough.

LIGHTWEIGHT DUTCH OVENS

We love traditional Dutch ovens because of how versatile they are. We stock dozens of our top-rated models in the test kitchen, routinely using them to boil, braise, bake, fry, and more. Most Dutch ovens are made from enameled cast iron, and they're quite heavy—we've tested options that weigh more than 18 pounds. In most cases, this heft is helpful: Heavy cast iron retains heat well, which makes it ideal for baking picture-perfect, crusty loaves of bread as well as deep frying. It's also great for searing and braising meat and making soups and stews. But cast-iron cookware can be too heavy for some home cooks, especially those with disabilities, arthritis, or otherwise diminished hand, arm, or back strength. So we set out to find a lightweight pot that is just as versatile and dependable as a cast-iron Dutch oven and that doesn't sacrifice quality for lightness.

Our research led us to conclude that there aren't many criteria a pot has to follow to be dubbed a Dutch oven. Manufacturers throw the label on pots made from any material you can think of, from cast iron to stainless steel, aluminum, and even ceramic. Many have enameled or nonstick coatings. Some products are labeled "stockpots" or "casseroles" as well as or instead of being called a Dutch oven. For this review, we focused less on name and more on certain characteristics.

We rounded up and tested eight lighter-weight options to find an alternative that was just as versatile and dependable as a traditional Dutch oven. We selected pots made from stainless steel and aluminum, with sides no higher than 6 inches, since higher sides can keep cooks from being able to reach and manipulate food. We included models that held from 6 to 7 quarts—the size we call for in most of our recipes—and that weighed less than 6.5 pounds, which is far less heavy than our cast-iron winner. Some of these pots seared meat as evenly and quickly as cast-iron pots. But what we gained in maneuverability, we lost in heat retention. The lightweight models couldn't radiate enough heat to produce crusty, well-browned loaves of bread. Some were also unable to successfully trap steam and moisture, which is also necessary for bread baking, as well as braising. We still suggest using a cast-iron Dutch oven for baking bread, but the lightweight options we found are versatile enough to sear, braise, and fry, and we recommend them for people who prefer a lighter pot. Our top two options are listed below in order of preference (prices are what we paid at the time of testing).

HIGHLY RECOMMENDED	PERFORMANCE		TESTERS' COMMENTS
ALL-CLAD D3 Stainless Stockpot with Lid, 6 Quart MODEL: 8701004424 PRICE: $294.99 MATERIALS: Fully clad stainless steel with aluminum core CAPACITY: 6 qt WEIGHT: 3 lb, 13 oz (pot); 1 lb, 4 oz (lid) COOKING SURFACE DIAMETER: 10 in INTERNAL HEIGHT: 3⅞ in	COOKING EASE OF USE DURABILITY	★★★ ★★★ ★★★	This reliable pot performed almost as well as a traditional cast-iron Dutch oven. Its fully clad construction ensured stellar heat retention and distribution, helping it sear meat efficiently and evenly. Its broad cooking surface meant that we didn't have to sear meat in extra batches, and its large, easy-to-grip handles and low, straight sides allowed us to maneuver and reach down into the pot with ease. It was large enough to fry in, and it baked bread adequately, though its loaf was not as satisfyingly browned and crusty as those from our favorite cast-iron pots.

RECOMMENDED			
TRAMONTINA 6 Qt Tri-Ply Clad Stainless Steel Covered Sauce Pot MODEL: 80116/040DS PRICE: $119.95 `BEST BUY` MATERIALS: Fully clad stainless steel with aluminum core CAPACITY: 6 qt WEIGHT: 3 lb, 14 oz (pot); 1 lb, 1 oz (lid) COOKING SURFACE DIAMETER: 8 in INTERNAL HEIGHT: 5 in	COOKING EASE OF USE DURABILITY	★★★ ★★ ★★★	Our Best Buy lightweight Dutch oven is constructed from three layers of durable stainless steel and aluminum, which radiated and distributed heat efficiently and evenly. This led to a great sear on meat and beautifully cooked rice. We also liked its large, secure handles and tight-fitting lid. But it had one drawback: Its cooking surface is 2 inches smaller than that of our winner, so it took more batches (and more time) to sear food.

AIR FRYERS

Despite their name, air fryers don't fry your food. They're essentially small convection ovens with powerful fans that circulate hot air around food to approximate the crisp and juicy results of deep frying. They require less oil—mere tablespoons, as opposed to quarts—and are less messy than deep frying. Air fryers generally cook food 5 to 10 minutes quicker than conventional ovens. They need to be preheated for only a few minutes, if at all, and they won't heat up your entire kitchen. Throughout years of testing air fryers, we've concluded that even the best models can't achieve the crispiness that deep frying offers, but some come impressively close. We tested three styles: drawer-style models with baskets that pull out from the front; flip-top models with lids that lift up from the top to reveal the baskets inside; and bigger, cube-shaped models with doors that swing open in the front and multiple racks inside like an oven. The oven-style models often include revolving rotisserie baskets or propeller-shaped auto-stir attachments, both of which automatically rotate to toss food around, supposedly for more-even heating and crisping. Our top five models are listed below in order of preference (prices are what we paid at the time of testing).

HIGHLY RECOMMENDED	PERFORMANCE	TESTERS' COMMENTS

INSTANT Vortex Plus 6-Quart Air Fryer
MODEL: n/a
PRICE: $119.95
STYLE: Drawer
CONTROLS: Digital
HEIGHT: 12½ in

COOKING ★★★
SAFETY ★★★
CAPACITY ★★★
EASE OF USE ★★½

Our winning air fryer was the first model we've tested that delivers on its promise to offer an extra-large capacity. Though it's only a foot tall, this drawer-style model was large enough to fit four chicken cutlets or two 15-ounce bags of frozen french fries, cooking everything to crispy, golden perfection. We were even able to cook a whole 4-pound chicken in it. A quick 2-minute preheat ensured that the interior was hot when we added food. The wide drawer-style basket was easy to remove and insert—and our hands were safeguarded from the heating element—and its sturdy handle allowed us to shake its contents for easy redistribution. Intuitive digital controls (including a simple knob to set the time and temperature) were brightly lit and easy to operate. This fryer is a great option for a family of four or anyone who is looking for more cooking space without adding much bulk.

PHILIPS Premium Airfryer with Fat Removal Technology
MODEL: HD9741/99
PRICE: $249.95
STYLE: Drawer
CONTROLS: Digital
HEIGHT: 11¼ in

COOKING ★★★
SAFETY ★★★
CAPACITY ★★
EASE OF USE ★★★

We love this machine's slim, compact footprint, and we liked that its nonstick cooking basket was simple to clean and had a removable bottom for deeper cleaning. Its digital controls and dial-operated menu made setting the time and temperature easy and intuitive. It automatically stopped cooking as soon as the set time was up, and its drawer allowed us to remove its cooking basket without exposing our hands to the heating element. While it can't hold as much food as our winner can, it can handle small batches of frozen foods or air-fryer recipes intended to serve two people.

RECOMMENDED

GOWISE USA 3.7-Quart 7-in-1 Air Fryer
MODEL: GW22621
PRICE: $75.15 `BEST BUY`
STYLE: Drawer
CONTROLS: Digital
HEIGHT: 13 in

COOKING ★★★
SAFETY ★★★
CAPACITY ★★
EASE OF USE ★★½

While this air fryer's digital controls weren't quite as intuitive as those of our favorite models, it was still easy to set the time and temperature once we got the hang of the multiple buttons. It cooked foods quickly, and its display was bright, large, and easy to read. Its drawer and automatic shutoff were a boon to safety, and its nonstick interior was easy to clean. Its small capacity wouldn't work for a crowd, but it cooked our recipes for two and small batches of frozen fries without issue.

PHILIPS Premium Analog Airfryer
MODEL: HD9721/99
PRICE: $169.95
STYLE: Drawer
CONTROLS: Analog
HEIGHT: 11 in

COOKING ★★★
SAFETY ★★★
CAPACITY ★★
EASE OF USE ★★

This small model's stature and footprint make it easy to store, but it's still large enough to cook small batches of frozen foods and our recipes evenly and quickly. Its nonstick interior was easy to clean, but its analog temperature and timer dials weren't as precise as digital controls.

ROSEWILL RHAF-15004 1400W Oil-Less Low Fat Air Fryer - 3.3-Quart (3.2L), Black
MODEL: RHAF-15004
PRICE: $60.20
STYLE: Drawer
CONTROLS: Analog
HEIGHT: 12 in

COOKING ★★★
SAFETY ★★★
CAPACITY ★★
EASE OF USE ★★

Another smaller, drawer-style air fryer that could fit easily under cabinets, this analog model had simple controls that were intuitive to set. While it cooked food well and cleaned up easily, testers struggled a bit when sliding the basket into the machine, and it required some jiggering to lock in. As with other analog models, its temperature dial was less precise, and it was easy to knock slightly away from the target temperature.

SMART OVENS

Over the past few years, smart countertop ovens have arrived with a splash. However, this appliance category still has only a handful of players and remains a bit amorphous, since each company promises that its oven can accomplish a range of cooking tasks with very different technologies. All smart ovens claim to produce expertly cooked food with hands-off convenience. Typically, smart ovens have apps that let you control cooking, peruse a library of built-in recipes, and purchase accessories; some also allow you to order meal kits. The ovens use sophisticated software in a variety of ways, whether to identify foods you put in them or run cooking programs that incorporate traditional and innovative cooking technologies, alone or in combination, to optimize results. While you can operate them exactly like a standard oven, smart ovens offer many more functions. They also guide you step by step as you prepare recipes: They monitor and adjust cooking time and temperature (some via built-in temperature probes), offer helpful videos and tips, transmit images or graphs of your cooking progress on their apps or oven displays, and scan packaged retail foods or the company's own meal kits for one-step preparation. Some offer access to a community of users who share recipes and tips. All the ovens periodically update software and add features, just like your phone or laptop does. Most also link to Siri, Alexa, or Google Assistant, so you can operate them by voice. After testing a lineup of five ovens, we discovered that three failed to live up to their promises. Some of the programming didn't work. For instance, even after we'd entered the exact weight of our whole chicken in ounces, as requested, one oven roasted it until the exterior leg and wing meat was as hard as plastic. Another took 8 minutes (and three separate cooking stages) to toast a slice of bread and still failed. It also took 3 hours to roast a small (4-pound) chicken. A third unpredictably burned toast after previously completing a successful session. To earn its place in our kitchen, we expected each smart oven to cook competently in every mode—and hopefully with less effort or time than conventional appliances. Our top two choices are listed below in order of preference (prices are what we paid at the time of testing).

HIGHLY RECOMMENDED	PERFORMANCE	TESTERS' COMMENTS

JUNE Smart Oven (3rd Generation)
MODEL: JCH03
PRICE: $999.99 (Premium package)
EXTERIOR: 19¾ x 18½ x 12¾ in
INTERIOR: 16 x 12 x 8 in
FUNCTIONS AND FEATURES: Toast; Bake; Convection Bake; Roast; Broil; Air-Fry; Grill; Pizza; Proof; Keep Warm; Dehydrate; Reheat; Slow Cook; Food ID; cook programs for packaged foods; customizable heating elements; app that includes oven controls, notifications, recipes, and guided cooking; live video monitoring; data and temperature charts of current and recent cooking projects
ACCESSORIES: Baseline model ($599.00) includes food-temperature probe, wire rack, and baking sheet; Premium package adds 3 air-fry baskets, enameled cast-iron grill/griddle, baking peel, 1 extra baking sheet, 2 roasting racks, and "pro" metal food-temperature probe

PERFORMANCE ★★★
ACCURACY ★★★
EASE OF USE ★★★
CLEANUP AND DURABILITY ★★★

We highly recommended the previous version of the June oven, and this newest model, the 3rd Generation, follows suit with hardware and software tweaks. We loved that we could either operate it entirely as a traditional countertop oven or let its food-recognition wizardry, attached probe thermometer, and preprogrammed settings take over and simplify cooking, all while keeping us informed of progress with its internal camera and notifications from its rock-solid, user-friendly app. We tested the Premium package, which includes the oven and the extra accessories noted at left. Everything it produced, from juicy, crispy-skinned whole roast chicken and vegetables to air-fried cod and potatoes; gorgeous, crusty pizza; toasted bagels; crispy bacon; baked tofu; broiled asparagus; grilled chicken breast; and tender barbecued ribs—and even an egg simply placed on the oven rack to hard-cook in the shell—came out beautifully cooked. The functions weren't all fancy: We threw in a slice of leftover pizza, and it recognized it and reheated it to perfection. Our favorite feature: All this happened with very little effort on our part. Cleanup was easy, too. We didn't want to put this oven away when testing was done.

RECOMMENDED

TOVALA Smart Oven
MODEL: Gen 2
PRICE: $299.00 `BEST BUY`
EXTERIOR: 18.25 x 11.75 x 12 in
INTERIOR: 13.25 x 10.5 x 8.75 in
FUNCTIONS AND FEATURES: Toast; Bake; Convection Bake; Steam; Broil; Toast; Reheat; Scan-to-Cook packaged foods; Tovala Meal Kits; app with guided recipes, controls, and notifications
ACCESSORIES: Wire shelf, enameled rimmed baking sheet, measuring cup (to add water to steam chamber)

PERFORMANCE ★★½
ACCURACY ★★★
EASE OF USE ★★½
CLEANUP AND DURABILITY ★★★

This compact oven, well designed and easy to operate, combines steam and conventional cooking. It uses just 1 cup of tap water to generate steam, which helps baked goods rise and foods remain moist as they reheat or cook. Overall, the oven and app performed well. Toast came out nicely browned. Our quibble was that the oven was a bit cramped: The surface of its baking sheet measures just 10 by 8.5 inches, so a whole butterflied chicken barely fit, and we could cook only a half rack of barbecued ribs. The company bills itself as a meal kit service with an oven, but kits are optional (starting at $11.99; each serves one). The kits we tried were surprisingly fresh and flavorful and easy to prep. Menus varied weekly, and kits arrived promptly; you can customize their frequency. This oven is a solid choice for small households—and for people who don't like to cook.

KITCHEN TIMERS

When cooking or baking, you can certainly use the timers on your smartphone, smart speaker, oven, or microwave—but there are good reasons to have a dedicated kitchen timer. Unlike most of the alternatives, a dedicated timer can be carried into another room so that it's always visible and within earshot. A kitchen timer is also often easier to set than the timers on appliances, and you don't have to worry about dirtying your phone with food. We prefer digital models to old-fashioned dial-face timers because they tend to be more precise, easier to set, and easier to read. The simplest digital models track a single set time and beep when that time is up. Most are considerably more complex. Many are "multiple-event," which means they can track multiple times simultaneously. Most can count up (like a stopwatch) in addition to down. It's also common for timers to have adjustable volume settings (sometimes including a silent setting) and flashing lights so that there's a visual alert, too. We rounded up nine (both single- and multi-event) models and compared their accuracy, ease of use, and durability. Our top four models are listed below in order of preference (prices are what we paid at the time of testing).

HIGHLY RECOMMENDED	PERFORMANCE	TESTERS' COMMENTS

THERMOWORKS Extra Big & Loud Timer

`BEST SINGLE-EVENT TIMER`

MODEL: TX-4100-YL
PRICE: $33.00
NUMBER OF EVENTS: 1
MAXIMUM DURATION: 99 hr, 99 min, 99 sec
DIMENSIONS: 3½ x 5 x 1 in
TRACKS ELAPSED TIME: Yes
EXTRA FEATURES: Stopwatch, adjustable volume, memory, magnets, splash-resistant

ACCURACY ★★★
EASE OF USE ★★★
DISPLAY AND ALERTS ★★★
CLEANUP AND DURABILITY ★★★

The big digital screen and clearly labeled buttons made it easy to read and use this simple, intuitive timer. The digits on its screen were some of the largest in our lineup, and the entire screen flashes when the timer goes off. Splash-resistant and sturdy, this timer looked as good as new at the end of testing. The timer has a wide base and can be tilted up on a kickstand so that it is easy to read from above. It also has magnets and can be positioned on a refrigerator or other magnetic surface.

OXO Good Grips Triple Timer

`BEST MULTI-EVENT TIMER`

MODEL: 11303700
PRICE: $25.00
NUMBER OF EVENTS: 3
MAXIMUM DURATION: 99 hr, 59 min, 59 sec
DIMENSIONS: 3 x 4¼ x 2¼ in
TRACKS ELAPSED TIME: Yes
EXTRA FEATURES: Stopwatch, adjustable volume, unique beep pattern for each timer, memory

ACCURACY ★★★
EASE OF USE ★★½
DISPLAY AND ALERTS ★★★
CLEANUP AND DURABILITY ★★★

This compact triple-event timer is accurate and easy to use. The screen displays all three events at once (no scrolling required). It's easy to set and adjust the individual events because each one has its own button, and a pair of horizontal bars on the screen brackets the event being modified. We like that each event makes a unique sound—one beep for the first event, two beeps for the second event, and three beeps for the third event—and that the volume is adjustable. Our only quibble is that the digits on the screen are slightly smaller than ideal.

THERMOWORKS TimeStack

MODEL: TX-4400-GR
PRICE: $59.00
NUMBER OF EVENTS: 4
MAXIMUM DURATION: 99 hr, 99 min, 99 sec
DIMENSIONS: 4 x 6¾ x 2¼ in
TRACKS ELAPSED TIME: Yes
EXTRA FEATURES: Stopwatch, voice recordings, adjustable volume, silent mode, unique beep pattern and flashing light for each timer, backlight, memory, magnets, splash-proof

ACCURACY ★★★
EASE OF USE ★★½
DISPLAY AND ALERTS ★★★
CLEANUP AND DURABILITY ★★★

This big, sturdy quadruple timer has a tilted display with big digits and sports an impressive number of extra features. In addition to having dedicated "set" and "start/stop" buttons, each of its four set times has its own flashing light and a unique beep pattern. You can even record custom voice memos such as "check the chicken" or "rotate the cookies." This timer takes some getting used to because it has so many buttons and settings, so we appreciated that the instructions for recording and clearing the voice memos are printed on the bottom of the timer. It's a great option for busy cooks who routinely prepare multiple dishes at once.

MARATHON Commercial Grade Direct Entry Table Timer

MODEL: TI030018BK (Black)
PRICE: $20.00
NUMBER OF EVENTS: 1
MAXIMUM DURATION: 99 hr, 99 min, 99 sec
DIMENSIONS: 4½ x 4½ x 2 in
TRACKS ELAPSED TIME: Yes
EXTRA FEATURES: Stopwatch, adjustable volume, silent mode, memory, interval timer, clock

ACCURACY ★★★
EASE OF USE ★★★
DISPLAY AND ALERTS ★★½
CLEANUP AND DURABILITY ★★★

With a full keypad and a screen with big digits, this timer is simple and easy to use. It beeps, and a red light flashes when the time is up, but the light was small and easy to miss from across the room. It has four memory settings, which are useful when preparing recipes that you make frequently. It has an interval timer feature, which can be handy for workouts, studying, and other activities that require timing events of multiple lengths back-to-back. When the timer isn't in use, you can toggle over to a clock setting.

INEXPENSIVE CHEF'S KNIVES

A good chef's knife is a cook's best friend. It's arguably the most important tool in the kitchen, an essential all-purpose blade that can do everything from small, precise tasks (mincing garlic) to minor butchery (breaking down a whole chicken, filleting a fish) and a whole lot in between. Many say that if you buy just one knife, let it be a chef's knife. We've recommended our favorite chef's knife for almost three decades, retesting it repeatedly since new knives enter the market all the time. To see if our favorite still held up to the competition, we tested it against a fresh crop of nine options. Since our favorite doesn't cost much—usually less than $40—we set the price cap for our lineup at $75. We focused on knives with blades measuring about 8 inches, as we've found this length to be the most useful and versatile for most cooks. We limited our lineup to knives with stainless-steel blades because they are the easiest to care for. Our top five knives are listed here in order of preference (prices are what we paid at the time of testing).

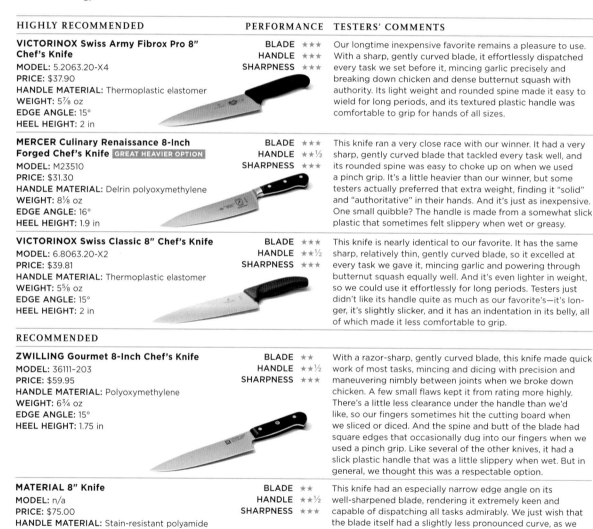

HIGHLY RECOMMENDED	PERFORMANCE	TESTERS' COMMENTS
VICTORINOX Swiss Army Fibrox Pro 8" **Chef's Knife** **MODEL:** 5.2063.20-X4 **PRICE:** $37.90 **HANDLE MATERIAL:** Thermoplastic elastomer **WEIGHT:** 5⅞ oz **EDGE ANGLE:** 15° **HEEL HEIGHT:** 2 in	BLADE ★★★ HANDLE ★★★ SHARPNESS ★★★	Our longtime inexpensive favorite remains a pleasure to use. With a sharp, gently curved blade, it effortlessly dispatched every task we set before it, mincing garlic precisely and breaking down chicken and dense butternut squash with authority. Its light weight and rounded spine made it easy to wield for long periods, and its textured plastic handle was comfortable to grip for hands of all sizes.
MERCER Culinary Renaissance 8-Inch **Forged Chef's Knife** `GREAT HEAVIER OPTION` **MODEL:** M23510 **PRICE:** $31.30 **HANDLE MATERIAL:** Delrin polyoxymethylene **WEIGHT:** 8⅛ oz **EDGE ANGLE:** 16° **HEEL HEIGHT:** 1.9 in	BLADE ★★★ HANDLE ★★½ SHARPNESS ★★★	This knife ran a very close race with our winner. It had a very sharp, gently curved blade that tackled every task well, and its rounded spine was easy to choke up on when we used a pinch grip. It's a little heavier than our winner, but some testers actually preferred that extra weight, finding it "solid" and "authoritative" in their hands. And it's just as inexpensive. One small quibble? The handle is made from a somewhat slick plastic that sometimes felt slippery when wet or greasy.
VICTORINOX Swiss Classic 8" Chef's Knife **MODEL:** 6.8063.20-X2 **PRICE:** $39.81 **HANDLE MATERIAL:** Thermoplastic elastomer **WEIGHT:** 5⅝ oz **EDGE ANGLE:** 15° **HEEL HEIGHT:** 2 in	BLADE ★★★ HANDLE ★★½ SHARPNESS ★★★	This knife is nearly identical to our favorite. It has the same sharp, relatively thin, gently curved blade, so it excelled at every task we gave it, mincing garlic and powering through butternut squash equally well. And it's even lighter in weight, so we could use it effortlessly for long periods. Testers just didn't like its handle quite as much as our favorite's—it's longer, it's slightly slicker, and it has an indentation in its belly, all of which made it less comfortable to grip.

RECOMMENDED		
ZWILLING Gourmet 8-Inch Chef's Knife **MODEL:** 36111-203 **PRICE:** $59.95 **HANDLE MATERIAL:** Polyoxymethylene **WEIGHT:** 6¾ oz **EDGE ANGLE:** 15° **HEEL HEIGHT:** 1.75 in	BLADE ★★ HANDLE ★★½ SHARPNESS ★★★	With a razor-sharp, gently curved blade, this knife made quick work of most tasks, mincing and dicing with precision and maneuvering nimbly between joints when we broke down chicken. A few small flaws kept it from rating more highly. There's a little less clearance under the handle than we'd like, so our fingers sometimes hit the cutting board when we sliced or diced. And the spine and butt of the blade had square edges that occasionally dug into our fingers when we used a pinch grip. Like several of the other knives, it had a slick plastic handle that was a little slippery when wet. But in general, we thought this was a respectable option.
MATERIAL 8" Knife **MODEL:** n/a **PRICE:** $75.00 **HANDLE MATERIAL:** Stain-resistant polyamide composite **WEIGHT:** 7⅝ oz **EDGE ANGLE:** 13° **HEEL HEIGHT:** 1.9 in	BLADE ★★ HANDLE ★★½ SHARPNESS ★★★	This knife had an especially narrow edge angle on its well-sharpened blade, rendering it extremely keen and capable of dispatching all tasks admirably. We just wish that the blade itself had a slightly less pronounced curve, as we found that we had to raise our arms and wrists awkwardly when rocking the blade from tip to heel. The spine and butt of the blade were also squared off, so they occasionally dug into our hands. And like several other knives, the handle was made of plastic that got slippery when wet, though it was otherwise comfortable to grip in different positions.

HAND MIXERS

Hand mixers strike a happy medium between combining ingredients by hand and hauling out a heavy stand mixer every time you want to mix. We use them in the test kitchen for whipping cream; beating egg whites into meringue; and combining ingredients for single batches of cookies, cakes, or pies. We think a hand mixer is an especially good option for people looking to get into baking without making a huge investment; people who don't have much storage space; and people with arthritis or certain disabilities that prevent them from lifting a larger mixer. While hand mixers make many baking projects much easier, we've found that they are not powerful enough to mix most bread or pizza doughs, despite some manufacturers' claims. Still, we think they can be an important and convenient addition to your kitchen arsenal. All hand mixers include two standard beater attachments; some also include one or two whisk attachments and a pair of spiral-shaped dough hooks. After first testing all eight of the models in our lineup with their beaters, we tested them equipped with their whisk attachments by preparing an additional batch of meringue. Finally, we outfitted our top two models with their dough hooks and mixed Bagel Bread. Along the way, we evaluated their speed and ability to effectively mix ingredients of different textures and densities, how easy they were to operate, clean, maneuver, and store, and how well they held up to repeated use and cleaning. Our top three models are listed here in order of preference (prices are what we paid at the time of testing).

HIGHLY RECOMMENDED	PERFORMANCE	TESTERS' COMMENTS

BREVILLE Handy Mix Scraper
MODEL: BHM800BTR1AUS1
PRICE: $129.95
EXTRA FEATURES: 2 whisk attachments, 2 dough hooks, timer, pause button, light, storage case
WEIGHT: 2 lb, 10.8 oz
BEATER HEAD DIAMETER: 2¼ in
LOWEST SPEED: 353 rpm
HIGHEST SPEED: 1,310 rpm

PERFORMANCE ★★★
EASE OF USE ★★★
DURABILITY ★★★

This mixer performed exceptionally well. It was speedy, creaming butter and sugar and whipping meringue faster than any other model, and it muscled through dense cookie dough with ease. Its beater heads are the widest in the lineup, making for efficient mixing and zero clogging, and they're silicone tipped, so they didn't clang around in the bowl. This mixer is thoughtfully designed with several features that make mixing more efficient and convenient, including a timer, a light that shines into the mixing bowl, a pause button, a well-positioned display screen, and a plastic storage case that locks onto its base.

CUISINART Power Advantage Plus 9 Speed Hand Mixer with Storage Case
MODEL: HM-90S
PRICE: $79.95 **BEST BUY**
EXTRA FEATURES: 1 whisk attachment, 2 dough hooks, storage case, cord wrap
WEIGHT: 2 lb, 4.4 oz
BEATER HEAD DIAMETER: 2 in
LOWEST SPEED: 349 rpm
HIGHEST SPEED: 1,285 rpm

PERFORMANCE ★★★
EASE OF USE ★★★
DURABILITY ★★★

This mixer performed the same as our winner, just without the bells and whistles. It offered a wide range of speeds, from slow to lightning fast, allowing it to tackle both lighter and denser ingredients with ease. Its controls, which consisted of a simple on/off button and two buttons to select speeds, as well as a small display screen, were the most intuitive to operate in the lineup. It was also one of the fastest models, losing only to our winner when creaming butter and sugar and beating egg whites for meringue. While it doesn't offer all the special features and conveniences of our winner, it is a fantastic option for home bakers.

RECOMMENDED

KITCHENAID 5-Speed Ultra Power Hand Mixer
MODEL: KHM512AQ
PRICE: $49.99
EXTRA FEATURE: Cord wrap
WEIGHT: 2 lb, 0.3 oz
BEATER HEAD DIAMETER: 1¾ in
LOWEST SPEED: 288 rpm
HIGHEST SPEED: 1,107 rpm

PERFORMANCE ★★
EASE OF USE ★★½
DURABILITY ★★★

This mixer's lowest speed was ideal for whipping cream or adding flour without flinging those ingredients everywhere. We were able to adjust the speed easily using a simple slider. This mixer ran into a bit of trouble when mixing oats and chocolate chips into stiff cookie dough—even at its fastest speed it took a few seconds to really get going—but it eventually powered through and mixed everything efficiently and effectively. We especially liked how light it was, which made it easy to maneuver while mixing.

NUTRITIONAL INFORMATION FOR OUR RECIPES

We calculate the nutritional values of our recipes per serving; if there is a range in the serving size, we used the highest number of servings to calculate the nutritional values. We entered all the ingredients, using weights for important ingredients such as meat, cheese, and most vegetables. We also used our preferred brands in these analyses. We did not include additional salt or pepper for food that's "seasoned to taste."

RECIPE	CALORIES	TOTAL FAT (G)	SAT FAT (G)	CHOL (MG)	SODIUM (MG)	CARBS (G)	FIBER (G)	SUGARS (G)	PROTEIN (G)
CHAPTER 1: SOUPS AND SALADS									
Tanabour (Armenian Yogurt and Barley Soup)	289	15	8	65	686	27	5	6	13
Madzoon ov Kofte (Armenian Yogurt and Meatball Soup)	500	22	10	91	963	50	7	9	26
Chorba Frik	270	13	3	40	850	25	7	3	13
Multicooker Hawaiian Oxtail Soup	520	29	10	170	1090	14	4	4	53
Vegetarian Chili	485	13	2	0	1239	77	22	11	22
Beef Yakamein (New Orleans Spicy Beef Noodle Soup)	624	25	8	185	1480	55	4	7	45
Jamaican Stew Peas with Spinners	512	21	14	48	1108	50	16	4	34
Okra and Shrimp Stew	302	17	5	108	1474	13	4	3	24
Crispy Lentil and Herb Salad	213	19	3	6	185	8	0	6	4
Roasted Butternut Squash Salad with Creamy Tahini Dressing	309	24	3	2	615	24	6	5	5
Shredded Swiss Chard Salad with Prosciutto, Basil, and Blue Cheese	167	12	3	18	654	9	1	4	8
Tomato and Chickpea Salad	439	27	3	0	729	40	13	11	15
Lao Hu Cai (Tiger Salad)	61	4	1	0	182	5	2	2	2
Chopped Vegetable and Stone Fruit Salad	110	5	1	0	250	15	3	11	2
CHAPTER 2: STARTERS									
Lemon Pepper Wings	924	74	13	258	743	26	1	4	41
Lumpiang Shanghai with Seasoned Vinegar	390	31	6	66	38	16	1	1	13
Hot Cheddar Crab Dip	217	15	9	78	430	6	1	3	15
Air-Fryer Romesco	130	9	1	0	240	10	3	2	3
Air-Fried Whole-Wheat Pita Chips with Salt and Pepper	70	1	0	0	260	14	0	1	4
Oysters on the Half Shell	162	5	1	100	230	10	0	0	19
Red Wine Vinegar Mignonette Granité	6	0	0	0	2	1	0	0	0
Lime-and-Soy-Marinated Scallions	4	0	0	0	110	1	0	0	0
Roasted Oysters on the Half Shell with Mustard Butter	249	14	7	125	243	10	0	0	19
Carciofi alla Giudia (Roman Jewish Fried Artichokes)	475	47	4	0	118	13	7	1	4
Spiced Cauliflower Fritters	300	20	6	100	660	21	3	3	10
Pakoras (South Asian Spiced Vegetable Fritters)	340	29	2	0	290	15	3	2	4
Carrot-Tamarind Chutney	15	0	0	0	200	3	1	2	0
Cilantro-Mint Chutney	146	12	1	0	242	9	3	2	3
CHAPTER 3: SIDE DISHES									
Braised Asparagus with Lemon and Chives	88	7	1	0	172	5	2	2	3
with Orange and Tarragon	91	7	1	0	172	6	3	2	3
with Sherry Vinegar and Marjoram	88	7	1	0	172	5	2	2	3
Roasted Cauliflower with Mint and Olive Sauce	382	35	5	0	705	16	6	5	6
Sautéed Radishes and Scallions with Garlic, Dill, and Capers	111	9	6	23	411	8	3	3	2
Leeks Vinaigrette	196	14	3	3	243	14	2	3	4

RECIPE	CALORIES	TOTAL FAT (G)	SAT FAT (G)	CHOL (MG)	SODIUM (MG)	CARBS (G)	FIBER (G)	SUGARS (G)	PROTEIN (G)
CHAPTER 3: SIDE DISHES (continued)									
Pa amb Tomàquet (Catalan Tomato Bread)	215	9	1	0	330	29	2	2	5
Roasted Okra	58	3	0	0	269	8	4	2	2
Spicy Red Pepper Mayonnaise	*109*	*11*	*1*	*4*	*70*	*3*	*1*	*1*	*1*
Stewed Okra	93	6	2	10	298	7	2	2	3
Roasted Kale with Garlic, Red Pepper Flakes, and Lemon	120	8	1	0	285	11	4	3	5
with Coriander, Ginger, and Coconut	*189*	*15*	*7*	*0*	*308*	*13*	*6*	*3*	*6*
with Parmesan, Shallot, and Nutmeg	*195*	*13*	*4*	*13*	*335*	*11*	*4*	*3*	*12*
Hasselback Potato Casserole	483	22	11	54	890	50	4	4	22
Lentilles du Puy with Spinach and Crème Fraîche	170	10	2	7	732	14	1	6	7
Instant Pot Barbecue Beans	790	32	12	80	3220	85	12	37	45
Grits with Fresh Corn	260	12	7	30	720	32	3	7	7
Jellied Cranberry Sauce	144	0	0	0	51	37	1	33	0
with Ancho Chile	*149*	*0*	*0*	*0*	*99*	*38*	*2*	*33*	*0*
with Lemon and Rosemary	*145*	*0*	*0*	*0*	*51*	*37*	*2*	*33*	*0*
with Orange and Cardamom	*146*	*0*	*0*	*0*	*51*	*37*	*1*	*33*	*0*
CHAPTER 4: PASTA, SANDWICHES, AND MORE									
Gnocchi à la Parisienne with Arugula, Tomatoes, and Olives	471	26	20	223	500	25	2	3	13
Pesto di Prezzemolo (Parsley Pesto)	490	51	8	10	450	4	2	1	7
Linguine with Pesto di Prezzemolo	*770*	*52*	*8*	*10*	*450*	*61*	*2*	*4*	*17*
Pasta Cacio e Uova (Pasta with Cheese and Eggs)	177	15	5	82	353	1	0	0	10
Cauliflower Pasta with Browned Butter–Sage Sauce	510	23	8	30	1110	64	7	5	14
Ultracreamy Spaghetti with Zucchini	550	22	9	35	920	69	5	7	22
Maftoul with Carrots and Chickpeas	410	9	1	0	930	70	7	8	13
Cheddar-Crusted Grilled Cheese	590	41	23	104	893	31	2	4	24
with Bacon and Pepper Jelly	*756*	*45*	*24*	*119*	*1234*	*59*	*3*	*23*	*30*
with Tomato	*614*	*43*	*23*	*107*	*959*	*32*	*3*	*4*	*26*
Gruyère-Crusted Grilled Cheese with Smoked Salmon	*653*	*42*	*22*	*118*	*1297*	*31*	*3*	*4*	*37*
Air-Fryer Make-Ahead Lentil and Mushroom Burgers	350	14	2	0	490	47	6	6	12
Tartiflette (French Potato and Cheese Gratin)	649	42	21	110	924	41	5	5	22
Briam	320	25	3	0	503	24	5	6	4
Skillet Tomato Cobbler	270	14	6	25	430	31	3	15	4
Instant Pot Savory Oatmeal with Sautéed Wild Mushrooms	560	26	6	20	840	64	11	4	16
Air-Fryer Hearty Vegetable Hash with Golden Yogurt	400	18	3	5	720	52	10	15	13
CHAPTER 5: MEAT									
Pastelón (Puerto Rican Sweet Plantain and Picadillo Casserole)	318	18	2	21	197	35	3	17	8
Smoked Prime Rib	690	57	21	145	990	2	1	1	38
Smoked Prime Rib Sandwiches with Green Chile Queso	1070	80	26	155	1860	39	2	6	46
Kousa Mihshi (Lebanese Stuffed Squash)	600	38	11	55	1330	46	7	20	22
Zucchini-Cucumber Salad with Pine Nuts and Mint	*154*	*15*	*2*	*0*	*261*	*6*	*2*	*2*	*2*
Kalbi (Korean Grilled Flanken-Style Short Ribs)	1375	125	54	259	595	10	0	8	50
Stir-Fried Beef and Gai Lan	412	27	8	120	633	4	0	1	36
Mehshi Bazal	310	9	4	40	430	44	4	23	14
Wine-Braised Spareribs with Garlic and Rosemary	1305	110	33	333	1107	4	1	0	65
Sisig	1220	110	37	320	2730	13	1	1	43
Garlic Fried Rice	*390*	*11*	*2*	*0*	*290*	*68*	*0*	*0*	*6*

RECIPE	CALORIES	TOTAL FAT (G)	SAT FAT (G)	CHOL (MG)	SODIUM (MG)	CARBS (G)	FIBER (G)	SUGARS (G)	PROTEIN (G)
CHAPTER 5: MEAT (continued)									
Kimchi and Ham Steak Fried Rice	532	18	4	79	3670	52	3	2	38
Short-Grain White Rice	*160*	*1*	*0*	*0*	*200*	*35*	*1*	*0*	*5*
Honey-Glazed Pork Shoulder	486	28	10	139	743	18	0	18	39
Pan-Seared Thick-Cut, Bone-In Pork Chops	272	14	5	110	88	0	0	0	33
Creamy Apple-Mustard Sauce	*144*	*3*	*0*	*0*	*1034*	*28*	*4*	*23*	*4*
Maple Agrodolce	*155*	*0*	*0*	*0*	*86*	*28*	*1*	*23*	*1*
Multicooker Abgoosht (Persian Lamb and Chickpea Stew)	295	16	6	47	369	23	4	3	17
CHAPTER 6: POULTRY AND SEAFOOD									
Tunisian Tajine with White Beans	500	29	9	500	840	15	3	2	45
Chicken Parmesan Meatballs	1008	65	30	280	2275	34	5	11	73
Grilled Chicken Souvlaki	487	28	10	196	619	4	1	0	53
Msakhan	590	29	7	115	910	37	3	8	45
Baharat	*10*	*0*	*0*	*0*	*0*	*1*	*1*	*0*	*0*
Chicken Teriyaki	505	35	9	194	821	7	0	3	34
Pollo a la Brasa (Peruvian Grill-Roasted Chicken)	670	45	13	225	1960	4	0	1	57
Ají Verde (Peruvian Green Chile Sauce)	*140*	*15*	*3*	*10*	*170*	*1*	*0*	*0*	*1*
Ají Amarillo (Peruvian Yellow Chile Sauce)	*130*	*14*	*2*	*10*	*400*	*0*	*0*	*0*	*0*
Chicken Francese	350	18	7	175	990	12	0	1	29
Blackened Chicken	349	16	7	168	508	5	2	1	46
Porchetta-Style Turkey Breast	694	36	10	256	1032	4	2	0	85
Holiday Smoked Turkey	538	20	5	251	1269	8	1	6	76
Duck Breasts with Port Wine–Fig Sauce	210	5	2	88	605	14	1	12	23
Salmon Peperonata	652	45	9	125	1078	14	4	5	49
Tuna Poke	299	18	2	44	713	4	1	1	30
Salmon Teriyaki Poke	344	23	5	62	731	8	3	3	25
Fisherman's Pie	582	33	19	235	1103	35	3	3	36
Garlicky Broiled Shrimp	247	13	8	245	965	8	0	5	24
Hot Honey Broiled Shrimp	*259*	*13*	*8*	*245*	*980*	*11*	*0*	*9*	*23*
Smoky, Spiced Broiled Shrimp	*246*	*14*	*8*	*245*	*966*	*7*	*1*	*5*	*24*
CHAPTER 7: BREAKFAST, BRUNCH, AND BREADS									
Çilbir (Turkish Poached Eggs with Yogurt and Spiced Butter)	188	14	8	211	311	3	0	3	12
Omelet with Cheddar and Chives	380	30	14	602	435	2	0	1	26
Asparagus, Leek, and Goat Cheese Quiche	436	32	20	178	454	24	2	3	14
Matzo Brei	370	22	12	317	401	30	2	3	13
with Cinnamon and Sugar	*358*	*22*	*12*	*317*	*290*	*27*	*2*	*2*	*12*
with Mushrooms and Chives	*354*	*22*	*12*	*317*	*345*	*26*	*1*	*1*	*13*
with Smoked Salmon and Dill	*386*	*23*	*12*	*320*	*441*	*30*	*2*	*3*	*16*
Breakfast Burritos with Chorizo and Crispy Potatoes	788	59	19	451	1350	28	1	2	36
with Bacon and Crispy Potatoes	*766*	*60*	*18*	*437*	*1025*	*27*	*1*	*3*	*30*
with Poblano, Beans, Corn, and Crispy Potatoes	*701*	*45*	*11*	*401*	*674*	*46*	*6*	*4*	*28*
Alu Parathas (Punjabi Potato-Stuffed Griddle Breads)	490	21	9	33	561	68	3	2	9
Tamatya-Kandyachi Koshimbir (Tomato-Onion Salad)	*51*	*1*	*1*	*0*	*300*	*10*	*3*	*6*	*2*
Kesra Rakhsis (Semolina Flatbread)	361	16	2	0	252	46	3	1	9
Pan Boxty	266	14	8	33	399	32	2	2	5
Jalapeño-Cheddar Scones	358	21	12	70	241	35	1	8	8

RECIPE	CALORIES	TOTAL FAT (G)	SAT FAT (G)	CHOL (MG)	SODIUM (MG)	CARBS (G)	FIBER (G)	SUGARS (G)	PROTEIN (G)
CHAPTER 7: BREAKFAST, BRUNCH, AND BREADS (continued)									
Fresh Corn Muffins	336	12	7	58	289	52	2	19	6
Cardamom–Brown Sugar Butter	*80*	*8*	*5*	*20*	*29*	*3*	*0*	*3*	*0*
Shokupan (Japanese White Bread)	304	5	3	11	296	54	2	5	10
Kanelbullar (Swedish Cinnamon Buns)	319	13	8	49	226	45	2	22	6
CHAPTER 8: DESSERTS									
Orange Upside-Down Cake	423	19	11	92	257	62	2	46	4
Ice Cream Cake	660	42	24	160	210	68	3	56	9
Pâte Sucrée Tart Shell	197	10	6	43	67	24	1	8	3
Milk Chocolate Crémeux Tart	537	36	22	164	196	46	2	26	8
Fruit Hand Pies	505	30	19	100	361	55	2	18	6
Cherry Hand Pie Filling	*80*	*0*	*0*	*0*	*40*	*19*	*0*	*17*	*0*
Peach Hand Pie Filling	*50*	*0*	*0*	*0*	*35*	*13*	*1*	*11*	*0*
Pineapple Hand Pie Filling	*60*	*0*	*0*	*0*	*35*	*14*	*1*	*9*	*0*
Blueberry Cream Pie	510	32	18	85	360	53	0	32	5
Apple-Blackberry Betty	294	10	6	23	404	47	6	26	5
Pear Crisp with Miso and Almonds	516	22	12	54	226	76	6	46	5
Peanut Butter–Stuffed Chocolate Cookies	318	14	5	25	175	48	2	34	5
Alfajores de Maicena (Dulce de Leche Sandwich Cookies)	272	13	9	53	109	35	1	20	4
Dulce de Leche	107	3	2	11	66	18	0	18	3
Struffoli (Neopolitan Honey Balls)	579	29	6	86	192	76	2	48	7
Breton Kouign Amann	343	19	12	49	224	41	1	16	4
Vegan Chocolate Mousse	277	18	3	0	39	31	3	24	3
Whipped Coconut Cream	*271*	*28*	*25*	*0*	*17*	*6*	*0*	*2*	*3*

DULCE DE LECHE

CONVERSIONS & EQUIVALENTS

Some say cooking is a science and an art. We would say that geography has a hand in it, too. Flour milled in the United Kingdom and elsewhere will feel and taste different from flour milled in the United States. So while we cannot promise that the loaf of bread you bake in Canada or England will taste the same as a loaf baked in the States, we can offer guidelines for converting weights and measures. We also recommend that you rely on your instincts when making our recipes. Refer to the visual cues provided. If the bread dough hasn't "come together in a ball" as described, you may need to add more flour—even if the recipe doesn't tell you so. You be the judge.

The recipes in this book were developed using standard U.S. measures following U.S. government guidelines. The charts below offer equivalents for U.S., metric, and imperial (U.K.) measures. All conversions are approximate and have been rounded up or down to the nearest whole number. For example:

1 teaspoon = 4.929 milliliters, rounded up to 5 milliliters

1 ounce = 28.349 grams, rounded down to 28 grams

VOLUME CONVERSIONS

U.S.	METRIC
1 teaspoon	5 milliliters
2 teaspoons	10 milliliters
1 tablespoon	15 milliliters
2 tablespoons	30 milliliters
¼ cup	59 milliliters
⅓ cup	79 milliliters
½ cup	118 milliliters
¾ cup	177 milliliters
1 cup	237 milliliters
1¼ cups	296 milliliters
1½ cups	355 milliliters
2 cups	473 milliliters
2½ cups	591 milliliters
3 cups	710 milliliters
4 cups (1 quart)	1 liter
4 quarts (1 gallon)	4 liters

WEIGHT CONVERSIONS

OUNCES	GRAMS
½	14
¾	21
1	28
1½	43
2	57
2½	71
3	85
3½	99
4	113
4½	128
5	142
6	170
7	198
8	227
9	255
10	283
12	340
16 (1 pound)	454

CONVERSIONS FOR INGREDIENTS COMMONLY USED IN BAKING

Baking is an exacting science. Because measuring by weight is far more accurate than measuring by volume, and thus more likely to achieve reliable results, in our recipes we provide ounce measures in addition to cup measures for many ingredients. Refer to the chart below to convert these measures into grams.

INGREDIENT	OUNCES	GRAMS
Flour		
1 cup all-purpose flour*	5	142
1 cup cake flour	4	113
1 cup whole-wheat flour	5½	156
Sugar		
1 cup granulated (white) sugar	7	198
1 cup packed brown sugar (light or dark)	7	198
1 cup confectioners' sugar	4	113
Cocoa Powder		
1 cup cocoa powder	3	85
Butter†		
4 tablespoons (½ stick, or ¼ cup)	2	57
8 tablespoons (1 stick, or ½ cup)	4	113
16 tablespoons (2 sticks, or 1 cup)	8	227

* U.S. all-purpose flour, the most frequently used flour in this book, does not contain leaveners, as some European flours do. These leavened flours are called self-rising or self-raising. If you are using self-rising flour, take this into consideration before adding leavening to a recipe.

† In the United States, butter is sold both salted and unsalted. We generally recommend unsalted butter. If you are using salted butter, take this into consideration before adding salt to a recipe.

OVEN TEMPERATURES

DEGREES FAHRENHEIT	DEGREES CELSIUS	GAS MARK (imperial)
225	105	¼
250	120	½
275	135	1
300	150	2
325	165	3
350	180	4
375	190	5
400	200	6
425	220	7
450	230	8
475	245	9

CONVERTING TEMPERATURES FROM AN INSTANT-READ THERMOMETER

We include doneness temperatures in many of our recipes, such as those for poultry, meat, and bread. We recommend an instant-read thermometer for the job. Refer to the table above to convert Fahrenheit degrees to Celsius. Or, for temperatures not represented in the chart, use this simple formula.

Subtract 32 from the Fahrenheit reading, and then divide the result by 1.8 to find the Celsius reading.

EXAMPLE:

"Roast chicken until thighs register 175 degrees."
To convert:

175° F – 32 = 143°
143° ÷ 1.8 = 79.44°C, rounded down to 79°C

INDEX

S

DUCK BREASTS WITH PORT WINE–FIG SAUCE